7 Ch + I + P

CHINESE
COMMUNIST
ESPIONAGE

KAZAKHSTAN

RUSSIA

Lake Baikal

MONGOLIA

Ulaanbaatar

Harbin

Changchun

Shenyang

NORTH KOREA

Pyongyang

Seoul

SOUTH KOREA

Almaty

Bishkek

KYRGYZSTAN

Urumqi

XINJIANG

Hohhot

Beijing

Tianjin

Dalian

Weihai

Kashgar

TAJIKISTAN

AFGHANISTAN

PAKISTAN

Chinese line of control

Indian claim

Xining

Yan'an

Lanzhou

Xi'an

Jinan

Qingdao

Zhengzhou

Yellow Sea (Huang Hai)

Huang He (Yellow River)

CHINA

Nanjing

Shanghai

TIBET

Lhasa

Chang Jiang (Yangzi River)

Chengdu

Wuhan

East China Sea (Dong Hai)

New Delhi

NEPAL

Thimphu

BHUTAN

Kathmandu

Chongqing

Changsha

Nanchang

Ruijin

Fuzhou

INDIA

BANGLADESH

Dacca

Guiyang

Kunming

Guangzhou

Nanning

Macau

Hong Kong

Taipei

TAIWAN

BURMA

Hanoi

LAOS

Vientiane

Haikou

Sanya

HAINAN

VIETNAM

South China Sea (Nan Hai)

PHILIPPINES

Manila

Rangoon

THAILAND

Bangkok

0   250   500 Kilometers

0   250   500 Miles

CHINESE

COMMUNIST

ESPIONAGE

An Intelligence Primer

———

PETER MATTIS AND **MATTHEW BRAZIL**

Naval Institute Press
Annapolis, Maryland

Naval Institute Press
291 Wood Road
Annapolis, MD 21402

Library of Congress Cataloging-in-Publication Data
Names: Mattis, Peter L., author. | Brazil, Matthew J., author.
Title: Chinese Communist Espionage : An Intelligence Primer / Peter L. Mattis and Matthew J.
Brazil.
Description: Annapolis, Maryland : Naval Institute Press, [2019] | Includes
 bibliographical references and index.
Identifiers: LCCN 2019020106 (print) | LCCN 2019981671 (ebook) | ISBN
 9781682473030 (hardcover) | ISBN 9781682473047 (ebook)
Subjects: LCSH: China. Guo jia an quan bu—History. | China. Gong an
 bu—History. | Zhongguo gong chan dang—History. | Espionage,
 Chinese—History. | Espionage, Communist—History. |
 Espionage—China—History. | Intelligence service—China—History.
Classification: LCC UB271.C6 M38 2019 (print) | LCC UB271.C6 (ebook) |
 DDC 327.1251—dc23
LC record available at https://lccn.loc.gov/2019020106
LC ebook record available at https://lccn.loc.gov/2019981671

♾ Print editions meet the requirements of ANSI/NISO z39.48–1992 (Permanence of Paper).
Printed in the United States of America.

27 26 25 24 23 22 21 20 19   9 8 7 6 5 4 3 2

◆ Contents ◆

◆ Preface ◆

T his book is the result of collaboration between Peter Mattis, an analyst of the modern People's Republic of China (PRC) intelligence community, and Matthew Brazil, a historian of early Chinese Communist Party (CCP) intelligence operations and a former corporate investigator. We hope that this material will be of interest to those seeking a clearer understanding of how China conducts espionage. Even though "everyone spies," the methods by which the PRC pursues secret intelligence are too often shrouded in unnecessary mystery. This can lead to miscalculation, misunderstanding, and prejudice by governments protecting national security information and businesses protecting trade secrets. Perhaps more importantly, it distorts and harms bilateral relations between China and its important diplomatic and trading partners, particularly the United States and Japan.

The mystery is partly of our own making. This field is neglected by China watchers, sometimes to avoid somehow upsetting commerce or other institutional relations with China, but also because of the thin veil of the Chinese language. Many recently published works on Chinese espionage in English failed to pierce that veil or even to give it a fair go, using few if any Chinese-language sources. It is as if someone in Beijing wrote a book about the U.S. intelligence community without examining English-language sources.

As the reader can see in our bibliography, we have consulted numerous Chinese publications, books, and other materials. However, we believe that we have only scratched the surface. Few are more aware than the handful of authors who have delved into this arena of the vast and unexplored range of published Chinese-language works on intelligence, unofficial samizdat-type literature, and unopened archives that will eventually bring additional clarity to this murky world.[1] However, we hope that we have begun a more critical analysis of this darker corner of Chinese communist history and governance than is evident in the increasingly mythologized accounts that have come out of Beijing in recent times.

In writing a reference guide, we do not intend to provide the definitive answers but rather to introduce the history of intelligence within the CCP and the modern party-state. Systematically sketching the key figures, organizations, and espionage cases invites readers to draw their own conclusions about PRC intelligence services, their activities, and their methods. By contrast, much of the existing analysis and commentary about Chinese intelligence is anecdotal or drawn from the observations of security professionals who cannot speak freely. The experience of these professionals often is limited to a fraction of the PRC's clandestine activity. Focusing only on economic espionage, the activities of intelligence services, united front work, or theft in cyberspace would result in misleading conclusions about what the PRC does in each of the other areas—reminiscent of the parable of the elephant and the blind men.[2] By contrast, we make a broader attempt to explain what today's PRC intelligence services do and the roots of their work in CCP history.

The value of a reference guide lies in making a lot of data easily accessible. Between the limitations of English-language works and the narrow lens through which most security professionals look at PRC intelligence, there is a need to shine a light across the breadth and historical depth of this activity. The needs of the present often require journalists and analysts to emphasize the new rather than the continuous. We hope this reference guide enables those who must meet the needs of today to see both continuity and novelty with greater clarity.

We are particularly grateful to David Chambers, James Mulvenon, Bob Suettinger, Frederick Teiwes, and two anonymous reviewers for their comments on large portions of the manuscript. We are also grateful for the advice of Børge Bakken, Michael Dutton, Roger Faligot, João Guedes, Jianye He, Philip J. Ivanhoe, Wendell Minnick, Dahlia Lanhua Peterson, Steve Tsang, Bruce Williams, Peter Wood, Miles Maochun Yu, and the staffs of the C. V. Starr East Asian Library, University of California, Berkeley, and of the University Services Center at the Chinese University of Hong Kong.

While those mentioned above and others who prefer anonymity provided generous help, we take responsibility for errors or omissions. The views expressed in this book are the authors' alone and not those of the U.S. Government, CECC, or anyone in them.

CHINESE
COMMUNIST
ESPIONAGE

Introduction

For the employees of a certain Chinese government ministry in Beijing, the coldest day of 2011 was not in winter. It was on the morning that all personnel were ordered to view the execution of one of their comrades, who had been exposed as a spy for the Central Intelligence Agency (CIA), and his pregnant wife. The two were shot in the ministry's interior courtyard, the proceedings shown on closed-circuit television.

The man's sentence was only one of a dozen or more lethal warnings to the Chinese bureaucracy between late 2010 and December 2012. The state and the ruling Chinese Communist Party (CCP) would not tolerate disloyalty by those entrusted with its secrets. There would be no mercy, even for the unborn child of a traitor. The forces of state security had destroyed CIA networks in China, and woe to anyone who tried to revive them.

Why does the CCP react in such a vociferous and lethal manner to a crime that would draw only a prison sentence elsewhere? One answer lies in how close the party has come to being destroyed by betrayal, whether from allies or spies within.

For Americans and others in the West, foreign espionage and related "intelligence failures" have been perilous but have not really been threats to national existence. The Japanese attack in Hawaii on December 7, 1941, shook the U.S. government and especially its intelligence establishment, which vowed never to be so surprised again—though September 11, 2001, might qualify as a reminder. In both cases the United States may have stumbled, but these intelligence setbacks did not prevent the nation from recovering and fighting back hard.

3

The CCP had its own versions of Pearl Harbor and September 11, but by contrast they almost destroyed communism in China. They underline how intelligence (defined as useful information and analytic products to guide decisions regarding an enemy)[1] and security (protective measures against hostile acts)[2] began to blend in Chinese party and state organizations. On April 12, 1927, the party was surprised almost to death by what it called a "counterrevolutionary coup." The perpetrators were the CCP's erstwhile allies, the Chinese Nationalist Party (KMT), whose soldiers and police rounded up and executed thousands of communists in Shanghai and other cities. The Nationalists called it "the 1927 party cleansing," when they rid themselves of infiltrators who intended to subvert and overthrow the KMT leadership. At the end of the coup, the CCP had only 2,000 to 3,000 soldiers remaining, and its overall membership dropped from 60,000 to 10,000.[3] But two decades later Mao Zedong's CCP kicked the Nationalists out of mainland China, in part by planting countless spies inside the Nationalist government to rot it from within.

The "April 12 incident" in 1927 led to the birth of the Red Army on August 1 and the founding later that year of clandestine operations, assassination squads, and finally a professional intelligence service that absorbed them, the Special Services Section (SSS).[4] Today's Ministries of State Security and Public Security consider the SSS to be their predecessor. The struggles of the SSS to survive and gather enemy intelligence form important parts of the party's founding narrative. The successes celebrated today are not entirely hyperbole and are vital to understanding both the history of Chinese communism and the behavior of the contemporary Chinese party-state with its impressive surveillance apparatus.

The early years of the SSS were marked by hard-earned gains and lucky breaks to collect intelligence on the KMT and maintain the party's underground presence inside China's cities. In April 1931 the SSS's greatest operational success clashed with its greatest failure. From 1929 the service ran a small three-man spy ring, now known as the Three Heroes of the Dragon's Lair (龙潭三杰, *longtan san jie*), in the heart of the KMT's intelligence apparatus. The intelligence provided by these men, Qian Zhuangfei, Li Kenong, and Hu Di, allowed the communists operating in the cities to stay a step ahead of KMT security organs. Qian in particular furnished actionable intelligence, because his talent and origins earned him a job as the private secretary for Xu Enzeng (U. T. Hsu), the chief of KMT intelligence. From this vantage point, he saw everything that crossed Xu's desk and more.

Assassinations and mayhem, however, were as much the province of the SSS as any delicate intelligence operation. The SSS operations section (*xingdong ke*) murdered collaborators, set off car bombs, and assassinated KMT officials. These "red brigades" or "dog-beating squads," as they became known, attracted at least as many thugs as committed communists. Gu Shunzhang, its guiding light who doubled as SSS director, was one of the former, despite his labor activism.[5] A talented magician and master of disguise, Gu also participated directly in the section's operations. In April 1931 local KMT security officials in Wuhan recognized and arrested him. Gu knew as well as anyone that he faced torture and death at the hands of the KMT and agreed to cooperate. He warned his captors, however, that they should remain silent about his arrest until he could be brought to KMT intelligence headquarters in Nanjing. Gu knew of Qian and the two other "heroes" but did not identify them.

Gu's captors ignored his advice and cabled Nanjing, crowing over their success in capturing the CCP's head spy. The telegrams arrived at Xu's office after he had departed for the day and fell into the hands of Qian Zhuangfei. CCP knowledge of Gu's capture and agreement to cooperate spurred a frantic rush to vacate urban hideouts. Gu had a detailed knowledge not just of his section and its work but also of the CCP's underground infrastructure across China's cities. Communist safe houses, communications protocols, true names and aliases, cover organizations, and spies within the KMT all were in Gu's head. Qian, Li, and Hu's cover may have been blown, but not before Qian gave the CCP at least a twelve-hour head start. That lead time allowed the communists to begin destroying relevant documents and ordering cadres to flee the city.

The Three Heroes of the Dragon's Lair saved the urban CCP leadership in spite of the failure of vetting and indoctrination to identify Gu Shunzhang's unreliability. Meanwhile, Mao and the Red Army remained safely out of reach in the remote mountains of Jiangxi, to which the leadership retreated. However, the damage Gu wrought nearly destroyed the party's urban presence. The KMT central government rounded up thousands of communists in the cities, though key figures such as future premier Zhou Enlai, future five-star general Chen Geng, and Chen Yun escaped the dragnet. As a number of party luminaries, such as Mao Zedong and Marshal Ye Jianying, would later note, the Three Heroes spy ring changed the course of the Chinese revolution by saving key cadre. The episode has engendered countless books, essays, and movies, because it is a place where historical truth and propagandistic convenience overlap.

The party narratives, however, are less forthcoming about the subsequent collapse of the SSS even as they applaud the KMT's execution of Gu some time in 1935. Gu's defection critically weakened SSS operations, and the party disbanded the unit in 1935. As the locus of CCP power shifted to the countryside and the Jiangxi soviet, so too did the party's intelligence apparatus. Many of those brought in to run the Political Protection Bureau (PPB) under the Central Committee, and the Second Bureau of the Central Revolutionary Military Commission (CRMC)—the forerunner of today's Central Military Commission (CMC)—began their intelligence careers in the SSS. Qian Zhuangfei ran the bureau's training program in radio interception and analysis. Li Kenong also served as a CRMC deputy director and as head of the Jiangxi province branch of the PPB. Others, such as Chen Yun, Kang Sheng, and Pan Hannian, would fight a rearguard action in the cities to preserve the CCP's intelligence operations before fleeing to communist base areas.

The CRMC Second Bureau would become similarly legendary for saving the party during the KMT Encirclement Campaigns (1930–34) and the Long March. Although the impact of this military intelligence department cannot be denied, most approved Chinese sources obfuscate the reasons for the Second Bureau's successes in exploiting KMT communications. For many years, the KMT did not encipher their communications, sending messages entirely in the clear. This allowed the Second Bureau to intercept enemy radio traffic, build a comprehensive order of battle, be alert to enemy operations, and locate their units. As the KMT introduced ciphers, the Second Bureau did not develop a strong deciphering capability but rather learned to exploit captured and stolen codebooks. The successes of Red Army operations during the Long March seem to correlate directly with where the Second Bureau could rely on its existing order of battle knowledge and enemy ciphers.

If SSS operations demonstrated the value of intelligence in protecting the party, then the Second Bureau showed the value of integrating command and intelligence to seize the initiative and use the smaller Red Army effectively against superior forces. The CRMC Second Bureau began the history of the People's Liberation Army (PLA) intelligence apparatus. Today's Intelligence Bureau in the Joint Staff Department and Strategic Support Force would see themselves as direct descendants. Although the history of military intelligence falls strangely silent for much of the period between the end of the Long March in 1935 and the founding of the People's Republic of China (PRC) in 1949, intelligence remained an important brace for Red Army leadership. During the Liao-Shen campaign (1948) in the northeast, Lin Biao would travel with intelligence personnel as part of his command train. Peng Dehuai, while in command of the Eighth Route Army in 1940 in eastern China, told newly arrived civilian intelligence personnel that they reported to him and his intelligence chief rather than to their own headquarters in Yan'an.[6] In short, the CCP early on understood the value of intelligence for the party's security and military operations.

Understanding these early years is critical for two reasons. First, since 1927 the CCP has considered intelligence a professional activity that requires dedicated organizations to conduct it. Even as these organizations were established and eventually eroded, another organization always arose to take up the mantle. The SSS was absorbed into the Political Protection Bureau, which also shared personnel with the CRMC Second Bureau. Some officers in each moved into the successor Social Affairs Department, the Red Army's general staff, the Eighth Route Army's intelligence units, and so on, almost to the present day. Only after the founding of the PRC in 1949 did clearer lines start to emerge between the party, state, and military intelligence units with distinct career patterns.

Second, the heroes of these operations and veterans of these organizations played key roles in Chinese intelligence until their deaths. This founding generation of intelligence officers remained active into the 1980s. Premier Zhou Enlai, the first SSS director, involved himself in domestic and foreign intelligence operations almost until his death in 1976. Liang

Guangpu, who led the General Staff Department's intelligence bureau from 1978 to 1982, ran the CRMC Second Bureau's wireless training academy in Ruijin in the early 1930s. Li Kenong, one of the Three Heroes of the Dragon's Lair, would wear both party and military intelligence hats throughout the rest of his career until his death in 1962, and he contributed to the first operational histories and training materials as Chinese intelligence professionalized in the late 1930s. Many other names—for example, Ye Jianying, Wu Xiuquan, Liao Chengzhi, Luo Qingchang—appear repeatedly throughout this history for their roles in shaping the relationship between decisionmakers and intelligence officers as well as the process of intelligence.

Troubled Politics, Troubled Intelligence

Looking back at the history of the CCP since its founding in 1921, several themes emerge that are useful to understand the effect of Chinese communist intelligence and security operations on the party's development and on modern China itself. Closely weighing these themes has helped us separate the CCP's propaganda line from what can be discerned from reliable and validated data and what can be inferred and from matters where only an informed guess is possible.

The first theme is often termed "red versus expert." This widespread tension between those of proven political loyalty and the technically competent was evident early in the revolution and took different forms that did not specifically denigrate expertise per se until after 1956.[7]

A variant on this theme that heavily influenced CCP intelligence is tension between the party's ideologues and counterspies on the one hand and its intelligence professionals and the highly trained secret agents they dispatched on the other. Intelligence officers and agents who were successful in gathering enemy secrets did so in part by cultivating contacts with the other side, including liars, thieves, smugglers, drug dealers, and of course traitors. In a stinging irony, by successfully stealing enemy secrets, these communist officers and agents exposed themselves, in the best of times, to doubts about their loyalty. In the worst of times, ideologues and counterspies who seldom if ever had to leave the safety of the CCP's base areas purged their own intelligence people for doing their jobs, motivated at least in part by the radical policy prescriptions, and at times the paranoia, of

Mao Zedong.[8] This was the fate of senior intelligence official Pan Hannian after he confessed in 1955 to not reporting an important meeting twelve years earlier with Wang Jingwei, the leader of the Japanese puppet government. Between eight hundred and one thousand CCP intelligence officers and agents were demoted, fired, or imprisoned in the subsequent purge ordered by Mao.

The 1955 intelligence purge was just the first wave in a series of losses in the ranks of the PRC intelligence community. Later that year Zhou Enlai conceived and Mao Zedong approved a reorganization that led to the founding of the party's first permanent foreign intelligence organ, the Central Investigation Department (CID). In the following decade the organization grew, built standard procedures, and forged interagency cooperation. But when the Cultural Revolution began in 1966, the CID was not exempted from the chaos. Rival Red Guard factions formed within the department, each competing with the other to represent true adherence to Mao's "thought." As the radical left under Mao's wife, Jiang Qing, and the Cultural Revolution Group ascended, almost the entire senior leadership of the CID was purged. Fighting within forced Zhou and Mao to engineer a military takeover of the department in March 1967 to protect its secrets from leaking off premises and into Red Guard newspapers.

The death of Mao in 1976 and the end of the Cultural Revolution did not end purges in the intelligence field. The next housecleaning was directed against an unknown number of Cultural Revolution "beneficiaries," chiefly Luo Qingchang, the new CID director and the only senior intelligence leader from 1966 who survived the deluge. But Luo hung on for years, just as in the rest of society leftists did not simply withdraw in shame and fear with the December 1978 return of Deng Xiaoping to the party's core leadership. In fact, Luo resisted change. Notably, he encouraged subordinates to ignore a speech made by Deng at a foreign affairs conference the next summer where he urged intelligence reforms and enhanced clandestine operations outside of PRC embassies.

Luo was finally ousted for good in 1983 with the formation of the Ministry of State Security (MSS), though to this day he retains an inexplicably honored place in CCP intelligence history. However, the three purges in 1955, 1967, and 1983 produced an unmeasured decline in talent available to the PRC intelligence community as it shifted from a place in the party to a government ministry under the state council. These purges, extending even beyond Mao Zedong's rule, reflect how the party's struggle-criticism-transformation ideal continues to drive events.[9] That often-gruesome influence on Chinese communist intelligence operations can still be observed.

Intelligence into the Modern Era

The politics of the MSS's establishment in 1983 coincided with Deng Xiaoping's policy of reform and opening that increased China's engagement with the outside world. In 1975 Deng began drafting plans for the "Four Modernizations"—agriculture, industry, science, and national defense—to make China rich and powerful. These modernization programs required importing technical and managerial knowledge from advanced capitalist economies. How to do this was unknown. China's break from the Soviet Union in the 1950s led to policies of self-sufficiency and undermined the party leaders' ability to understand the outside world. With relatively few important diplomatic relationships and weakened intelligence resources, Deng's China needed to both experiment diplomatically and to educate its own leadership about the outside world.

China's intelligence apparatus, however, was ill prepared to support these intelligence needs. The aforementioned purges had reduced the size and the operational knowledge of the civilian intelligence cadre. Moreover, when the civilian ministries and the party bureaucracy were disbanded in 1967, one of two things happened. Either agents lost contact with their handlers and, in some cases, only reconnected a decade later with mixed successes in maintaining the intelligence relationship, or the PLA General Staff Department's Second Bureau (2PLA) took over the handling of many CID agents, and there is no sign that the agents necessarily returned to civilian control when the party bureaucracy stood back up. When the MSS was created a few years later, its personnel came predominantly from the counterintelligence elements of the Ministry of Public Security (MPS). Even the first minister, Ling Yun, came from an internal security background.

Although the information is sketchy, Deng Xiaoping appears to have turned to his friends in the military for intelligence. During Deng's brief rehabilitation in 1975 as the PLA chief of the general staff, he brought intelligence veteran and former diplomat Wu Xiuquan back as a deputy chief of the General Staff Department and as 2PLA director. Wu expanded 2PLA's open-source intelligence in 1979 by creating the Beijing (now China) Institute for International and Strategic Studies to collect and analyze the strategy of the Soviet Union and other major countries.[10] Other significant 2PLA leaders, such as Liu Guangfu (1978–82), Zhang Zhongru (1982–85), and Cao Xin (1985–88), began their careers under the CRMC Second Bureau or the Eighth Route Army, and some, such as Cao and Wu, served directly with Deng.

These connections are not the only indicators that Deng relied on the military for intelligence. The PLA dominated the major externally facing leading small groups, most notably those for Taiwan and foreign affairs, which set overall policy guidance. The minister of state security would not join the foreign affairs leading small group until the mid to late 1990s, isolating the ministry. Although the MSS chiefs were politically reliable, there is no indication that they were the kind of political heavyweights who did not need a formal position to be influential.[11] In 1985 the Ministry of Foreign Affairs, echoing Deng's 1979 speech on foreign affairs, argued the MSS presence in official missions should be reduced and operationally restricted, lest the discovery of its operations derail the foreign relationships critical to Deng's modernization program.[12]

Deng's reliance on the PLA cemented the military's role as the primary foreign intelligence provider, but it had a few unintended consequences that reverberate to the present day. Focusing on foreign intelligence advanced the careers of 2PLA defense attachés, creating a cadre of military intelligence leaders led by Xiong Guangkai who had little to no experience in military operations. From 1988 to 2006, the defense attachés led PLA intelligence, even overseeing the signals intelligence apparatus. In one sense, this new generation of intelligence officers were PLA outsiders. For example, Xiong spent much of his early career abroad as a defense attaché and in analytic positions at 2PLA headquarters. He served and was educated entirely within military intelligence. His predecessor as deputy chief of the general staff with the intelligence portfolio, Xu Xin, however, served in a broader range of positions. Xu originally was an infantry officer serving in Deng's division in the Eighth Route Army and was a veteran of the Korean War.

Ironically, Deng's reliance on the PLA at the expense of the MSS created the conditions for the politicization of military intelligence in the 1990s. The rise of 2PLA's role in foreign intelligence—2PLA for years was known as "China's CIA"—dragged the military intelligence apparatus further away from military operations.[13] As Xiong rose to the top and saw little room for advancement, he attached himself to CCP general secretary Jiang Zemin. As an outsider himself, Jiang needed to know more about the PLA leadership and whether to trust them. With Deng's help, Jiang faced down a military coup in 1993 and, thanks in part to PLA actions, initiated crises with the United States in 1995, 1996, 1999, and 2001.[14] The limited records of these crises suggest the PLA was less than forthcoming with Jiang if not at times outright deceptive. Xiong reportedly availed himself of the PLA's signals intelligence department to spy on other military leaders and furnish Jiang with reporting on what the military leadership was actually doing. Jiang even tried to move Xiong to take over the MSS in 1998, but other leaders balked at the idea of a clear partisan running the MSS, and Xiong stayed in the military.[15] The Jiang-Xiong relationship cemented the military's role at the center, leaving little room for other ministries to play a meaningful role in foreign intelligence.

Absent political interest to remove the MSS's operational restrictions and expand its presence abroad, the ministry largely focused on domestic consolidation. When the MSS was created in 1983, it consisted of the central headquarters and a small number of local state security departments. The MSS covered only about half the country at the provincial level by the end of the 1980s and even less at local levels. The 1990s, however, saw the final consolidation across the provincial and local levels. Most of the expansion came at the expense of the MPS. Many MPS officers were police one day, intelligence officers the next. Current minister of state security Chen Wenqing was one of those officials. Chen began his career in counterespionage at the Sichuan public security department but was moved into the Sichuan state security department when it was created around 1993–94.[16]

The consolidation of PLA intelligence to support China's leadership and the MSS domestic expansion did little to resolve some of the major challenges for Chinese intelligence. Except for tactical intelligence embedded with operational units, military intelligence oriented itself to support policy rather than military operations. U.S. and Allied military operations in the Persian Gulf War in 1991 demonstrated that modern militaries needed robust, real-time intelligence capabilities to exploit missiles and precision-guided munitions, and militaries without those capabilities were dangerously vulnerable.[17] Party leadership, however, trumped military decisionmakers, even as the latter began formulating aggressive modernization programs to make the PLA capable of information-enabled operations comparable to those executed by the United States and other advanced militaries.

The influx of MPS personnel into the MSS highlighted the need for better training and education programs. Although much of the MSS's work on a day-to-day basis qualified as internal security and counterintelligence with directly transferable skills, domestic intelligence skills are not as readily transferable to foreign operations or handling foreign sources. Minister of state security Jia Chunwang (1985–98) began commissioning research for unclassified books and articles to capture the historical legacy and lessons of CCP intelligence by 1992, but these works would not begin appearing until several years later.[18]

The PLA and the MSS, however, started making investments in the mid-1990s that would pay off much later. Companies such as Beijing TOPSEC Network Security Technology Company (founded in November 1995) and Venustech (founded in 1996) reportedly received start-up funding from the government. These early network security firms produced China's first indigenous security tools, such as network sensors and firewalls. They also were brought into a network of companies around the China National Information Technology Security Evaluation Center (CNITSEC), which was established in 1997. Ostensibly a national standards center for evaluating vulnerabilities, CNITSEC appears to be the public-facing organization for the MSS bureau responsible for computer network exploitation and network defense. These organizations became the center of a web of public-private partnerships and contracts that China's intelligence services use to obscure their activities in cyberspace. At the time, however, these were just long-term bets on a handful of bright researchers. This bet would become fundamental to Chinese intelligence a decade later, but the results would be especially important for the MSS.

The reform and opening era for Chinese intelligence was a time for rebuilding, and Beijing's leaders went with the capabilities they had. Relying heavily on the military intelligence apparatus created imbalance across the system. Without a large number of experienced intelligence professionals, the MSS more closely resembled another national police force than a sophisticated intelligence service with worldwide reach. The MSS never quite escaped the consequences of its predecessors' past politics and purges, ceding the field to military intelligence.

Emerging as a Global Intelligence Power

As the millennium turned, China's economic dynamism and international presence steadily increased and then accelerated after China's accession to the World Trade Organization in 2001. In 2005 U.S. deputy secretary of state Robert Zoellick gave a remarkable speech clarifying the purpose of the U.S.-China relationship. Zoellick stated the U.S. goal should be to integrate China into the international system as a "responsible stakeholder." The specifics of the speech were less relevant than Washington's recognition that Beijing was a force with which to be reckoned and on the way to becoming an equal. There was no sign, however, that Chinese intelligence was keeping pace with the country's needs.

Military intelligence was still captured by the needs of the central leadership, even as PLA writings about modernization highlighted an outsized role for intelligence in modern operations.[19] Some MSS provincial departments were rumored to have started special training programs for foreign intelligence operations, but nothing in the publicly available espionage case records suggests that a newfound sophistication started to emerge.

The mismatch between China's intelligence capabilities, their organizational distribution, and requirements for intelligence support would begin to shift shortly after the baton was passed from Jiang Zemin to Hu Jintao. This process began in 2002 with the Sixteenth Party Congress, when Hu replaced Jiang as the CCP general secretary. Jiang, however, held on to the chairmanship of the CMC, giving him effective control over the PLA. The Jiang-Xiong relationship consequently continued to shape military intelligence, and there was little Hu could do about it. The two power centers, however, created a command problem for the PLA, because the CMC chairman decided military policy and signed off on operations, while the PLA ostensibly was loyal to the party general secretary. The PLA helped engineer Jiang's formal retirement from the CMC in September 2004, paving the way for the PLA (and probably Hu) to sideline Xiong for the purpose of redirecting its intelligence organizations toward PLA priorities.

The retirement of Lieutenant General Xiong Guangkai, the deputy chief of the general staff with the intelligence portfolio, in December 2005 provided the first public indicator that change was coming. Xiong's replacement, Zhang Qinsheng, came to the position without any intelligence background. This introduction of an operations officer into senior intelligence roles was the first of several changes to career pathways as the PLA slowly reasserted itself over its intelligence apparatus. Although Zhang only stayed in the position for a short time before his promotion to command the Guangzhou Military Region, his successors—Ma Xiaotian, Qi Jianguo, and Sun Jianguo—all came from outside military intelligence. Just as significantly, senior military intelligence officers started to find experience and promotions outside of intelligence. Where intelligence careers were once stovepiped and terminal, officers with intelligence experience moved into deputy commander and deputy chief of staff positions throughout the PLA. One of the first to move was former 2PLA director Chen Xiaogong, who became a deputy air force commander in 2009. His successor at 2PLA, Yang Hui, became chief of staff of the Nanjing Military Region and continued through 2017 as chief of staff for the Eastern Theater Command. Other figures from technical reconnaissance and signals intelligence also started moving, such as signals intelligence chief Wu Guohua, who in 2011 became a deputy commander of the Second Artillery, China's conventional and strategic missile force.[20]

On November 26, 2015, Xi Jinping announced a wide-ranging set of organizational reforms that affected the PLA from the CMC down to the lowest soldiers. These reforms fundamentally reshaped the PLA's organization of intelligence. The technical reconnaissance or collection elements within 2PLA and the General Staff Department's Third Department (3PLA) were moved into the newly created Strategic Support Force alongside other electronic and information warfare elements. Technical reconnaissance bureaus from the military services also moved under this new force, leaving only a limited capacity within the theater commands. The Strategic Support Force centralized tactical and operational intelligence, making it easier from a technical and organizational perspective to fuse intelligence for battlefield commanders.

Minus its technical components such as the Aerospace Reconnaissance Bureau, 2PLA became the Intelligence Bureau of the Joint Staff Department. The implications of the change remain unknown because of a dearth of information. One knowledgeable Chinese interlocutor suggested the Intelligence Bureau would be a more focused body for supporting the CMC and other top-level decisionmakers, undistracted by the immediate needs of warfighting and battlefield support. This individual thought that, if anything, the influence of the Intelligence Bureau would increase.[21] One of the potential downsides of moving the technical collection resources into the Strategic Support Force, however, would be breaking up China's all-source intelligence capability. When everything existed under the General Staff Department, the deputy chief responsible for intelligence could provide an all-source perspective to the leadership. This may have been one of the reasons for the influence of leaders such as Wu Xiuquan and Xiong Guangkai. For this loss not to be felt under the new organizational structure, the PLA—or at least Xi Jinping and the CMC—would need to have established a national intelligence priorities framework and ensured that Strategic Support Force intelligence also would flow to the Intelligence Bureau. Whether these developments occurred, unfortunately, is unknowable.

As military intelligence began its realignment, the MSS adopted a more aggressive posture toward collecting foreign intelligence. All signs pointed toward an opportunity for expanding the ministry's role overseas. With the PLA turning inward even as China's "Going Out" policy subsidized Chinese firms pursuing economic opportunities abroad, China's interests were expanding without a commensurate expansion of intelligence capabilities.

The MSS bet on cyberspace, made in the 1990s, and a similar though less successful military effort became critical components of China's intelligence power. Computer network exploitation became the easiest way to have a turnkey collection capability without the investment of time and money in training case officers and analysts to understand and operate in a foreign environment, especially with the past intelligence purges weakening China's human intelligence capability.

The movement of information into digital form and its storage on computer networks created a "*Dreadnought* moment" worldwide for signals intelligence collection and close-in technical operations.[22] Just as the 1906 launch of HMS *Dreadnought* with its long-range guns reshaped naval warfare and nullified the British naval advantage over Germany, the emergence of computer network exploitation reshaped technical collection. During the Cold War, the Western and Soviet bloc intelligence services engaged in a no-holds-barred competition to collect secrets. As new technical operations were uncovered by the adversary, each side learned new techniques and turned them around in the field against third-country targets. Creating bugs for typewriters and listening devices inside wall panels became an artisanal craft. China's autarkic, self-reliance policies under Mao after 1949 isolated China's intelligence services from most of this experience, and spying domestically never required the same degree of technical sophistication that Western and Soviet bloc intelligence needed to apply.

Just as importantly, the 1930s and 1940s saw the emergence of machine encryption requiring the use of early computers to break. The achievements of the CRMC Second Bureau were not primarily in the field of cryptography. The bureau exploited captured codebooks and direction-finding rather than learning how to organize a systematic code-breaking effort comparable to the U.S. and U.K. efforts to break German and Japanese codes. With the 1960 Sino-Soviet split, Beijing lost much of its access to modern technologies. Cold War signals intelligence, however, required the resources of an advanced industrial state, and China lagged behind. The PLA reportedly would not learn about modern techniques such as telemetry analysis until Washington approached Beijing for cooperation in replacing the U.S. listening facilities lost in the Iranian Revolution of 1979. Actually breaking computer-encrypted communications remained beyond the reach of Beijing's spy apparatus.

Computer network exploitation changed everything for Chinese intelligence, both civilian and military. The craft of technical operations shifted from the elegance of the device and its delivery to the elegance of the software. Moreover, the Internet enabled global reach without a global network of listening posts, satellites, and intelligence officers. Chinese military and intelligence thinkers understood this shift in the 1990s, but a decade would pass before the scope of Chinese activity became clear. Leaks from the U.S. government suggested Chinese intelligence was targeting U.S. military and corporate networks as early as 2003 in a series of intrusions collectively known as Titan Rain. The British government, probably in cooperation with the United States, also identified the same hackers getting inside government networks, including the Foreign Office and the House of Commons.[23] Forensic investigations beginning in the late 2000s would reveal far-reaching networks of infected hosts across the private and public sector. The first public report to reveal the scope of this activity came from the Canada-based Citizen Lab in 2009, which investigated Chinese intrusions into computers owned by the Tibetan government in exile. As the investigators unraveled the command and control network and traced infected machines, they found more than 1,000 infected hosts in 103 countries. These exploits allowed the Chinese side to access and edit files, surreptitiously use microphones and web cameras, and collect emails.[24] This intrusion set, called GhostNet, would soon be followed by public exposure of other wide-ranging efforts for intelligence collection and intellectual property theft, notably Aurora in 2010 and Shady RAT in 2011.[25]

These widespread intrusion sets marked the clear emergence of computer network exploitation as a go-to part of the Chinese intelligence toolkit. Most importantly, some of the Chinese intrusions clearly focused on providing operational support to other intelligence operations at home and abroad. In the penetration of Google's networks in Operation Aurora, Chinese hackers sought files on the Google accounts related to Chinese individuals that were covered by a legal intercept warrant. This information would show whom the Federal Bureau of Intelligence (and other parts of the U.S. intelligence community) was tracking inside the United States.[26] The breaches of Anthem Insurance and the Office of Personnel Management made public in 2015 compromised the personal information of more than 20 million current and former U.S. government employees. Although attribution of the attack was never firmly settled publicly, U.S. counterintelligence officials admitted that China appeared to be using the data to target U.S. officials for recruitment.[27] The data taken in these intrusions suggests the MSS was behind them, because the PLA would not necessarily have human intelligence capabilities for follow-on exploitation. This operational integration showed China posed a different intelligence threat than it once did, marrying sophistication to scope and scale.

One of the striking points of Western reporting on Chinese computer network exploitation is focus on the PLA almost to the exclusion of the MSS. The intrusion sets such as Titan Rain amalgamated a large amount of activity coming out of China but rarely specified whether the MSS or its military counterparts were behind them. The PLA became more exposed because digital forensics married with organizational mapping of the military's cyber units.[28] This combination is what allowed the U.S. Department of Justice to issue an indictment for five PLA hackers working for 61398 Unit of 3PLA. The PLA simply was louder, and its greater organizational transparency allowed foreign analysts to trace activity directly back to military office complexes. The MSS, however, was significantly more discreet. The first conclusive public trace of an intrusion to the MSS did not occur until May 2017.[29] Consequently, it is doubtful anyone outside the ministry has a clear sense of how successful it has been at collecting intelligence abroad.

A new minister, Geng Huichang, took over in August 2007 after a mistress-related scandal toppled several government ministers, including MSS chief Xu Yongyue. Unlike his predecessors, Geng was an intelligence professional focused internationally rather than domestically. The beginnings of his career are murky, but he may have entered the CID before becoming one of the principal America watchers at the MSS bureau known publicly as the China Institutes of Contemporary International Relations.[30] When he took over the MSS, Geng may have been the right man at the right time for his service. The PLA was turning inward, and the bureaucratic shifts offered the MSS an opportunity to showcase its growing sophistication abroad. One Western study of Chinese foreign policymaking during this time suggested MSS influence on foreign policy was on the rise, due in part to its domestic power. Such influence on the part of intelligence services usually occurs because they are useful contributors to the process.

The MSS also strung together a solid decade of counterintelligence successes against Taiwan and the United States beginning in 2003. The most significant MSS success was the dismantling of CIA operations in China between late 2010 and late 2012. In 2010 the MSS began running a series of dangles at CIA and allied intelligence services to draw out case officers. One of the more believable efforts harvested a throwaway covert communications system from the CIA. Using an expendable system with an agent whose bona fides are suspect is normal operational practice. However, the CIA reportedly connected that system to the Internet-based system that it was using for its vetted and committed Chinese agents. Before the connection was shut down, the MSS in cooperation with military signals intelligence generated a large number of operational leads that it subsequently tracked down. At least twenty Chinese agents working for the CIA were arrested and executed.[31]

From the vantage point of 2018, Chinese intelligence has arrived as an indisputable global power. Other intelligence systems may be superior in specific ways or in specific capabilities, but Chinese capabilities across the board cannot be dismissed or underestimated. The Chinese services have demonstrated the ability to collect intelligence abroad using creative methods and to shut down the principal intelligence threats operating inside China.

Putting It All Together

The evolution of the CCP and PRC intelligence apparatus demonstrates that bureaucracy and politics mark this history at least as much as the prurient sensationalism that accompanies much writing about intelligence. China's intelligence officers of today may be the inheritors of the *Sunzi Bingfa* (*Art of War*), but ancient tradition is a poor substitute for practical experience. The CCP eminence grise Zhou Enlai told Henry Kissinger as much during the latter's secret mission to Beijing in July 1971. As Kissinger waxed lyrical about the mystery of China, Zhou admonished him: "You will find [China] not mysterious. When you have become familiar with it, it will not be as mysterious as before."[32]

These broad brush strokes of Chinese intelligence history show the perils of ideological politics and dramatic changes. Although the definitive work of Chinese intelligence history cannot be written until the archives become available, the performance of CCP intelligence during the Mao years is decidedly mixed. In closing his noteworthy study of European intelligence performance from World War I through World War II, the historian Ernest May observed that the organization of intelligence services seemed to have no bearing on the success or failure of those services. The intelligence services, however, that frequently reorganized and rewired themselves consistently underperformed.[33] It is doubtful the history of Chinese intelligence will show differently.

The current structure of Chinese intelligence, dating to the establishment of the MSS in 1983, has proven the most durable since the CCP first created professional intelligence units in 1927. Beijing has used it as the foundation to support intelligence and covert action missions concerning Taiwan, Falun Gong, and now counterterrorism, with ad hoc interagency task force–like agencies.[34] The current structure has proven stable, at least in part because it contained enough flexibility with a broad structure stretching from Beijing to the provinces and into the localities.

The language Chinese intelligence uses reflects its Marxist-Leninist and revolutionary heritage. The lexicon suggests (as has been borne out in interviews with former officials who had routine contacts with their Chinese counterparts) that the intelligence services are bastions of faith in the CCP. Although they may be practical in terms of techniques and methods to acquire intelligence, this information is filtered through a Marxist-Leninist lens. The implication is that foreign targets are viewed in the worst possible light. The CCP's method of developing policy from objective and scientific laws of social-economic development means that policy failures are often viewed as the result of external interference. The Chinese intelligence services, judging from our research, have internalized that perspective and indeed may be the chief instrument through which Mao Zedong's paranoia is reinforced.

The most important implication of this finding is that intelligence analysis within the Chinese intelligence services may not resemble the empirical, positivist tradition that permeates Western intelligence. Instead, routine intelligence analysis may be politicized by highlighting reporting that reinforces the future anticipated by "scientific" Marxist analysis. Conversely, the CCP has proven durable precisely because the party has demonstrated flexibility in the face of unwanted realities. Both the MSS and its military counterparts have demonstrated several ways around this politicization. According to one knowledgeable foreign intelligence officer, MSS analysis is conducted by close advisors of the vice ministers and ministers from within their offices. Such analysis is given directly to the leaders, with limited dissemination. The standing of vice ministers and ministers allows more direct and truthful evaluation than would otherwise be possible.[35] Additionally, a number of recent espionage cases highlight the case officers asking their sources to provide their assessment of large intelligence questions based on reading and interviews. This allows the intelligence service to relay such reports without having to commit ideological infractions that might have political consequences later.

Notes on Bibliography

We avoided most online references except for official CCP and PRC government websites, but even these were used sparingly in favor of published books and articles. Though the online Chinese encyclopedia *Baidu Baike* (百度百科), which some consider semiofficial, often contained relevant material, its articles were used only in a few cases, because footnotes are sometimes inconsistent and the articles can be edited by any registered user. By contrast, the *Wenku* (文库, or library) section of *Baidu* contains portable document format files with more useful published articles.

How to Use the Primer

This volume has sections that will appeal to both general interest readers who wish to better understand modern China and espionage in general and to specialists in fields such as intelligence and security, recent Chinese history, and the politics of the PRC. "Foreign guests" who travel to and live in China, whether as tourists, diplomats, businesspeople, or others, often wonder about surveillance and how it works. In chapter 7 they will find factual information, as opposed to the usual rumors, about how the host government conducts surveillance. Students of the Chinese language will benefit from the combined use of Chinese characters with *pinyin* romanization throughout, especially in the web-based glossary of Chinese espionage and security terms that shows how the jargon has evolved over the decades. A timeline reveals how Chinese communist intelligence operations have influenced history (and vice versa). Reference chapters on operations, cases, and notable spies reveal the Chinese Communist Party's focus on intelligence and security as a "core business" from its early days.

Wherever possible, we have cross-referenced findings between communist and noncommunist sources. When it was not, we have carefully examined available evidence and excluded points that appear mistaken or exaggerated. We welcome inquiries from scholars who can point out errors and omissions.

The endnotes include URLs in some instances. These can quickly change, but articles on this topic, once posted, are more often moved by a web administrator than censored and deleted. Therefore, if a URL does not work, try using keywords to search for the reference; quite often, the article you seek will appear on another page or site.

Beyond the pages of this book you will find an online reference, a glossary of Chinese espionage and security terms, at ccpintelterms.com. We had only limited access to official Chinese lists of terms, such as *Shiyong Gong'an xiao cidian*, an unclassified public security dictionary. However, the bibliography shows that we examined many other works on CCP intelligence and security history for relevant phrases. The resulting product should be of use not only to students of the Chinese language but also to a broad range of others interested in China and in espionage. We expect to expand this list in coming editions as more material emerges on the Chinese services, allowing improved understanding of this hitherto underexplored topic.

• ONE •

Chinese Communist
Intelligence Organizations

Soviet agents in Shanghai helped organize fledgling Chinese Marxists even before the founding of the Chinese Communist Party (CCP) in July 1921. They schooled its leaders in clandestine methods—though not all were apt students. After the CCP was formed, Moscow used the Communist International (Comintern), their wholly controlled instrument, to orchestrate policy and even some operations. An often contentious secret relationship was born. After 1949 it became the Sino-Soviet "friendship," lasting until 1960. This interpretation is no anticommunist trope: CCP-approved literature, published in China, presents many details.[1]

The organs of CCP intelligence also had direct help from Russian advisors, an even more inconvenient truth given the assassinations and other violence associated with the OGPU (Unified State Political Directorate), NKVD (People's Commissariat for Internal Affairs), KGB (Committee for State Security), and their modern successors.[2] A significant number of Chinese intelligence officers, possibly hundreds, were trained in Russia— starting in 1926 with Chen Geng and Gu Shunzhang. In the 1930s Zhou Enlai loaned Chinese comrades to Soviet military intelligence (the GRU, or Main Intelligence Directorate). They were trained and deployed in networks that kept tabs on Japanese forces in China.[3]

However, the CCP's espionage services should not be characterized as a tool of the Russians, especially after 1939 when Kang Sheng took formal control. With the approval of Mao Zedong, Kang and his deputy Li Kenong aggressively spied on the GRU station in Yan'an in 1940–44. Moreover, Mao approved the removal of Russian advisors from inside the CCP security services over a year before the Sino-Soviet split of 1960.

Afterward, there is no evidence of other foreign advisors, only intelligence liaison, such as with the Americans between the Richard Nixon visit in 1972 and the end of the Cold War. The main subject: information about their common enemy, Russia.

Foreign influence notwithstanding, CCP intelligence organizations have consistently focused on contemporary problems and perceived threats: a nearly fatal lack of intelligence capability (1927), the need to reestablish clandestine networks in enemy-occupied cities (1934–39), an outmoded revolutionary organization retooled for the needs of a nation-state but interrupted by the Korean War (1949–53), an incomplete and fractured foreign intelligence structure needing consolidation as China sought its place in the world (1955), and an intelligence and counterintelligence community, shattered by the Cultural Revolution, facing renewed foreign espionage threats with the opening of China (1983). In 2016 China's seven military regions were replaced by five theater commands, and military intelligence was reorganized. Analysts have wondered whether the other shoe would drop: another reorganization of civilian intelligence, the Ministry of State Security (MSS), and possibly of the national police, the Ministry of Public Security (MPS). Accelerated campaigns to combat corruption inside the party-state and to counter foreign spying heralded at least rearranged tasks for the MSS and the MPS, with the former renewing its focus on counterintelligence at home and foreign espionage abroad.

Our thesis about CCP intelligence organizations says that they regularly struggled to keep up with the times and reorganized their way forward, like the services of many other nations. This idea runs contrary to the Beijing-approved narrative found in books, television programs, and movies. The script for public consumption emphasizes the heroics of friends and the atrocities of enemies. At times it reads like an updated rendition of *The Water Margin* (水浒传, *Shui hu zhuan*), one of the four great classical novels of Chinese literature. The CCP-scripted drama of their "hidden battlefront" (隐蔽战线, *Yinbi zhanxian*) boosts the party's legitimacy, showing that patriotic Chinese support the CCP no matter who is in charge or what deed is expected. It seems to tell today's citizens that just as it was patriotic to be a communist before 1949, so it is today. This belief system underlines that mistakes will eventually be corrected, and loyalty to the party will be rewarded.

In this chapter, we seek to clarify how CCP intelligence organs developed, declined, and renewed, how they succeeded and failed. We hope to move closer to an understanding of how intelligence became a core business of the party and will remain so for the foreseeable future. To check the CCP's official narrative, we sought validation with other sources from Taiwan, Hong Kong, and elsewhere.

1927: Central Military Department Special Operations Branch (特务工作处, *Zhongyang junwei teke*), May–August 1927

After narrowly escaping the April 12 Nationalist coup d'état in Shanghai, Zhou Enlai set up the Special Operations Branch in Wuhan under the Central Military Department in late May 1927.[4] Gu Shunzhang took charge of daily operations. The already extant Wuhan-based Special Operations Work Division (特务特务工作处, *Tewu gongzuo chu*), a VIP protection unit formed a year earlier, may have been folded into the new organ.[5] The new Protection Section (保卫股, *baowei gu*), with sixty members, took over this vital function, and half of their number were soon packed off to Moscow for training. An Intelligence Section (情报股, *qingbao gu*) produced a daily report of all available information in Wuhan based on agent material. One of their sources was the chief of police in Wuhan.[6]

The Special Operations Section (特务股, *Tewu gu*), which probably started later than the others, was responsible for assassinations of enemies and turncoats (renegades: 叛徒, *pantu*). It eventually came to be called the Red Squad or, more frankly, the Red Terror Squad (红队; 红色恐怖队, *hong dui; hongse kongbu dui*). In August 1927 these intelligence and protection organs under the Central Military Department were abolished as the Central Committee prepared to move back to Shanghai.[7]

1927–35: Special Services Section (中央特别行动科, *Zhongyang tebie xingdong ke,* also known as 中央特别任务科 [abbreviated 中央特科 *Zhongyang teke*])

On November 14, 1927, the Central Committee directed Zhou Enlai to reorganize its subordinate departments and add a permanent urban intelligence organ.[8] Zhou took the existing general branch (总务科, *Zongwu ke*), responsible for clandestine accommodations and meeting places, and began building additional sections for intelligence (情报, *qingbao*), operations (行动, *xingdong*), and radio communications (无线 电通讯, *wuxiandian tongxun*). The consolidated result was known as the Special Services Section (SSS).[9] In Chinese it was commonly referred to as the *Teke* (特科), and this abbreviation is widely used today in publications and on the Internet.

The new organization protected the central leadership, assembled intelligence, assassinated and kidnapped enemies and turncoats, rescued imprisoned comrades, and maintained clandestine radio stations and ciphers.[10] Gu Shunzhang led the SSS from 1927 to 1931.[11] The organization was based in Shanghai and had officers in Tianjin, Beiping (now Beijing), and the Hong Kong–Macau region.

The SSS faced a mortal crisis in April 1931 when its leader, Gu Shunzhang, was apprehended in Wuhan by the KMT. Under threat of torture, Gu quickly defected and began naming names and places used as hideouts. As a result, many communists were caught and executed, including CCP general secretary Xiang Zhongfa. However, SSS clandestine operatives inside the central government managed to sound an alarm in time for many communists to escape capture (see Li Kenong and the Three Heroes of the Dragon's Lair). Their actions may have saved the CCP leadership and its urban assets from complete annihilation.[12]

In 1931–33 Chen Yun and Kang Sheng led the remnants of the urban networks in Shanghai, but the SSS gradually expired as aggressive KMT operations forced them into hiding or to evacuate, following the leadership to Red Army headquarters in Jiangxi. In the first six months of 1933, more than six hundred communists were detained in Shanghai, and fewer than five hundred members remained free. That January, SSS interim director Chen Yun departed the city for Jiangxi, and Pan Hannian (see chapter 3) left only four months later. By 1934 the CCP's urban intelligence networks were "ninety percent destroyed." In September 1935, near the end of the Red Army's Long March, the CCP formally disbanded its young spy organization.[13] Inside the Red Army at Ruijin, a successor was already in place:

the Political Protection Bureau (PPB), led by Deng Fa. It absorbed SSS officers including Li Kenong,[14] but the PPB was more focused on digging out internal enemies than on gathering intelligence.[15] While there were key successes (see Mo Xiong, chapter 3), urban and rural intelligence network building would not again be seriously addressed until the formation of the Social Affairs Department in February 1939.

1931–39: Political Protection Bureau
(中央政治保卫局, *Zhongyang zhengzhi baowei ju*)

In the last few months of 1930, party leaders in Shanghai decided to bring security work and the purging counterrevolutionary committees under more centralized control after Mao Zedong's Pyrrhic victory of purge and revenge known as the Futian incident. In roughly August 1931 the Central Political Protection Department (中央政治保卫处, *Zhongyang zheng-zhi baowei chu*) was founded in Jiangxi with Deng Fa, fresh from under-ground work in Hong Kong, as its leader.[16] The new organ was subordinate to the Red Army General Front Command. In November it was elevated to become the State PPB (国家政治保卫局, *Guojia zhengzhi baowei ju*) and given the responsibility to guard the party center. Li Kenong, Qian Zhuangfei, and other veterans of the SSS who had, like Deng Fa himself, recently fled the cities entered the PPB as division and section chiefs with responsibilities in the Red Army zones and in enemy areas.[17] This may have been the point at which genuine enemy intelligence (敌情, *di qing*) work began in the state PPB, broadening its scope from rear area security. The SSS continued its work in Shanghai, but now there was another central body with security and intelligence functions.[18] Their precise relationship requires further research.

In 1934 the state PPB included both civilian-focused units and one embedded in the Red Army. They appear to have been two sides of the same coin, led by Deng Fa and Li Kenong. The latter held positions in both.[19] Some prominent examples show how the PPB and Red Army military intelligence had a "revolving door" aspect: Luo Ruiqing, a politi-cal officer who became First Corps PPB head under Lin Biao and went on to higher office;[20] Zhang Shunqing, the Third Corps PPB head under

Peng Dehuai who also was an army political officer;[21] and Wang Shoutao, who was director of the Political Department of the Ninth Corps when the Long March began and was a short-lived PPB director in 1935.[22]

Given the background of Li Kenong and Qian Zhuangfei as SSS clandestine officers in KMT areas, one might suppose that they were assigned duties in Ruijin to control work behind enemy lines. However, CCP sources give few details of their daily work—mostly just noting their arrival and reassignment after having their identities revealed with the defection of Gu Shunzhang in April 1931. Sources agree that Li was head of the "implementation department" of the State PPB in Ruijin (国家政治保卫局执行部, *Guojia zhengzhi baowei ju, zhixing bu*) but give little information about what he actually did there, other than arranging for passage of personnel in and out of White areas. Qian Zhuangfei was assigned to a military unit as a PPB cadre and as head of the Intelligence Bureau of the Central Military Commission (CMC). He either died in a KMT air raid during the Long March or was captured and killed.[23] Both men would have been subordinate to Deng Fa. However, Li Kenong might have outshined his boss: upon arrival in Bao'an in 1935, Deng was reassigned, at least on paper, to be the lead of the Grain Department.[24] Li Kenong was on the rise.

A national PPB was maintained under the command of Mao Zedong and Zhu De in Ruijin before and during the Long March (1934–35). When they reached the Bao'an and Yan'an areas, they also called this organization the Northwest PPB (西北政治保卫局, *Xibei zhengzhi baowei ju*). A party historian opined that they were the same.[25] Wang Shoudao was appointed its director on October 30, 1935, and Zhou Xing took over in February 1936.[26] Zhou Xing was one of the handlers of Edgar Snow when he visited Bao'an that year and briefed the American on sensitive matters such as the number of political prisoners under detention.[27]

Though the PPB absorbed personnel from the Special Services Section (SSS) when it was disbanded in September 1935, the bureau was focused on protection of the leadership and "digging out" of perceived enemies (see *Chanchu* in the web-based glossary of terms).[28]

1939–49: Social Affairs Department
(中共中央社会部, *Zhonggong zhongyang shehui bu*)

In November 1937 intelligence veteran Kang Sheng arrived in Yan'an from Moscow on a Soviet aircraft with Wang Ming and Chen Yun. By August 1938 Kang was in charge of the CCP's existing security and intelligence assets: the PPB, the leadership guard force, and the shattered remnants of the recently abolished SSS.[29] Although direct evidence is lacking, Kang probably had Russian training in intelligence and security operations.[30] He may have carried instructions from Joseph Stalin to reorganize CCP intelligence after years of substantial casualties resulting from the 1930–31 Futian incident, the April 1931 defection of Gu Shunzhang, and the trials of the Long March (1934–35).

In 1939 the CCP held its safest base area to date and Mao Zedong was making strides toward consolidating party leadership, albeit under an ineffectual challenge from Wang Ming. But knowledge of the KMT enemy was lacking. The atmosphere was ripe for intelligence rebuilding and reorganization. On February 18, 1939, the Party Central Committee established the *Shehui Bu*, or Social Affairs Department (SAD), with Kang as its director. Over the next four years Kang spread SAD offices down to the local level in many communist-held areas; integrated intelligence, counterintelligence, and policing; systematized reporting and analysis; and established intelligence stations (情报站, *qingbao zhan*) in previously untouched regions. However, he is remembered today for using the SAD in 1942–44 to encourage bizarre mass struggles against innocents and imaginary enemies and carrying forth similar methods to help Mao Zedong wreak havoc two decades later during the Cultural Revolution.

The late Warren Kuo, a Taiwan historian who defected from the CCP South China Bureau in 1942 and eventually settled in Taiwan,[31] listed these functions for the SAD, similar to the CCP's less succinct founding announcement:[32]

- formulate CCP security policies and plans
- provide guidance to subordinate SAD elements
- direct security measures and purges within the party
- provide security-related guidance to the military, party, and other groups on public security (police) and intelligence

- assign cadres to perform espionage, enemy penetration, and other subversion outside the party
- devise codes and ciphers.[33]

The SAD was initially organized with a director, a deputy director, a secretary general, and subordinate sections: First Section, organization; Second Section, intelligence; Third Section, examination and trial; Fourth Section, analysis; a general services section; and a cadet training corps. After the short tenure of SAD deputy director Kong Yuan, Mao and Kang Sheng appointed Li Kenong (see chapter 2) and Pan Hannian as deputy directors in charge of espionage in the KMT-controlled regions and Japanese occupied zones—their respective areas of expertise.[34]

Two prominent party historians have written that the SAD and the Central Intelligence Department (中央情报部, *Zhongyang qingbao bu*, founded in 1941), became "one organization, two name plates" (一个 机构两块牌子, *yige jigou liang kuai paizi*). Kang Sheng (SAD director, 1939–46) and his successor Li Kenong (1946–49) headed both the SAD and the Intelligence Department while in office.[35] The Intelligence Department appeared focused on coordination with the Red Army, including intelligence tasks performed by the Eighth Route Army Liaison Offices. Besides coordination, this arrangement may have kept the military out of the SAD's business while promoting Kang's rise toward becoming CCP intelligence primus inter pares. The 1943 creation of the publicly known CCP Central Enemy Area Work Commission (中央敌区工作委员会, *Zhongyang diqu gongzuo weiyuanhui*) may have been driven by a similar motivation.[36] Coming at the same time as the 1943 Salvation campaign, it placed Kang Sheng firmly in charge of all intelligence activity, special operations, and counterespionage, the last including the antispy, antitraitor work that Kang carried to the point of madness in 1943.

Before 1943 Kang and his deputies focused in part on organization building and training. For example, in 1940 Zhao Cangbi used "Soviet materials and his own extensive experience" to deliver training in gathering and disseminating intelligence (怎样收集和专递情报, *zeyang shouji he zhuandi qingbao*), classroom and practical exercises in different settings of surveillance and countersurveillance (侦查与反侦查, *zhencha yu fan zhencha*), methods of securely carrying concealed information, battlefield intelligence collection, an understanding of enemy intelligence acquisition, and digging out enemy agents.[37]

Pan Hannian also ran systematic instruction after he returned to Yan'an and was reassigned to the SAD in early 1939. Needing people to revamp demolished urban networks in cities under Japanese occupation, Pan worked with Chen Yun to quietly survey the CCP party center's schools and other units to find students suitable for intelligence operations.[38] Recruits included university students, soldiers, peasants, and workers. For example, Pan recruited a young couple, who he believed were psychologically suited for long-term clandestine work, for insertion into Chongqing, the Nationalist wartime capital. They knew the Sichuan dialect and culture and could therefore more easily build an intelligence network of local people. They survived against the odds owing to their skills and adaptability.[39] While the writings available on Pan Hannian reveal no evidence of Russian influence on his work, accounts of Pan's "system" (潘汉年系统, *Pan Hannian xitong*) are reminiscent of contemporary Russian NKVD and GRU training for illegal agents—persons tutored before insertion to blend into the target society, passing themselves off as ordinary citizens.[40]

Zhou Enlai revealed in January 1942 that the party had more than five thousand agents in Sichuan, Guizhou, and Yunnan (probably including underground operatives). A prominent example was KMT Lieutenant General Yan Baohang, a military strategist for Generalissimo Chiang Kai-shek in Chongqing but secretly in charge of an SAD network.[41] There was at least one overseas agent, Ji Chaoding, who worked in the United States with the communist party there for a period in the early 1940s. After 1945 Ji became a CCP agent inside the KMT finance ministry in Nanjing.[42] After the revolution, in reference to the CCP's agents, Chiang Kai-shek wrote: "There was no space that they did not enter" (无空不入, *wu kong bu ru*). Mao claimed that "during the liberation war, intelligence work was the most successful" for good reason: by 1947 CCP intelligence networks in Nanjing and Shanghai were reporting on KMT military order of battle, weaponry, and base locations, their strategic battle plans, and the texts of meetings between the generalissimo and his top generals.[43]

Besides intelligence training and operations, "traitor weeding" (铲除汉奸, *chanchu hanjian*) to find and eliminate "enemy agents and

Trotskyites within the Party" remained a priority, not only because Stalin, Mao, and Kang thought it vital, but because Japanese and KMT intelligence targeted Yan'an.[44] Of special concern: the rapid expansion of the CCP's membership rolls with "petty bourgeois elements" from the cities after the July 1937 outbreak of the Anti-Japanese War. As pointed out by Michael Dutton, the CCP had a "string of 90 percent problems": 90 percent growth in membership from 1937–40; 90 percent of the 770,000 new communists were of petty bourgeois origin; and 90 percent of existing cadres lacked formal training in party schools and schooling in Marxist principles.[45] Accordingly, Mao, Chen Yun, Liu Shaoqi, and Kang pushed for a "Rectification" (政风, Zhengfeng) movement in late 1941, which officially began the following February.[46] Unlike the now-condemned 1943 Salvation campaign, Rectification is still considered a positive event by the modern CCP.[47]

Despite of the turbulence of Rectification (1942–44) and Salvation (1943), SAD intelligence operations continued. However, development of crucial insertion agents ("inner line," 内线, neixian) stalled as cadres hesitated to volunteer for duty that was doubly dangerous, both from enemy detection and, if they survived, from suspicion of being too close to the enemy.[48]

In mid-1943 the Soviet GRU liaison in Yan'an reported that the Salvation campaign, now thoroughly out of control, would target senior Chinese communists including Zhou Enlai and Bo Gu. Stalin responded in December 1943 with a telegram through his assistant Georgi Dimitrov. It directly criticized Kang Sheng's extreme measures during Salvation and urged Mao to cease persecuting CCP members (see the Dimitrov telegram in the web-based glossary).[49] Mao eased his campaign in 1944, and a popular backlash ensued. Mao was forced to apologize in at least four meetings late that year for the use of torture by the SAD, with Kang Sheng seated onstage in silence. Post-Mao official history has systematically shifted blame away from the chairman to Kang, even though the idea that Kang could have pursued his program without Mao's approval is ridiculous.[50]

After the 1945 Seventh Party Congress and the sudden surrender of Japan that August, Li Kenong and Pan Hannian worked to revive clandestine networks as the CCP prepared to take on the KMT enemy.[51] Mao gradually eased Kang out of power, sending him to Shandong province; Li Kenong officially took over the SAD on October 1, 1946, after the failure of the Marshall mission.[52] The SAD shifted focus to military intelligence, building networks from KMT officials who, as the regime became weaker from corruption and incompetence, became available.

In spite of its successes under Li Kenong during the closing years of the Chinese Communist Revolution, and perhaps because of its association with Kang Sheng, Mao Zedong decided to abolish the SAD in mid-1949. Counterespionage personnel became part of the new Ministry of Public Security, while people useful in building a foreign intelligence program were retained under Li Kenong but placed into interim bodies, mostly under the military. Although permanent reorganization was needed to serve the needs of a new nation-state, it would wait for five years while the new People's Republic endured the declining health of Mao's trusted intelligence chief Li Kenong, a renewal of spy mania at home, and the ordeal of the Korean War.

The People's Republic, 1949–Present: Ministry of Public Security (公安部, *Gong'an bu*, 1949–Present)

The MPS is China's national police agency with subordinate public security bureaus (PSBs, 公安局, *Gong'an ju*) in each province, county, and municipality, under which lie local police stations (公安派出所, *Gong'an paichusuo*). The ministry focuses on police work, but its mission statement includes antiterrorist operations, administering China's vast household registration and national identification system, guiding community security commissions, conducting border security and immigration work, issuing passports and visas, protecting sensitive venues and facilities, managing public events, and supervising "public information networks."[53]

MPS missions today are partly reminiscent of its early days in 1949, when the CCP and its new government faced millions of hostile people at home and powerful enemies abroad. To shift from revolutionary conquest to administering and pacifying the entire nation, Mao Zedong decided to split the Social Affairs Department (SAD) into two government ministries, one for public security and the other for intelligence. The latter was stalled (see the Multi-Agency Interim Period), but in June Mao convinced a reluctant Luo Ruiqing to become the first MPS minister. Luo chose his deputies from among former associates in the army and the PPB.[54] The party abolished the SAD that August and shifted personnel en masse from parts of the SAD and the army to the MPS.[55]

The MPS focused on enemies, from Beijing down to local police stations.[56] Luo spoke on November 1 about thousands of ex-Chinese Nationalists and enemy "special agents" (特务分子, *tewu fenzi*) across the nation. At the end of 1950, the ministry claimed to have "broken" (破获, *pohuo*) 2,070 spy cases, including plots to assassinate Mao and the mayors of Shanghai and Guangzhou.[57] Fears of a Nationalist counterattack were exacerbated when their Taiwan-based air force bombed Shanghai.[58] In April 1951 the MPS arrested an American, Hugh Francis Redmond, accusing him of spying for the United States. In November 1952 two CIA officers (see the Downey-Fecteau case) were captured when their aircraft was downed over China.[59]

There was also a serious systemic issue: unreliable and incompetent local police from the previous regime. The CCP reorganized them into public security bureaus subordinate to the ministry and injected more reliable communist recruits as replacements. However, the low number of police relative to the general population was not increased.[60]

To supplement their efforts, PSBs employed "mass line policing" and "surveillance and control" (管制, *guanzhi*) in which civilian volunteers helped to watch millions suspected of disloyalty in their workplaces. This saved the ministry from imprisoning them in the growing but overstretched MPS gulag.[61] To find these enemies, the CCP and the MPS pursued the Campaign to Suppress Counterrevolutionaries (1950–51), leading to 700,000 executions. Fearing a popular backlash, after 1953 the ministry shifted toward professional efforts to find actual hostile intelligence operatives, who were harder to dig out than ordinary people with suspicious backgrounds. These more serious counterintelligence cases were managed under MPS bureau chief Ling Yun, through "surveillance and control" by civilian party committees. When suspicions of clandestine contacts with foreign countries or Taiwan arose against senior or other notable communists (for example, Gao Gang, Rao Shushi, Yang Fan, Pan Hannian, and Sidney Rittenberg), MPS investigations were closely supervised by the party and followed institutional guidelines. However, intervention by Mao was the wild card. For instance, Mao's belief that Pan Hannian was untrustworthy and Luo's eagerness to obey the chairman's orders overrode the lack of evidence showing genuine treachery.[62] Yet unlike the Soviet NKVD and KGB under Stalin, the MPS was not given free rein to terrorize the party rank and file.[63] Mao and the Politburo held the reins.

The MPS drove programs that successfully made China a hard target for hostile intelligence agencies: mass surveillance and control through neighborhood committees, political campaigns that continually harassed real and imagined opponents, and the *hukou* household registration policy (居民户口政策, *hukou zhengce*), which recorded each citizen's home area, forbade their migration without permission, and recorded mere visits to other areas. In recent times the PRC has considered abolishing the *hukou* system, but even in 2018 it remained an obstacle for people who wished simply to take a job away from home.[64] Another carryover to today is that MPS and PSB officers, still fewer in number compared to police in other nations, total less than half per capita compared to police in the United States, highlighting the continued reliance on surveillance of society by grassroots CCP organizations and, increasingly, technical means.[65] Technology lately plays a major supporting role with web-based monitoring, highly accurate facial recognition, and associated technologies as the "world's biggest camera surveillance network" is deployed beyond levels found in other nations.[66] The advanced surveillance apparatus being tested in Xinjiang is perhaps a harbinger of a future heretofore imagined only by science fiction.[67]

The MPS hosted a small group of Soviet advisors beginning in late 1949 but did not rely on them except for selected technical guidance.[68] Due to Chinese irritations over "inappropriate, and at times even laughable" proposals from Russians who were unfamiliar with Chinese realities, the MPS decided in September 1958 to send home its Russian advisors a year before the Sino-Soviet split emerged into the open.[69] Only two years later, MPS internal documents referred to Soviets in China using the derogatory term *special agents* (特务, *tewu*).[70]

Until 1966 the MPS and other security organs worked to improve interagency coordination and common standards. Successful U.S. and Taiwan agent insertions declined as bureaucratic control over the majority

Han society increased, blunting the efforts of foreign adversaries. A notable exception occurred in October 1961, when CIA-supported Tibetan guerrillas ambushed a Chinese army convoy and recovered twenty-nine issues of a secret military journal, which they passed to the CIA.[71]

Xie Fuzhi became the second and longest-serving MPS minister (1959–72) when Luo Ruiqing was promoted to be PLA chief of staff. According to Michael Schoenhals, Xie was relatively ineffective and at first did not (or could not) appreciably change past policies. Then came the Cultural Revolution. In 1966–67 Xie purged the ranks at headquarters, brought in PLA officers, and ordered local PSBs to support the "revolutionary actions of the left." Among the newcomers was PLA general Li Zhen, who became Xie's vice minister. By 1968 MPS headquarters was reduced to 126 people, one-tenth of its previous strength. However, some provincial, municipal, and county PSBs stayed under local CCP control in defiance of the party's left wing, and Xie complained that some local bureaus supported "conservatives," though he managed to use Red Guards to purge others of "enemies within."[72]

Xie died of stomach cancer in March 1972 and was succeeded by General Li Zhen,[73] who supervised security when Richard Nixon visited China in February 1972; led the massive and controversial hunt for "May 16th" conspirators that year (which might have motivated many to wish him dead); conducted security for and surveillance of the growing number of foreign missions in Beijing, including the U.S. Liaison Office (USLO); and arranged logistics and security for the highly secret Tenth Party Congress in August 1973.[74] The month before, James Lilley arrived in Beijing as the openly declared CIA representative in the USLO. Lilley was closely watched during his tour but managed to scout out dead drop sites and encounter helpful Chinese without being declared persona non grata.[75]

In 1972, before Li Zhen's untimely demise, Mao began to send PLA officers in civilian ministries back to the army in the wake of the Lin Biao affair and the mounting problems of military control. This opened the ministry to its former workforce banished during the Cultural Revolution, which Li Zhen and his radical left vice minister, Shi Yizhe, may have opposed. Li's suspicious death in October 1973 left the minister's office empty and Shi ostensibly in charge.

Hua Guofeng (see chapter 2) led the investigation into Li's death, ruled it a suicide, and became MPS minister in 1975. The Central Committee only approved this verdict in March 1977, after Mao's September 1976 death and the overthrow of the radical left Gang of Four.[76]

Meanwhile, the MPS was challenged by a spike in criminal cases, making clear that military control of policing had failed. From fewer than 200,000 cases in 1969 (24 crimes per 100,000), the caseload rose to more than half a million in 1973 (60 per 100,000), the most dramatic increase since the 1959–61 great famine. The steady ascent in crime continued into the early reform era, with another high point in 1981. As early as 1970, Zhou Enlai complained about the lack of professionally trained MPS officers. In 1972 he sensed an opportunity when Mao was allegedly shocked by reports that torture was going on in MPS establishments. Zhou continued to bring back old MPS cadres and reinstated Deng Xiaoping, in part to take charge of dealing with crime on China's railway network (vital before the current era of more efficient highways and air travel).[77] The Beijing and Heilongjiang PSBs scored a major success in January 1974 when China expelled five Soviet diplomats for espionage and arrested Li Hongshu (李洪枢), said to be a longtime Soviet GRU agent. In April, Zhou Enlai underlined the point by warning all PSBs to be vigilant against Taiwan and foreign special agents and rely on mass organizations to enhance security.[78] Hua Guofeng accelerated the return of purged cadres upon becoming minister in 1975, steering policy away from class struggle.[79]

A month after Mao's September 1976 death, the Cultural Revolution was finished. Cadre returns to the MPS continued, and the ministry established an office to begin investigations into the activities of radical leftists. More MPS operations were devoted to "strike hard" campaigns against crime and spying and the "comprehensive management" of social order. Since police numbers remained low, this required the revival of local mass line security organs. Arrests soared. As Dutton points out, though crime was no longer politicized (condemning vice, graft, and violence as counterrevolutionary), police and the party began to criminalize political dissent, treating it as much of a crime "under the law" as assault, robbery, murder, and espionage. The category of "counterrevolutionary criminal" disappeared from the criminal code in 1997.[80]

In a signal case showing that the Cultural Revolution was permanently reversed within the MPS and nationwide, former Shanghai PSB director Yang Fan, arrested in the early 1950s as an enemy agent, was formally cleared in December 1983 after his release from prison five years earlier and praised for his counterintelligence work in post-1949 Shanghai[81] (see Luo Ruiqing, chapter 2, and Pan Hannian, chapter 3). But the state was not going soft on espionage: earlier that year, CCP general secretary Hu Yaobang announced that the authorities arrested two hundred Chinese citizens for spying on behalf of the Soviet Union in 1982.[82]

However, the national leadership criticized the MPS for a surge in spy cases as China opened its doors to foreign investment, and the ministry lost its counterespionage mission to the new Ministry of State Security in July 1983.[83] While the MSS gained the counterspy portfolio, the MPS continued managing foreigners on Chinese soil and maintaining a baseline of surveillance against them (see chapter 7). The MPS identifies some foreign businesses and other entities as "sensitive units" (敏感单位, min'gan dan-wei) if they meet certain criteria, from a foreign semiconductor factory[84] to one of its own municipal public security sub-bureaus.[85] Freed from catching spies, the MPS focused on more ordinary criminal cases, even though they continued to consider "intelligence work" such as recruiting clandestine sources as a vital part of the "hidden struggle."[86]

But crime includes a wider range of activity in China than elsewhere. The MPS First Bureau includes the large and secretive 610 Office, founded June 10, 1999. Originally tasked to suppress the Falun Gong, it now works against "heretical religions" not officially approved by the state, such as underground Christian, Muslim, and Buddhist groups.[87]

In recent times, the MPS has stressed the use of technology to enhance its efforts nationwide, inaugurating the 110 emergency number in 1996–97,[88] pushing out a DNA database to bureaus in 2000,[89] and placing a case management system down to the lowest level police stations later that decade, enabling officers to view cases not only under MPS purview but also some under that of the MSS.[90] Measures such as the Counterterrorism Law (2015) and the National Intelligence Law (2017) and improved management practices in general have made MPS, MSS, and PLA operations more efficient and coordinated in operations and intelligence.[91]

Depictions of the MPS are common on television and in films. The 2016 movie *Operation Mekong* (湄公河行动), a dramatic depiction of an MPS operation in the Golden Triangle border area after the 2011 murder of thirteen Chinese citizens, is one of the better examples.[92]

1949–55: The Multi-Agency Interim Period

In August 1949 the CCP abolished its Intelligence Department (founded in 1941) and Social Affairs Department (1939–49), which together had been "one organ, two nameplates" under the Central Committee.[93] In their place, the new leaders of the People's Republic planned government ministries instead of party departments for public security and intelligence. Policing and domestic counterintelligence were soon assigned to the new Ministry of Public Security (1949–present), but an equivalent intelligence body was not formed.[94]

In October through December 1949 former SAD director Li Kenong assumed the overt title of vice foreign minister and took two other jobs that were not publicized: director of the Central Military Commission Intelligence Department (CMC–ID, 军委情报部, *Junwei Qingbao bu*)[95] and secretary (书记, *Shuji*) of the CCP Central Committee Intelligence Commission (CC–IC, 中央情报委员会, *Zhongyang Qingbao Weiyuanhui*).[96]

That division of foreign intelligence duties has not yet been explained by Chinese sources. However, the party's leadership formed the beginning of an intelligence community over the first five years of the People's Republic, criticizing problems, making changes, and establishing intelligence tasking. An early intelligence work conference in April 1950 prioritized Taiwan, the United States, the United Kingdom, North Korea, and Japan as targets for agents dispatched abroad, and the CCP continued to follow its doctrine from earlier decades of using "single line" direction of agent networks (see *Danxian* in the web-based glossary). Zhou Enlai stressed a transition from "simple military intelligence" to military and political intelligence, economic intelligence, and technology acquisition.[97]

In the first half of 1950 Li Kenong supervised a team of writers to draft the history of CCP intelligence from May 1927 to October 1, 1949—"A preliminary summary of 22 years of Chinese Communist intelligence work" (中共二十二年情报工作的初步总结; *Zhonggong er shi er nian qingbao gongzuo de chubu zongjie)*. Perhaps more of an ideological guide than a historical review, it was never released publicly but has been described by party historians who use it as a reference. The Li Kenong study focused on 1937 to 1949, when Mao consolidated control of the party, and celebrated the importance of Marxism–Leninism–Mao Zedong thought in guiding CCP agencies. The official story indicates that CCP intelligence eschewed such Soviet and U.S. practices as honey traps, coercion and blackmail, paying off informants, and assassinating opponents.[98] But such claims are contradicted in particular by the Red Squad assassinations of 1928–34 and modern cases such as those of Bernard Boursicot and Paul Doumitt and the allegations against Katrina Leung.[99]

The Korean War intervened in June 1950, focusing attention on the U.S.-led counterattack that brought United Nations (UN)/U.S. forces near China's frontier. As already noted, the CMC–ID was formed under Li Kenong in December 1950 to improve intelligence work. But the organization lasted only until January 1953. Coincidentally, this period coincides with the long combat stalemate (July 1951–July 1953) in Korea, when a series of costly Chinese and UN offensives failed to yield significant gains to either side. That bloody period might have prompted reassessments of military intelligence operations. The CMC Liaison Department (CMC–LD, 军委联络部, *Junwei lianluo bu*), also supervised by Li, probably assumed foreign intelligence duties at this point.[100]

Li Kenong was assisted by Luo Qingchang, Zou Dapeng, Ma Ciqing, and Feng Xuan.[101] He must have delegated significant authority to them because of his simultaneous duties as a senior negotiator in Korea in 1951–53.

In March 1953 Li's long struggle with heart disease became a more serious issue. On March 5, Mao Zedong instructed him to seek treatment, and the next day the Chinese learned that Stalin had died in Moscow.[102] The Soviet leader had insisted that the Korean War should continue, but with his death China and the UN resumed the talks in Panmunjom, reaching a truce in July.[103]

These developments, taken together with other more mundane issues such as how to fund foreign intelligence housed in the CMC (1954), may have delayed the eventual consolidation of foreign intelligence operations.[104] However, by early 1955 intelligence stakeholders in the party and army were ready for a change.

1955–83: Central Investigation Department
(中央调查部, *Zhongyang Diaocha Bu*)

In 1955 Li Kenong, no longer busy with international negotiations, was considered the top choice to lead a consolidated PRC intelligence agency. Party central office director Yang Shangkun (杨尚昆) met on February 23 with Luo Qingchang and others, who proposed that "political intelligence" (政情, *zhengqing*) be placed in one department under the Central Committee, as it had been before 1949—a departure from the earlier idea of forming a government intelligence ministry under the State Council. Li Kenong agreed and held a meeting on March 4 with premier Zhou Enlai, Luo Qingchang, and Su Yu (粟裕), head of the PLA General Staff Department. They decided to separate some foreign intelligence functions from the Central Military Commission[105] and establish the CCP Investigation Department under the party's Central Committee, with Li as director, which Mao Zedong approved on April 8. CID personnel, many of whom came from the PLA General Staff Liaison Department (总参联络部, *Zongcan Lianluo Bu*), left the military in the transfer, effective July 1. Li Kenong's first deputies were Zou Dapeng and Feng Xuan, and his senior confidential assistants were Luo Qingchang, Mao Cheng, and Ma Ciqing. Li reported to Yang Shangkun, and major issues were delegated to Deng Xiaoping and Zhou Enlai in the Politburo.[106]

Perhaps because it was located inside the party, the existence of the CID remained a well-kept secret.[107] Those in the know referred obliquely to the "Organ in the Western Garden" (中直西苑机关, *Zhongzhi Xiyuan jiguan*), referring to its location in northwestern Beijing. Under secure circumstances, its name in plain language was *Diaocha bu* or *Zhongdiao bu* (调查部, 中调部).[108]

This is Beijing's official and vetted history of the events, but reality seems messier.[109] It unfolded amid a renewed spy mania that also gripped the CCP in earlier periods (for example, see Kang Sheng, chapter 2, and *Shencha ganbu* and *Qiangjiu Yundong* in the online glossary). From 1950 to 1953, tens of thousands of people were arrested as counterrevolutionaries and thousands of others as "spies" (特务, *tewu*), though not without concern over a genuine threat (see the Downey-Fecteau case, chapter 5). The party's overreaction was underlined by moves that party historians now call serious errors and by intervening events. Two former PSB municipal directors, Yang Fan in Shanghai and Chen Bo in Guangzhou, were falsely charged in 1954 with being enemy agents. Then came two even more stunning developments: the arrest of a hero of the "hidden battlefront," Pan Hannian, on April 3, 1955, accused (like Yang Fan) of treason, and the Kashmir Princess bombing case: the April 11 destruction over the open ocean of Air India passenger flight 300 on which premier Zhou Enlai was originally booked, headed for the Bandung conference. The Chinese investigation showed that the aircraft was blown up in midair by a KMT time bomb planted in Hong Kong.[110]

Pressure to find more counterrevolutionaries followed, though this was perhaps as much a symptom of the times, and of the reign of Mao Zedong, as a reaction to contemporary events. The center suggested that staff in institutions be examined to "thoroughly clean out hidden counterrevolutionary elements" (彻底肃清暗藏的反革命分子, *Chedi suqing ancang de fan geming fenzi*).[111] More than 18 million people were investigated in the *sufan* (cleansing) campaign that followed, though ultimately only 257,551 were purged.[112] In the PRC intelligence community, eight hundred to one thousand people were demoted, transferred, or arrested, primarily because they had been associated with Pan Hannian, who ran CCP espionage networks in the Japanese-occupied zones of China during 1937–45.[113] It was perhaps symptomatic of Mao's previous and subsequent tendency to brand masses of people as guilty by association.

Li Kenong's biographer claims that he was a lone dissenter on Pan's arrest, writing a two-part report issued in May and July 1955—just as the CID was being established—summarizing Pan's career and clearing him of treason.[114] In September 1955 Chairman Mao ignored this evidence but continued to place trust in Li as CID director and personally promoted him to the rank of general (上将, *shangjiang*).[115]

Party historians do not comment on how these alarming developments affected the founding of the CID between March and July. It is not surprising that the details remain hidden from view, but it is notable that

Li managed to keep organization building on track during this tumultuous period.

Early CID priorities were its enemies in Taipei and Washington, and for good reason: the CIA continued its work to infiltrate the mainland from Taiwan and the Nationalist-held islands near the mainland.[116] In 1955 the CID set up municipal and provincial bureaus in Shanghai and Guangdong, areas troubled by KMT remnants.[117] Further study is needed to define how the CID cooperated with MPS counterintelligence work through these bureaus, whether the CID exposed hostile foreign operations, and the extent to which the department worked inside China.

In 1955–69, the number of foreign countries willing to establish diplomatic relations with China doubled, from twenty-six to fifty.[118] This "second upsurge in the establishment of diplomatic relations" after the 1955 Bandung conference meant more opportunities for the CID in posts overseas and prompted an internal debate: could covert operations be supplemented with overt ones without tipping off adversaries to China's intelligence requirements? On one side was Xiong Xianghui, director of the CID's Second Bureau and a veteran CCP intelligence covert operative from the Chinese civil war. He hinted that covert operations were stalled and argued that positive conditions, particularly in Europe, should allow operatives to pursue overt contacts for intelligence. Ma Ciqing argued that such contacts could be beneficial but posed security problems, while covert work remained essential. Zhou Enlai, who was the final arbiter, agreed with Ma: covert operations would remain the priority.[119] Zhou's choice may have set the direction for the CID for the rest of its existence: to remain unacknowledged, and even unspoken, outside of those within the party with a need to know.

Relations with Soviet intelligence after 1949 began well, with Russian advisors based inside the CID. But for unclear reasons Moscow withdrew its KGB officers from the CID and the MPS in September 1958, a year before the Sino-Soviet split and the departure from China of the main body of Russian advisors.[120]

The CID conducted internal seminars and meetings to promote standardization and discuss problems. The December 1955 Second Political Intelligence Work Conference (第二次政治情报工作会议, *Di er ci zhengzhi qingbao gongzuo huiyi*) included the MPS, the CID, and the CCP Inspection Commission. Zhou addressed the meeting, stressing securing socialist construction and the people's democratic dictatorship at home, and peace on China's periphery[121]—predictable themes but indicative of a defensive stance, in contrast to the promotion of revolution a generation before by the Comintern in Moscow. Nonetheless, Chinese efforts to assist national liberation movements, notably in Southeast Asia, became more active in the 1950s and 1960s.[122] The CID role in them requires further research in hitherto closed archives.

As had been true during the revolution ending in 1949, the CCP gave some intelligence officers cover jobs as journalists. Those posted abroad were commonly backstopped as Xinhua (New China News Agency) correspondents, allowing them to travel, ask questions, and cultivate contacts for plausible reasons. Xinhua offices with intelligence officers under cover during at least some of their tenure were established in Prague (1948), London and Cairo (1956), Paris (1957), and Japan (1964). The office in Hong Kong took on activities beyond intelligence and grew into the PRC's unofficial consulate in the British colony,[123] and Xinhua also established such a presence in the Portuguese enclave of Macau.[124]

Other CID work meetings (调查部工作会议, *Diaocha bu gongzuo huiyi*) followed. One in February-March 1959 included CID officers stationed overseas. Another on October 20, 1961, was the All China Intelligence Work Conference (全国情报工作会议, *Quanguo qingbao gongzuo huiyi*), which may have been a key interagency coordination session. Participants included the CID, the MPS, the Ministry of Foreign Affairs, PLA intelligence (军情, *junqing*) the PLA General Political Department, the State Council Foreign Affairs Office, and the PRC Overseas Chinese Affairs Commission. Apparently, the CID had an expanding array of stakeholders and perhaps some rivals: the meeting also discussed "how to rectify intelligence work and the division of labor among the various systems" (如何整顿情报工作和各系统的分工, *ruhe zhengdun qingbao gongzuohe ge xitong de fengong*).[125]

In October 1957 Li Kenong fainted, fell, and suffered a stroke, making Kong Yuan the acting director. Li made a brief recovery in 1961 but passed away in February 1962. Kong formally assumed leadership that November.[126]

Yang Shangkun's diary includes only scant detail of his supervision of intelligence operations but contains occasional tidbits. For example, from October 11 to December 10, 1962, he met with Kong Yuan and other senior CID officers on nine occasions, a comparatively high frequency probably associated with Kong's assumption of formal leadership and early U.S. efforts to infiltrate Tibet. Kong's promotion may have been celebrated at a dinner in the Diaoyutai state guesthouse on November 16, when, in Yang's words, "CID invited a [Chinese] diplomat stationed overseas, and we almost got drunk!" (中调部请驻外使节，几乎喝醉了! *Zhongdiao bu qing zhu wai shijie, jihu he zui le*).[127]

Besides being a CID deputy director, Luo Qingchang was deputy of the office of the Central Committee Taiwan Leading Small Group, and he worked in Zhou Enlai's executive office with the lead on intelligence matters.[128] Luo's obituary lauds his role in discovering a Nationalist Chinese plot to kill PRC president Liu Shaoqi during the state visit to Cambodia in April 1963 and for work to convince former KMT general Li Zongren to defect to the mainland from Switzerland in 1964.[129] These accounts of Luo's life omit that he was also closely tied to Wang Dongxing, head of Mao's bodyguards, and to radical polemicist, vicious operator, and intelligence veteran Kang Sheng, under whom Luo directly worked in Yan'an during the Anti-Japanese War. Both of these men became prominent Cultural Revolution beneficiaries who protected and utilized Luo Qingchang in the storm to follow. Inside the CID, officers came to call them the "trinity" (三位一体, *san wei yi ti*).

When the Cultural Revolution entered its chaotic period in August 1966, Mao removed political control of the CID from the embattled Deng Xiaoping, turning it over to Kang.[130] For the next seven months Kong Yuan and his deputy Tong Xiaopeng tried to insulate the CID from the frantic politics of the time and keep operations on track, but Red Guard factions soon formed within the department, just as they did in other organizations, apparently leading to leaks (see Classified Materials Theft, 1966–67, chapter 5).[131] Unlike Chinese efforts to construct nuclear weapons and missiles, intelligence operations were not kept isolated from the ravages of Mao's last revolution.

Luo Qingchang took over the CID in December 1966, deposing Kong Yuan.[132] A month later, the radical Central Case Examination Group, headed by Jiang Qing, opened an investigation against Kong, who had undergone months of struggle with the CID's Red Guard Rebel faction (造反派, *zaofan pai*). Kong and his deputies were forced into labor camps or worse, except for one—Luo Qingchang—who continued on post even during the military takeover of the department in April 1967, and later when the CID was absorbed by the PLA Second Department (Intelligence) on June 13, 1969.[133]

Xiong Xianghui possibly headed 2PLA, and Luo may have become a deputy. As hostility between China and the Soviet Union reached its peak, Mao explored ending isolation from the West, leading to rapprochement with the United States. CID officers began returning to their overseas posts concurrent with the PRC's admission to the UN in 1971. In March 1973, when the CID was formally reestablished as a Central Committee Department, Luo was back in charge.[134] Perhaps not coincidentally, this occurred at the same time as Mao agreed to Zhou Enlai's proposal to restore Deng Xiaoping to political office (March 9), and discussions ensued (February–June) between Zhou Enlai and Henry Kissinger on opening diplomatic missions in Beijing and Washington, giving CCP intelligence organs new opportunities for overseas operations.[135]

Zhou Enlai passed away on January 8, 1976. While terminally ill in hospital on December 20, 1975, Zhou summoned Luo Qingchang, whose rank was too low for a routine meeting, to his bedside. Zhou asked for news of old friends in Taiwan and requested that the CID transmit his wish that they "not forget to work in the people's interests." The Chinese accounts of this dramatic scene do not indicate whether it went beyond the symbolic.[136]

After the September 1976 death of Mao, his successor Hua Guofeng revived the national open-source "intelligence/information" (*qingbao*) system and pursued other measures to evaluate and import foreign technology (see Hua's entry, chapter 2).[137] Unfortunately for the new leader, he was blamed for an overambitious ten-year plan, unveiled in February–March 1978, that other senior leaders including Deng Xiaoping had agreed to pursue. Deng Xiaoping used its Maoist style to discredit Hua and began his own ascent toward the leadership in December.[138]

Six months afterward, on July 7, 1979, Deng Xiaoping, now ranked as a vice premier but with significantly greater influence, made a speech at a work conference convened by the Ministry of Foreign Affairs. Deng suggested that the CID cease using diplomatic cover for its officers overseas—a suggestion Deng said had originated with Zhou Enlai in 1964. However, Luo Qingchang avoided formally promulgating Deng's speech. Instead, he worked against it by expanding six regional units and sending additional officers to overseas diplomatic posts. During internal briefings, Luo urged cadres to ignore Deng's policy direction, saying that it represented a return to "class struggle" and "anti-intelligence-ism," seemingly rhetorical charges. Although Luo presented the appearance of compliance beginning in August 1979, he avoided implementing change and retired in 1983, when Deng engineered a reorganization that forced him out of office.[139] The fact that it took Deng so long to get rid of Luo, a notorious Cultural Revolution beneficiary, and that Luo remains a respected figure even today speaks to his lingering influence, and perhaps that of the radical left.

Though Luo was an irritant to Deng, serious disappointments in the U.S.-China relationship may have more strongly influenced the intelligence reorganization of 1983. PRC leaders hoped for a period of consolidation and stability following the January 1979 diplomatic normalization with the United States, but problems followed that must have generated security concerns: the military debacle with Vietnam in February 1979, the enactment of the U.S.-Taiwan Relations Act in April that contained unexpected provisions for the island's defense if attacked by China, and U.S. President Jimmy Carter's defeat in November 1980 by Ronald Reagan, an avowed friend of the KMT government on Taiwan.[140]

Counterintelligence concerns likely mounted. Chinese citizens with previously dormant consumer ambitions were becoming more vulnerable to cash incentives, at the same time as more foreigners began wandering the cities without official escort and foreign consulates multiplied on Chinese soil.[141] Counterintelligence was under the purview of the MPS, but it was left to premier Zhao Ziyang, a liberal reformer in the CCP context, to express concerns about rising crime, "intolerable political and ideological apathy" by security personnel, and the need to "suppress counterrevolutionary activities." This led to a crackdown on crime in the summer of 1983 and to campaigns against "bourgeois liberalization" and "spiritual pollution" later that year. Deng Xiaoping may have promised in 1978 to renounce class struggle, but struggle against enemies remained a part of the CCP playbook.[142]

Continued spying competition came to characterize the U.S.-China relationship, in spite of other cooperation that developed. An internal party debate developed in early 1981 about the risks of Westernization and the dangers of relying on a foreign power, themes that echo even today under Xi Jinping with his antispy campaign (2014–present) and the Made in China 2025 initiative.[143]

If Deng and Zhao perceived that the MPS was not up to catching spies as China opened to the outside world, this would help explain the creation of a new agency able to consolidate espionage abroad and counterespionage at home, the MSS, proposed by Zhao himself and approved by the National People's Congress in July 1983.

1955–2015: Second Department of the PLA General Staff Department (2PLA, 总参二局, Zongcan Er Ju)
2015–Present: Intelligence Bureau of the PLA Joint Staff Department (联合参谋情报局, Lianhe Canmou Qingbaoju)

For sixty years, 2PLA—also known as the Military Intelligence Department of the General Staff Department (GSD)—was the Chinese military's primary intelligence organization. Both 2PLA and its companion, the GSD Third Department for technical reconnaissance, were successor organizations of the Central Revolutionary Military Commission's Second Bureau and the Eighth Route Army's intelligence organs.

2PLA reported to a GSD deputy commander who oversaw the portfolio that included intelligence and foreign affairs. This officer was the PLA's chief diplomat, participating in a broad range of military-to-military exchanges, as well as its senior intelligence officer. In the latter role, the deputy chief was one of at least two PLA representatives typically present on externally oriented CCP leading small groups: Hong Kong and Macau

Affairs, Taiwan Affairs, and Foreign Affairs. This officer also served as president of the China Institute for International Strategic Studies (CIISS, 中国国际战略学会, *Zhongguo guoji zhanlue xuehui*) beginning in 1979 with its founder, Lieutenant General Wu Xiuquan.

According to various sources, 2PLA was composed of six or seven bureaus divided into three systems. The first managed 2PLA's clandestine human intelligence operations. Most sources agree that the headquarters component was the First Bureau with five subordinate liaison bureaus in Beijing, Shanghai, Guangzhou, Shenyang, and Tianjin. This system may also include offices in several other cities, based on descriptions released in Taiwanese prosecutions of espionage cases. No information, however, is available on whether such offices reported to the local liaison bureau or directly to 2PLA headquarters.

The second system managed scientific research and ran the technical side of 2PLA operations, including unmanned aerial vehicles (UAVs), technical sensors, and satellites. This system probably is the most readily identifiable part of 2PLA, because each major component, including its Second Bureau, had military unit cover designators that are occasionally referenced in public. These included the Aerospace Reconnaissance Bureau (航天侦察部), Beijing Remote Sensing Institute, and tactical UAVs. Most importantly, this bureau guides the operations of tactical reconnaissance and intelligence elements within the military regions.[144]

The third system managed defense attachés overseas and overt human intelligence collection and conducted analysis of foreign affairs.[145] This system probably included the Third, Fourth, Fifth, and Sixth bureaus.[146] One of them probably served as the desk for defense attaché offices in overseas diplomatic posts (colloquially known as the 武官处, *wuguanchu*), and the other three had responsibilities divided into three geographic areas of analytic coverage: Russia, former Soviet Union, and Eastern Europe; United States and Western Europe; and Asia.[147]

In addition to its internal bureaus, 2PLA also oversaw two very different think tanks: CIISS and the China Foundation for International Strategic Studies (CFISS, 中国国际战略研究基金会, *Zhongguo guoji zhanlue yanjiu jijinhui*). According to its official description, CIISS serves the Chinese government and military beyond 2PLA. The think tank offers "consultancy and policy advice to and undertake research projects for relevant departments of the Chinese Government, the military and other institutions and enterprises and play the role as their think tank in the interests of national security, economic development, international security, and world peace and development."[148] The staff of CIISS includes a mix of serving 2PLA officers drawn primarily from the defense attaché and analytic ranks, retired senior intelligence officers, and permanent research staff.[149] If CIISS is primarily a research institute, then CFISS is an exchange-related think tank that may have a more operational role for 2PLA. Former 2PLA officer Zhai Zhihai founded CFISS in 1989 before handing it over to Chen Zhiya (son of Chen Geng; see chapter 2) in the early 1990s. GSD deputy chief Xiong Guangkai directed CFISS's most notable research into crisis management and decisionmaking to build the intellectual foundations for a revamped policy process modeled on the U.S. National Security Council. The project ultimately led nowhere, but CFISS continued working with foreign interlocutors into the late 2000s to explore related issues.[150]

On November 26, 2015, Chinese president and CMC chairman Xi Jinping announced a major overhaul of the PLA. The reforms particularly relevant to 2PLA overhauled the first-level departments (such as the GSD) reporting to the CMC and created the Strategic Support Force (SSF, 战略支援部队, *Zhanlue zhiyuan budui*). The first reform renamed the GSD the Joint Staff Department (JSD). The principal shift was that the GSD would no longer serve as both the PLA's general staff and the ground forces' headquarters component. The latter was carved into a separate entity, and 2PLA itself was downgraded from a department to a bureau to become the JSD Intelligence Bureau. The second reform had more far-reaching effects, for it moved technical and tactical reconnaissance into the SSF along with the GSD's Third Department.[151] Although new data is not yet available on the JSD Intelligence Bureau, the basic features of 2PLA remain intact. There is still a JSD deputy chief who oversees intelligence and foreign affairs. CIISS was not touched, and no Chinese news reporting suggests the Intelligence Bureau has given up its role in managing defense attachés and analysis. To the contrary, Chinese interlocutors believe the bureau will continue to play an important role in informing China's leadership.[152]

1983–Present: Ministry of State Security
(国家安全部, *Guojia anquan bu*)

At the first session of the sixth National People's Congress (NPC) on June 20, 1983, delegates approved premier Zhao Ziyang's proposal for the establishment of a state security ministry "to protect the security of the state and strengthen China's counterespionage work." The next day, the NPC voted to appoint Ling Yun as the first minister.[153] The MSS held its inaugural meeting on July 1 to announce the formal establishment of the ministry. Central Political-Legal Commission chairman Chen Pixian delivered the opening speech to outline the goals of the new ministry: "Doing state security work well will effectively promote socialist modernization and the cause of realizing the unification of the motherland, opposing hegemonism, and defending world peace."[154] Cloaked in Chen's euphemistic language was the first public hint that the MSS would conduct foreign intelligence operations and covert action to influence events abroad in addition to taking over domestic counterespionage.

The creation of the MSS marked a clear departure from past CCP practices by placing intelligence and counterespionage completely outside the party and under the State Council (that is, the PRC government). In an earlier interview as a vice minister of public security, Ling Yun told Xinhua that "we are firmly against resolving ideological questions and the problem of dissidence by judicial or administrative means." According to Ling, doing so was the kind of exploitation of intelligence and counterespionage only done by Kang Sheng and the leftist "Gang of Four."[155] The chief intelligence organization may have shed its role as the ideological enforcer, but pure party loyalty remained vital.[156]

Chen Pixian's speech set forth five requirements for MSS personnel related to party loyalty: purging the influence of Kang Sheng, Xie Fuzhi, and the extreme left; adhering to Deng Xiaoping's exhortation of "emancipating one's mind, summing up experience, [and] actively conducting reforms"; "never neglecting either [party work or professional work]"; "maintaining a unanimous political position" behind CCP leadership; and adhering to party discipline.[157]

The MSS generally appears to have adhered to the depoliticization of the service. This is not to say that the corruption has not impacted the organization. MSS elements, particularly at local levels, often have provided protection services for the business dealings of CCP officials or their well-connected friends.[158] However, the ministry rarely appears connected to any elite political maneuvering or purges. Since 1983 only the purges of Beijing party secretary Chen Xitong (1995) and Shanghai party secretary Chen Liangyu (2006) were rumored to involve the ministry.[159] In the wholesale purges after the fall of Bo Xilai and Zhou Yongkang, the Beijing State Security Bureau chief Fang Ke and Vice Minister Qiu Jin were ousted precisely because they exploited MSS resources to back particular leaders in their political struggles against each other.[160]

Creating the MSS in 1983 was the easy part. The first two ministers, Ling Yun and Jia Chunwang, faced the challenge of turning a small ministry with only a handful of outlying provincial departments into a nationwide security apparatus. The expansion occurred in four waves. The original departments (or those created within the first year) appeared to be the municipal bureaus or provincial departments of state security for Beijing, Fujian, Guangdong, Guangxi, Heilongjiang, Jiangsu, Liaoning, and Shanghai. A second wave appeared shortly thereafter between 1985 and 1988, including Chongqing, Gansu, Hainan, Henan, Shaanxi, Tianjin, and Zhejiang. The third wave from 1990 to 1995 completed the expansion of the ministry across the country at provincial levels, bringing in Anhui, Hunan, Qinghai, and Sichuan provinces.[161] The fourth wave of MSS expansion was vertical. The provincial-level departments either took over local public security bureaus or established subordinate municipal or county bureaus. For many local PSB officers, they were police one day and state security the next. When MSS minister Jia left in 1998 for the MPS, the MSS was a nationwide organization at every level.

From the national level to the local levels, the MSS and its subordinate departments and bureaus report to a system of leading small groups, coordinating offices, and commissions to guide security work while lessening the risk of politicization on behalf of CCP leaders. At present, the two most important of these are the Political-Legal Commission (政法委员会, *Zhengfa weiyuanhui*) and the Central State Security Commission (CSSC, 中央国家安全委员会, *Zhongyang guojia anquan weiyuanhui*). The Political-Legal Commission is chaired by a Politburo member, currently former public security minister Guo Shengkun, at the central level and a deputy party secretary at lower levels. The commissions oversee all state security, public security, prisons, and procuratorate (judicial) elements for their level. Xi Jinping announced the creation of the CSSC in the Third Plenary Session of the Eighteenth Party Congress in November 2013. The CSSC held its first meeting on April 15, 2014. The purpose of this new commission was twofold. First, it was intended to balance internal political power created by the expansion of the security services and their capabilities in the 2000s. Second, the commission orients the MSS and other security forces toward planning for and preempting threats to the party-state.[162] At lower levels, provinces, counties, and municipalities have state security leading small groups (国家安全领导小组, *guojia anquan lingdao xiaozu*). The political-legal commissions and state security leading small groups overlap in personnel but not perfectly. And they combine with defense mobilization committees and 610 offices to create a kind of system of systems that oversees local security and intelligence work.

MSS headquarters is organized into numbered bureaus and spread across at least four compounds in Beijing. At present, the MSS is believed to possess at least eighteen bureaus. Unlike the People's Liberation Army (PLA), where military unit cover designators offer a way to track units, MSS elements are not so readily identified. The following designations are ones in which we possess a modicum of confidence:[163]

- First Bureau: "secret line" operations by MSS officers not under covers associated with Chinese government organizations
- Second Bureau: "open line" operations by MSS officers using diplomatic, journalistic, or other government-related covers
- Third Bureau: unknown
- Fourth Bureau: 台港澳局, Taiwan, Hong Kong, and Macau Bureau
- Fifth Bureau: 情报分析通报局, Report Analysis and Dissemination Bureau
- Sixth Bureau: unknown
- Seventh Bureau: 反间谍情报局, Counterespionage Intelligence Bureau, gathers information and develops intelligence on hostile intelligence services inside and outside China

- Eighth Bureau: 反间谍侦察局, Counterespionage Investigation, runs investigations to detect and apprehend foreign spies in China
- Ninth Bureau: 对内保防侦察局, Internal Protection and Reconnaissance Bureau, supervises and monitors foreign entities and reactionary organizations in China to prevent espionage
- Tenth Bureau: 对外保防侦察局, Foreign Security and Reconnaissance Bureau, manages Chinese student organizations and other entities overseas and investigates the activities of reactionary organizations abroad
- Eleventh Bureau: 中国现代国际关系研究所, China Institutes of Contemporary International Relations, performs open-source research, translation, and analysis. Its analysts also meet regularly with foreign delegations and spend time abroad as visiting fellows.
- Twelfth Bureau: 社会调查局, Social Affairs or Social Investigation Bureau, handles MSS contributions to the CCP's united front work system
- Thirteenth Bureau: Network Security and Exploitation (also known as the China Information Technology Evaluation Center [中国信息安全测评中心, *Zhongguo xinxi anquan ceping zhongxin*]), may manage the research and development of other investigative equipment
- Fourteenth Bureau: 技术侦察局, Technical Reconnaissance Bureau, conducts mail inspection and telecommunications inspection and control
- Fifteenth Bureau: Taiwan operations linked to the broader Taiwan Affairs work system. Its public face is the Institute of Taiwan Studies at the China Academy of Social Sciences.
- Sixteenth Bureau: unknown
- Seventeenth Bureau: unknown
- Eighteenth Bureau: U.S. Operations Bureau for conducting and managing clandestine intelligence operations against the United States.

◆ TWO ◆

Chinese Communist Intelligence Leaders

T he men who have led the Chinese Communist Party's (CCP) intelligence and security services (and they have all been men) have
shared few traits. Besides being male, their common attribute is
loyalty to the party. From there it diverges. Zhou Enlai, an intelligence
leader from the early days until his death, founded the effort in 1927. In
the words of Chen Yun decades later, before then the party "did not know
how to organize intelligence."[1] Zhou, who hailed from an intellectual family, maintained an expertise in tradecraft and operations management
even after ascending the heights of party leadership. In modern times he
retains the most respect—cultivated by modern propagandists to the level
of a saint—of any of the figures discussed in this volume. Gu Shunzhang, a
not particularly ideological Russian-trained special operative and assassin,
was a trusted servant of the leadership until he was captured in 1931. He
quickly turned traitor to save himself from torture and death. Kang Sheng,
an organization and intelligence specialist and later a polemicist of "Mao
Thought," is another black sheep of CCP intelligence history. Kang was
unswervingly loyal to Mao Zedong, but the CCP posthumously expelled
him for being the chairman's all-too-willing sword during the Cultural
Revolution. Li Kenong started as a clandestine officer in a key network and
later became a highly capable intelligence generalist and enemy negotiator. He led CCP intelligence during the civil war and the early PRC. Luo
Qingchang, allegedly a brilliant analyst, aligned himself with Kang during the Cultural Revolution, opposed Deng Xiaoping's 1979 intelligence
reforms, and was forced out in 1983. Curiously, the CCP continues to

cultivate Luo's image for achievements before 1966 while ignoring everything afterward.

The leaders of the post-Deng era (1992–present) are also a mixed lot, linked by party loyalty albeit infected by corruption. However, the man with the most lasting influence arguably remains chairman Mao Zedong himself. He sought primary authority over CCP intelligence and security work from about 1930 and consolidated control in 1935–39. Intelligence became Mao's machine. He approved every leader and was the final arbiter of policy until his 1976 death.

Mao was the unnamed and unindicted coconspirator in what the party now calls the "three major left deviations in the history of public security and protection" (公安保卫史上的三次大的左倾, *gongan baoweishi shang de sanci dade zuoqing*). In the first of these, the so-called Futian incident of 1930, Mao used Red Army security forces as secret police to attack his enemies inside the party and the army. The CCP leadership criticized him and his influence temporarily declined, though he recovered during the Long March (1934–35). Mao then enhanced his power by pursuing two more "left deviations," the Salvation campaign (1943) and the Cultural Revolution beginning in 1966.[2]

Forty years after his death, these "deviations" obscure Mao's continuing legacy in PRC intelligence and security work. The Ministry of State Security is not only a foreign intelligence organization. It has also been used to investigate internal opposition to the regime and corruption inside the party, though more sparingly than were the NKVD and KGB under Stalin. The Ministry of Public Security (MPS) is not only a police force but has also purged deviant noncommunist political activists and religious practitioners. Though the torture regularized under Mao's three major left deviations is condemned today by regime propaganda, it is still employed by the intelligence and security services and the party's internal discipline body.

Marxist political sensibilities still drive policy and analysis, and China's current leader, Xi Jinping, has returned to Mao's policy of demanding personal loyalty from his security services and the rest of the party and state apparatus. The past seems to be prologue in another sense: at least some of the leaders outlined in this chapter are subjects of study and emulation by new intelligence recruits in China. As in previous times, their examples are molded to show the current leadership in the most legitimate and favorable light.

These entries are in alphabetical order by family name. While less information exists about some contemporary figures, others are well known to specialists.

Chen Geng (陈赓, 1903–61)

A native of Hunan, Chen Geng was an early member of the Chinese Communist Party and a famous communist general of the revolution. In his early days as a revolutionary, he pursued intelligence duties in Shanghai from 1928 to 1931 in the Special Services Section (SSS). His son, Chen Zhiya, was a senior intelligence officer in the 1990s.

Following a brief stint with a warlord battalion in Hunan,[3] Chen Geng joined the CCP in December 1922.[4] After some university study in Shanghai and protest activity in Hunan, representatives of the nascent Whampoa Military Academy (黄埔军校, Huangpu junxiao) recruited him. Chen graduated from Whampoa, the Nationalist Army's officer school, in November 1924.[5] He saw action against local warlords and according to CCP accounts saved the life of Chiang Kai-shek in October 1925, earning the KMT leader's lasting regard.[6]

After Chen fought for the first month of the Northern Expedition in July 1926, the CCP sent him and Gu Shunzhang to Moscow, Khabarovsk, and Vladivostok for instruction on explosives, interrogation, marksmanship, field investigations, political protection operations, and armed rebellion. In February 1927 the pair returned to Shanghai and reported to Zhou Enlai, who was preparing for the arrival of the KMT's Northern Expedition. Zhou sent Chen to Wuhan in March, where he became the commander of a special operations battalion (特务营, tewu ying) under KMT general Tang Shengzhi. After the KMT-CCP split on April 12, Chen worked to protect CCP leaders in Wuhan and secretly traveled to Nanchang, where he participated in the August 1 uprising, which is regarded as the birth of the Red Army. During the subsequent retreat, Chen took three bone-breaking bullets in the left leg on September 1. Evacuated through Shantou and Hong Kong, Chen arrived in Shanghai in October. The party arranged hospitalization and therapy under an assumed identity, though Chen had to flee when recognized by a KMT loyalist. When he could walk again in April 1928, the CCP assigned Chen Geng to take up espionage work with the newly formed SSS.[7]

Chen led the SSS Second Section, Intelligence (情报科, *Qingbao ke*), which infiltrated KMT intelligence bodies, police, foreign consulates, newspapers, press associations, and criminal syndicates, mostly in Shanghai but also in Wuhan, the Beiping-Tianjin region, and Hong Kong.[8] The SSS achieved a number of successes but waged a losing battle, reflected partly in CCP circulars 25 and 69 (December 1927 and October 1928) urging faster insertion of agents into the KMT special services and forbidding captured communists from betraying secrets, and each other, on pain of execution.[9]

In this desperate time, lauded in modern propaganda as one of optimistic heroism, Chen Geng's intelligence section managed to achieve some significant successes, including the use of Dr. Ke Lin in assassinating the turncoat Bai Xin in 1929[10] and the *Longtan sanjie* (龙潭三杰, Three Heroes of the Dragon's Lair) infiltration of the KMT in 1930–31.[11]

Chen Geng may have been most intimately involved in the operation to run Yang Dengying (also known as Bao Junfu) inside KMT intelligence.[12] Tang—Cantonese, somewhat literate in Marxism, and having a propensity to make friends in high places[13]—volunteered to the CCP as a "walk-in" in February 1928. Chen Geng personally cultivated the fledgling agent,[14] who managed to infiltrate the KMT party's intelligence service, the *Zhongtong* (中统), ultimately becoming its liaison with the British International Settlement authorities in Shanghai.[15] Yang delivered information on KMT and foreign concession police operations against the CCP[16] until SSS director Gu Shunzhang defected to the KMT in April 1931, exposing Chen, Yang, and many others.[17]

Gu's defection on April 25 was a major disaster for the communists, albeit a victory for those who escaped thanks to the early warning from the Three Heroes. Nonetheless, it became impossible for Chen and others to remain in Shanghai. He departed on September 21, 1931, for the Ouyuwan Soviet area, yielding his position in the Intelligence Section to Pan Hannian, while Chen Yun and Kang Sheng assumed other SSS leadership posts.[18]

Chen was wounded in the right leg on September 5 while in command of the Twelfth Division, Fourth Army. Following treatment and a series of adventures, Chen made his way to Shanghai to obtain better treatment and receive new orders.[19]

On March 24, 1933, the night before his scheduled departure from Shanghai, Chen went to see a movie and was spotted by his former comrade Chen Liansheng (no relation), who had defected to the KMT. Chen Liansheng followed him out of the theater and tried to convince Chen Geng to defect. He fled but was arrested and imprisoned at the International Settlement jail with Liao Chengzhi. Before long they were transferred to KMT custody in the Chinese city.[20]

At this time the KMT was urging some CCP members to seek forgiveness and defect, as opposed to the usual approach of a one-time offer of mercy followed by torture and execution. Chiang Kai-shek transferred Chen to Nanjing, plying him with gifts and offers of clemency. After Chen was transferred to a Nanjing hotel, two underground CCP members helped him escape.[21]

Chen fled to the Jiangxi soviet area and resumed military duties. On the Long March he held combat commands and performed VIP protection work, including being in charge of leadership security at the Zunyi conference in January 1935. During and after the rest of the 1930s and 1940s Chen went on to a distinguished military career. In 1950 he briefly served as military advisor to Ho Chi Minh and fought in Korea (1951–52), later becoming a PLA deputy chief of staff (1954) and vice minister of defense (1959).[22] Like Li Kenong, Chen developed heart disease in his later years.[23] Also like Li, Chen's early death at age 58 may have spared him from being labeled an enemy spy during the Cultural Revolution.

Chen Kaiceng (陈开曾, ?–2008)

Chen Kaiceng of Shanghai served as director of the Second Bureau of the PLA General Staff Department (2PLA) from 1999 to 2001 after being promoted to major general in 1990. No other information is available in English or Chinese.

Chen Wenqing (陈文清)

Chen Wenqing is the fifth and current head of the Ministry of State Security (MSS), appointed on November 7, 2016, during a session of the National People's Congress.[24]

Chen Xiaogong (陈小工)

Chen Xiaogong of Shandong province served as director of the 2PLA for less than eighteen months in 2006 and 2007, when he was promoted to assistant chief of the general staff. He currently sits on the foreign affairs committee of the National People's Congress after retiring from the PLA in 2013.[25] Chen finished his military career as a lieutenant general and a deputy commander of the PLA Air Force, where he moved in 2009. Chen was the first of several senior intelligence officers transferred to operational or warfighting deputy positions around the PLA rather than letting his career top out.[26] Chen's father was the diplomat Chen Chu, who served as Beijing's first ambassador to Japan after the normalization of relations in 1972.

Chen came late to military intelligence after beginning his career as an infantry officer and serving in the periodic conflicts during the early 1980s that punctuated the Sino-Vietnamese border following the 1979 war. He reportedly saw combat as a regimental commander, and his unit suffered heavy casualties. Chen's entry to intelligence, according to one account, was as the PLA's program manager to support the U.S. covert action program in Afghanistan in the mid-1980s. One quasi-official biography states that Chen entered 2PLA in 1986 and rose successively as a deputy branch chief, branch chief, deputy bureau chief, and then bureau chief.[27] Sometime after joining 2PLA, Chen came to Washington, DC, as a visiting fellow at the Atlantic Council.

During the mid-1990s Chen served as the 2PLA Fifth Bureau director, overseeing analysis of the United States and Western Europe.[28] From 1999 to 2001 he was defense attaché to Cairo. Chen then served for two years beginning in September 2001 as defense attaché in Washington, DC, but was frozen out of regular contacts by the Pentagon because of the April 2001 EP-3 incident.[29]

Chen returned unusually early from the United States in September 2003 and took a position in the CCP Central Committee's foreign affairs office as deputy director. He would have been a key player in organizing the Central Foreign Affairs Work Conference in 2006, and he was eventually appointed as assistant chief of the general staff.[30]

Chen Youyi (陈友谊, 1954–)

Chen Youyi became director of the 2PLA in December 2011. As of September 2018, no information suggested that he was replaced in the new Intelligence Bureau (情报局) of the Joint Staff Department. He previously served as a 2PLA deputy director and director of the peacekeeping office within the Ministry of National Defense. The latter is the outward-facing name for a 2PLA bureau and presumably remains so after the 2015–16 reorganization.[31] Chen was promoted to major general in July 2010 while serving as a deputy director. Known as an expert on the former Soviet Union, Chen earned a doctorate from the Institute of Eastern Europe, Russia, and Central Asian Studies within the Chinese Academy of Social Sciences in 1995.[32]

Deng Fa (邓发, 1906–46)

From 1931 to 1935 Deng Fa was Mao's head of secret police. He is known abroad for mention in Edgar Snow's *Red Star Over China*. Like Gong Changrong (see chapter 3), Deng was a colorful figure whose life story might eventually become the subject of a biographical action film, particularly if today's leadership wishes to further sanitize the darkest elements of CCP intelligence and security during the revolution.

Deng was born in Yunfou county, near Guangzhou. He had no formal education, but his father insisted that the children study for two hours each evening. Deng helped support the family by working in a rural factory rolling firecrackers, and he studied on his own.[33]

In 1921, the year the CCP was founded, the teenaged Deng left home for Guangzhou, finding employment as a cook on British ships into Hong Kong. The 1922 seaman's strike drew him into leftist and union politics, and Deng became a propagandist. In 1923 he joined the CCP.

During the 1926–27 Northern Expedition, he commanded a small unit of youths in Guangzhou. After the April 12 Nationalist coup d'état, Deng continued propaganda work underground. Along with Ye Jianying and others, he participated in the disastrous Canton (Guangzhou) uprising of December 1927, commanding a district combat unit and then a worker "Red Guard" detachment (赤卫队, chiwei dui). Though defeated, Deng again eluded his enemies and returned to his home to write a critique of the campaign.

In 1928 Zhou Enlai was building the newly established SSS, the CCP's first intelligence organization. Deng Fa was in Hong Kong working as the CCP secretary at the Taikoo dockyards (太古船坞, Taigu chuanwu), and Zhou gave him the additional duty of handling SSS matters.

Deng's responsibilities soon multiplied. Known to both the British in Hong Kong and KMT authorities in Guangzhou, Deng nonetheless made himself publicly visible in Hong Kong demonstrations and physical confrontations. When captured by the British in late 1930, he managed to bluff his way out by pretending to be an ordinary peasant, repeatedly answering questions with his own query, "Who is Deng Fa?"

However, more than a few Hong Kong police had seen Deng. In December 1930 he left the colony to lead the CCP military and special services (intelligence and special operations) committees of the Fujian-Guangdong-Jiangxi border area in the southernmost part of Red Army territory.[34]

The timing was extraordinary. Deng plunged into a turbulent atmosphere of Nationalist opposition to CCP expansion in the region by a local unit of pro-Nationalists calling itself the AB Corps (A B 团, tuan). Within the CCP, Mao Zedong took the opportunity to brand rivals as reactionary supporters of the AB Corps, leading to the Futian incident: large-scale executions of alleged AB Corps members, Red Army cadre, and even some "base area founders."[35]

Deng did well in this gruesome work and was promoted in November 1931 to head the new State Political Protection Bureau (PPB). At about this time, Li Kenong, Qian Zhuangfei, and other SSS intelligence officers, recently evacuated from the cities, joined the PPB. In 1932–34, this may have moved the PPB at least slightly from its focus on internal security toward broader concerns.[36] The period also marked the decline of the SSS, which was formally abolished in 1935. Though party historians blame the excesses of Futian and its aftermath on the influence of Mao's opponent, Wang Ming, Deng Fa is acknowledged to have carried out much of them. He became one of the most hated men in the party leadership but was promoted to the CCP Central Executive Committee (中央执行委员, *Zhongyang zhixing weiyuan*) in January 1934.[37]

Subsequent events forced the PPB to refocus. In September 1934 Mo Xiong, a CCP agent on the KMT army staff, learned that the Nationalist Army was about to begin its fifth "encirclement" campaign with force that might defeat the Red Army. Mo's network acquired and delivered the KMT army's attack plans through the lines to the communist headquarters in Ruijin.[38]

The Red Army escaped the encirclement and began their famous Long March in October 1934. The PPB never stopped "weeding" (铲除, *chanchu*) the party's perceived enemies, but its priorities shifted toward tactical military tasks such as reconnaissance, signals intercept, and analysis.[39] Li Kenong began taking a leading role on the Long March; apparently he was more skilled at these functions than Deng.[40] At the end of the march in November 1935, Deng was shifted to lead the Grains Department.[41] In spite of this change of vocation, he met Edgar Snow in Xi'an in June 1936 while disguised as a Nationalist officer and facilitated his passage to Mao's headquarters.[42]

Deng may have retained some security duties but was laterally transferred if not demoted. Though he could read and write and was good-humored and trustworthy, Deng was less of an intelligence specialist than a loyal enforcer: brave, physically capable, experienced at protection and intimidation, and a servant of those holding power in the party, not a clever politician. In early 1937 the party sent him to Moscow where he participated in the work of the CCP's delegation to the Comintern under Wang Ming and Kang Sheng, studied Marxist-Leninist revolutionary theory, and gave talks such as "The Worker Movement in China." He also lobbied for accelerated delivery of promised Soviet military assistance.[43]

That July, Japanese attacks in northern China led to all-out war. The Chinese Communists and Nationalists entered into an uneasy "Second United Front" against Japan. Stalin decided that Wang Ming, Kang Sheng, and Deng Fa should return to China—Wang and Kang to join the CCP Politburo in Yan'an and Deng to take the place of Chen Yun as CCP representative in Dihua (迪化, now Urumqi, Xinjiang). Deng was further than ever from intelligence management, but after returning to China in September 1937 he was named to the CCP's ruling Politburo in December as a nonresident member based in Dihua, but now part of that elite body.[44]

Deng stayed for two years in Xinjiang. Clandestine skills undoubtedly came in handy for survival. In a second transfer of extraordinary timing, Deng was sent to Yan'an in mid-1939 to take over the Party School.[45]

That year the party leadership's paranoia about enemy infiltration was growing by the month. Deng was to ensure that his students, including many new party members, were thoroughly schooled in Marxist precepts to resist the temptations of the old society. However, by early 1942 Mao had decided that a large-scale examination of party member attitudes was necessary. Deng Fa, ever the loyal apparatchik, stayed in the Party School. Mao opened his Rectification campaign with a speech, "Reorganizing Party Work Style," in February 1942. Deng spoke after Mao, promising to help root out potential opponents in the lower ranks, including students at the Party School.[46]

Deng left the Party School to lead the CCP Labor Commission (中央职工委员会, *Zhongyang zhigong weiyuanhui*) in the spring of 1943, just as the infamous Salvation campaign of Mao and Kang began, forcing hundreds of false espionage confessions.[47] Confirmation is elusive, but this move suggests that Deng was intentionally sidelined.

While Mao Zedong emerged from the Seventh Party Congress (April–June 1945) with unprecedented power and influence, Deng Fa lost his Politburo seat and his place on the Central Committee, as did others associated with the more brutal aspects of security work.[48]

Adding to the impression that Mao wanted his former secret police chief out of sight while he united the CCP to defeat the Nationalists, Deng was sent to Paris (December 1945), Manila, and Shanghai (January 1946) to represent China at labor meetings and publicize the CCP's version of current events.

On April 8 an aircraft from Chongqing to Yan'an carrying four American crewmen and seventeen passengers including Deng Fa, Bo Gu, and General Ye Ting overshot its destination by 134 kilometers and crashed into Black Tea Mountain (黑茶山, *Heicha shan*) in Shanxi province. Rumors of sabotage have existed for years but without conclusive evidence.[49]

Geng Huichang (耿惠昌, 1951–)

Geng Huichang of Hebei was the fourth head of the Ministry of State Security (MSS), a position he held from August 30, 2007, to November 2016. He was the first MSS leader with a foreign-oriented career rather than having internal security or domestic political experience, even though the depth of this experience is almost impossible to gauge. Geng's official biography identifies his birthdate, that he is a college graduate, the date he became minister, and the two subsequent National People's Congress (NPC) confirmations of his position in 2008 and 2013.[50] Reportedly, in addition to being an expert on the United States, Geng is knowledgeable about Japan and economic espionage.[51]

Geng's publicly available career data is sparse, with two major gaps that cannot be filled due to a lack of available information in Chinese or English. The first gap is Geng's early career. Prior to publishing an article on the U.S. presidential election in the journal *Contemporary International Relations* (现代国际关系), Geng's career is a black hole.[52] In 1985 he became the deputy director of the Institute of American Studies (美国研究所) at the China Institutes of Contemporary International Relations (CICIR, 中国现代国际关系研究院). From 1985 to 1994 Geng steadily advanced up CICIR's ranks, becoming its president in 1993—a bureau-level position within the MSS—before disappearing once again.[53] That second gap ended sometime in the late 1990s or early 2000s when Geng was brought back to the MSS headquarters in Beijing as an assistant minister or vice minister.[54]

Gu Shunzhang (顾顺章, 1895–1935)

A native of the Shanghai region, Gu Shunzhang may be China's best-known traitor for his 1931 defection to the Chinese Nationalists while serving as head of the CCP SSS. Gu betrayed countless party members, addresses, and methods of clandestine work, which almost annihilated the urban party. Clear photos of him are impossible to find.

Sorting fact from fiction about Gu remains a work in progress, as Beijing's propagandists have a strong interest in presenting him in the worst possible light. A lot of material probably remains classified. After he joined the CCP in 1924 and participated in union organizing and strike work, the party sent Gu and Chen Geng to Moscow, Khabarovsk, and Vladivostok in December 1926 for three months of instruction in clandestine work.[55] The pair studied explosives, interrogation, marksmanship, field investigations, political protection operations, and armed rebellion. On their return to China in February 1927, both served in related functions: Chen as the head of a special operations unit in Wuhan,[56] and Gu as head of the Military Special Commission (军事特别委员会, *Junshi tebie weiyuanhui*),[57] the nascent CCP organization supervising clandestine work. They also participated in training new intelligence operatives in 1928–30, as the party's intelligence organization expanded after the April 1927 split with the Nationalists.[58]

The two remained comrades until Gu's April 1931 defection, yet the CCP depicts them as polar opposites even before that fateful day: Chen as a fresh-faced youth and competent optimist, Gu as the evil opportunist, drug user, womanizer, and shadowy figure with wild ambitions, disciplined by Zhou Enlai for his excesses. Yet on the eve of his defection, Zhou and the party leadership trusted Gu, accompanied by Dong Jianwu, to escort Zhang Guotao, a top communist, on a five-hundred-mile trip from Shanghai to the Hubei-Henan-Anhui (*Eyuwan*) soviet.[59] This throws doubt on today's dark depiction of Gu before his defection but clarifies nothing about his true characteristics and actual contributions to CCP intelligence operations.

After Gu and Dong delivered Zhang to the Eyuwan soviet in mid-April 1931, Gu headed back toward Shanghai, passing through Wuhan for a clandestine rendezvous on April 25. He was disguised that day as the "All-Transforming Magician" Hua Guangqi, alias Li Ming, a favorite cover that he apparently used often. By chance, a former communist in the employ of the KMT spotted Gu, and authorities arrested him. Gu decided to cooperate with the innocuously named Central Statistics Bureau (CSB, 中统局, *Zhongtong ju*), the KMT organ charged with catching communists, as his alternative was death by torture.[60] Gu offered his captors limited information about the local CCP organization but promised more in exchange for a meeting in Nanjing with Generalissimo Chiang Kai-shek, who agreed to see Gu the following Monday.[61]

To their credit, the CSB office in Wuhan immediately issued six encrypted reporting telegrams to their chief, Xu Enzeng (徐恩增, U. T. Hsu), in Nanjing. However, Xu could not be reached that weekend. A CCP agent on the CSB headquarters staff, Qian Zhuangfei, saw the telegrams first, and alerted the CCP (see *Longtan Sanjie*, Three Heroes of the Dragon's Lair).[62]

In response, Zhou Enlai, Chen Yun, Li Kenong, and other top communists met on April 26 and issued instructions for CCP members in Shanghai and Jiangsu to shift accommodations that night. Within two hours Chen Yun sent more than one hundred posters with Gu's picture to party branches so that they could watch out for him as they pursued evasive measures.[63] The CCP Central Committee had Zhou confront Gu's family, asking if they intended to join him in Nanjing. When Gu's wife said that she would be obligated to follow her husband, her callers murdered her and ten other members of the family, sparing only an infant boy.[64] Their bodies were not discovered until weeks later, but they may have been killed that Sunday or Monday night (April 26–27), just as Gu was asking Chiang Kai-shek to protect them. No one seems to know what happened to the boy.

According to the CCP's "Order the Arrest of Gu Shunzhang, A Traitor to the Revolution," Gu gave the KMT information on how to find CCP general secretary Xiang Zhongfa and other ranking officials, which they promptly did. Gu also handed over the locations of CCP offices in Hubei, the identities of more than a dozen previously unknown communists including people already in custody, and general information about CCP operations.[65]

Though CCP accounts hint that Zhou Enlai arranged an effort to assassinate Gu four years later, Frederic Wakeman indicated that KMT records on Taiwan show that Gu decided to rejoin the CCP and was executed by the KMT CSB when they discovered this.[66]

Though parts of Gu's life remain obscured and available accounts must be critically examined, it is easy to understand why he remains a focus for modern-day CCP-approved histories. His defection almost destroyed the party, and he was a dramatic and mysterious figure. Most of all, the fate of his loved ones, buried beneath an urban patio until the stench of their bodies drew inquiries, was a signal warning to those who would betray the CCP: the party has its revenge in the end.

Hua Guofeng (Hua Kuo-feng, 华国锋, 1921–2008)

Famous as China's transitional leader between Mao Zedong and Deng Xiaoping, Hua Guofeng is less well known for overseeing China's security services and its science and technology (S&T) organizations as PRC technology acquisition efforts were revived after the Cultural Revolution. Hua's career included an early stint doing tactical intelligence and reconnaissance. In Mao's last years, Hua performed little-known sensitive duties, including inquiries into the 1971 defection of Lin Biao and the death two years later of minister of public security Li Zhen.

Rumors targeting Hua Guofeng have existed for decades,[67] and parts of his personal history are unclear.[68] Hua joined the CCP in 1938 at age seventeen and became a guerrilla fighter in Shanxi. His unit provided tactical intelligence to the Eighth Route Army in 1940–41: disguised as a local peasant, Hua occasionally scouted behind enemy lines and was reportedly imaginative in designing improvised explosive devices against Japanese patrols. These and other stories of Hua's exploits might be exaggerated, but in 1942 Hua was promoted, indicating success.[69]

In the Chinese civil war, Hua again ran tactical intelligence and sabotage work, sending spies against Nationalist General Yan Xishan's units to reconnoiter, poison food and water, and disseminate propaganda.[70]

In 1949 Hua was fortuitously transferred to Mao's native place in Xiangtan county, Hunan province. He vigorously implemented land reform, beginning a pattern of loyally adhering to Mao's directives, with occasional exceptions.[71] When the Great Leap Forward began in 1958, Hua sent Beijing favorable reports of radical policy success, which Mao used against critics reporting famine. The chairman named Hua as Hunan party secretary a year later. In 1961 Hua was transferred back down to Xiangtan—perhaps less a demotion than a placement into the sensitive post of running Mao's home county during the height of the famine. Hua undertook projects to impress Mao and managed to keep the leader's home area insulated from the unfolding disaster.[72]

Hua became Hunan province CCP secretary in 1964 and broadened his portfolio to include province-level security work by improving militia units and speaking on the U.S. threat. Mao viewed Hunan under Hua's control as one of the five provinces that supported his rural program.[73]

Hua faced Red Guard opposition in Hunan during the Cultural Revolution and was detained in its capital, Changsha, by a "revolutionary rebel" workers' group in mid-1967. Zhou Enlai negotiated his release, but Hua only returned to power later following military intervention. Loyalty to Mao's programs and administrative skill made Hua attractively "red and expert" during a shortage of officials after widespread purges—not the last time that this combination would lead him upward. Now a prominent "survivor," Hua was appointed a member of the Central Committee at the Ninth CCP Congress in 1969.[74]

In October 1971 Mao transferred Hua to Beijing to handle agricultural, financial, and commercial affairs. Mao urged Hua to develop a "political nose" but trusted him, giving Hua at least three sensitive tasks: assess the attempted "coup" by Lin Biao in September 1971, conduct a review of dismissed former cadres claiming wrongful treatment,[75] and lead the investigation of the mysterious death inside MPS headquarters of its minister, Li Zhen, on October 22, 1973.[76] Hua judged Li's death to be a suicide. The event caused considerable suspicion and contention inside the leadership, placing Hua in a hot seat where he apparently excelled.[77]

Hua was elected to the Politburo in August 1973 and formally appointed to be MPS minister and vice premier in charge of political and legal work in January 1975.[78] In successively higher offices, Hua oversaw intelligence and security work and simultaneously had purview over the acquisition of foreign science and technology.[79] Further study is needed to define matters, but the following information indicates that Hua Guofeng either agreed to or influenced renewed coordination between PRC technology acquisition and foreign intelligence operations.

In 1975 the National Science and Technology Information Work Meeting met for the first time in twelve years, and Hua worked with Deng Xiaoping to overhaul the Chinese Academy of Sciences. Among their goals were to speed the import of foreign technology, support basic research, and cut back on ideological interference. Their effort was stalled by Mao's criticism of Deng that November and by further radical opposition in early 1976.[80]

Barely a month after Mao's death on September 9, 1976, Hua performed arguably the most important security function of his career as the decisive actor in the arrest of Jiang Qing and her radical associates, the so-called Gang of Four, on October 6.[81]

With the radical left disabled, Hua oversaw the revival of the national open-source intelligence/information (*qingbao*) system, founded in 1956 but sidelined during the Cultural Revolution. A national S&T development plan was released in 1977, and a year later the National People's Congress ratified the Four Modernizations. That same year saw renewed efforts by the China Society for S&T Information, the Institute of Scientific and Technical Information of China, and the military, which founded an open-source document service. Partly as a result, in 1980 the Fifth National Science and Technology Information Work Meeting resolved to tie intelligence work to economic construction and S&T development.[82] Unfortunately for Hua, these achievements in boosting Chinese technology were tarnished by the Ten-Year Plan, unveiled in February–March 1978. Later that year, Deng Xiaoping, once again on the rise, used the plan's reliance on Mao era–type goals to discredit Hua,[83] even though Deng himself had agreed to it.[84]

Hua Guofeng lost his influence and high offices in 1980–81, but unlike officials who fell during Mao's time, he was not imprisoned or disgraced and even retained a Central Committee seat until death.[85] Under his five-year tenure as China's senior leader, close coordination of foreign intelligence and technology acquisition resumed. His work to rebuild these capabilities and to strengthen internal security continued under subsequent leaders.

Huang Baifu (黃柏富)

Huang Baifu of Zhejiang province served as Second Department of the PLA General Staff Department director from late 2003 to early 2006. Prior to becoming director, he served as 2PLA's political commissar.[86] Following his retirement from the military he served as deputy director of the 2PLA-managed think tank, China Institute for International Strategic Studies (中国国际战略学会), where he worked from at least 2008 through late 2015.[87]

Ji Shengde (姬胜德, 1948–)

Ji Shengde, son of Chinese diplomat Ji Pengfei, served as 2PLA director from 1995 to 1999. He also served as a deputy director and oversaw the department's military attachés working overseas.[88]

He is currently imprisoned on a commuted death sentence for his role in the 1999 Yuanhua smuggling scandal. For many years prior to his arrest, Ji maintained a flamboyant lifestyle, even flaunting foreign luxury cars in front of colleagues and foreign officials.[89] General Ji also was involved in funneling Chinese money into the 1996 U.S. elections, reportedly giving $300,000 to Johnny Chung to give to the Democratic Party and its candidates.[90]

Jia Chunwang (贾春旺, 1938–)

Ling Yun's unexpected departure in 1985 over Yu Qiangsheng's defection ushered in a new era for the Ministry of State Security. During his thirteen-year tenure, Jia Chunwang oversaw the MSS's expansion and evolution into a nationwide organization with departments and bureaus down to the local level. Jia is unique among the ministers of state security for having a career beyond the ministry and being a rising star at the time of his selection.[91]

Jia shares his pedigree with the luminaries of his generation's elite, such as Hu Jintao. Jia belonged to the Tsinghua clique cultivated by university president Jiang Nanxiang. After graduating in the mid-1960s, Jia stayed on as a "double-load cadre" serving as Tsinghua CCP official. According to his official biography, he was sent down to the countryside for six years during the Cultural Revolution before returning to Tsinghua University in 1972. For the next decade, Jia served as secretary of the China Youth League committee at the university and served on the latter's party committee from 1978 to 1982.[92] In 1983 Jia was one of the young officials chosen for a senior position (as Beijing deputy party secretary) when Deng sidelined older cadre. Jia's career prospects probably rose when he became an acolyte of vice premier Qiao Shi. In 1987 Qiao became a Politburo member, overseeing the Central Party School and the CCP Secretariat. Jia reportedly became one of Qiao's most trusted aides as the latter rose to lead the Central Political-Legal Commission and the NPC.[93] These connections probably gave Jia the protection and the political power to involve the MSS in the takedown of Beijing party secretary Chen Xitong in 1995.[94]

The MSS began as a central-level ministry and only a handful of provincial departments. By the end of Jia's tenure, the MSS covered every province and provincial-level city and countless municipalities. The expansion took place in four distinct waves, finishing in the mid-1990s (see Ministry of State Security). The first three waves (1983–84, 1985–88, 1990–95) were largely horizontal, extending the ministry's reach across the provinces. The fourth wave, which ran concurrent with the third, extended the MSS reach down into the localities. This was accomplished largely by taking over portions of existing public security bureaus. Building up the MSS made Jia a candidate for the Politburo ahead of the 1997 party congress.[95]

As head of the MSS, Jia's second-most important contribution was launching a historical research program. Beginning in the early 1990s, Jia started commissioning histories of Chinese intelligence and its leaders to help educate younger officers. According to the MSS general office in the foreword of a book on Li Kenong, the point of these histories was at least in part to teach younger officers about the legacy that they inherited. Because of the three purges within CCP intelligence in the mid-1950s, the Cultural Revolution, and the forming of the MSS, younger officers or those brought over from the MPS lacked a sense of history or being part of a rich tradition.[96]

However, Jia's further political ascension was not to be. Qiao's control over the security establishment and political-legal apparatus—which he had built up since the mid-1980s—incited the concern of top political leaders Jiang Zemin and Li Peng. Instead of advancing, Jia was transferred—maybe forcibly—to the MPS in a seemingly lateral move. Arguably, Jia's move began the ministry's political rise that culminated when Politburo member Zhou Yongkang became minister of public security in 2003. Some rumors indicated Jia was removed for intelligence failures on Taiwan and Tibet.[97] Jia finished his government career as minister of public security (1998–2003) and then as chief of the People's Supreme Procuratorate (2003–8).

Kang Sheng (康生, 1898–1975)

Kang Sheng is among China's most famous intelligence figures, but his deservedly villainous reputation and exaggerated record are used to sanitize in official CCP history. The full support given to him, even for his darkest deeds, by Mao Zedong, Liu Shaoqi, Chen Yun, and other senior leaders is seldom acknowledged. While Kang's role in the political campaigns of 1942–44 caused great damage, his efforts to build the party's espionage apparatus during that decade helped the CCP to achieve its 1949 victory.

Like many communists, Kang Sheng changed his name several times, seemingly to mark life transitions. At birth he was Zhang Zongke, from a Shandong landlord family near Qingdao.[98] As Zhang Yun, a Shanghai University student, he joined the CCP in early 1925, conducted union organizing, participated in the May 30 movement, and left school in 1926 to become the CCP Organization Department's Shanghai director.[99] He helped lead the March 1927 Shanghai uprising during the Northern Expedition.[100]

After the April 12, 1927, anticommunist coup, the urban CCP went underground. Kang became head of the party's organization department in 1931[101] and assisted with the frantic evacuations after the April 25, 1931, defection of Gu Shunzhang.[102]

However, Kang's career was boosted by the disastrous events that year. Zhou Enlai appointed Kang (as Zhao Rong) to the CCP Central Committee and to the Central Special Services Commission that provided political oversight of intelligence and security. Kang became deputy of the SSS under Chen Yun and the director of their Third Section, the Red Squads, which were responsible for assassinating enemies.[103] Zhou Enlai fled Shanghai in December 1931, and a few months later, when Chen Yun departed, Kang Sheng took over all SSS work, gaining the nickname "the boss" (老板, *laoban*). However, the CCP almost completely evacuated Shanghai the following year. Kang fled to Moscow in July 1933,[104] adopting his final nom de guerre, Kang Sheng.[105]

While in Moscow from August 1933 to November 1937, Kang was the assistant to CCP delegation leader Wang Ming. He watched Joseph Stalin consolidating the Soviet security services into one body, the NKVD, in 1934, using them in the Great Terror (1936–38) to rid the Communist party of perceived enemies.[106] Though details are scarce, Kang received professional security training from the NKVD in Moscow,[107] identifying fellow Chinese he supposed to be traitors and Trotskyites.[108] Today's CCP narrative claims Kang persecuted loyal comrades to keep secret his bourgeois past, curry favor with the senior leader Wang Ming, and obtain revenge against others.[109] However, his victims included others. In 1935 Kang may even have called for the execution of Ho Chi Minh (Nguyen Ai Quoc), then a Comintern trainee in Moscow. Kang may simply have been following the Stalinist example to advance himself, avoid being named a counterrevolutionary, and learn the tricks of the terror trade.[110]

Though Wang Ming tried to secure the party leadership when he and Kang returned to China in November 1937, Kang chose Mao's side within a year. In early 1938 he alleged in a *Liberation* article that the former CCP leader Chen Duxiu was a follower of Trotsky and a spy, helping eliminate a rival to Mao's drive toward party leadership.[111] That summer, Kang vouched for the background of the controversial actress Jiang Qing, whom Mao wished to marry in spite of suspected KMT connections.[112] Mao rewarded Kang with appointments as head of the PPB in December 1937, the Central Party School in March 1938, and the Military Intelligence Department that August. When CCP intelligence was reorganized in February 1939, Kang became director of the Central Social Affairs Department (SAD), now elevated to become a Central Committee department. In spite of Moscow's expressed disapproval in March 1940, Kang accrued other leadership roles, including chair of the committee to pursue "cadre screening" (审查干部, *shencha ganbu*) in autumn 1941.[113] During the infamous "traitor weeding" activity of the Rectification (整风, *Zhengfeng*, 1942–44) and Salvation (抢救, *Qiangjiu*, 1943) movements, Kang worked directly under the Central Committee and Mao, who described enemy spies in Yan'an being "as thick as fur."[114]

After receiving reports from their resident GRU officer in Yan'an, Moscow sent Mao the "Dimitrov telegram" on December 22, 1943, demanding that Mao cease purge activity against reliable party members.[115] The telegram, almost certainly written with clearance from Stalin, specifically mentioned Mao's intelligence chief: "I also feel doubts about the role of Kang Sheng. . . . He is taking abnormal measures that only arouse mutual suspicion and strong dissatisfaction by ordinary Party members and the masses, which [might] help the enemy and collapse the Party."[116]

Mao at first resisted but eventually yielded to Moscow's admonishments amid widespread outrage in Yan'an against Kang. Mao sidelined his security chief but protected him, sending Kang to lead land reform work in Shanxi in the spring and summer of 1947 after replacing him as head of the Intelligence Department and the SAD in October 1946.[117] Not long afterward, Kang was posted to his native Shandong province to work in the East China Bureau as its third secretary, under Rao Shushi—a severe demotion.[118]

While Kang was working in Shandong (1948–56), his ranking on the Politburo varied between number six and as a mere alternate member. In 1955 his former subordinate Pan Hannian was arrested, accused of being an enemy agent. Purges and demotions of up to one thousand intelligence cadres followed, and that year the CCP Central Investigation Department (CID) was founded, devoted entirely to foreign intelligence. In September 1956 Mao brought Kang back to Beijing to participate in the first plenum of the CCP Eighth Congress. While party records indicate Kang played no role in the CID, he retained personal connections with Li Kenong and Luo Qingchang.[119]

Kang focused on Sino-Soviet relations in the late 1950s, tasked by Mao to work alongside Deng Xiaoping to oppose Moscow's de-Stalinization—perceived in Beijing as opposing Mao's personality cult. In the leadup to

the Cultural Revolution (1966–76), Kang allied with Jiang Qing to identify targets for ideological criticism. Kang supplanted Deng Xiaoping as
the political overseer of CCP intelligence organs in August 1966[120] as the
chaos began, branding the heads of the Central Committee Propaganda
and Organization Departments as enemy agents.[121] Kang claimed to have
the power to detect enemy spies without objective evidence, nowadays
denounced as "mysticism" (神秘主义, shenmi zhuyi).[122] In April 1967
chaos within the CID imperiled the security of classified documents—
Red Guard newspapers were beginning to publish confidential material.
Mao approved a plan by Zhou Enlai to hand over CID people and assets to
2PLA (military intelligence), possibly a temporary setback for Kang since
Lin Biao controlled the army.

In the wake of the Lin Biao incident of September 13, 1971, when
Marshal Lin fled China and was killed in a plane crash, Kang Sheng became
clinically depressed, and in May 1972 he was diagnosed with bladder cancer. Now truly ill, Kang stayed on the Politburo for symbolic reasons as an
old revolutionary, though his activity drastically declined.[123] Close to death,
Kang asked Zhou Enlai and Deng Xiaoping, with whom he retained close
relations, to tell Mao that Jiang Qing and Zhang Chunqiao had betrayed
the CCP in the 1930s and might still be spies for Taiwan.[124] Mao responded
that Kang was seeing "spies under the bed."[125]

Kang's condition worsened, and he died in December 1975. Marking
a byzantine end to the drama of CCP security and intelligence under Mao,
Kang and Xie Fuzhi, the former minister of public security, were together
posthumously expelled from the CCP in 1980 as coconspirators with
Jiang Qing.

Kang Sheng left lasting and tragic legacies. He refined the existing CCP
"struggle culture" of the 1930s into a tool for Mao to consolidate control
and grew the intelligence organs even as he eschewed competent expertise
in actual espionage disciplines. A practice attributed to Kang, *bi gong xin*
(逼供信; forcing confessions by torture and believing them), continues
to be employed by PRC security forces in modern times. However Kang's
uncritical support of Mao, always striving to anticipate his preferences, was
not so unique: other senior leaders were as compliant. A crucial difference

was that Kang's personal relations with the chairman were consistently good.[126]

Kong Yuan (孔原, 1906–90; Spouse: Xu Ming [许明])

The last director of the CCP Central Investigation Department before the Cultural Revolution was Kong Yuan of Jiangxi province, the highest-ranking intelligence officer purged in its chaotic opening period.[127] A CCP-approved summary says that Kong "made great contributions to Party organization, PRC Customs work, foreign affairs, foreign trade, work on Taiwan, and on the hidden battlefront."[128] In reality he mostly performed espionage work, but according to a Taiwan scholar, Kong and many other officers had cover assignments for which they were well qualified and that they might actually have performed.[129]

As an eighteen-year-old student activist in Changsha, Kong Yuan had no intelligence duties but operated secretly due a hostile local warlord, joining the Communist Youth League and then the party itself in quick succession (1925). Just as the KMT Northern Expedition entered Changsha in September 1926, Kong organized worker "pickets" to provide armed support.

When Changsha was secured, Kong was appointed the chief judge on a special court to try landlords.[130] He was on a mission to buy firearms in Wuhan during April 1927 when the KMT staged its anticommunist coup. Afterward, Kong participated in the Nanchang uprising of August 1, 1927, and joined the newly formed Political Protection Office (政治保卫处, *Zhengzhi baowei chu*), performing bodyguard work and possibly some intelligence tasks.[131]

After a brief posting to Shanghai in 1928 in another trade union position, the CCP sent Kong to Moscow in March 1929 for about eighteen months of instruction at the Communist University of Toilers of the East. His curriculum may have included a standard one-year military and political course, leaving six months for other specialized training that has not yet been identified.[132] In October 1930 Kong returned to China and became secretary (秘书, *mishu*) to Kang Sheng—the Organization Department head who began his own intelligence duties the following year.[133]

The KMT rapidly hunted down urban communists in 1931–34, and Kong was constantly on the move. He became the party committee head of nearby Jiangsu province and acted as Central Committee representative for northern China. In the spring of 1935 he was back in Shanghai, appointed to the Central Committee as an alternate member and as White Area party representative.[134] He was one of the few active communists left in China's largest city at that time. His presence and that of some others in Shanghai, such as Pan Hannian and Gong Changrong, indicate that CCP intelligence operatives were the last to evacuate the cities and the first to return during 1931–36.

In July 1935 with the CCP's urban networks almost extinct, Kong was evacuated to Moscow, ostensibly to attend the seventh congress of the Comintern. He entered the Lenin Institute in Moscow for an advanced course that lasted perhaps as long as three years, but this account is vague and may have been a cover for other training.[135] These were the same years when Wang Ming and the notorious Kang Sheng were the CCP's Moscow representatives at the Comintern. Kang pursued a purge of Chinese Communists resident there, shopping them to the NKVD as politically unreliable traitors—but Kong Yuan somehow survived.

In August 1938 Kong returned to China a full year after the start of the Sino-Japanese War. He was initially posted to Xinjiang as an army political instructor. Kong probably had substantial intelligence training and experience by this time, because in April 1939 he was appointed deputy director of the Social Affairs Department, the CCP's newly consolidated intelligence organ.[136]

In October of that year Kong published an essay lauding the "struggle against subversive agents" that presaged the Rectification Movement (1942–44) and Salvation (1943) antispy campaign.[137] However, Li Kenong replaced Kong Yuan as SAD deputy director in May 1940, allowing Kong to depart for Chongqing with Zhou Enlai, where Kong's spouse Xu Ming was "performing secret work." According to one source, Kong spent about four months undercover in Chongqing "setting up secret organizations" (建立秘密机关, *jianli mimi jiguan*). However, he was discovered by the KMT, and Zhou transferred him to an overt, official position in the CCP's

Eighth Route Army Liaison Office, taking on the southern bureau work of the recently departed Bo Gu, a much more senior party member.[138]

In January 1941 the New Fourth Army incident marked the effective end of KMT-CCP military cooperation in the field. The CCP's liaison office in the Nationalist capital of Chongqing continued to operate, albeit like a diplomatic mission in an adversary nation. Kong and others built armed underground networks that were instructed to accumulate weapons, shun contact with overt CCP members, and practice "the three diligences" (三勤：勤业, 勤学, 勤交友, *san qin: qinye, qinxue, qin jiaoyou*): diligently build careers, study, and cultivate contacts.

In late 1942 Kong inadvertently met Gao Qing, a CCP member on loan to the GRU (Soviet army intelligence). Gao was engaged in clandestine work against the KMT in Chongqing and expressed the strong desire to meet Zhou Enlai. He did, and Kong became Gao's case officer.[139]

In June 1943 the Salvation (*Qiangjiu*) campaign in Yan'an prompted a recall to headquarters of Zhou Enlai, Kong Yuan, their spouses, and one hundred others. Upon reaching Yan'an on July 16 Kang Sheng accused Kong and Xu Ming of being "turncoats" (叛徒, *pantu*) and "enemy agents" (特务, *tewu*) who falsely "waved the red flag." Kong's problems likely lasted until the Dimitrov telegram of December 22, 1943, when the Russians strongly suggested that Mao rein in Kang Sheng and stop attacking Zhou Enlai and others. Kong survived, but his protectors Zhou Enlai and Ye Jianying emerged with surprisingly low party ranks (twenty-third and thirty-first, respectively) at the Seventh Party Congress (April 23–June 11, 1945).[140]

One root of Kong's problems during the 1943 Salvation campaign, as for many others in the intelligence business, was the "lack of clarity" in his time doing clandestine work, when party cadres sitting safely in the rear area could not directly observe him. Twenty years later, during the Cultural Revolution, Kong Yuan, Xu Ming, and others would again suffer baseless but devastating accusations because they actually performed their jobs as clandestine officers.[141]

Though Kong would not again hold a senior intelligence position until 1957, the Japanese surrender brought him back into the business. In September 1945 he trekked on foot and horse with Xu Ming and other intelligence officers to the Shenyang SAD detachment. Kong simultaneously resumed intelligence duties and also became a senior municipal party committee official. As the Chinese civil war resumed in 1947, Kong was dispatched to various posts, including Jilin and Yanbian near the Korean border, where he drove conscription for the communist forces. Once Manchuria was secured and the KMT armies were in retreat, Kong was appointed first in Jilin and then in Fushun as municipal party secretary in 1948–49 and was noted for his efforts to dig into the details of governance: restoring the economy, developing agricultural and industrial production, encouraging commerce, and hunting for enemies within each urban household.[142]

As the communist victory approached, the party brought Kong back to the center of power in July 1949, but not to an intelligence assignment. The Central Committee appointed Kong as a member of two important finance commissions[143] and as chief of PRC customs and excise. These were politically sensitive posts and unlikely to have been cover jobs. Besides building China's first unified and fully sovereign customs organization since the end of the First Opium War (1839–42), Kong pursued an internal rectification program to ensure loyalty to the CCP's program.[144]

Kong's foreign affairs responsibilities expanded during the 1950s. He became a vice minister of foreign trade in 1953, focused on building commercial relations with the Warsaw Pact countries, North Korea, and Vietnam. Afterward, Kong was appointed to the highly sensitive Central Committee Leading Small Group on Taiwan Work, and in 1957 he returned to the senior intelligence ranks as deputy director of the CID, the PRC's first foreign intelligence organization.[145] Within a year Kong became the State Council Foreign Affairs Office deputy director responsible for overseeing foreign contacts with government organizations.[146] It was consistent with a continuing presence of CCP intelligence officers when foreigners came into contact with the party during these isolated years (see Li Kenong, Pan Hannian, Zhou Enlai, and Luo Qingchang).

Kong probably became acting director of the CID when Li Kenong was sidelined by a cerebral hemorrhage in October 1957,[147] formally taking charge when Li died in February 1962.[148] In 1967 the radical left Central Case Examination Group, charged with substantiating the suspicions of the chairman against his old comrades, opened a case on Kong Yuan.[149] He and Xu Ming were struggled against as "enemy spies," accused of tipping off their children to Mao's preferences in the struggle among Red Guard factions. Both attempted suicide, and under unclear circumstances Xu Ming died while Kong Yuan lived. He was imprisoned for seven years.[150]

Kong again surfaced in 1975, just before Mao's death and during the time of Deng Xiaoping's brief comeback, as a political committee member of a unit under the PLA General Staff. Possibly semi-retired and recovering from imprisonment, Kong was named as a PLA General Staff advisor in 1980 and in 1983 as a member of the Leading Small Group on State Security that established the new ministry of that name. Kong also provided advice to PRC customs in the 1980s.

After a long and colorful life, Kong Yuan passed away in September 1990.[151] Unlike other prominent intelligence heroes with similarly distinguished records, little has been openly published about him, for reasons that remain unclear.

Li Kenong (李克农, 1898–1962)

The exploits of Li Kenong make clear that Chinese communist intelligence used standard espionage techniques from its early history. Cited today as a unique revolutionary hero and called a "guiding personage" (卓越人物, *zhuoyue renwu*) by his official biographer, Li led the first important espionage ring inside the Chinese Nationalist enemy, rose to the top of the CCP spying apparatus during the communist revolution ending in 1949, and led foreign intelligence in the early years of the People's Republic.[152] Li is officially depicted as the loyal, competent, and honorable face of CCP intelligence in contrast to its villains such as Kang Sheng. While Li did move CCP intelligence, in fits and starts, away from secret police activity and toward espionage, he survived by striving to anticipate the preferences of Mao Zedong, and he did not hesitate to assist in some of Kang's, and Mao's, worst acts.

Li Kenong was born in Chao county, Anhui, and raised in nearby Wuhu. Part of the "May Fourth Generation," he was exposed early to nationalist politics through his family, progressive journals, and local demonstrations. He joined the CCP in 1926, assisted the Northern Expedition when it arrived, and fled to Shanghai after the CCP-KMT split of April 1927.[153]

Li performed cultural and propaganda work in Shanghai in 1927–29 with Pan Hannian and was probably an officer in the CCP Special Services Section by 1928. In November 1929 he met Hu Di, a fellow communist from his hometown, who introduced him to Qian Zhuangfei, the newly hired confidential assistant to H. T. Hsu (徐恩增, Xu Enzeng). Hsu was the recently appointed director of the KMT's Investigations Bureau, charged with hunting communists. Li reported this to Zhou Enlai, and in December the SSS established a "special small group," or a spy ring, inside the KMT security service. Their work probably reduced CCP casualties for the next sixteen months. In 1930 Li also recruited Mo Xiong, a KMT army staff officer whose information five years later enabled the Red Army in Jiangxi to escape the KMT's fifth encirclement campaign.[154]

Luck ran out for the "Li Kenong small group" (李克农小组, *Li Kenong xiaozu*) on April 25, 1931, with the defection of SSS director Gu Shunzhang, who told the KMT everything he knew, including the identities of Li, Qian, and Hu. However, the quick action of Li's ring gave the CCP between twelve and thirty-six hours to evacuate from locations that would quickly become compromised[155] (see *Longtan sanjie*, Three Heroes of the Dragon's Lair).

Li, Qian, and Hu fled to the Red Army headquarters in Jiangxi and were transferred to jobs in the PPB, subordinate to Deng Fa. At that time the PPB was mostly focused on internal security.[156] However, the military necessities of the Long March (1934–35) made intelligence on the enemy as important as internal security, and Li showed himself to be more qualified than Deng Fa, who was widely resented for his role in earlier purges. Deng Fa was sidelined, and Li helped expand the PPB's work to include protection of key leaders, internal investigations, apprehending deserters, and tactical military intelligence.[157] However, the PPB's mission to "dig out" (铲除, *chanchu*) or "weed" traitors remained prominent.[158]

In 1935 Edgar Snow noted that Li was chief of the communications department of the foreign office, perhaps a genuine function but certainly a cover for his intelligence duties.[159] Li further expanded his portfolio during the 1936 Xi'an incident, taking on a negotiator role for which he later became known abroad: in united front talks with the KMT in 1936–37, in the CCP-KMT negotiations during the 1945–46 Marshall mission, in the 1951–53 Panmunjom peace talks, and during the Geneva talks of 1954.[160]

Kang Sheng's return to China in November 1937 once again altered the CCP intelligence landscape. The higher ranking Kang took over PPB and reorganized it as the SAD in 1939, eventually strengthening its presence in the party organization and expanding networks nationwide to face the Japanese invasion. At first, Kong Yuan was Kang's deputy director, but Li Kenong and Pan Hannian replaced him in early 1941, with Pan running espionage work in Japanese-occupied areas and Li managing the rest of China from headquarters in Yan'an.[161] Li established a series of Eighth Route Army Liaison Offices charged with CCP-KMT liaison (1937–46) in Nationalist cities.[162] Each liaison office had senior representatives for the CCP's core functions: organization, propaganda, military, and intelligence. The offices served as a model for early PRC diplomatic missions after 1949.[163]

Even as a senior officer, Li took time for occasional operations of his own, such as wooing the third Soong sister, Soong Ailing (wife of KMT finance minister H. H. Kung), to support the united front in 1937. It was characteristic of CCP efforts to assign intelligence officers to united front influence work, taking advantage of the intelligence officer's skills in spotting and assessing candidates for recruitment, arranging secret information exchanges, and maneuvering someone to the point where discreet, mutual cooperation could be established.[164]

In 1942 Zhou Enlai revealed that the CCP had five thousand agents in the Nationalist areas of Sichuan, Guizhou, and Yunnan. They included KMT lieutenant general Yan Baohang, a military strategist for Generalissimo Chiang Kai-shek who was secretly running his own CCP network.[165] After the revolution, Chiang Kai-shek himself wrote that "there was no space that they [the CCP's agents] did not enter" (无空不入, *wu kong bu ru*).[166]

In spite of these successes, 1942 to 1944 were dark years for the CCP's espionage apparatus at the party center in Yan'an as Mao and Kang Sheng, assisted by Li Kenong, began the Rectification (1942–44) and Salvation (antispy, 1943) campaigns. The latter included countless false denunciations and confessions through torture (see *bi gong xin*, 逼供信).[167]

Opium may also have been a blot on the record of Li Kenong. The Soviet author Peter Vladimirov, who was the GRU representative in in Yan'an, wrote that CCP Politburo member Ren Bishi briefed him in September 1943 on the "vanguard, revolutionary role" played by the drug in the difficult economic situation, asking the Russian to solicit Moscow's understanding. Li Kenong allegedly played an important role by maintaining liaison with criminal secret societies in the KMT and Japanese areas in order to assure safe passage and sale of the product.[168] Research by Chen Yung-fa two decades after publication of Vladimirov's diaries supported the allegations of opium trafficking, concluding that shipments of the "special product" (特产, *techan*) from the CCP base area were of significantly higher value than others. While Mao later considered planting this "certain thing" (某物, *mowu*) to be a mistake, the Red Area economy would have suffered a considerable setback without it.[169]

In December 1943 the Russians convinced Mao, via the Dimitrov telegram, to cease the antispy campaigns.[170] Mao's brief flirtation in 1944 with the U.S. Dixie mission was only a temporary counterweight. Spying remained important. Colonel David Barrett, the Dixie mission commander, wrote: "There were no police in Yenan. Police were probably unnecessary, for as we came to know later, the whole of Chinese Communist society is pervaded with spies, snoops, and informers. Such persons, of course, were not in evidence. . . . it is likely we never went anywhere that someone did not follow us, but we were never aware of it."[171]

Popular resentment against Kang Sheng for the excesses of the 1943 Salvation campaign led Mao to publicly apologize and gradually ease Kang out of his top positions. Mao ordered Li Kenong back from Beiping to Yan'an in October 1946 to take over the Intelligence Department. He formally replaced Kang as SAD director less than two years later. Another new era in CCP intelligence began.[172]

With civil war looming, Li Kenong moved away from internal investigations to focus on espionage for critical military intelligence. On the day Japan surrendered, Li called an "emergency conference" to urge organs to place "inner line" (内线, *neixian*) agents inside the KMT. But recruitment was hard because the job posed a double hazard: if not apprehended by the Nationalists, an agent might face problems later inside the CCP for having been associated with the enemy.[173]

In spite of this, the weaknesses on the Nationalist side and the skills of Li Kenong and Pan Hannian resulted in comprehensive penetration of the KMT military and government in 1947–49.[174] As it did earlier in the decade, the CCP kept hostile intelligence services at bay in their occupied areas, a legacy that carried over into the People's Republic. Foreign espionage organs found it difficult to impossible to sustain agent networks in China's core areas.

In 1949–50 Li Kenong wrote an account of intelligence work during the revolution. It remains classified and unavailable to foreign researchers, but it probably informs the work of the CCP historians cited herein. Before the outset of China's involvement in Korea in October 1950, Mao decided to split his intelligence and security functions into two State Council (government) ministries. The Ministry of Public Security (August 1949–present) took over domestic counterintelligence from the SAD, which was abolished at the same time. Li was to head an intelligence ministry, but consolidation was postponed in favor of letting the military take the lead, for reasons that remain officially unstated. Li's worsening heart ailment, his role as a chief negotiator in the Panmunjom peace talks until July 1953, and the war itself may have delayed the reorganization that eventually followed.[175]

The year 1955 finally brought movement, albeit coincident with a devastating purge of the intelligence ranks. Between March and July, Zhou Enlai, Yang Shangkun, and other leaders agreed to appoint Li as head of a reorganized and consolidated foreign intelligence organ directly subordinate to the Central Committee, the Central Investigation Department. However, also in March, arrests began that led to the demotion, transfer, or imprisonment of eight hundred to one thousand intelligence officers. The root cause of this disaster was, as it had been in 1931 and 1943, Mao himself. The chairman decided that Pan Hannian was the leader of a "counterrevolutionary clique" for not reporting a meeting in 1943 with the puppet government leader Wang Jingwei.[176]

Flying solo, Li attempted to deflect the chairman's rage, writing two reports asserting Pan's innocence dated April 29 and July 29.[177] They too remain classified and are difficult to validate. However, the events that followed are thought-provoking: from April through July, the leadership discussed reorganizing the PRC intelligence services and purging enemies within. In July and August the CID was formally albeit secretly established as the PRC's first foreign intelligence agency, with Li Kenong as director. In September, Li was promoted to general (上将, *shangjiang*).[178] If the approved CCP narrative is to be believed, Li's bravery in disputing Mao's suspicions of Pan Hannian somehow did not hinder his career.

Official accounts seem to prioritize preserving the legitimacy of Mao Zedong. By placing blame for problems on a few villains and glorifying other figures such as Li Kenong, we are left with a scripted narrative of CCP espionage. Nonetheless, Li accomplished much in spite of declining health and a difficult political situation. In October 1957 he suffered a fall that resulted in a cerebral hemorrhage, and he was sidelined from duty until his death in February 1962.[179]

According to his biographer, Li garnered one final duty when he partially recovered in July 1961: assembling historical materials and interviewing veterans in order to assess the lessons drawn from the decline of the SSS in 1932–35, an encore to his still-secret study in 1949–50. Li's last small group worked in Shanghai during the autumn and wrote a text of 80,000 characters. It and much else remain under wraps.[180]

His death in 1962 spared Li Kenong from the misery that followed. His biographer claims that Mao rebuffed a January 1967 attempt by Kang Sheng to posthumously condemn Li. However, in 1978, two years after the end of the Cultural Revolution, Li Xiannian suggested that if Li Kenong had been alive in 1966, "he would surely have been branded a big *tewu* [spy]" by leftist radicals.[181] Research continues to better define the life of this significant figure.

Li Zhen (Li Chen, 李震, 1914–73)

Army Major-General Li Zhen was a Central Committee member and head of the Ministry of Public Security when he was found hanged to death at the ministry's Beijing headquarters on October 22, 1973.[182] His death shocked the CCP Politburo and may have contributed to the postponement of the Fourth National People's Congress. The limited material on Li Zhen describes his positive military record but condemns him as a counterrevolutionary.[183] Li's death was officially termed a suicide, but at least one leading party historian still considers Li's case unresolved, and the circumstances of his death raise questions.[184]

Li Zhen joined the CCP in August 1937. After a united front assignment, he filled a series of army political commissar posts, first with a local guerrilla unit and later with the Eighth Route Army at the brigade and military district levels. During the Chinese civil war (1946–49), Li was a senior political commissar in the Central Plains Field Army under General Chen Yi and Xie Fuzhi.[185] During the Korean War (1950–53), Li headed the political department of the Twelfth Army of the Chinese People's Volunteers. Afterward, he moved to the Shenyang Military Region headquarters (1954–66), eventually becoming its deputy political commissar.[186]

In September 1966, just after the Cultural Revolution entered its chaotic phase, Li Zhen was transferred to the MPS in Beijing, probably because of his wartime association with its minister, Xie Fuzhi. Li became deputy minister (*fu buzhang*)—number two in the organization. There are few details of Li's activities at MPS, but his continued association with Xie indicates support for the radical left program that led to widespread chaos, purges, and torture. Soon after the attempted defection in September 1971 of Mao's heir apparent, Lin Biao, Xie Fuzhi died in March 1972, and Li took over the ministry.[187]

In the last months of his life, Li Zhen was at the height of his powers, being both a minister and a Central Committee member since the 1969 Ninth Party Congress. At the Tenth Party Congress (August 1973), Mao's dominance and his Cultural Revolution policies were confirmed by delegates who were summoned at the last minute and were brought to the Great Hall of the People through underground passageways.[188] It was a routine that fit with the times when "everything was a state secret,"[189] and possibly because of the increasing number of foreign diplomats and journalists, including Americans, staying a block away at the Beijing Hotel.[190]

In the midst of this strained atmosphere, Li Zhen had a powerful and sensitive duty that official accounts hint was linked to his death. He was

Zhou Enlai's deputy leading the central group monitoring the massive investigation against the "May 16 conspiracy." The campaign, approved by Mao and driven by Zhou, originally targeted extremist Red Guard leaders attacking the premier in 1967. However, it gradually expanded to include thousands of Red Guards in an effort to stop the chaos of 1967–68. By the time Li Zhen took over day-to-day supervision in February 1972, the same month that Richard Nixon visited China, the hunt for conspirators was under way nationwide.[191]

The May 16 investigation is officially viewed today as a massive overreach that persecuted millions of innocents. Li Zhen's death is termed by the same officialdom as suicide because he was allegedly afraid of being exposed as a May 16 element himself. Zhou Enlai initially thought that Li's death was murder, perhaps because so many had suffered under the May 16 investigation. If viewed through the lens of motive, means, and opportunity, the circumstances carried reasonable suspicion of foul play left unaddressed by available accounts.[192]

Of those who led the investigation, three agreed on suicide: Hua Guofeng, Liu Fuzhi, and Yu Sang. All attained higher office after Mao Zedong passed away in September 1976. By contrast, Wang Hongwen, who dissented, was arrested a month afterward as a member of the Gang of Four. The May 16 investigations stopped a year later. Since official accounts of Li Zhen's life and death are scarce, and untold numbers of people may have benefitted from his demise, the official suicide verdict seems incomplete.

Ling Yun (凌云, 1917–2018)

Born in Jiaxing, Zhejiang, Ling Yun had a long career in counterintelligence work before becoming the first leader of the new MSS in 1983. In spite of that expertise, irony prevailed: Ling was fired in 1985 due to the high-level defection of a bureau chief under his command.

Ling joined the CCP in 1938 and was a cadre with the SAD, probably first trained as an interrogator at SAD headquarters in Zaoyuan, Yan'an. Details of his career are scant, but after the CCP victory in 1949 Ling joined the MPS and became a bureau chief, probably in charge of counterintelligence work. On April 4, 1955, one day after the arrest of Pan Hannian,

Ling Yun visited Sidney Rittenberg in prison to inform the American of his release and to apologize for an unjust six-year imprisonment.[193]

When the Cultural Revolution began in 1966, Ling was an MPS vice minister, still in charge of counterintelligence. Late in 1967 he was arrested along with two other vice ministers, Xu Jianguo and Xu Zirong. The trio were tortured in 1968 with the object of forcing confessions that they had spied for the enemy. Only Ling Yun survived.[194] He later attributed his treatment to an accusation by Kang Sheng.

Ling's rehabilitation after the Cultural Revolution put him in line for office when CID director Luo Qingchang was forced out in 1983. Ling was appointed by the Politburo to lead the MSS, assembled from the now defunct CID, the counterintelligence units of the MPS, the United Front Work Department, and possibly others. However, his tenure was cut short by the defection of his foreign affairs bureau chief, Yu Qiangsheng (俞强声), to the Americans.[195]

Relieved from office, Ling appears to have been excused without punishment. He has made at least one appearance in CCP-approved espionage literature without hint of disgrace, but his life has remained largely undocumented, unlike other major figures in CCP intelligence history.[196] In Ling's official obituary from March 2018, his dismissal from the MSS after the Yu Qiangsheng defection was not mentioned—only his appointment in 1983 and retirement in 2004, mirroring continued official reticence to discuss Ling's career.[197]

Luo Ningdong (罗宇栋, 1943–)

Luo Ningdong of Chongqing twice served as director of 2PLA, filling the position from 1992 to 1995 and from 2001 to 2003. Major General Luo also held the position of deputy director at the 2PLA-managed think tank, the China Institute for International Strategic Studies (中国国际战略学会), between his stints at the top of 2PLA.

Luo entered the PLA in 1960 and graduated from the Zhangjiakou School of Foreign Languages. Much of his career is mysterious, but he reportedly worked at the Nanjing International Relations Institute (国际关系学院) on at least two occasions and served as its head beginning in 1995.[198]

Luo Qingchang (罗青长, 1918–2014)

Known for his extensive knowledge of the enemy, Luo Qingchang of Sichuan was possibly the most resilient survivor in CCP civilian intelligence during and after the rule of Mao Zedong. In the chairman's twilight years, Luo served as director of the Central Investigation Department (*Zhongyang Diaocha Bu*) and retained that office until the 1983 intelligence reorganization. Luo was forced out that year, curiously without significant retaliation for siding with the radical left during the Cultural Revolution.

Luo joined the Communist Youth League in 1932 at age fourteen and the CCP in 1936. He survived the Long March (1934–35) and performed political work among youth. Afterward in the Fourth Front Army he worked under Wu Defeng, an experienced intelligence cadre. Wu recommended Luo, then barely twenty, for the Central Party School. He graduated in July 1938 and was sent straight to a Central SAD intelligence training course. Luo's class was the second batch of intelligence students and the first with youthful trainees. The comprehensive five-month course was a departure from previous shorter, ad hoc classes and was meant to remedy the shortage of capable intelligence cadres after the Long March.[199]

When the course ended in December 1938, Luo was posted to the Xi'an Eighth Route Army Liaison Office under the cover of being a confidential assistant (机要秘书, *jiyao mishu*), though his actual duties were to work with the CCP's clandestine intelligence network in Xi'an. Unlike other such figures with similar duties, there are few stories about Luo's achievements during this time, although in 1938–39 he supposedly coordinated the penetration of KMT commander Hu Zongnan's headquarters. Luo was posted back to Yan'an in 1941 and became an intelligence analyst, earning accolades as a "famous living archive" (有名的活档案, *you ming de huo dang'an*) after coming to Mao's attention for supplementing intelligence reports with an encyclopedic memory. SAD director Kang Sheng replaced Luo as head of Xi'an operations with Wang Shijian, who six years later became one of the most infamous turncoats in CCP intelligence history.[200]

After Mao abolished the SAD in August 1949, Luo was assigned to head both the First and Fourth Bureaus of the Central Committee's Intelligence Department (中央情报部, *Zhongyang qingbao bu*) in the reorganization. After October 1949 he also joined the Central Military Commission's Liaison Department and was eventually promoted to its head. In 1955 Luo concurrently joined premier Zhou Enlai's office as deputy director responsible for intelligence matters—which may have saved him a decade later during the Cultural Revolution. That same year the premier supposedly asked Luo to research the record of Pan Hannian, who had just been arrested as a traitor (see also Li Kenong). Between 1955 and 1961 Luo became chief of staff (秘书长, *mishu zhang*, literally "chief secretary") of the newly created CID and one of its deputy directors, possibly in charge of analysis, and deputy of the office of the Central Committee's Taiwan Leading Small Group.[201] In the last role, Luo's obituary lauds his part in discovering a Nationalist Chinese plot to kill PRC president Liu Shaoqi during a state visit to Cambodia in April 1963 and for work to convince Li Zongren, the former KMT general, to defect to the mainland in 1964.[202]

In 1967 the radical Central Case Examination Group opened an investigation against CID director Kong Yuan, who was already under pressure from the Red Guard rebel faction (造反派, *zaofan pai*). He and his deputies were forced out of the CID and into labor camps or worse, except one—Luo Qingchang—who apparently continued on post during the military takeover of the department (April 1967) and when the CID was absorbed by the PLA in June 1969.[203] It remains unclear what Luo did to avoid the fate of his colleagues, but some sources say that he was close to not only Zhou Enlai but also Kang Sheng and Wang Dongxing, both Cultural Revolution beneficiaries.

As China and the Soviet Union became increasingly hostile, Mao explored ending the PRC's radical isolation. CID officers returned to their overseas posts concurrent with the PRC's admission to the UN in 1971; by this time Luo may have held the number one or two spot in the organization, perhaps under a military officer.[204] However, the CID was not fully reestablished as a department of the Central Committee until March 1973,[205] coincidentally at the same time as Mao agreed to Zhou Enlai's proposal to restore to office Deng Xiaoping (March 9) and during discussions between Zhou Enlai and Henry Kissinger on opening diplomatic missions with the United States. Luo was named CID director.[206]

On December 20, 1975, Zhou Enlai was terminally ill in hospital. Bucking protocol, he summoned Luo for a final conference.[207] More events than can be recounted here rapidly followed, notably Zhou's death on January 8, 1976, popular protests in Tian'anmen Square against the left, the second fall of Deng Xiaoping, and the rise of Hua Guofeng in April. Mao died on September 9, and a month later the radical left was in disgrace and the Cultural Revolution was finished.[208]

Deng Xiaoping's resumption of responsibility for foreign affairs in July 1977 was the writing on the wall for Luo, in part because his protector Wang Dongxing was losing positions during the period. For over a year Deng had more important matters to attend to, including the brief but disastrous attack against Vietnam in early 1979.[209] But on July 7, 1979, Deng turned his attention to the CID and Luo. In a speech to the Foreign Affairs Work Conference, Deng suggested that the CID move away from diplomatic cover for its overseas officers, urging them to instead rely more on secret, illegal cover and make greater use of foreign agents; he claimed that this guidance originated with Zhou Enlai just before the Cultural Revolution.[210] It was somewhat reminiscent of Li Kenong's push in 1945–46 urging intelligence cadres in comfortable positions in the rear area to volunteer for more dangerous clandestine agent insertion work.

However, Luo resisted. He avoided promulgating Deng's speech, dispatched additional personnel abroad under diplomatic cover, and told subordinates it was imperative to resist Deng's "class struggle and anti-intelligence" views. In September Luo was forced to reverse himself and support Deng. Luo later supported the rehabilitation of Pan Hannian, not something to be expected of a hard-core leftist.[211]

However, Deng remained frustrated with Luo, who continued to avoid change. Luo retained his position until the 1983 intelligence reorganization abolished the CID and replaced it with the MSS. Luo perhaps was saved again as Deng struggled with other matters such as moving aside Hua Guofeng in September 1980, arranging the trial of Jiang Qing and the rest of the Gang of Four (November 1980–January 1981), and other matters.[212] Luo's ability to survive was nonetheless notable and requires further study.

After Luo was pushed out of intelligence leadership in July 1983, he remained active as the deputy (and later as an advisor) on the Central

Committee Leading Small Group on Taiwan Work.[213] Luo's passing in 2014 was marked with memorial services befitting a veteran revolutionary close to Zhou Enlai. His children include a PLA general and other officials, and he remains an unusual case among prominent Cultural Revolution beneficiaries.[214]

Luo Ruiqing (Lo Jui-ch'ing, 罗瑞卿, 1906–78)

Luo is praised today as a dedicated communist, an accomplished army political commissar and security officer during the revolution, the first minister of public security (1949–59), and the PLA chief of staff (1959–65) who pursued professionalism in the military against the rising dominance of Mao Thought. Less discussed are Luo's vigorous pursuit of the escalating antispy struggle of the 1950s and his subsequent oversight of the unjust prosecutions ordered by Mao Zedong against senior CCP intelligence figures. Mao and defense minister Lin Biao engineered Luo's denunciation in December 1965, accusing him of opposing People's War. Luo thus joined Beijing vice mayor Wu Han as one of the earliest senior leaders to fall in the leadup to the Cultural Revolution.

Luo graduated in November 1926 with the fifth class of Whampoa Military Academy (黄埔军校, *Huangpu junxiao*) at its Wuhan branch campus. He participated in the Nanchang uprising of August 1, 1927, and was admitted to the CCP in 1928.[215] Luo became one of the Red Army's first political commissars and eventually joined Zhu De and Mao Zedong's base at Jinggangshan (井冈山) in Jiangxi.[216]

Wounded in 1932, Luo was sent to the Soviet Union for medical treatment and may have been trained at that time in security matters. When he returned to Jiangxi, Luo became the director of the PPB for Lin Biao's First Army Corps. After the Long March (1934–35), Luo continued in senior commissar positions. In 1937 he became part of a five-man committee that oversaw traitor elimination (锄奸, *chujian*) and political protection work (政治保卫工作, *zhengzhi baowei gongzuo*), and he became dean of studies at the Anti-Japanese Military and Political Academy. Luo served in a senior commissar position in the Eighth Route Army in 1940–44 and returned to Yan'an for the 1945 Seventh CCP Congress that cemented Mao's position as unchallenged leader. During the Marshall mission (1946), Luo was on the staff of Ye Jianying in Beijing. After its failure in 1947 he returned to duty in the Nineteenth Army Group as one of the most senior political commissars in northern China. Luo hoped to return to his native Sichuan to participate in the PLA's final offensives there when Zhou Enlai told him of Mao's impending order to lead the new MPS. Luo responded that someone like Li Kenong, who headed the SAD, would be a better candidate. Zhou warned that Mao had already decided on Luo, adding that "everyone has their own matters, Li Kenong has Li Kenong's" (各人有各人的事，李克农有李克农的事, *ge ren you ge ren de shi, Li Kenong you Li Kenong de shi*). Over a dinner that evening, Mao further cajoled Luo, who accepted the draft.[217]

The establishment of the MPS was well under way at the founding of the PRC on October 1, 1949, but was formally inaugurated on November 1. That month, the MPS accepted five Soviet advisors at headquarters but retained its own structure and methods. Luo's immediate focus was to secure China's borders and the newly occupied areas, and the minister was especially concerned about foreign espionage. A week later the Shanghai Public Security Bureau arrested seventeen Nationalist operatives who planned to assassinate mayor Chen Yi. On November 12 Beijing authorities apprehended three more Nationalist agents. Air attacks on Shanghai by B-24 bombers based in Taiwan followed in January and February 1950, killing more than five hundred people. Further arrests in Beijing and Tianjin followed, and public security bureaus joined in coastal defense work as agent landings were reported opposite Taiwan.[218]

Besides antispy work, Luo pursued police reforms, building about thirty-five police academies in the first years of the PRC in order to achieve a large-scale officer replacement program. Thousands of ideologically dependable "revolutionary police" took the places of "bad elements" ejected from municipal PSBs—that is, holdovers from the Nationalist regime.[219]

This turbulent atmosphere, leading up to China's entry into the Korean War in October 1950 and the political campaigns that followed, was the backdrop to Luo Ruiqing's later investigation of Shanghai PSB director Yang Fan. A month after the PLA entered Shanghai in May 1949, Yang, a senior CCP intelligence officer seconded from the now defunct SAD, was appointed deputy director of the new Shanghai PSB. Yang was promoted to director in 1950, but a damaging defection to Taiwan that year of former Nationalist agents working for him drew Luo's attention to a more high-ranking former Nationalist on Yang's staff, Hu Junhe. Luo visited in December 1951 to investigate the appointment of Hu and began criticism of Yang that eventually led to his arrest.[220]

With the Korean armistice and peace, Luo continued to focus on countering espionage.[221] Mao began to travel more, and Luo worked closely with Wang Dongxing, director of the Central Guards Bureau, to coordinate the chairman's security. Wang became a vice minister of MPS for this function in 1955. A major challenge for Mao's security team was the chairman's tendency to make sudden plans that he would change on a whim. This behavior during a visit to Wuhan in the company of Luo, Wang, and other senior officials led to the Yellow Crane Pavilion incident (February 1953), when a crowd recognized Mao, leading to a brief loss of control by his security team and Luo's humiliating apology.

Mao Zedong began his Great Leap Forward (大跃进, Da yue jin) campaign in January 1958, demanding extreme increases in agricultural and industrial production. Luo led the ministry and local PSBs in taking their own "great leap" in investigating cases and in making arrests and detentions. This led localities to strive to go further, instituting overly ambitious goals such as drastically reducing reported fires and even the number of recorded family arguments. Powers such as gathering intelligence and detention of suspects were pushed downward to lower level police stations and neighborhood committees and communes.[222] Luo attempted to rein in this trend in late 1958, but politics soon intervened: as a result of the purge of Marshal Peng Dehuai at the Lushan plenum in summer 1959, Luo was transferred back to the PLA to become chief of staff in September and was replaced at the MPS by Xie Fuzhi. During Xie's early tenure some communes organized their own reform through labor camps, where inmates worked as slaves.

Luo offered advantages over Peng Dehuai: he had criticized Peng in Yan'an during the 1942–44 Rectification campaign, was close to Mao, and while MPS minister had concurrently held the post of commander and political commissar of the PLA's Public Security Forces.[223] As PLA chief of staff (1959–65) Luo planned the border war with India (1962) and Chinese assistance to Vietnam in the face of the U.S. escalation in Indochina

(1962–65). However, in November 1965 Luo came under criticism for opposing People's War because he had prioritized military skills alongside political training, placing him at odds with defense minister Marshal Lin Biao and the chairman himself. Luo disappeared that same month and was stripped of his positions in December.[224] At the MPS, minister Xie Fuzhi pointed to Luo's example and alleged a criminal conspiracy, leading to further purges inside the ministry in early 1966. In August 1966 the MPS Cultural Revolution Group took charge of the ministry leadership and began purges of municipal PSBs that led to a breakdown of order throughout the country.[225]

Luo attempted suicide that March by jumping out a third-story window. He broke both legs but survived and received continued abuse. However, Mao's general remained stubbornly loyal. Even after his release in 1974, Luo went to Tian'anmen Square to offer a sincere salute to Mao's giant portrait.[226]

Luo once famously said: "Enemy intelligence work is like a knife, if used well it can kill the enemy, if used badly it also might injure oneself" (特情工作好像一把刀子, 用得好可以杀害敌人用得不好也可以伤害自己, *Teqing gongzuo haoxiang yi ba daozi, yongde hao keyi shahai diren, yongde buhao ye keyi shang hai ziji*).[227] Released in 1974, Luo died in August 1978 of a heart attack while in Germany for medical treatment.[228]

Luo's ultimate fate was ironic. As China's top security official in the 1950s, he followed Mao's instructions without question, persecuting hundreds if not thousands of loyal intelligence officers in response to the chairman's paranoia. Luo escaped the fate of Pan Hannian and others because he lacked a vulnerable period in his career of human intelligence work of rubbing elbows with the enemy. Therefore, Luo escaped loyalty questions until just before the Cultural Revolution. Mao did not protect him after 1965, probably because of his efforts to maintain military professionalism just as the chairman and Lin Biao sought to make Mao Thought and People's War the focus of military indoctrination.

Xie Fuzhi (Hsieh Fu-chih, 谢富治, 1909–72)

Xie Fuzhi, of Hubei province, became a full member of the CCP Politburo in 1969 after serving as a vice premier of the State Council (1965–72) and head of the MPS. He was MPS minister from 1959 until his death in March 1972—the longest-serving incumbent in that office. Before assuming these high posts, Xie was an experienced and valued army political officer—and political acumen may have contributed to his survival in the Cultural Revolution (1966–76). Xie was buried with full honors in 1972 but was posthumously disgraced, alongside Kang Sheng, for supporting radical left politics in his final years.

Xie Fuzhi joined the Red Army in 1930 and the CCP in 1931. He quickly rose to the political officer ranks from being a common soldier and small unit leader, attaining division level assignments during and after the Long March (1934–35). Xie served in other division and army level billets in the Anti-Japanese War (1937–45) and saw combat. After Japan surrendered, Xie was second in command to General Chen Yi when their forces caught tens of thousands of enemy prisoners. During the Chinese civil war (1946–49), Chen and Xie's forces participated in major operations and captured hundreds of thousands of Nationalist soldiers, culminating in the conquest of Chongqing.[229] Xie also became closely associated with Deng Xiaoping.[230]

After the 1949 victory, Xie Fuzhi continued in high-level military political assignments and also became the CCP first secretary of Yunnan province. In September 1955 he was promoted to general and a year later was elevated to the CCP Central Committee.[231]

Upon becoming minister of public security in 1959, Xie did not significantly change policies inherited from his predecessor Luo Ruiqing. He urged officers to "train hard to perfect skills" and oversaw increasing use of law enforcement equipment—not an indication that he prioritized ideological purity over expertise.[232]

However, in 1966 Xie became an ally of Jiang Qing and the Central Cultural Revolution Group. He enthusiastically carried out Mao Zedong's radical left program while avoiding significant criticism of his old comrade, Deng Xiaoping, when the latter was purged in August 1966. As a member of the Central Case Examination Group, Xie held control over personnel files and participated in the purge of many senior party figures, possibly including his old boss, Chen Yi. Xie issued the "Six Regulations of Public Security" (January 1967) that authorized security forces and others to torture and abuse millions in blacklisted classes and categories, including senior figures such as Liu Shaoqi.[233] That same month Xie attacked the sons and daughters of condemned officials as "counterrevolutionaries," earning the ire of at least one powerful Politburo member, Li Xiannian. Also in January, Xie suspended use of agents and safe houses in MPS counterintelligence operations and launched inquiries into them. For the remainder of Xie's active career, the "mass line" was preferred to professional norms in counterintelligence work.[234]

In July 1967, during the height of the Cultural Revolution's chaotic period, Xie flew to Wuhan to help quell a mutiny of army units that became known as the July 20 (or Wuhan) incident. Years later, his traveling companion, Wang Li, said that Xie "bungled things" by making unnecessary public appearances and incendiary speeches during confrontations between Red Guard groups and dissatisfied military units, leading to greater tensions, armed conflict, dozens of deaths, and the evacuation from Wuhan of Mao himself, who was on a secret visit.[235]

Nonetheless, Xie became an alternate member of the Politburo in 1966 and a full member at the 1969 Ninth Party Congress. Though at the peak of his power when he died of cancer in March 1972, Xie was posthumously expelled from the CCP in 1980 along with Kang Sheng, their verdicts linked together and with the deposed Gang of Four. In January 1981 the Supreme People's Court condemned Xie as a counterrevolutionary coconspirator of Lin Biao and Jiang Qing.[236]

Xie's tenure as a high official illustrates how a nation's security apparatus can be harnessed for a radical political program, used to commit mass atrocities, and help trigger large-scale instability.

Xu Yongyue (许永跃, 1942–)

Xu Yongyue of Zhenping county, Henan, was the third minister of state security, serving from 1998 to August 2007, when he was removed in a shakeup ahead of the Seventeenth Party Congress. By official and Hong Kong media accounts, Xu had little experience in intelligence and security prior to his assignment in 1994 as chairman of the Hebei Provincial Political-Legal Commission. Xu graduated in 1960 or 1961 from the Beijing People's Public Security School (now known as the Public Security

University), where he also worked as a "double-load cadre" before transferring to the Chinese Academy of Sciences' General Office.[237] There is, however, largely no record of Xu's activities in the 1960s. He joined the CPP in 1972 and subsequently began a nineteen-year career as a private secretary (秘书, *mishu*) at the Ministry of Education in 1975. After his minister was denounced by the Gang of Four in late 1975, Xu spent eight years working for Zhu Muzhi at the Propaganda Department and then the Ministry of Culture. In 1983 Xu began working for Chen Yun, whom he would serve until the latter's death in 1994.[238] His earlier patron now deceased, Xu appeared to have been the safe choice for minister. Then-general secretary Jiang Zemin reportedly tried to install his close ally, deputy chief of the general staff (intelligence) Xiong Guangkai, but met with resistance from other Chinese leaders and/or the People's Liberation Army (PLA).[239] Xu's involvement in a corruption scandal surrounding minister of finance Jin Renqing reportedly led to his dismissal in August 2007, despite the official explanation that Xu had reached retirement age and thus could not remain until the National People's Congress (NPC) in 2008.[240]

During Xu's tenure at the MSS, the ministry's influence appears to have waned in favor of the MPS.[241] First, Xu was not confirmed as a Central Committee member until the Sixteenth Party Congress in 2002 and therefore was outranked by his MPS counterparts. At the same time Xu joined the Central Committee, the minister of public security, Zhou Yongkang, joined the Politburo. Second, Xiong joined the Taiwan Affairs Leading Small Group in his military intelligence role and became its secretary-general—a possible indictment of the ministry's intelligence operations against Taiwan. Third, China's entry into the World Trade Organization (WTO) in 2001 promised to open the doors even further to foreigners. Monitoring the increasing number of aliens in China was a major reason for the creation of the MSS in 1983. However, at a Central Political-Legal Commission conference in 2000, Politburo Standing Committee member Wei Jianxing stated China's impending WTO ascension required better "public security [公共安全, *gongong anquan*]," rather than "state security [国家安全, *guojia anquan*]," work.

Xu had a reputation within the MSS of being a "country bumpkin [土包子, *tu baozi*]" but, according to a retired senior foreign intelligence official who met Xu on several occasions, this was largely an act to disarm potential bureaucratic opponents within the ministry. This official asserted Xu probably was one of the smartest senior intelligence officials with whom he had interacted.[242] Xu's reputation for concealing his true abilities went back to the 1980s, when he gave a reportedly "electrifying" speech that received national circulation on the need for better governance rather than relying on police power.[243]

Yang Hui (杨晖, 1963–)

Yang Hui of Qingdao, Shandong province, served as 2PLA director from 2007 to 2011, when he became a deputy chief of staff of the Nanjing Military Region. Prior to the reorganization announced by Xi Jinping in November 2015, Yang was a lieutenant general (military region deputy leader grade) and chief of staff of the Nanjing Military Region.[244] He currently occupies an undefined leadership position in the Eastern Theater Command.[245]

Yang was educated at the Nanjing Foreign Language Institute (南京外国语学院, *Nanjing Waiguo Yu Xueyuan*) and joined the PLA in 1981. He later earned his MA and PhD in literature in Yugoslavia and, according to some sources, a second PhD in law from the Chinese Academy of Social Sciences. He served in the military attaché offices in Yugoslavia, the Soviet Union, Russia, and Kazakhstan.[246] Yang reportedly served as a deputy director of 3PLA, China's signals intelligence service, from 2001 to 2006, but at least one article places him at 2PLA during this time as a deputy director.[247] In addition to his intelligence work, Yang served as the deputy commander of the Thirty-first Group Army just prior to becoming 2PLA director.

Zhou Enlai (Chou En-lai, 周恩来, 1898–1976)

Zhou is known as the long-serving premier of the People's Republic of China and its first foreign minister. He is also revered by Beijing as the founder of CCP intelligence. Zhou built the first espionage and covert action organizations, ran some early operations, and maintained political oversight for long periods. He lost sway over intelligence management as Mao Zedong rose toward unchallenged power during the Anti-Japanese War (1937–45). Afterward, Zhou regained influence in this field until the

Cultural Revolution began in 1966. Zhou's struggle to maintain control of foreign intelligence in the last ten years of his life was a bellwether of the wider difficulties of the period.

Early in his revolutionary career at Nankai University, Zhou Enlai was not yet inclined to observe clandestine habits, openly organizing and risking arrest.[248] But he may have begun adopting secret practices in 1921 when he joined the CCP in France and came under Comintern (Russian) leadership.[249] In 1923 when the Comintern ordered the CCP to ally with the Nationalists (KMT) in the First United Front, Zhou Enlai returned to China and became the political commissar at the KMT's Whampoa Officer Academy (黄埔军校, *Huangpu jun xiao*). Zhou may have had his first brush with military intelligence in June 1925 when he entered the camp of a nearby enemy warlord unit to negotiate a truce—experiencing what it was like to peer behind enemy lines.[250]

In early 1927 Zhou was in Shanghai to support the arrival of the Nationalist Army's Northern Expedition.[251] His effort came to a brutal end when conquering Nationalist Army units simultaneously attacked communists across China on April 12—a failure that contributed to the founding of the party's first real espionage organ. Zhou narrowly escaped and made his way to Wuhan, where he formed a VIP protection unit with Nie Rongzhen under the CCP military commission.[252] However, Chen Yun recalled decades later that before 1927, the party "did not know how to organize intelligence."[253]

About this time Zhou came down with malaria and went to Hong Kong to recuperate.[254] In September a clandestine body that later became the First Branch of the CCP SSS began procuring housing for CCP leaders returning to live "underground" in Shanghai.[255]

On October 18 the leadership discussed the failed postcoup uprisings in Hunan, Hubei, Guangdong, and Jiangxi, and sent a message to Zhou that he should return to Shanghai for consultations. On November 14 with Zhou present, the Politburo ordered him to reorganize the departments under the Central Committee: organization, propaganda, military, special services (intelligence and security work), communications, and others, indicating that intelligence was now a core task. Over the next two weeks, Zhou organized the SSS directly under the party leadership, with branches (科, *ke*) handling general services (总务科, *zongwu ke*), intelligence (情报科, *qingbao ke*), operations (行动科, *xingdong ke*), and radio communications (无线电通讯科, *wuxiandian tongxun ke*). Their missions were to protect the central leadership, assemble intelligence, suppress defections and hit enemies, rescue imprisoned comrades, and establish clandestine radio stations.[256] Zhou was in charge,[257] although Gu Shunzhang ran day-to-day affairs.[258]

Chinese mainland sources paint a saintly picture of Zhou Enlai taking three roles in CCP intelligence over the following decades: high-level political oversight, master trainer and operations guru, and ad hoc organizer of important networks. While Zhou was crucial in intelligence organization building, this narrative obscures the roles of others.

From 1928 to 1930 Zhou, Chen Geng, Gu Shunzhang, Li Weihan, Ren Bishi, and Deng Xiaoping wrote key directives, taught seminars, and arranged field training on intelligence tradecraft, self-defense, White Area (enemy) underground operations, and carrying out attacks.[259] Zhou also assisted Gu Shunzhang in founding the "Red Squads" or Red Guard (红队, 赤卫队, *hong dui, chiwei dui*), which protected VIPs and punished turncoats.[260]

In 1929–31 Zhou oversaw Gu Shunzhang, Li Qiang, and Chen Geng as they managed operations. For example, on August 24, 1929, Nationalist authorities arrested the communist rural organizer Peng Pai after being tipped off by a CCP defector, Bai Xin.[261] The KMT raid that netted Peng targeted a clandestine meeting that Zhou Enlai was to attend, but he was waylaid by other business, making a narrow escape.[262]

Zhou Enlai called an emergency meeting that night and ordered the SSS to rescue the detainees and plan Bai's assassination. Gu Shunzhang and Chen Geng were placed in charge, and the SSS put all available resources into the rescue attempt.[263] Gu Shunzhang commanded the rescue force in the guise of a movie crew, according to a Taiwan source.[264] Li Qiang later reminisced that twenty Red Squad members were included because of the scale of the task. Foul-ups and bad luck foiled the operation on August 28, and Zhou Enlai called off the rescue attempt.[265] But time was up. Peng Pai and his three comrades were executed at Shanghai Longhua prison two days later.[266] The assassination plan against Bai Xin went on, and he was shot in November (see Chen Geng and Ke Lin, chapter 3).[267]

On April 26, 1931, Zhou was faced with even worse news: Gu Shunzhang's sudden defection to the KMT (see *Longtan sanjie*, Three Heroes of the Dragon's Lair, chapter 5). Zhou, Chen Yun, Li Kenong, Nie Rongzhen, and Li Qiang met that evening and issued instructions for CCP members to evacuate offices and change accommodations.[268] The Central Committee had Zhou test the loyalty of Gu's family. Operatives found his wife at home and asked her if she intended to join Gu with the Nationalists in Nanjing. Taken by surprise, she replied that she would be obligated to follow her husband. Her callers murdered her and ten other members of the family on the spot, sparing only an infant boy.[269] Their bodies were not discovered until weeks later, but they may have been killed that Sunday or Monday night (April 26–27), just as Gu requested the Nationalists to protect his loved ones.[270] The ultimate fate of the baby remains unknown.

Zhou quickly left Shanghai, and others—Chen Yun, Kang Sheng, and Pan Hannian—took the reins of espionage and covert action work in the city. Accounts grow thin of Zhou's role in managing intelligence and security work once he arrived in Jiangxi, but there are hints that he retained influence.[271] Zhou's investigation of the Futian incident is one such sign. After attacks against the Red Army in Jiangxi by pro-KMT groups dubbed the AB Corps, a series of violent CCP purges from December 1930 to July 1931 left more than ten thousand dead—not the KMT enemy, but Mao's antagonists in the Red Army as he took the opportunity to identify and kill enemies within. Zhou's intervention in December 1931 on behalf of the Central Committee wound down the purges. During the October 1932 Ningdu Conference, Ren Bishi, Xiang Ying, and Deng Fa criticized Mao for his "guerrilla mentality" and "right opportunism." The future chairman lost his position as general political commissar, replaced by Zhou, who nonetheless was also criticized as an "appeaser."[272]

In China, the Futian incident and associated clashes have been called the first of "three major left deviations in the history of public security and protection," the others being the Yan'an Salvation campaign (1943, see *Qiangjiu yundong*) and the Cultural Revolution (1966–76).[273] Each of the three resulted in setbacks for Zhou in managing intelligence. Mao's political protection units, which carried out many of the killings, were reorganized into the new State PPB in mid-November 1931. Deng Fa, one of Mao's critics, became its director, a move that enhanced CCP control of internal security.[274] In the meantime, Zhou's urban SSS networks slowly expired. Though a few agents were left, the SSS was abolished in 1935.

Mao's setback did not discourage the future chairman in his drive toward military and party leadership. His fortunes reversed for the better in January 1935 at the famous Zunyi conference, three months into the Long March. Mao criticized the failures of the march and laid them at the feet of Zhou and others. Though Zhou retained his general political commissar title for a few more months, Mao became the more influential first front army commissar. Outmaneuvered, Zhou switched to Mao's side.[275]

Deng Fa was eased out of the PPB after the remnants of the Red Army arrived in Bao'an, Shaanxi, on October 10, 1935. Signs indicate that Zhou briefly recovered some control over intelligence and related operations. In April 1936 Zhou and one of the Three Heroes of the Dragon's Lair, Li Kenong, conducted negotiations with the KMT "Young Marshal" Zhang Xueliang, whose army hemmed in the Reds under orders from the Nationalist Central Government. In spite of Generalissimo Chiang's objections, they reached an informal truce in the name of jointly resisting Japan.

In another successful influence operation, Zhou and Li were among the first to receive the American reporter Edgar Snow when he arrived in July 1936 to interview Mao and other leaders.[276] When Marshal Zhang Xueliang kidnapped Chiang Kai-shek a few months later in December, it was a surprise to everyone including Mao, Zhou, and Stalin. Mao wanted to place Chiang on trial and execute him, but Stalin intervened: Chiang had to live to keep China united and the Japanese too busy to threaten Russia. Zhou and Li were on the beat again, leading talks with the Nationalists. Both men continued in these enemy negotiation roles as long as each was active.[277]

In the wake of the Xi'an incident, Zhou and Li negotiated acquisition of Yan'an as the communist base. It brought the welcome changes of city life (rather than the small and dusty village of Bao'an) and a usable airfield.

The arrival by plane from Moscow of Kang Sheng and Wang Ming in November 1937 altered the power balance in the CCP leadership. Wang, who had been a Comintern official in charge of Asian affairs, had a following among those such as Bo Gu who had studied in Moscow. He was not willing to subordinate himself to Mao, and a leadership challenge was in the offing.[278]

However, Wang made a serious tactical error. On December 18 he traveled with Zhou Enlai and Bo Gu to Wuhan for united front negotiations with the Nationalist Central government.[279] Wang established the Yangtze Bureau, hoping to replace Yan'an as the center of CCP leadership—an obsolete idea from the days when the party was headquartered "underground" in Shanghai. This left both the military and the party's security services in Yan'an with Mao and Kang Sheng.

Zhou suffered political setbacks: he lost his position on the Secretariat at the Politburo conference of December 9–13, 1937, when Wang Ming, Kang Sheng, and Chen Yun were added.[280] Zhou continued to support Wang until May 1939, according to his later self-criticism.[281] In September 1939 the Politburo named Kang as head of the Social Affairs Department, its new reorganized intelligence body. In September 1941 Kang was also appointed head of the newly established CCP Intelligence Department, which provided guidance to the CCP Eighth Route Army Liaison Offices, including by Zhou Enlai in Chongqing.[282]

Zhou's new portfolio included intelligence management, but at the lower level of the CCP Southern Bureau, based in the Chongqing Eighth Route Army Liaison Office (April 1939–September 1946). This was the largest of the fifteen liaison offices and the one with the heaviest workload and broadest scope, since it was in the Nationalist wartime capital. Though seemingly in the CCP political wilderness and far from the emperor, Zhou had a staff of more than one hundred people, including Ye Jianying and Dong Biwu. From the Chongqing office Zhou controlled an unknown number of intelligence assets. They included Zhang Luping (张露萍, 1921–45), who reported to Ye Jianying and controlled a seven-person spy ring inside Nationalist intelligence.[283] Southern Bureau agents also probably contacted and recruited Sidney Rittenberg, the American soldier who eventually joined the CCP and stayed on in China after World War II.[284]

Zhou also conducted and managed united front work to attract Chinese and foreigners repelled by the increasing corruption of the KMT.

In these influence operations, Zhou hosted important foreigners such as Ernest Hemingway and Martha Gellhorn and the American journalist Theodore White, leaving a positive impression in sharp contrast with the corrupt, ostentatious Nationalist elite. Afterward, Hemingway told State Department officials that he thought the communists would defeat the KMT after the war.[285]

In spite of these achievements, Zhou may have been in the cross-hairs of Kang Sheng, targeted as part of Mao's purge of the leadership that was only stopped by the Dimitrov telegram of December 1943. In it, the Russians specifically criticized Kang for overreaching and requested that Mao protect Zhou.[286]

Zhou Enlai may have resumed political oversight of intelligence once Kang Sheng was sidelined in October 1946, due in part to the widespread resentment of Kang.[287] Giving Zhou oversight was logical: the CCP had a civil war to fight and win, and the new SAD and Intelligence Department director Li Kenong needed support to build agent networks inside the KMT enemy.

In 1949 Zhou chaired a meeting on July 8–9 that discussed how to structure the party's intelligence and security services after victory. The SAD was abolished a month later. Li Kenong was given charge of all foreign intelligence activity in a drawn-out transition period before the more permanent CID was formed five years later. During the interim, Li became the head of the military's intelligence department. Zhou became foreign minister (1949–58) and prime minister (1949–76), and Li reported to him in his overt position as a vice minister of foreign affairs.[288]

In practice, Yang Shangkun and Deng Xiaoping handled routine political issues with CID director Li and his successor Kong Yuan. Luo Qingchang was based in the premier's office as a direct liaison for intelligence matters.[289] Zhou became the face of the PRC to the world and led the country's most important negotiations, including at the Geneva Conference of 1954. In 1955 he requested background on Pan Hannian from Li Kenong (see their entries) to answer Mao's questions about Pan's loyalty. Li's two reports exonerated Pan but did not convince the chairman to spare the veteran spymaster.

During the first half of the Cultural Revolution (1966–76), Zhou once again lost some, albeit not necessarily all, influence to Kang Sheng (see Classified Materials Theft, 1966–67). Also pushed out of the party's political supervision of intelligence were Deng Xiaoping and Yang Shangkun, purged as the radical left dominated politics while the CID itself was riven by factional disputes.

When Kang Sheng's health began to fail in 1971, Zhou may have recovered some political oversight of intelligence and security, but the situation requires further study (see Hua Guofeng and Li Zhen).[290]

Negotiations with adversaries remained an important priority. Besides Zhou, others who met with foreign leaders sometimes had intelligence backgrounds. Zhou Enlai and Ye Jianying, each with substantial intelligence experience, led negotiations with the United States in 1971–72. Zhou's assistant in the negotiations, Xiong Xianghui, was a veteran SAD officer who penetrated the staff of Nationalist general Hu Zongnan in 1936.[291]

On December 20, 1975, Zhou Enlai was terminally ill in hospital and summoned his old aide, Luo Qingchang. Zhou asked for news of old friends in Taiwan and requested that the CID transmit his wish that they "not forget to work in the people's interests." The Chinese accounts of this dramatic scene do not clarify whether its significance went beyond the symbolic.[292]

Zhou's death on January 8, 1976, triggered national mourning and antileft demonstrations in Tian'anmen Square. Though he had been loyal to Mao since 1939, Zhou in death became a symbol of popular resistance to radicalism, an echo of his opposition to the chairman's policies in 1931 and 1938.

◆ THREE ◆

Notable Spies of the Chinese Revolution and the Early PRC

In publications approved by the Chinese Communist Party (CCP), the people who did the dangerous work of spying on the party's enemies during the Chinese revolution are called its "countless nameless heroes" (无数无名英雄, *wu shu wu ming yingxiong*). This is partly because so many died anonymous deaths and because of the difficulty of documenting their clandestine activities when records were often purposely not maintained. In party-approved literature, only a select few are described. This may indicate that there are more than a few black sheep and shameful traitors yet to be revealed. Nonetheless, these tales do not contradict accounts from KMT and Taiwan sources.

Many CCP intelligence officers and other operatives were persecuted after 1949 for doing their jobs in the revolution too well—that is, cultivating close contact with enemy agents and officials in order to obtain quality intelligence information. On the U.S. side during the same period, Americans such as David Barrett, commanding officer of the 1944 Dixie mission U.S. Army Observer Group, Yan'an, also suffered after the communist victory, one of those blamed during the 1950s Red Scare for "losing China."[1] The political fight in the United States over blame for the rise of communism was a disastrous ordeal for the victims. However, their situation was less harsh compared to the executions, imprisonments, and other hardships borne by the far greater number of communist undercover officers and agents such as Pan Hannian and Dong Jianwu, particularly during the Cultural Revolution (1966–76).

The blame for the CCP's witch hunts against its own intelligence officers and the greater population rests with Mao Zedong more than any other person. His almost continual "white scare" lasted decades and helps illustrate the deep and seemingly endless suspicions of one of the most paranoid leaders in world history.

What follows are our modest first steps to examine the lives of the foot soldiers of China's "secret war"; we hope that other scholars will be inspired to further explore this understudied area.

Adler, Solomon (艾德勒)

See Coe, Virginius Frank.

Cai Xiaogan (蔡孝乾, 1908–82)

A native of a rural area near Taichung, Taiwan, Cai Xiaogan matriculated at Shanghai University at the age of sixteen in 1924, where he became acquainted with CCP founders including Qu Qiubai and Ren Bishi. Already fluent in Japanese from his early education in Taiwan (then a Japanese colony), Cai's language skills, knowledge of Taiwan, and academic prowess doubtless made him an attractive candidate for CCP recruitment. By 1926 he was back in Taiwan, an underground CCP operative organizing left-wing activities to educate fellow youth. In 1928 he helped organize the Communist Party of Taiwan.

The rapidly escalating Japanese threat on the Chinese mainland may have contributed to the CCP decision in 1934 to call Cai Xiaogan to the Red Army base in Ruijin, Jiangxi, where he was trained in army political work. The Long March began that October, and Cai survived the year-long journey to China's northwest—the only Taiwanese to do so. When the Anti-Japanese War began in 1937, Cai was employed to interrogate Japanese prisoners. As the war went on, Cai stayed in Yan'an; there is no information about how he fared during the infamous Rectification and Salvation campaigns of 1942–44, but in 1945 he attended the Seventh CCP Congress.

Cai's star rose in the wake of Japan's surrender. In August the CCP formed the Taiwan Provincial Work Committee (台湾省工作委员会, *Taiwan sheng gongzuo weiyuanhui*). In March 1946 the East China Bureau formally established the Taiwan committee as an operational entity to develop espionage and sabotage networks on the island in preparation for an eventual invasion. In July Cai and his team of six-plus people secretly deployed to Taiwan. They begin forming clandestine cells in Taipei, Keelung, Kaohsiung, and a number of rural and mountain districts.[2]

In early 1947 Cai's network had about seventy operatives. History intervened on February 28 when the KMT arrested a woman merchant in Taipei, sparking a revolt fueled by local resentment against Taiwan's new masters. In response, Generalissimo Chiang Kai-shek sent reinforcements that landed in Keelung and Taipei on March 9, beginning a brutal mopping up campaign that killed between 18,000 and 28,000 local people.[3] This led to a recruiting bonanza for the CCP underground in Taiwan: two years later, Cai's Taiwan Provincial Work Committee network had grown to 1,300 operatives.[4]

However, Cai's good fortune was soon reversed. On August 14 the KMT Secrets Preservation Bureau arrested his cell in Keelung City. Over the next seven months they nabbed at least eighty others, including Cai himself.[5] In March 1950 Cai defected and assisted in mopping up the remainder of his own comrades.[6] CCP intelligence operations on Taiwan may not have fully recovered until increased economic integration with the mainland in the 1980s allowed more cross-straits exchanges and therefore opportunities to recruit Taiwanese people visiting, or living on, the mainland.

Coe, Virginius Frank (柯弗兰, 1907–80), and Adler, Solomon (艾德勒, 1909–94)

Frank Coe and Solomon Adler were former U.S. Treasury Department officials who lived in China beginning in 1958 and 1962, respectively, and who contributed to the English translation of Mao's writings. However, their role as KGB assets in the United States during World War II, presumably trained in clandestine methods, poses unanswered questions about their activities for the CCP, before and after arrival in Beijing.

While working at Treasury during World War II, Coe and Adler were members of the Nathan Silvermaster group, a Soviet spy ring of at least eleven persons. At first controlled by Earl Browder of the U.S. Communist Party, they were placed under the direct control of the KGB in 1944 due to the increasingly critical nature of their reporting.[7]

Coe and Adler were hired into the Treasury Department by Harry Dexter White, a senior official there who cooperated with the Silvermaster group or was at least a "trusted individual" of Moscow.[8] Ji Chaoding met Adler in the 1930s when he worked at the Library of Congress and also knew Coe, who became the department's director of monetary research. In 1941 Adler was assigned to the U.S. Embassy, Chongqing, as Treasury attaché, where he supposedly continued to report to KGB via unknown means. Harry Dexter White helped place Ji into the Chinese Nationalist Ministry of Finance there, where he was an agent of influence controlled by Zhou Enlai. After Coe and Adler came under FBI scrutiny during the Joseph McCarthy era, Ji invited at least one of them, Adler, to China.[9]

After Coe moved to China in 1958 and Adler in 1962, they assisted with the translation of volume four of Mao's works, more of a prestige job than one suited to their backgrounds. Coe may have been based in the CCP International Liaison Department and was responsible for reading and summarizing reports in the Western press and writing propaganda.[10] Adler's main assignment was in the Institute for the World Economy in the Chinese Academy of Sciences and as an advisor to the Ministry of Foreign Trade. Indicating strong trust by the CCP, by 1964 Coe and Adler were at "the top of the pagoda" in Beijing, tasked with passing along party policy to other foreigners in the Chinese capital. In August 1970 during one of the Cultural Revolution's dreariest periods, they greeted Edgar Snow when he visited Beijing, though they may have suffered in its more manic period in 1966–68; Zhou Enlai personally apologized to Coe and Adler at a 1973 dinner for "the injustices they suffered over the years."[11] After writing a laudatory article in 1976 calling Mao the greatest Marxist of the modern era, Coe passed away three years later in Beijing. Adler survived until 1994, unhappy with the direction China took under Deng Xiaoping's reforms.[12]

Their unique lives as assets serving first Moscow and then Beijing remain an unexplored topic with potential to further illuminate CCP influence operations and intelligence history.

Dong Hui (董慧, 1918–79)

Recruited into the Social Affairs Department because of her hometown connections in Hong Kong, Dong Hui later married Pan Hannian and suffered with him after his 1955 purge.

At the beginning of the Anti-Japanese War in 1937, Dong Hui was a college student in Beiping (now Beijing). Forced by the war to leave the city, she decided to relocate to Xi'an. After arriving, she enrolled in the Northwest United University (西北联合大学, *Xibei Lianhe Daxue*).

However, the rapidly unfolding events of 1937 moved the nineteen-year-old Dong to leave ordinary studies behind. She approached the CCP's de facto embassy and intelligence station in Xi'an, the Eighth Route Army Liaison Office. There she was given an entry test for schools in the CCP's Yan'an base area and probably assessed for suitability to adapt to the communist cause. Dong was admitted to the Yan'an Revolutionary School (革命学校, *Geming Xuexiao*) and began classes in November.

Like hundreds of other newly arrived youth at the time, Dong was quickly admitted (January 1938) to the CCP during its membership expansion that began at the start of the anti-Japanese struggle. In July 1938 she entered the Marxist-Leninist Institute (马列学院, *Malie Xueyuan*), where she became the classmate and roommate of Jiang Qing, the future spouse of Mao Zedong.[13]

When Dong graduated in mid-1939, the CCP assessed her background and noted connections to Hong Kong elite society—partly via her father, the general manager of the Dao Heng Bank. Dong was recruited into the SAD, posted to Hong Kong, and placed under the supervision of Pan Hannian.

While in Yan'an, Dong Hui criticized Jiang when the former Shanghai actress began to pursue Mao, so she suffered not only when Pan was arrested in 1955, but also during the Cultural Revolution (1966–76) when Jiang Qing exacted revenge against perceived enemies.

Dong Jianwu (董健吾, 1891–1970)

Dong Jianwu was made famous in Edgar Snow's *Red Star Over China* as "Pastor Wang." Known by this and other aliases, Dong began service with CCP intelligence in 1928, already equipped with the natural cover of an

Episcopal minister. He was one of the few active communist agents who survived the high tide of arrests and executions in the cities from 1931 to 1936 and became an important liaison between the CCP and KMT during the Anti-Japanese War. Among other missions, in January 1936 he carried a message from Song Qingling to Mao and Zhou indicating the Nationalists were ready to negotiate an anti-Japanese united front, and he guided Snow to a rendezvous in Xi'an with Deng Fa, who took the American leftist journalist to his historic meetings with CCP leaders.

After the communist victory in 1949, questions arose about Dong's relations with the KMT that have not been adequately addressed by CCP historians. Though he remained free, Dong came under suspicion of collaboration with the Nationalists and was unable to find gainful employment. Persecuted during the Cultural Revolution, Dong died in 1970 and was posthumously rehabilitated in 1978–79.[14]

Gong Changrong (龚昌荣, 1903–35)

It would not be surprising if a movie or television drama is made about Gong Changrong. Gong was born in rural Guangdong with the surname Li, but his poor peasant father sold him to an overseas Chinese named Gong, whose gave him that new surname. The movement of May 4, 1919, radicalized the teenager, and during the Canton–Hong Kong strike (June 1925–October 1926), Gong joined the CCP-organized pickets (纠察队, jiucha dui) in Guangzhou, their group trained and equipped for street fighting. In 1926 they were reorganized into a Red Guard (赤卫队, chiwei dui), and Gong became a member of their "dare to die" (敢死队, gan si dui) company. During the Guangzhou uprising of December 1927, Gong was assigned to guerrillas under Ye Jianying who briefly controlled the city. After that disastrous action, Deng Fa praised Gong for his bravery under fire and tally of enemy dead.[15]

In July 1930 Gong was transferred briefly to Hong Kong to take charge of the "Dog Beating Squad" under the municipal CCP committee. Within three months he had killed a number of turncoats and special operatives of the pro-KMT Guangdong warlord Chen Jitang whom the British allowed into the city to track down communists. Notably, Gong was also reportedly responsible for killing Hong Kong police sergeant Tse On (谢安, Xie An), a member of the Police Anti-Communist Squad, while Tse was attempting to gather intelligence at a meeting in the Nga Lok restaurant in Yaumatei.[16]

To maintain close relations with China's small working class, the CCP leadership had chosen to stay in Shanghai, the country's largest city. However, they lived a precarious underground existence, with increasing pressure from Nationalist authorities. The party decided that Gong could be usefully employed in Shanghai to perform protection work. He was instrumental in arranging movement and protection of the party leadership in the aftermath of the Gu Shunzhang defection of April 1931. In subsequent years the CCP gradually withdrew from the city, but the secret war continued. Gong led a number of assassinations of Nationalist security officials, including the killing of Huang Yonghua (黄永华) in July 1933, whom Gong personally shot while racing by on a bicycle.[17]

Though Gong's heroics were a bright spot for the communist movement, the KMT was closing in on urban communists. His last big assignment came in November 1934: to execute Xi Guohua (翕国华), a defector from the Shanghai CCP bureau. Gong's team of four operatives only wounded Xi on their first try, but they finished him off as he lay recovering in the Renji hospital of Jiaotong University.[18]

The capture of one of his close comrades led the Nationalists to the home of Gong and his spouse, who along with three other communists were arrested, offered the opportunity to defect, and tortured when they refused. After spending almost five months in what was probably a brutal confinement, Gong and his three comrades were executed in Nanjing by strangulation.[19] Their capture and deaths marked the effective end of CCP intelligence operations in Shanghai until they were slowly revived after the 1934–35 Long March.

Ji Chaoding (冀朝鼎, Chi Ch'ao-ting, 1903–63)

Ji Chaoding may have been the first CCP member with espionage duties overseas, albeit before there was an intelligence organ, and likely was controlled by Zhou Enlai. He attended Qinghua (Tsinghua) University on a Boxer indemnity scholarship at the time of the May 4 movement of 1919 and was radicalized like many of his generation by China's plight at the hands of Japan and the Western powers. According to a reference by his brother, Mao's famous interpreter Ji Chaozhu, Chaoding met and befriended Zhou and joined the Chinese Communist Party "at its very beginnings." The party was formally founded in July 1921, about nine months after Zhou left for France, so circumstances indicate they met in 1919 or 1920.

Ji was assigned to travel to the United States in 1923 or 1924. He secretly remained a Chinese communist after the 1927 Nationalist-Communist Chinese split while ostensibly becoming a loyal member of the Chinese Nationalist Party (KMT), gathering intelligence against them under Zhou's direction. While in the United States, Ji was associated with the American officials Solomon Adler and Frank Coe, who were implicated as Soviet spies in the Venona intercepts, worked to weaken U.S. support for the KMT, and were eventually exposed during the Red Scare of the 1950s. Coe moved to China in 1958 and Adler in 1962.[20]

In 1939 Ji returned to China and continued his secret work as an asset of Zhou Enlai's network run out of the Eighth Route Army Liaison Office in the KMT's wartime capital, Chongqing. Harry Dexter White, the same senior U.S. Treasury Department official who hired Adler and Coe, influenced the Chinese Nationalist Ministry of Finance to employ Ji Chaoding in a senior position.[21] Ji managed to survive an investigation by the KMT counterespionage agency, the Central Bureau of Investigation and Statistics (中央调查统计局, *Zhongyang diaocha tongji ju*, abbreviation *Zhongtong*), and became the confidential secretary to KMT finance minister H. H. Kung. In January 1949 Ji may have assisted in negotiating the peaceful surrender of Beiping (Beijing) to the PLA, and he became a prominent economist in the new People's Republic. Ji died of a cerebral hemorrhage in Beijing in 1963. Like Li Kenong, Ji was perhaps spared persecution during the Cultural Revolution (1966–76): in spite of his wife Luo Jingyi's association with Kang Sheng, Ji's long overseas service may have become the subject of suspicious accusations.[22]

Ke Lin (柯麟, 1901–99)

Dr. Ke Lin of Guangdong is credited with enabling a noted assassination in Shanghai in 1929 and for critical work in Macau from 1935 to 1951. He is the subject of a five-part CCTV documentary, presenting an idealized and informed but probably incomplete accounting of his twenty-three-year intelligence career ending in 1951.[23]

Just after becoming a medical doctor, Ke Lin joined the CCP in January 1926. He was assigned to the Fourth Revolutionary Army in 1927 and participated in the Guangzhou uprising that December, escaping to Shanghai after its defeat.[24]

By mid-1928, Ke Lin was directly reporting to Special Services Section intelligence section leader Chen Geng, who had him establish cover as a noncommunist physician at the Wuzhou clinic (五洲药房) under the pseudonym Ke Dawen (柯达文). After the August 24, 1929, capture of CCP rural organizer Peng Pai, Zhou Enlai determined that CCP member Bai Xin (白鑫) had defected and helped the KMT apprehend Peng. Though Bai quickly disappeared, the SSS determined that he was in Shanghai, so all hands were on the lookout for him. After a failed rescue attempt led by Gu Shunzhang, Peng and three other communists were executed on August 30.[25]

Only two days after Peng's capture, Bai Xin entered Ke Lin's Wuzhou Clinic by chance, seeking treatment for malaria. Dr. Ke recognized him, but Bai slipped away too quickly for capture. Chen Geng established a liaison point (*lianluo dian*) nearby in case Bai called again, since it appeared that he and his KMT handlers were too cautious to enter a major hospital for treatment. Two weeks later, Bai's condition worsened and he telephoned Ke, requesting treatment at a hotel in the French Concession. Bai decided to trust Ke and allowed a follow-up house call at his sanctuary, the house of KMT intelligence officer Fan Zhengbo.[26] With this knowledge, the SSS staked out Fan's residence and assassinated Bai on November 11 as he departed to board a ship for Italy.[27]

In the wake of the operation, Ke Lin left, probably in haste, for south China, at one point settling in Xiamen. At this point, if not earlier, Ke was a classic illegal operative in the Russian tradition, living a carefully backstopped cover identity in a genuine vocation but spending significant time pursuing intelligence duties. Unlike another officer with natural cover, Dong Jianwu, Ke Lin was apparently never suspected as a communist spy. Though details about the next four years are scarce, he engaged in further SSS operations but had to flee Xiamen in 1934 when the KMT broke up the city's communist networks. Upon arrival in Hong Kong, Dr. Ke established the South China Clinic (华南药房, *Huanan yaofang*). At this point, communist networks all over urban China had been compromised in large measure, and Ke may have been one of the few who were operational—not dead, hiding, or in prison. However, he did not stay still for long. In September 1935 Pan Hannian ordered Ke to move to Macau, establish another medical practice, and make contact with ex-Red Army general Ye Ting, whom Dr. Ke had known during the 1927 Guangzhou uprising. Ye was hiding in Macau with his family, and Ke's mission was to renew their friendship and bring Ye back to the communist cause. Ke's work took time: Ye Ting finally departed Macau in October 1937, months after the outbreak of the second Sino-Japanese War, to take command of the communist New Fourth Army.[28]

Ke Lin stayed in Macau and continued clandestine operations for sixteen more years. In 1942 he was a key link in the evacuation of leftist intellectuals from nearby Hong Kong. In 1950, at the request of Ye Jianying, Ke coordinated the diversion from a Macau warehouse of tons of aviation equipment belonging to two Chinese Nationalist firms. Most importantly, Ke cultivated and recruited Macau business figures such as Ho Yin and Ma Man-kei to the communist cause.[29]

With Japan's surrender in August 1945, the KMT surrounded Macau, as had the Japanese before them, and placed operatives in factories and among guilds of herbalists, barbers, and hotel employees.[30] In the midst of regular KMT bombings and shootings against Macau communists, Ke Lin and others such as Ho Yin appealed to the Portuguese for protection. The Portuguese, albeit from an increasingly weaker position, tolerated both KMT and CCP operations as long as they did not disturb public order.[31]

Ke Lin became an administrator in 1943 and later the director of Kiang Wu hospital (镜湖医院, *Jinghu yiyuan*), turning it into a center of CCP influence until the founding of China's unofficial liaison, the Nam Kwong Company (南光公司, *Nanguang gongsi*), in August 1949—headed by Ke Ping (柯平, also known as Ke Zhengping, 柯正平), Ke Lin's younger brother.[32]

With the CCP's 1949 victory, Ke Lin publicly revealed his CCP membership, though his exploits as a CCP intelligence officer remained hidden until the 1980 *neibu* (内部, internal reference only) publication of *Chen Geng in Shanghai*. In 1951 Ke Lin left Macau for Guangzhou, where he became director of the Zhongshan Teaching Hospital (广州中山医学院, *Guangzhou zhongshan yixueyuan*). Suffering unspecified difficulties in the Cultural Revolution, Dr. Ke was sheltered in Beijing, returning to his Guangzhou post in 1980 at the age of seventy-nine. He retired four years later and passed away in 1991.[33]

Li Qiang (李强, 1905–96)

Born in Changshu, Jiangsu (江苏常熟; originally surnamed Zeng Peihong [曾培洪]), Li Qiang is praised today as a tough and highly intelligent individual. While a young man, he played a crucial role in the founding of CCP intelligence, including its Red Squads and the party's clandestine radio communications. During the Anti-Japanese War (1937–45) and the civil war (1946–49) he was an official in the communists' fledgling defense industry. After 1949, Li was admitted to the Chinese Academy of Sciences and held senior government positions, including as minister of foreign trade.

As a child, Li was inspired by the May 4, 1919, movement and was drawn to anti-imperialist and antifeudal ideas. In 1924 he joined the Chinese Nationalist Party but was attracted to talks by communist activists at Shanghai University. He participated in the May 30, 1925, movement and joined the Communist Youth League (CYL) and the CCP that same year, possibly at this time discarding his original name to become Li Qiang. Li became the secretary of the Pudong, Shanghai, CYL branch in early 1926, which grew rapidly in what was then a center for ship repairs.[34]

In February 1926 Luo Yinong (罗亦农), the head of the neighboring Jiangsu area CCP, was one of the party's overseers of security work. He appointed Li as the head of the nascent CCP Changshu Special Branch (中共常熟特别支部), placing the young activist in charge of the coming armed uprising in his hometown. Meanwhile, Luo Yinong became head of the CCP's Military Special Commission (军事特别委员会, *Junshi tebie weiyuanhui*) under the CCP Shanghai executive committee. A month later the special commission was taken over by Gu Shunzhang (顾顺章).[35] These were antecedents of the security organs that followed, albeit narrowly focused on armed action and VIP protection.

For much of the rest of 1926 Li Qiang, who had some training in chemistry, oversaw the manufacture of bombs and grenades that were sent to communist uprisings in Jiangxi and that would be used locally in support of the Northern Expedition. With the April 12, 1927, anticommunist coup, Li Qiang secretly returned to Shanghai and connected with Gu Shunzhang's clandestine organization, where he was put to work destroying documents, transferring personnel and records to safe locations, and building up stores of arms and ammunition.[36]

When the party headquarters temporarily evacuated to Wuhan in May, Li joined the short-lived Military Commission Special Operations Section (军委特务科, *Junwei tewu ke*) under Gu Shunzhang, becoming head of its Special Operations branch (特务股, *tewu gu*). In a 1981 interview, Li said that he performed "Red squads work" (assassinations of enemies and VIP protection).[37] In November 1927 the party formed its first comprehensive intelligence and security organ, the Special Services Section (SSS). Li served in Shanghai as a clandestine operative performing various tasks, including visiting Chen Geng while he was laid up in a Shanghai hospital.[38]

In June 1928 the CCP Sixth Congress decided to set up long-distance wireless communications to link the party Central Committee with outposts in China and Moscow. Li Qiang was put in charge of this effort and named as leader of the SSS Fourth Section (Communications; 交通科, *Jiaotong ke*, later renamed 通讯科, *Tongxun ke*).[39] He and his small staff also established connections with railway, bus, and shipping firms for handling couriers and other clandestine nonradio communications, and they set up channels for transporting people and funds.

The Nationalist central government kept strict controls on communications equipment and radio textbooks written in Chinese, but Li Qiang read and spoke enough English to use books and schematic diagrams in that language. He made friends with a group of foreign amateur radio operators in Shanghai. Following their example of building their own equipment, he used them to find essential parts. After months of patient work, Li put the CCP's first clandestine radio on the air in 1929 at a house that still stands in Shanghai off of Yan'an West Road.[40] Later that year and again in January 1930, Li traveled to Hong Kong to set up a second clandestine station. While there he met another CCP traveler in transit, Deng Xiaoping.

Li took the opportunity to teach China's future paramount leader how to encrypt messages and follow radio procedures. [41]

This account highlights the practical obstacles faced by CCP urban operatives of the time. The dangers were also many. During this period the CCP sent four students to the Soviet Union to study radio technology and arranged for another, Zhang Shenchuan (张沈川), to secretly enroll in a Shanghai radio school. Once Zhang was trained, Li set up clandestine classes in October 1930 at the Fu Li electric appliance factory in Shanghai. He taught radio theory, and Zhang trained students on how to set up and operate the equipment. However, that December foreign concession police, following up on a lead concerning suspicious activity, arrested five instructors and fifteen students. Li Qiang and the survivors split up and later resumed the training under more clandestine conditions.[42]

Perhaps Li Qiang's most dramatic, albeit jinxed, operation was the attempted rescue of the CCP rural organizer and Politburo member Peng Pai, who was arrested on August 24, 1929, after being betrayed by a defecting communist, Bai Xin (白鑫). Gu Shunzhang and Chen Geng planned the operation with Li Qiang, who assembled a team of twenty men disguised as a movie crew. Various foul-ups and bad luck foiled the operation on August 28, and Zhou Enlai called off the rescue attempt.[43] There were no more chances to effect an escape; Peng Pai and four others were executed at Shanghai's Longhua prison on August 30.[44]

The disastrous defection of SSS chief Gu Shunzhang in April 1931 made it impossible for Li Qiang to remain in Shanghai. Like many others, he fled within the month.[45] The Comintern took the opportunity to bring him to Moscow for further training in radio technology and communications, which he took in English with a class of other international communists.[46] Li apparently stayed in Russia for seven years, only departing Moscow on December 12, 1937. His biographer notes that by the time he left, Li was one of the seven most prominent radio experts in the Soviet Union. This explains his later admission as a fellow of the Chinese Academy of Sciences, but his other activities outside of the study of radio remain unknown. Li was among the last of those from China studying wireless communications to depart Russia.[47]

Li's activities are unclear between 1938 and 1940, but in 1941 he became chief of the CCP's Military Industry Bureau (军工局, *Jun gong ju*), subordinate to the CCP Central Military Commission (CMC). He oversaw production of weaponry, ammunition and explosives, cotton, metals, coal, wood, and other products useful to the communist forces.[48] He was concurrently the head of the Yan'an Academy of Natural Sciences (延安自然科学院).

During the Chinese civil war (1946–49), Li continued in similar military industrial roles and expanded into his expertise on radio as the director of the CMC General Communications Administration and deputy director of the Central Broadcasting Management Section. At the request of Liu Shaoqi and Zhu De, he built and operated the CCP's first shortwave broadcast station, the New China News Service Radio. After 1949 he joined the Ministry of Posts and Telecommunications and expanded China's ability to send short- and medium-wave broadcasts abroad. He also negotiated trade and communications agreements with the Russians in the early years of the PRC as a vice minister of foreign trade.[49]

Liu Ding (Liu Ting, 刘鼎, also known as Dai Liang, 戴良, 1902–86)

Liu Ding, "the dean of military ordnance industry and hero of the United Front," was born Kan Sijun (阚思俊) to an intellectual household in Nanxi, Sichuan, on December 15, 1902. Liu became a major figure in weaponry research and manufacturing and was the deputy of the Second Ministry of Machine Building. Liu also played a part in CCP intelligence history and is remembered especially for his clandestine role in the Xi'an incident.[50]

Liu Ding went to Europe in 1924 on a work-study program and was recruited to the CCP in Germany by Zhu De, who later became marshal of the PLA. Liu went to Russia to study, teach, and translate at the Soviet Air Force Machinery School and the Moscow University of the East, where he graduated in 1928—one of the earliest CCP members to be trained outside of China in science and technology, focused on weaponry manufacture.[51]

Liu may also have had some intelligence training in Moscow,[52] because the next year he was in Shanghai as the deputy of the intelligence branch of the Special Services Section under Chen Geng.[53] In 1931 the Shanghai French Concession police captured a CCP courier but could not read his collection of top secret (绝密, *juemi*) documents. They asked Yang Dengying, posing as a rich, pro-Western businessman but really one of Chen and Liu's agents, to find an expert to evaluate the captured material. Yang produced a disguised Liu Ding, who examined the papers and pronounced them to be worthless Marxist study texts. The French accepted this assessment and Liu spirited the documents away.[54] In 1933 when the KMT and the colonial police in Shanghai were arresting more communists, Liu fled Shanghai for Fujian and Ruijin. He started a successful 35-millimeter mortar assembly line in Ruijin that stayed in production until the Long March began in October 1934.[55]

Liu Ding's clandestine talents were again required after the CCP finished the Long March. In late 1935 the "Young Marshal" Zhang Xueliang and his Fengtian army held a position, under orders from the Nationalist army, on the southern flank of the CCP's base area in Bao'an. In December, during a trip to Shanghai, Zhang secretly voiced his dissatisfaction with Chiang Kai-shek's policy of first destroying the communists before confronting the Japanese invaders—the Young Marshal's father Zhang Zuolin had fallen victim to a Japanese assassination plot four years earlier. Liu Ding learned of Zhang's dismay through Song Qingling. After Liu reported this development to CCP headquarters in Bao'an, Liu and Li Kenong were dispatched to Xi'an in March 1936 to assess Zhang Xueliang's intentions. When they met, Liu gave Zhang a good first impression—he was "an erudite man with whom one could talk"—charming Zhang into further negotiations and a closer relationship. After an initial agreement was struck (see the Xi'an incident), Liu was accepted by Zhang on his staff as CCP liaison. On December 11, 1936, Zhang gave Liu a few hours' warning of his plan to kidnap the generalissimo the next day, and Liu immediately informed the Bao'an headquarters.[56]

In March 1941 Liu became chancellor of the newly founded Taihang Industrial School (太行工业学校), near Yan'an, the party's first effort to regularize ordnance instruction and manufacture.[57] Liu left that post in September 1943 due to the political turmoil of the Salvation (*Qiangjiu*) campaign.[58] Accounts of this time do not reveal if Liu was one of its victims.

After the 1945 Seventh Party Congress, when those sanctioned during the Salvation movement were rehabilitated en masse, Liu Ding again returned to ordnance manufacturing, focused on artillery, grenade, and small arms production. In 1950 Liu and Xu Xiangqian negotiated with the Soviet Union for arms assistance to fight the Korean War, and Liu became a vice minister of heavy industry. In 1957 he was promoted to be the deputy minister of the Second Ministry of Machine Building—charged with narrowing the gap with foreign countries in precision machining, electronics, materials, and defense research.[59]

In the Cultural Revolution Liu Ding was purged along with Luo Ruiqing as a "big spy." He survived seven years of torture and internal exile, and he was later praised for writing ten million words in technical papers and summaries while imprisoned.[60]

Perhaps because of his value to the military, Liu was rehabilitated earlier than most, in February 1978. In his twilight years, Liu consulted for the Ministry of Aviation Industry and the China Ordnance Society before passing away from an illness in mid-1986.[61]

Mo Xiong (莫雄, 1891–1980) and Xiang Yunian (项与年, 1894–1978)

Mo Xiong was a Nationalist general and clandestine agent of CCP intelligence for nineteen years, a rare survivor of the wholesale roundup of communist spies in the early 1930s. In October 1934 he and his controller Xiang Yunian warned the Red Army of an impending attack that might otherwise have crushed the communist movement in China.

Mo Xiong was born in Yingde county, Guangdong, famous for its black tea. Eschewing that industry, he began a military career at age seventeen and later joined the Nationalists. According to a Taiwan source he was a member of *Tongmenghui* (同盟会, 1905–12), the secret society formed by Sun Yat-sen to oppose the Qing Dynasty.[62]

In about 1921 Mo joined the Nationalist army, became an officer, and participated in the Northern Expedition (1926–27). As a KMT brigade commander in December 1927, he helped put down the CCP's Guangzhou uprising. Mo ascended the ranks of the KMT army in his home province and held numerous posts including head of the Guangdong garrison command and commander of the Guangdong Fourth Army, where he was promoted to major general (少将, *shaojiang*).[63] However, Mo had a secret.

In September 1934 Generalissimo Chiang called a meeting of his commanders at Lushan, where he unveiled his fifth "encirclement" campaign: 800,000 troops were to be deployed in a final attempt to surround and annihilate the CCP Red Army. The planning was so intricate that one set of documents weighed two kilograms. Unfortunately for the KMT, Mo Xiong was in attendance and had full access. His secret: Li Kenong of the SSS had recruited him in 1930.[64]

As soon as Chiang Kai-shek's planning conference for the fifth encirclement campaign was dismissed, Mo Xiong handed over a selection of documents to his controller Xiang Yunian, a Fujianese and veteran of SSS operations in Shanghai. Xiang worked overnight with two others in the ring to summarize the plan and render it into secret writing (密写墨水, *mixie moshui*), which they hid in the margins of four student dictionaries.

Disguised as a teacher burdened with books, Xiang departed and headed for Red Army headquarters in Ruijin. But Nationalist army controls were strict at the frontier checkpoints facing the communists; Xiang could see that only itinerant local people were being allowed through, so he knocked out four of his front teeth with a stone, sullied his clothing, and made himself appear like a roughed-up beggar. Disguised thus, he approached a checkpoint. When challenged, Xiang told of being beaten and chased by dogs at a rich man's house. It was enough for the Nationalist sentries to allow him through without a search that might have changed the course of modern Chinese history.

Xiang arrived in Ruijin at Red Army headquarters on October 7; Li Kenong and Zhou Enlai, whom he had previously known him from his SSS service in Shanghai, barely recognized him. Three days later, the Long March began. Xiang left with the Red Army but before the new year was dispatched to Hong Kong to help rebuild the CCP's urban intelligence networks.[65]

Meanwhile, Mo Xiong stayed in the Nationalist Army until the evacuation of Guangzhou in 1949, when he finally went over to the communist side. He suffered from accusations of enemy collaboration in 1951 but apparently was cleared and served in posts in Guangdong until the Cultural Revolution.[66] Career details of both Mo and Xiang are otherwise scant, and they require further study.

Nie Rongzhen (Nieh Jung-chen, 聂荣臻, 1899–1992)

Nie's career led him into the center of the CCP military and the top of the PRC government. Born in Sichuan, he studied in Belgium and France and knew Zhou Enlai and Deng Xiaoping. While in Belgium, he worked in an arsenal and munitions plant, on an automobile line, and in an electrical equipment factory, harbingers for his later duties in building China's advanced defense systems. Nie joined the party in 1923, was trained in the Soviet Red Army Academy in 1924, and was a political officer under Zhou Enlai at the Huangpu Academy in 1925–26. Nie participated in the Guangzhou (Canton) uprising of December 1927 and made his way to the Red areas after a brief stint in the SSS during 1930–31. Nie participated in the Long March (1934–35) and supported Mao at the Zunyi conference.[67]

Foreign observers in the Yan'an period wrote that he was "the brains and driving force" behind the Jin-Cha-Ji border region government, and his leadership was promoted as a model in communist propaganda. In spite of these achievements, Nie may have come under attack by Kang Sheng during the *Qiangjiu* (Salvation) campaign in October 1943 as a "dogmatist" and supporter of Wang Ming. At one point soon afterward, Nie personally saved Mao's life during an air attack and was key to the defense of Yan'an from the Nationalists after the 1945 surrender of Japan.[68]

As one of China's most experienced military officers, Nie became acting chief of the PLA general staff just before the Korean War (1950–53). In July 1950, after the North Korean invasion but before Chinese involvement in October, he sent more than one hundred Chinese intelligence officers into the conflict to keep tabs on Pyongyang's offensive. Nie became a marshal of the People's Liberation Army (PLA) in 1955 and three years later was placed in charge of China's nuclear weapons and missile programs, leading the National Defense Science and Technology Commission. Besides this work, the commission and its successor, the Commission of Science, Industry, and Technology for National Defense, became important in acquiring foreign technology. At the apex of his career, Nie was a vice premier.[69]

Nie's SSS special operations work in 1930–31 was as intense as it was brief. He joined the Shanghai Red Squads in May 1930. Posing as "Mr. Li," a journalist, Nie engaged in overnight operations to punish and kill opponents of the CCP underground. He instructed his wife, Zhang Ruihua (张瑞华), to abandon their residence if he did not return by dawn. On these sleepless nights, she nervously awaited a secret knock heralding his return, causing anxiety that she suffered from into her old age. When Nie's boss, SSS director Gu Shunzhang, defected to the Nationalists in April 1931, Nie assisted Zhou Enlai to move cadres away from known hideouts and destroy secret documents.[70] Afterward, he and Zhang fled to Jiangxi, where he resumed military duties.

Pan Hannian (P'an Han-nien, 潘汉年, 1906–77)

Pan Hannian is celebrated today as a highly successful intelligence leader and negotiator during the Chinese Communist revolution, but his name is synonymous with tragedy. For matters that were arguably professional errors and disagreements, Mao Zedong had Pan arrested for treason in 1955, leading eventually to his trial, life sentence, and death in prison. Eight hundred to one thousand intelligence cadres were affected in the wake of Pan's arrest. A forthcoming biography in English of Pan Hannian will detail his life and times and will shed much light on CCP intelligence history and the nature of secret party deliberations.[71]

Pan Hannian was born into a declining household with ancestors who had passed the imperial examinations. His father was a teacher, and Pan was an academic achiever at an early age. As their home in Yixing, Jiangsu, was rustic and isolated, at age fifteen Pan was sent to Changzhou for further schooling. At age eighteen he briefly taught elementary school and enrolled in a program in Wuxi to study classical Chinese.[72]

In 1925, at age nineteen, Pan arrived in Shanghai, a young man of letters. He became an editor and publisher of magazines that opposed foreign imperialism and that year joined the CCP. Focused on literary and propaganda work, Pan published so many periodicals that he was nicknamed *xiaokai* (小开), the "young boss." He kept this as an alias in later decades.[73]

As the Chinese Nationalist Party began their Northern Expedition to unite China and defeat local warlords, Pan joined the General Political Department of the National Revolutionary Army. Sent to Nanchang and Wuhan, he published the Revolutionary Army Daily (革命军日报, *Geming jun ribao*) in the first half of 1927. After the April 12 anticommunist coup that made mortal enemies of the Chinese Nationalist and Communist parties, the CCP sent Pan back to Shanghai to continue propaganda and cultural work, but now in the clandestine underground. He became an important part of the left literary movement that blossomed in 1929–30 and helped start the League of Left-Wing Writers in 1930, becoming an acquaintance of Lu Xun.[74]

In April 1931 the head of CCP intelligence, SSS director Gu Shunzhang, defected to the Nationalists. In a situation where so many had to flee Shanghai, Pan apparently was judged survivable and competent enough to head SSS intelligence collection operations.[75] Modern accounts credit Pan with quickly recruiting replacement intelligence sources for those compromised by Gu and organizing the retaliatory murders of several KMT police and security officials and CCP defectors.[76] However, it is likely that others such as Chen Yun and Kang Sheng also played major roles in these counterattacks.

Pan continued operations for about a year, but his position became increasingly less secure. When he departed Shanghai in early 1933, it may have been in the nick of time—a few months later, the KMT arrested his brother, who would be held until 1937. Pan made it to the Red Army base in Ruijin, Jiangxi, where he became the head of the Central Bureau Propaganda Department.[77] He played a major role in negotiations with leaders of the Fujian rebellion in 1933. In October 1934, after CCP agent Mo Xiong acquired plans by the KMT army for a fifth encirclement campaign, Pan helped establish the modus vivendi with Guangdong warlord Chen Jitang that allowed the Red Army to escape and begin the Long March.[78]

After the Zunyi conference in January 1935, CCP general secretary Zhang Wentian sent Pan to Moscow to reestablish contact with the Comintern. Pan departed the march near the Guizhou-Yunnan border and traveled overland through Guangxi and Hunan. In the spring he reached Shanghai and contacted Song Qingling (Madame Sun Yat-sen), who connected him with others who supported the Red Army. Part of Pan's mission was to assess whether any SSS networks remained in Shanghai, but he found that they were in disarray. In August, Chen Yun also arrived in Shanghai, and he and Pan departed by ship for Vladivostok—ordered to report directly to the Comintern and its CCP representatives, Wang Ming and Kang Sheng.[79]

In early 1936, when the Comintern learned of the warlord Zhang Xueliang's desire to cooperate with the CCP against Japan (see the Xi'an incident), Pan opened preliminary negotiations with the Nationalist central government, concurrently with efforts by Li Kenong to reach a separate CCP agreement with Zhang. In May, Pan traveled to Hong Kong and Nanjing and reported to Mao Zedong in Bao'an that August. Pan also pursued negotiations with the KMT following the December 1936 Xi'an incident, which pushed the two sides closer to forming the Second CCP-KMT United Front, this time against Japan, in 1937.[80]

Following the February 1939 establishment of the CCP's reorganized intelligence and security organ, the Social Affairs Department, Pan was appointed as one of two deputy directors and sent to Hong Kong. He developed an urban espionage network concentrated in Shanghai, Hong Kong, and Macau that became known in the party's innermost circles as the Pan Hannian system (潘汉年系统, *Pan Hannian xitong*), reporting directly to Central SAD headquarters in Yan'an. As in other CCP intelligence groups of the time (see Intelligence Stations and Eighth Route Army Liaison Offices), strict procedures governed recruitment and agent running, including central vetting of agents and operational plans, with stress on the principle of single line control (单线联系指导, *danxian lianxi zhidao*) to minimize compromise if any individual operative was captured.[81]

Between 1939 and 1943 Pan achieved successes in a number of operations. His networks identified, recruited, trained, and inserted agents into Japanese-occupied cities; ran an agent in the Hong Kong office of a Nationalist intelligence research institute;[82] traded intelligence on Japan with the Hong Kong offices of the Northeast Anti-Japanese Army and the Soviet Far East Intelligence Bureau;[83] conducted "private liaison" with Hu Egong, who worked in Hong Kong for the KMT finance minister H. H. Kung (Kong Xiangxi); confirmed an earlier report from Chongqing of German plans to invade Russia two days before the attack;[84] reported months before Pearl Harbor that Japan intended to push into the South Pacific and Southeast Asia and not advance north toward the Soviet Union;[85] and ran a clandestine agent who regularly visited the household of Li Shiqun, the deputy in the Chinese puppet secret police organization.[86] In autumn 1942 Pan became the head of the CCP Central China Bureau Intelligence Department (中共中央华中局情报部, *Zhonggong zhongyang Huazhong ju qingbao bu*), reporting to bureau chief Rao Shushi in addition to SAD director Kang Sheng.[87]

In spring 1943 Pan also managed to meet Li Shiqun himself and, fatefully, Wang Jingwei, head of the collaborationist regime.[88] Pan chose not to report the unplanned Wang Jingwei meeting to his superiors, perhaps because that summer he was criticized as a "liberal" (自由主义者, *ziyou zhuyi zhe*) by his boss, Rao Shushi. This was in the midst of Kang Sheng's Salvation campaign (*Qiangjiu yundong*), centered in the CCP's wartime headquarters of Yan'an, which wildly sought enemies in every corner of the Chinese Communist movement.[89] His decision had devastating consequences a decade later.

Pan travelled to Yan'an for the Seventh Party Congress (April-June 1945) and then returned to Hong Kong. He worked there for most of 1945–49, becoming a member of the CCP's Hong Kong Bureau. The agents in Pan's network recruited increasing numbers of Nationalist military and civilian officials as the fortunes of the Nationalist central government declined, regularly reporting on events inside the KMT via their clandestine radio in Shanghai.[90] In 1948–49 Pan directed the exfiltration from Hong Kong to north and northeast China of more than three hundred prominent non-communists, many of whom participated in the founding meetings of the Chinese People's Political Consultative Conference and served in state and mass organizations after 1949. His network also played an important role in arranging the defection of KMT pilots with their aircraft from Nanjing and Canton as the communist victory approached.[91]

In the first two years of the People's Republic, Pan was vice mayor of Shanghai, supervising security, intelligence, and united front work. He might have become the next mayor but was shifted to less sensitive duties after minister of public security Luo Ruiqing criticized Pan's subordinate Yang Fan, the Shanghai Public Security Bureau (PSB) director, for allowing former enemy agents into Shanghai's counterintelligence operations. However, Pan retained his rank after enduring criticism, and in 1954 his status still seemed secure as number three in Shanghai's CCP hierarchy.

Pan's shocking downfall came in April 1955 between two key party meetings in Beijing.[92] Mao opened the CCP national conference on March 21 with a speech that focused in part on the supposed Gao Gang–Rao Shushi "anti-party conspiracy," during which he mentioned Yang Fan as a coconspirator of Rao.[93] Mao then distributed a document specifically discussing Yang Fan's "mistakes" in public security work during 1949–51, when Yang was Pan's subordinate.[94]

Pan was troubled not only by this development but also by the news that his former agent, Hu Junhe, had been detained and was under interrogation: Hu had witnessed Pan's unreported 1943 meeting with the Japanese puppet government leader Wang Jingwei.[95]

A perfect storm of anguish hit Pan. According to his friend Xia Yan, when the congress ended on March 30, Pan sorrowfully said that there was a matter that he needed to clarify with Shanghai mayor Chen Yi. By coincidence, the next day, Rao Shushi was formally arrested. Pan, apparently hoping to be spared the harshest judgment of one who had stubbornly hidden the truth, confessed to Chen his unreported 1943 meeting in Shanghai with Wang Jingwei. The shocked mayor of Shanghai had Pan write a confession. The next day, Chen saw Mao Zedong at his Zhongnanhai residence and handed him the document. Mao's reaction was immediate and devastating. He wrote into the margins, "This man can no longer be trusted" (此人从此不可信用, *Ci ren congci bu ke xinyong*), and ordered Pan's arrest.[96]

On the evening of April 3, while Pan was in his room at the Beijing Hotel, he received a telephone call asking him to report to the lobby. Minister of public security Luo Ruiqing was there to serve an arrest warrant and detain him.[97]

Though evidence was lacking, Mao became convinced Pan was guilty of sabotage and treason, simultaneously an agent of the Japanese, the KMT on Taiwan, and the U.S. Central Intelligence Agency. His suspicions may have been aggravated by the April 11 destruction by a KMT time bomb of the Kashmir Princess, an aircraft scheduled to carry Zhou Enlai, who changed his flight, to the Bandung conference.[98] On April 12 Pan was formally charged with leading the "Pan-Yang Counterrevolutionary Clique."[99]

As party officials were secretly informed of Pan's arrest, they fell in line due to the chairman's prestige and power. Only Li Kenong, who was Pan's colleague under Kang Sheng during the Yan'an period, made a formal attempt to persuade the chairman that he had overreacted. At Zhou Enlai's direction, Li assembled a report that was delivered to the Central Committee in two parts, on April 29 and July 29. Apparently to retain credibility, Li pointed out problems in Pan's record, including the unreported Wang Jingwei audience in 1944 and Pan's failure to make an agreed on clandestine meeting in Beiping (Beijing) late that year. But Li's report also detailed evidence that Pan had otherwise been loyal: he informed the center of his recruited agents and contacts with the KMT, received agreement for operational decisions, provided high-grade intelligence, and had kept secret the details of the final assault on Shanghai in 1949, which he logically would have leaked to the KMT if he really was their man.[100]

Mao ignored the report but promoted Li Kenong and placed him in charge of the reorganized Central Investigation Department. In conjunction with a subsequent, wider movement beginning in July–August 1955 to weed out counterrevolutionaries (肃反运动, *sufan yundong*), between eight hundred and one thousand intelligence professionals associated with Pan were transferred, fired, or imprisoned.[101] It was a tragic irony that underground and intelligence work by loyal communists, which led to close contact with enemies at great peril, had prompted accusations once victory was achieved.[102] No one in the leadership, including Zhou, urged the chairman to reconsider.

In May 1962, three months after Li Kenong's death, Mao approved the Ministry of Public Security's (MPS) recommended findings that Pan was "a longtime hidden traitor within the party" who committed serious crimes. Pan was convicted and sentenced a year later.[103] In March 1967 during the Cultural Revolution, Pan was sent to a Hunan labor camp. He died of liver cancer and medical neglect in 1977—still incarcerated in spite of the death of Mao the previous year. In 1982 Pan was posthumously cleared in the 1980s Rehabilitation of Intelligence Cadres, long delayed due to the sensitivity of publicly admitting past errors by Mao Zedong.[104]

Pan Jing'an (潘靜安, also known as Pan Zhu, 潘柱, 1916–2000)

A native of Panyu district near Guangzhou and a longtime resident of Hong Kong, Pan (no relation to Pan Hannian) joined the revolution in 1936 and in 1938 was inducted into the CCP. About a year later he joined the Hong Kong Eighth Route Army Liaison Office under Liao Chengzhi as an officer of the Social Affairs Department (SAD). When Hong Kong fell to the Japanese in 1942, Pan was a key part of the operation to evacuate cultural elites and democratic personages to the mainland. This work won the attention of Zhou Enlai, and Pan was awarded the title of "exemplary member" of the Communist Party.

From 1958 to 1982 Pan was the head of the CCP Central Investigation Department (CID) station in Hong Kong and therefore was in charge of Beijing's espionage operations in the British Crown colony during most of the Cold War. In his cover job as deputy auditor of the Bank of China in Hong Kong, Pan could easily move in various social circles to benefit his intelligence duties.

When Pan returned to the mainland in 1982 at age sixty-six, he lived in Beijing and held sufficiently high party rank to become a delegate to the fifth through eighth sessions of the Chinese People's Political Consultative Conference. During this time he was named the vice chair of the conference historical materials committee. It is unclear if Pan worked full or part time in the CID and Ministry of State Security (MSS) headquarters in the 1980s, but due to his age he may have been retired or semiretired.[105]

Song Qingling
(Soong Ch'ing-ling, 宋庆龄, Madame Sun Yat-sen, 1890–1981)

The widow of Sun Yat-sen and sister of Madame Chiang Kai-shek, Song Qingling was an enthusiastic noncommunist supporter of the CCP. She lent great legitimacy to the People's Republic after 1949 and remains a major figure in both popular imagination and twentieth-century Chinese political history. Less appreciated is Song's role in intelligence, underground work, and influence operations.

Song's marriage in 1915 to the father of modern China, Sun Yat-sen, brought her to instant national prominence that lasted beyond his death in March 1925. She became a leader of the KMT left in Wuhan and a voice for equality of the sexes, saying in 1926 that "even though Chinese women have undergone two thousand years of oppression, they cannot stay out of the revolution."[106] After the April 12, 1927, Nationalist coup against the CCP, hostile Nationalist troops approached Wuhan.[107] In July Song and those close to her, including the left KMT's foreign minister Eugene Chen (陈友仁, Chen Youren), fled to Shanghai. Their Soviet advisor, Mikhail Borodin, left overland for Siberia and Moscow.

Song Qingling stayed less than a month in Shanghai, where she was placed under heavy if inept British and French surveillance at her residence in the French Concession (now a museum).[108] Before Borodin left Wuhan, he urged Song to head for Moscow and demonstrate a break with Chiang Kai-shek, leader of the KMT and the April coup. Taking his advice, Song wrote an essay accusing Chiang of betraying Sun Yat-sen's revolution. It was published on August 22, 1927, in the Shanghai *Shenbao* newspaper and was later reprinted in *The Nation* magazine in the United States.

The morning Song Qingling's essay appeared in Shanghai, she had already sailed on a Russian ship for Vladivostok in a plan organized with her friend and secretary Rayna Prohme, an American communist. Song's departure was part of a larger Russian operation to evacuate communists and leftists valuable to Moscow. Their freighter also carried seventy students, a dozen Russian military and other advisors, Eugene Chen, and the wife of Borodin.[109] They reached Vladivostok a week later and continued by train to Moscow.[110]

Symbolizing the often personal struggles behind the Nationalist-Communist split, Qingling's sister, Meiling, married the CCP's deadly enemy, Chiang Kai-shek, on December 1.[111]

Song Qingling received a hero's welcome in Moscow, where she participated in ceremonies marking the tenth anniversary of the October Revolution. Reflecting Song's value in Soviet eyes and her future in the People's Republic, she was befriended by Mikhail Kalinin, a prominent albeit powerless member of the Soviet Politburo. She stayed there for two years.[112]

Perhaps the novelty of life in Moscow wore thin, or Song and the Russians might have agreed that she should return to China. When Chiang Kai-shek invited Song to Nanjing for the interment ceremony of her late husband, she did not hesitate. To make clear that she was not endorsing the KMT or Chiang's leadership, Song made statements indicating that she would not participate in any Nationalist Party work.[113]

Indeed, Song became an implacable, brave, and outspoken opponent of Chiang. Though the generalissimo regularly ordered the assassination of political opponents, he did not allow harm to come to her, fearing public condemnation if not personal retribution from Song's siblings. Song Qingling remained free to travel (including to Germany and Moscow in 1930) and to speak, write, and march in public protests, though Chiang occasionally considered ways to intimidate her.[114]

In 1931 Song lobbied Chiang Kai-shek and world opinion itself for the release of the "Noulens couple," Comintern agents captured in Shanghai by the KMT, whose names were Jakob Rudnik and Tatiana Moissenko. After their conviction, Song and Agnes Smedley took care of the couple's son, who like his parents eventually repatriated to the Soviet Union.[115] In 1933, with Lu Xun, Song formed the Chinese League for the Protection of Human Rights in response to KMT assassinations. That March, in the name of the league, Song successfully lobbied for the release of the CCP underground leader Liao Chengzhi.[116] Considering that rescuing CCP members from jail was an important mission of the SSS, these operations may represent early examples of Song Qingling's employment as a CCP intelligence asset.

Other anecdotes highlight Song's occasional value to intelligence operations, in spite of how closely she was watched by the Nationalist security services. In December 1935 Marshal Zhang Xueliang (see the Xi'an incident), responsible for bottling up the CCP from his base in Xi'an, was in Shanghai; he told a friend of Song Qingling that he was open to talks with the CCP. Song notified Liu Ding, a veteran CCP intelligence operative staying in town. As a result, the CCP initiated talks that led to Chiang's kidnapping a year later.[117]

In January 1936 the veteran SSS operative Dong Jianwu visited Song in her apartment to obtain documents that she had acquired from an unnamed source. In that meeting Song provided Dong with identification documents that would allow him to pose as an official of the KMT finance ministry—perhaps not coincidentally, her brother, T. V. Soong, and then her brother-in-law, H. H. Kung, held the finance ministry port-folio during this period. Shortly afterward, Song helped to identify Edgar Snow and George Hatem as sympathetic to the communist cause, result-ing in an invitation to the CCP's headquarters at Bao'an.[118] Later that year, Dong Jianwu assumed the guise of Pastor Wang to meet Snow and Hatem in Xi'an and passed them to Deng Fa for clandestine transit to the CCP's nearby headquarters.[119]

The Xi'an incident and the outbreak of the Anti-Japanese War (1937–45) altered the lives of many Chinese, including Song Qingling. With Shanghai threatened by the Japanese, she moved to Hong Kong. In June 1938 Song helped found the China Defense League (保卫中国同盟, *Baowei zhongguo tongmeng*), a KMT-CCP joint effort to raise funds from abroad for the war effort. The outbreak of the Pacific War in December 1941 immediately threatened Hong Kong, so Song flew to Chongqing and established herself in the Nationalist wartime capital.[120] While there, Song established "close liaison" (亲密的联系, *qinmi de lianxi*) with Zhou Enlai and others in the CCP's de facto embassy.[121]

When Mao became the chairman of the Central People's Government in 1949, he chose as his chief deputies Liu Shaoqi, Zhu De, and Song Qingling.[122] This may not have indicated actual power for Sun Yat-sen's widow, but it did show her commitment to the new government—which she maintained in spite of the punishing political campaigns, executions, and humanitarian disasters that followed.

In the last years of her life, Song remained a noncommunist, though she was finally allowed to join the CCP on May 15, 1981, exactly two weeks before her death.[123] During the Nixon visit in February 1972, Song extolled Mao Zedong as a liberator of China's women.[124] If nothing else, her endorse-ment was an echo of Song's previous carefully crafted appeals to noncom-munist audiences. Lauding the chairman as a feminist seems ironic given what is now known about his sexual exploitation of some of the women around him. Yet Song's single-minded devotion to the CCP and her less than understood role as a clandestine operative, when matched with her charity work, make her presence on the Chinese stage singular and worth further study.

Tsang, John Chao-ko

See Zeng Zhaoke.

Wang Shijian (also known as Zhao Yaobin, 王石坚, 赵耀斌, 1911–?)

In 1947 the Chinese Nationalist government captured veteran CCP intelligence operative Wang Shijian and turned him to their side. In the midst of the numerous intelligence victories against the Nationalist enemy, it was a major setback. Wang went on to become a senior intelligence official on Taiwan until his death in the 1960s.

Wang Shijian, of Shandong, is one of several Benedict Arnold–like figures in the CCP intelligence pantheon. In contrast to Gu Shunzhang, Wang stuck with the KMT and survived to become one of their senior intelligence officials. Like the American revolutionary commander turned traitor, Wang distinguished himself early in the conflict. After capture and sentencing by the Nationalists in 1933, he participated in an underground party organization inside Suzhou military prison. When their group was discovered in 1935, he and other comrades were transferred to Nanjing for trial. However, Zhou Enlai negotiated the release of Wang and others two years later as a condition for joining with the Nationalists in the Second United Front (1937–45) to resist Japan.[125]

In 1940 Kang Sheng sent Wang to KMT-held Xi'an to replace Luo Qingchang as head of the regional intelligence network. Wang was directly subordinate to the CCP Intelligence Department in Yan'an and ran a network of agents that provided information on Nationalist forces. The network ranged from Beiping (Beijing) to Shenyang and from Xi'an to Lanzhou.[126]

In September 1947 Wang was "captured and turned" (see *Beibu panbian toudi*), providing the KMT with names of more than one hundred Communist Party members and dozens of secret party addresses used in north, east, and west China. An uncertain number of networks in these regions were blown, and five communists were killed, a major setback amidst other CCP advances during the Chinese civil war. The final communist victory came two years later in October 1949.[127]

Wang retreated to Taiwan with the Nationalist government and stayed in the intelligence field, becoming head of the Mainland Bandit Intelligence

Research Institute (大陆匪情研究所, *Dalu fei qing Yanjiu suo*). He passed away in the 1960s in Taiwan.[128]

Wang Xirong (王锡荣, 1917–2011)

One of the CCP's "countless nameless heroes" (无数无名英雄, *wu shu wu ming yingxiong*), Wang Xirong secretly couriered messages, firearms, and other materials between Weihai city, in Shandong, and the nearby countryside in the last three years of the Anti-Japanese War (1937–45). Her story of survival and courage became the basis for a popular film in 1978.[129] She was the occasional subject of newspaper write-ups about heroes of the revolution until her death at age ninety-four.[130]

Like many peasant women in traditional times, Wang originally had no formal name—she was simply called *Gengzi* (庚子), after the day of her birth, until 1946 when she took it upon herself to choose three characters she liked. During the war Wang was subordinate to the CCP Underground and Eighth Route Army intelligence, not the Social Affairs Department, which had less influence at that time in Shandong than the Eighth Route Army.[131]

Though she did not consider herself a spy, Wang was taught to observe and report, memorize and relay alerts, and disguise for transporting items such as pistols, written messages, and collections of documents. Among her favorite methods was wrapping an object in multiple layers of water-resistant cloth placed in the bottom of a large jar of thick and fragrant soy paste, carried on her back. She avoided hiding anything on her person.[132]

Wang knew her superiors in the Weihai liaison station (联络站, *lianluozhan*) network only by pseudonyms. She was approached for the job because her home lay along the courier line between more than twenty liaison points (联络点, *lianluodian*) organized under Weihai station. The station chief lived in the countryside at Yangting village, where Wang's mother resided, about thirty kilometers southwest of the city: there he commanded operations in the more dangerous urban center. Eighth Route Army cadres visited Wang's home with messages for the underground in Weihai. The liaison points along her route were mostly small shops. Wang's favorites were shoe stores, because people would come and go and not necessarily buy anything. Fruit shops were also used.[133]

Wang's new husband of the time became upset with the spectacle of numbers of men coming and going from her home. As her courier activities were secret, neighbors were allowed to believe the worst, socially speaking. Wang Xirong's husband left her before the end of the war, and she remarried a decade later.[134]

In her last years Wang lived a private life in a cramped apartment in downtown Dalian, attended to by her children and grandchildren. Ironically, the entrance to her building faced Ling Yun Street (凌云街), named for the first minister of state security.

Xiang Yunian (项与年, 1894–1978)

See Mo Xiong.

Ying Ruocheng (Ying Juo-ch'eng, 英若成, 1929–2003)

An actor known for films such as *The Last Emperor* (1987) and *Little Buddha* (1993), Ying was also a PRC vice minister of culture from 1986 to 1990. In his memoir *Voices Carry*, Ying wrote that he was recruited in 1952 to become a clandestine agent reporting on attitudes and activities of his foreign contacts in Beijing.[135] As a prominent person in the arts from an intellectual family, Ying was approached not by a public security officer of ordinary rank but by Beijing mayor Peng Zhen—who was also a member of the CCP Politburo. Michael Schoenhals observed that this approach was consistent with a policy to "respect the status, position, and dignity of the agent." The reporting relationship went on for years. Ying's family received food not ordinarily available to other urban Chinese in order to host foreigners in his residence—during a time, as his son observed, when "it was outrageous to have foreigners come to your home."[136]

The son, Ying Da, also became an actor and director. In 2009 he starred as an overweight intelligence officer of the Japanese puppet regime of Wang Jingwei in *The Message* (风声, *Fengsheng*) an espionage film set in 1942, directed by Feng Xiaogang (冯小刚).

Zeng Zhaoke (曾昭科; also known as John Tsang, Cantonese: Tsang Chao-ko, Tsang Chiu-fo, 1923–2014)

John Tsang was the most senior ethnic Chinese officer in the Hong Kong police force and was a noted marksman when he was arrested on October 3, 1961, accused of leading a Chinese communist espionage ring. The press dubbed him "Hong Kong's first spy" because none had been publicly named before then.

Zeng (Tsang) was born in Guangzhou of Manchu parentage. He attended primary school in Hong Kong and university in Japan, where he was exposed to Marxist writings, and he may have been recruited into the CCP at that time. In 1947 Zeng arrived in Hong Kong and began working for the police.[137]

British and Chinese sources have few details of the work done by Zeng's ring. However, his organization may have been the source of important intelligence, including the nature of the colony's defenses and internal security and matters such as the findings by British authorities concerning the 1955 bombing carried out by Taiwan agents in Hong Kong, targeting Zhou Enlai (see the Kashmir Princess Bombing).[138] Research has not uncovered their names or positions, but fourteen "foreign nationals" were arrested at the same time as Zeng, and four of these were expelled with him to China.[139]

Zeng's access was notably broad. He was a rising star in the Hong Kong police force and according to one Chinese media report was the senior CCP agent in Hong Kong. At one point a bodyguard for the Hong Kong governor, he became the deputy commandant of the police training school at Aberdeen in 1960, the post he held when arrested a year later.[140]

On October 1, 1961, a CCP intelligence courier entering Hong Kong from Macau was discovered carrying microfilm and a large amount of cash after an off-duty Hong Kong police detective observed him transferring a wad of $100 banknotes from one pocket to the other. Under interrogation, the courier revealed his affiliation with mainland Chinese authorities and his destination: the home of a woman later determined to be Zeng's mother.[141]

Police arrested Zeng on October 6 and interrogated him for more than fifty days. Instead of placing him on trial, Hong Kong authorities deported the ex-policeman to China on November 30. Due to his fluency in Japanese and English and academic training in Japan and Britain, Zeng became a professor of English at Jinan University in Guangzhou, where he worked before and after the Cultural Revolution. In his later years, Zeng was head of the English department at the university and a member of the Guangdong Provincial People's Congress.[142] According to one Chinese media report lauding Zeng's accomplishments, he also "assumed remote personal command of the Hong Kong and Macau intelligence networks" after arriving in Guangzhou,[143] though it remains unstated how long he held such duties and where he spent most of his work day.

In the 1980s Zeng was one of the few official Chinese contacts in Guangzhou with whom foreign diplomats could freely associate, possessing an imprimatur to hang out with foreigners that was not unusual for Chinese intelligence figures at that time. An urbane, tall, and smiling man in his sixties of notable vitality, Zeng cut a swath through the foreign community with a personality "much different from the dour functionaries we usually met," according to a diplomat based there at the time. Zeng had great command of detail and was frank in his opinions. At one point, when asked about the influx of new members of the National People's Congress (NPC) who were not the workers, peasants, and soldiers of the Mao era, Zeng opined, in his British-accented English: "Do you think we want to be ruled by a bunch of peasants?"[144]

Zeng's funeral honors in 2014 included indications that he had worked for the party before the 1949 communist victory and a wreath from CCP head Xi Jinping.[145] If Zeng was already an underground or intelligence operative when he arrived in Hong Kong in 1947, the party may have instructed him to obtain employment that included useful access to secrets, such as with the police.

In the absence of details about Zeng's specific activities, one can consider why the British decided to deport him rather than place him on trial. The Zeng affair in October-November 1961 came in the midst of China's great famine. In November 1960 China began supplying Hong Kong with much-needed fresh water, and in July 1961 Chinese authorities began to allow easier access to Hong Kong by mainland refugees fleeing famine.[146] The circumstances may have allowed the Chinese side to pressure the

British at a time when they were considering what to do with "Hong Kong's first spy."

Zhang Luping (张露萍, 1921–45)

Born in Beiping (Beijing) in 1921 as Yu Weina (余微娜), Zhang's parentage nonetheless made her a girl "from" Chongqing, and she was probably raised speaking Sichuanese as well as Mandarin.

Since the Nationalist wartime capital was in Chongqing, Zhang's origins may have held an appeal that contributed to her recruitment for training at age sixteen. Then known by another name, Li Lin (黎琳), she joined the CCP a year later in October 1938 while in Yan'an attending the Anti-Japanese Military and Political University (抗日军政大学, *Kangri junzheng daxue*).

In November 1939 the SAD sent her to Chongqing as a secret operative to lead the KMT Military Statistics Bureau Telecommunications Office Secret Party Small Group (国民党军统局电讯处秘密党小组, *Guomindang juntong ju dianxun chu mimi dang xiaozu*). In more plain language, this was a seven-person spy ring inside the Nationalist signal intelligence center. Members included a KMT lieutenant colonel, Feng Chuanqing, who commanded an around-the-clock operation with hundreds of radio intercept positions and perhaps a thousand operators and analysts. The spy ring did not last long, though; its members were apprehended in late 1940 and executed in July 1945. Zhang shouted slogans and swore at her captors as she was being executed.[147]

◆ FOUR ◆

Economic Espionage Cases

During the Cold War, the Soviet KGB's Directorate T and its Line X officers were noted foes of Western export controls and high-tech industries. Every year (with particularly notable success in 1980), they acquired thousands of technology samples, finished products, and other materials from the United States and its allies. These were clandestine transactions unlikely to have been approved for sale to the Soviet Union.[1]

In comparison to Russia's classic centrally controlled system for acquiring foreign technology, China's effort has some parallels but is unsurprisingly unique, including an element of post-Mao, Deng Xiaoping–inspired entrepreneurialism.

Beijing operates a centrally directed system that pursues technology through both open and clandestine means. Acquisition, control, and distribution efforts meet the science and technology development targets of the moment, both military and civilian—many are openly stated in the goals of the current PRC Five-Year Plan and in the now-famous Made in China 2025 program. At the same time Beijing allows other PRC organizations to pursue their own technology acquisition operations, all intended to help China catch up with and even surpass the West. It is an ambition with echoes from the past: the Self-Strengthening movement of the late Qing and the Great Leap Forward under Mao Zedong. However, Made in China 2025 is blessed with more rational and detailed planning.

A substantial part of today's catch-up effort is focused on open-source material that is publicly available in scientific journals and other publications. But the economic espionage cases outlined below were clandestine until discovered by law enforcement—a mix of operations run by CCP intelligence organs and those conducted independently by state-owned enterprises and overseas organizations, and even more independently by students and entrepreneurs.[2] However, we argue that evidence does not point to a "grains of sand" approach enlisting tens of thousands of ordinary Chinese in a worldwide effort. Rather, PRC technology acquisition is a hybrid phenomenon that is mostly secret and not made semipublic by calling upon all ethnic Chinese to pitch in. It includes both professional intelligence officers in clandestine operations (see Chung Dongfan below and Mak Chi in chapter 6) and Chinese state-owned enterprises running their own operations.

Beijing Dabeinong Technology Group
(大北农集团/北京大北农生物技术有限公司)

The Beijing Dabeinong Technology Group (DBN Group) and its subsidiary Kings Nower Seed Company were implicated in the theft of several strands of inbred seed lines from Monsanto, Pioneer, and LG Seeds. At least some of the indicted individuals were investigated under the Foreign Intelligence Surveillance Act (FISA), suggesting the FBI presented evidence to the FISA court that linked the DBN Group directly to the Chinese state. A Chinese government investment fund owned a 1.08 percent stake in the publicly listed company, according to an affidavit authored by a scholar at the University of Iowa, and the company also has the Chinese Communist Party (CCP) committee as part of its governance structure. In 2012 the DBN Group received a government grant to support research into a corn-focused genetic engineering project.[3] The company's website claims it has more than 18,000 employees and 67 subsidiaries; it is headquartered in the Haidian district of Beijing at Number 2 Yuanmingyuan West Road.[4]

Cai Bo (arrested 2013, pleaded guilty 2014) and
Cai Wentong (arrested 2014, pleaded guilty 2014)

Cai Bo was a Chinese national working at an unnamed PRC-based technology company. He and his cousin Cai Wentong, a Chinese national doing graduate studies at Iowa State University, attempted to export a controlled sensor with military applications from the United States to China. The angular rate sensors that the Cai cousins tried to acquire are used for line-of-sight stabilization and precision motion control systems. Cai Bo wanted to acquire the sensors on behalf of a Chinese client and contacted his cousin Cai Wentong to make inquiries. This put him in contact with an undercover federal agent who arranged for a December 2013 meeting in New Mexico with both of the cousins. In addition to the transfer of a sensor into the Cais' hands, the meeting was used to plot how to smuggle the sensors to China and was used as the basis for the charges against the Cais.[5] Cai Bo was sentenced to two years in prison and deportation following his release.[6]

Capener, Janice Kuang
(arrested 2012, pleaded guilty 2014)

Janice Kuang Capener was a Chinese national and employee at the Ningbo, Zhejiang, facility of a Utah-based irrigation company who stole trade secrets from her firm for Chinese competitors. Capener worked for Orbit Irrigation Products between 2003 and 2009—including as chief of operations for the company's manufacturing plant in China—and stole sales and pricing information to help her own company, Sunhills International LLC, and Zhejiang Hongchen Irrigation Equipment Company. They intended to undermine Orbit's market position based on the illegally gained knowledge of the company's pricing structures. Initially, a second Chinese national, Luo Jun, faced charges, but they were dismissed in 2012 shortly after the indictment was unsealed. In 2014, Capener was sentenced to 90 days in prison, 2 years of supervised release, and a $3,000 fine.[7]

Chan Kwan-chun "Jenny"
(arrested 2004, pleaded guilty 2005)

Chan Kwan-chun was a naturalized U.S. citizen and the controller of Manten Electronics, a New Jersey company that shipped approximately $400,000 worth of military-grade electronics to China without the required export license between 2003 and 2004. She is the wife of Chen Haoli (also known as Ali Chan). The electronic components shipped to Chinese research institutes played important roles within a variety of defense systems ranging from electronic warfare to missiles. Chan was sentenced to six months of home confinement as part of a two-year probation. Manten also forfeited the revenue from the illegal sales.[8]

Chang Huanling "Alice" (pleaded guilty 2014)

Chang Huanling was a Taiwanese national who attempted to export crystal methamphetamine from Taiwan to the United States and subsequently asked undercover FBI agents about the possibility of acquiring sensitive defense technology on behalf of a Chinese intelligence service. Chang's partner in this endeavor was Shen Huisheng. In a series of conversations beginning in 2012, Shen and Chang sought to acquire information on the E-2 Hawkeye reconnaissance aircraft, the stealth technology used in the F-22, missile engine technology, and unmanned aerial vehicles. The two sent the undercover agents a codebook to protect their communications and set up a Hong Kong bank account to handle related transactions.[9] In 2015 Chang was sentenced to time served and a $200 special assessment.[10]

Chang York-Yuan
(arrested 2010, suspended sentence 2010)

Chang York-Yuan (also known as David Zhang) was a naturalized U.S. citizen and businessman who attempted to transfer restricted defense technology to a research institute affiliated with the giant Chinese state-owned China Electronics Technology Group Corporation (CETC). Chang and his wife, Huang Leping, were co-owners of General Technology Systems Integration, Inc. (GTSI), based in Ontario, California. In 2009 GTSI entered into contracts with the Sichuan Institute of Solid-State Circuits— also known as the CETC Twenty-fourth Research Institute—to design and export two kinds of high-performance analog-to-digital converters. Under Chang and Huang's direction, GTSI hired two engineers to work on this project. Huang and Chang both separately lied to federal agents, telling them that this project had been cancelled after the two engineers were contacted by federal authorities in relation to the legality of the project, which would have required valid export licenses because the converters had national security applications.[11] Chang was sentenced to five years of probation.[12]

Chao Tah-wei (arrested 2008, pleaded guilty 2009)

Chao Tah-wei was a Chinese national and Beijing resident who attempted to export thermal-imaging cameras illegally to China. Chao and his coconspirator Guo Zhiyong were arrested at Los Angeles International Airport with a total of ten export-controlled, thermal-imaging cameras, manufactured by FLIR Systems, hidden in their luggage. Chao also shipped three similar cameras to Guo in October 2007 for which he earned a $900 commission. The ultimate consignees were the Ministry of Public Security (MPS) and the People's Armed Police. Chao pleaded guilty and was sentenced to twenty months' imprisonment.[13]

Chao Tze (indicted 2012, pleaded guilty 2012)

Chao Tze, a scientist at DuPont from 1966 to 2002, provided his former company's proprietary information as part of his consulting work for the Chinese firm Pangang Group. Chao began consulting for Pangang Group in 2003. Also, see Walter Liew.

Chen Haoli (arrested 2004, pleaded guilty 2005)

Chen Haoli (also known as Ali Chan), the husband of Chan Kwan-chun, was implicated in Manten Electronics' export control violations. Chen was sentenced to thirty months in prison followed by two years of supervised release.[14] Also, see Chan Kwan-chun "Jenny."

Chen Xiuling "Linda" (arrested 2004, pleaded guilty 2005)

Chen, a naturalized U.S. citizen and the spouse of Xu Weibo, was the purchasing agent of Manten Electronics. For conspiracy to violate U.S. export control laws, Chen was sentenced to eighteen months in prison followed by two years of supervised release.[15] Also, see Chan Kwan-chun "Jenny."

Cheng, George K. (arrested 1998, convicted 1999)

George Cheng was a Taiwanese national and U.S. permanent resident who shipped military equipment illegally to China in the 1990s. Cheng operated Telecomp Materials Recycling, a scrap metal company in New York. Prior to his arrest in 1998, U.S. authorities warned him several times as early as 1991 about possible export control violations. The military equipment he was charged with attempting to export without a license included navigational systems for the F-117 stealth fighter, thirty-five components for the navigational system of the F-111 fighter/bomber, tubes for the Navy's electronic warfare jamming devices, and hundreds of spare parts for M-16 and M-41 combat tanks.[16] In 1999 a federal court sentenced Cheng to two years in prison.

Cheng, Philip (indicted 2004, pleaded guilty 2006)

Philip Cheng, in collaboration with Martin Shih, attempted to circumvent export controls on night vision equipment for military use by establishing a company, SPCTEK, to hide their activities. The pair tried to manufacture the night vision equipment made by Shih's company, Night Vision Technology, in China. An informant tipped off U.S. authorities that Cheng and Shih would submit false end user documents claiming Taiwan as the destination while diverting the night vision cameras to China. Shih died of cancer before trial. Cheng was sentenced to two years in jail with a $50,000 fine.[17] Also see Shih, Martin.

Cheng Yongqing (arrested 2001, pleaded guilty 2005)

Cheng Yongqing, a naturalized U.S. citizen and vice president of Village Networks, conspired with Lin Hai and Xu Kai to steal proprietary software from Lucent Technologies. Specifically, Cheng and his coconspirators attempted to acquire switching software associated with Lucent's PathStar Access Server. The three men were starting their own company, ComTriad Technologies, in partnership with Datang Telecommunication Technology Industry Group, and they received between $500,000 and $1.2 million in startup capital from their Chinese partner. Cheng, Lin, and Xu originally sought venture capital financing in the United States but approached Datang after their U.S. interlocutors asked to see the product specifications based on the stolen Lucent software. In April 2001 the three electronically transferred their modifications on the Lucent PathStar software to China, presumably to Datang.[18] Cheng and Xu Kai avoided prison time as part of their plea agreement in 2005, but ComTriad paid a $250,000 fine.[19]

China Association for International Exchange of Personnel
(中国国际人才交流协会)

See the State Administration of Foreign Experts Affairs (SAFEA).

China Electronics Technology Group Corporation
(中国电子科技集团公司)

The China Electronics Technology Group Corporation (CETC) is one of China's leading defense industrial groups, overseeing a vast network of 150,000 employees, 18 state key laboratories, and 14 provincial- or ministerial-level key laboratories distributed across 18 provinces. CETC was formed in 2002 out of the research laboratories and enterprises administered by the now-defunct Ministry of Information Industries.[20] Three of CETC's research institutes—but not the organization as a whole—are on the U.S. Entity List for organizations that require additional licensing procedures to trade in specified items in the United States or with U.S. companies: the Fifty-fourth Research Institute in Shijiazhuang (also known as the Communication, Telemetry, and Telecontrol Research Institute), the Twenty-ninth Research Institute in Chengdu (also known as the Southwest Research Institute of Electronics Technology), and the Eleventh Research Institute in Beijing (also known as the North China Research Institute of Electro-Optics). All three research institutes and their subsidiaries have "presumption of denial" listed as their policy review guidance.[21]

China General Nuclear Power Group
(中国广核集团)

The China General Nuclear Power Group (CGNPG), formerly known as the China Guangdong Nuclear Power Company (CGNPC), is one of China's two major nuclear power companies. As a state-owned enterprise, CGNPG is administered by the State-owned Assets Supervision and Administration Commission. In addition to the company's nuclear energy business, CGNPG also operates wind, hydro, and solar power facilities. In 2016, the company and Allen Ho, an American nuclear engineer, were charged in U.S. courts for "conspiracy to unlawfully engage and participate in the production and development of special nuclear material outside the United States, without the required authorization from the U.S. Department of Energy." Conviction occurred in 2017.[22]

China International Talent Exchange Foundation
(中国国际人才交流基金会)

See the State Administration of Foreign Experts Affairs (SAFEA).

Chung, Dongfan "Greg" (arrested 2008, convicted 2009)

Dongfan "Greg" Chung, an aerospace engineer at Rockwell International (1973–96) and Boeing (1996–2006), was convicted of passing trade secrets related to the space shuttle, the C-17 military transport aircraft, and the Delta IV rocket. The indictment against him alleged Chung may have passed information related to the B-1 bomber. He held a secret clearance at the time of his arrest. Chung's motivation largely was to assist his home country, and he started receiving letters from officials in the Chinese aviation industry as early as 1979.[23] Chung was convicted in 2009 and sentenced to fifteen years in prison for passing trade secrets to assist the Chinese aviation industry. The investigative lead developed out of the Chi Mak case (see Mak, Chi, chapter 6), because an official from the Chinese Ministry of Aviation requested Chung pass his communications and materials through Mak's wife in the late 1980s. Chung's name was found on documents found in the Mak family residence.[24]

Datang Telecommunication Technology Industry Group
(大唐电信科技产业集团)

Datang Telecommunication is one of China's largest telecommunications equipment manufacturers alongside such companies as Huawei and ZTE. Datang is most known for its development of TD-SCDMA, an alternative Chinese standard for 3G mobile phones used by China Mobile, and TD-LTE, an alternative 4G standard. Datang benefitted from stolen switching software from Lucent Technology in 2000, but no evidence appeared in the legal proceedings against Cheng Yongqing, Lin Hai, and Xu Kai to suggest Datang knew it was receiving stolen software.[25]

Ding Zhengxing (arrested 2008, sentenced 2009)

Ding Zhengxing attempted to purchase and illegally export amplifiers that are export-controlled for military purposes (for digital radios and wireless area networks). Ding and his colleague Yang Su were arrested in Saipan, where they planned to take possession of the purchased amplifiers. A third person, Peter Zhu of Shanghai Meuro Electronics Company, was not caught. Ding was sentenced to forty-six months in prison after pleading guilty.[26]

Dorfman, Michael (pleaded guilty 2006)

Michael Dorfman was the son of Yale Dorfman and an employee of State Metal Industries. For his role in helping his father sell U.S. military components to China, he pleaded guilty to making false statements to the Department of Defense.[27] Also, see Yale Dorfman.

Dorfman, Yale (pleaded guilty 2006)

Yale Dorfman, the co-owner of State Metal Industries, attempted to export missile components that his company acquired through a contract with the U.S. Department of Defense. State Metal Industries had a contract from April 2003 with the Defense Department to smelt down surplus military equipment, including components of the AIM-7 Sparrow air-to-air missile. Dorfman hid AIM-7 components, including the radar guidance system, among other metal scrap in a cargo container bound for China.[28]

Du Shanshan (indicted 2010, convicted 2012)

Du Shanshan was an engineer at General Motors (GM) from 2000 to 2005 who stole company documents related to hybrid vehicles. GM later valued at roughly $40 million the thousands of pages of stolen documents that Du had emailed herself or backed up on a hard drive. She relayed the information to the company, Millennium Technology International, that she owned with her husband, Qin Yu. Qin then approached China's Chery Automobile to sell GM's research and engineering work on hybrid vehicles, and they pitched Chery on a joint venture to build hybrid cars.[29] Du was convicted for unauthorized possession of trade secrets and conspiracy and sentenced to one year in prison.[30]

Frank, Desmond Dinesh (arrested 2007, pleaded guilty 2008)

Desmond Dinesh Frank was a Malaysian freight forwarder based in Penang, Malaysia, who attempted to export controlled technologies (training equipment for the C-130 military transport aircraft) through his company, Asian Sky Support. He was also involved in money laundering and export violations related to Iran.[31] Frank was sentenced to twenty-three months in prison after pleading guilty in 2008.[32]

Ge Yuefei (arrested 2006, acquitted 2009)

Ge, a Chinese national, was an engineer at NetLogic Microsystems who stole proprietary chip technology to establish a business in China with Lee Lan. The pair stole circuit designs from NetLogic and Taiwan's Semiconductor Manufacturing Company to start a business backed by Beijing Electronic Development Company, which had links to the Chinese military.[33] Ge and Lee also reportedly planned to acquire funding dispersed through the 863 Program.[34] The federal jury deadlocked on the charges that the two stole trade secrets from NetLogic and acquitted them in 2009 on charges of stealing from Semiconductor Manufacturing Company.[35] Also, see Lee Lan.

Gormley, Timothy (pleaded guilty 2012)

Timothy Gormley was an export control manager at AR Worldwide who altered invoices and shipping documents to conceal the classification of microwave amplifiers manufactured and sold by his company. Gormley also listed false license numbers and lied to colleagues about the existence and status of export licenses. His behavior allowed more than fifty microwave amplifiers to be shipped to consignees in China, Hong Kong, Taiwan, Thailand, Russia, and other locations between 2006 and 2011. The consignees and end users remain unnamed. Microwave amplifiers can be used in weapons guidance systems and electronic warfare systems, including radar jammers. Gormley claimed to be "too busy" to apply for and properly manage export control licenses. In 2013 he was sentenced to forty-two months in prison.[36]

Gowadia, Noshir (arrested 2005, convicted 2010)

Noshir Gowadia, an Indian American and former Northrup Grumman engineer from 1967 to 1986, sold information about low observable (LO) technologies to China. Specifically, Gowadia helped design and create testing systems for a low signature, infrared-suppressing exhaust system for cruise missiles, based on the knowledge he developed working on the propulsion of the B-2 stealth bomber. At the time of his arrest, he had received roughly $80,000 of the $400,000 he expected for his services to the Chinese government, and he told the FBI that "at that time I knew it was wrong and I did it for the money."[37] From 2003 to 2005 Gowadia made six trips to China to consult on his infrared-suppressing exhaust system and to design test software to evaluate the cruise missile's performance against U.S. equipment. The State Administration of Foreign Experts Affairs arranged the visits and introduced Gowadia to the Chinese weapons engineers with whom he developed the missile.[38] A jury found him guilty in 2010 on charges relating to providing classified information to a foreign government, export control violations, and filing false tax returns. In January 2011 the court sentenced Gowadia to thirty-two years in prison.[39]

Gu Chunhui (indicted 2014)

Gu Chunhui (顾春晖) is one of five members of the Chinese signals intelligence unit (Unit 61398) indicted by the U.S. Department of Justice in May 2014. Gu managed domain accounts used to enable computer network operations and tested spear-phishing emails that would be used in targeting U.S. and other foreign companies.[40] Also see Huang Zhenyu, Sun Kailiang, Wang Dong, and Wen Xinyu.

Guo Zhiyong (arrested 2008, convicted 2009)

Guo Zhiyong, an engineer and a managing director at an unnamed Beijing electronics firm, attempted to acquire thermal-imaging cameras for his company's clients. Guo and his coconspirator Chao Tah-wei were arrested at Los Angeles International Airport with a total of ten export-controlled, thermal-imaging cameras, manufactured by FLIR Systems, hidden in their luggage. The cameras were intended for clients of Guo's technology firm, namely the MPS and the People's Armed Police.[41] Guo was convicted in a trial and was sentenced to five years in prison.[42]

Hanson, Harold Dewitt, and Yaming Nina Qi Hanson (arrested 2009, pleaded guilty 2009)

Yaming Nina Qi Hanson was a naturalized U.S. citizen who transported UAV autopilots to a Chinese aerospace firm. Although she lived in the United States and at overseas U.S. facilities where her husband was employed, Mrs. Hanson owned two properties in China and maintained close connections to family and former classmates there.[43] In 2008 the Hansons collaborated to import UAV autopilot devices from a Canadian company, MicroPilot, to the United States. As part of the import process, the Hansons signed an agreement with MicroPilot that they would only export the autopilots if they received approved U.S. government export licenses. Mr. Hanson reported the shipment missing in July 2008, but MicroPilot received a request in August for technical support on the autopilots from a Chinese company, presumably Xi'an Xiangyu Aviation Technical Group (西安翔宇航空科技股份有限公司), part of the Aviation Industry Corporation of China (中国航空工业集团公司) family of companies. MicroPilot alerted Canadian and U.S. authorities in October to a possible export control violation, because Mr. Hanson told MicroPilot that the autopilots were intended incongruously for a civilian model airplane club.[44] The devices had not gone missing; Mrs. Hanson had hand-delivered the autopilots in China without an export license. She told federal law enforcement that several former classmates provided $75,000 to purchase the MicroPilot parts; however, Yu Fang, president of Xi'an Xiangyu Aviation Technical Group, provided at least that amount toward the total purchase of approximately $90,000.[45] In November 2009 Mrs. Hanson pleaded guilty to making false statements, and the court sentenced her to time served. In November 2009, Mr. Hanson pleaded guilty to making false statements, and in February 2010 the court sentenced him to two years in prison.[46]

He, Philip Chaohui (indicted 2011, pleaded guilty 2013)

Philip Chaohui He, a Chinese national and former California Department of Transportation engineer, attempted to export radiation-hardened integrated circuits. He was caught at the port in Long Beach, California, with two hundred space-qualified and radiation-hardened circuits used in satellite communications systems concealed inside plastic infant formula containers. He arranged the purchase of the circuits through his company Sierra Electronic Instruments, and an unnamed Chinese coconspirator wired him roughly $490,000 toward the $549,654 total purchase. He presented the circuit manufacturer, Aeroflex, with false end user certificates that indicated the circuits would remain inside the United States. He also contacted Aeroflex under the alias "Philip Hope." A prior shipment of 112 circuits did go overseas to China, but the ultimate end user was unknown.[47] He was sentenced to three years in prison followed by three years of supervised release.[48]

Ho Szu-hsiung "Allen" (arrested 2016, sentenced 2017)

Ho Szu-hsiung, a naturalized U.S. citizen and nuclear engineer, was accused of helping a state-owned Chinese nuclear company develop and produce special nuclear material. Dr. Ho came to the United States in 1973 to attend the University of California, Berkeley, and earned a PhD in nuclear engineering from the University of Illinois in 1980. The indictment claimed that Ho provided illegal assistance to China General Nuclear Power Company (CGNPC) from 1997 to 2016 and enlisted half a dozen U.S.-based scientists to do the same.[49] Ho paid these scientists, including a senior executive at the Tennessee Valley Authority, to provide assistance to CGNPC, and he communicated the need for surreptitiousness to those he recruited. As a senior advisor to CGNPC and an owner of his own consulting firm, Energy Technology International, Ho told these still unnamed scientists that he had been tasked to gather U.S. nuclear expertise for CGNPC's programs. Specifically, he assisted the Chinese company's small modular reactor program (which are used primarily on submarines), advanced fuel assembly program, and fixed in-core detector system, and helped with verification and validation of nuclear reactor–related computer codes.[50] Ho was sentenced to twenty-four months in prison for violating the Atomic Energy Act in 2017.

Hou Shengdong (arrest warrant issued 2012)

Hou Shengdong was the vice director of the chloride-route titanium dioxide (TiO2) project department for the Pangang subsidiary Pangang Group Titanium Industry Company Ltd. Hou specifically requested Walter Liew and his company, USA Performance Technology Inc., provide proprietary DuPont blueprints for a TiO2 processing facility as a condition of working with the Pangang Group. An arrest warrant was issued in 2012 for the Chinese national, and Hou remains at large in China.[51] Also, see Walter Liew.

Hsu, You-Tsai "Eugene" (arrested 2001, sentenced 2002)

Naturalized U.S. citizen You-Tsai "Eugene" Hsu attempted to purchase sophisticated encryption devices used by the U.S. government and export them to China. He contacted Mykotronx, the manufacturer of encryption devices used to secure phone and fax transmissions, to inquire about the price of each unit. The Mykotronx device, KIV-7HS, was on the U.S. Munitions List and required approval from the National Security Agency for export.[52] The Columbia, Maryland–based company contacted federal law enforcement, which provided an undercover agent as an intermediary for Hsu. When the agent informed Hsu that the encryption devices were export controlled, Hsu proposed repackaging and disguising them for unlicensed export. His partner, David Tzu-Wei Yang, owned a freight forwarding business in California, and Hsu arranged for Yang to take possession and ship them via a Singaporean cutout to China.[53] Hsu received two concurrent forty-one-month prison sentences for his role in the conspiracy.[54]

Hsy, Howard (arrested 2003, pleaded guilty 2005)

Howard Hsy was a dual U.S.-Taiwanese citizen and former Boeing engineer who exported night vision equipment to China via an intermediary in Taiwan. Taiwan's Ministry of Justice Investigation Bureau arrested Hsy in 2003 and kept him under house arrest until his extradition to the United

States for his connection to an espionage case involving Yeh Yu-chen and Chen Shih-liang.[55] Hsy came to the attention of U.S. authorities in 2003 for his illegal export of plastic optical filters suitable for night vision lighting, night vision goggles with helmet mounts for fixed-wing and rotary aircraft, and liquid crystal displays that can be integrated into avionics.[56] Hsy and Donald Shull used forged documents to purchase night vision equipment that was shipped to an Auburn, Washington–based company that one of them owned before being transferred to China via Taiwan. The two men may have believed that the Taiwan connection was the end user.[57] In March 2006 Hsy was sentenced to two years of probation and fined $15,000.[58]

Hu Qiang (arrested 2012, pleaded guilty 2013)

Hu Qiang is a Chinese national and Shanghai resident who conspired to export dual-use pressure transducers from the United States to China. Hu, sometimes known as Johnson Hu, was the Shanghai sales manager for a subsidiary of MKS Instruments, an Andover, Massachusetts, company that manufactured the pressure transducers. The devices are controlled for export because they can be used in centrifuge cascades. Hu and his coconspirators allegedly obtained export licenses for thousands of trans-ducers, worth $6.5 million, to unauthorized end users in China by obtain-ing fraudulent end use certificates for existing MKS customers. They also used front companies to hide ultimate destinations and end use. In 2014 Hu was sentenced to thirty-four months in prison.[59]

Huang Jili (arrested 2012, pleaded guilty 2013)

Huang Jili was the chief executive officer of Ningbo Oriental Crafts Ltd. who conspired with one of his employees, Qi Xiaoguang, to steal cellular glass insulation. Huang and Qi attempted to purchase the formulas and manufacturing processes for FoamGlas from an employee at Pittsburg Corning for $100,000. The court ruled that the intended loss to Pittsburg Corning was more than $7 million, including the research, development, and protection of the proprietary information related to FoamGlas. The person whom Huang and Qi attempted to pay to break in to Pittsburg Corning's engineering department and steal this information was coop-erating with federal authorities. After an agreement was reached and the three met for a second time to exchange money and documents, the FBI arrested Huang and Qi. Huang was sentenced to 18 months in prison without parole and fined $250,000.[60] Also see Qi Xiaoguang.

Huang Kexue (pleaded guilty 2011)

Huang Kexue, a naturalized U.S. citizen who was a research scientist at a Dow Chemical lab in Indiana, stole company secrets in an effort to start his own company in China.[61] Prior to being fired in 2008, Huang had started sharing Dow Chemical intellectual property with Chinese researchers, and he obtained research grants to further his research at Hunan Normal University. Huang intended to develop and produce pesticides to compete with Dow Chemical inside China. After his dismissal from Dow Chemical, Huang worked at Cargill where he also stole details about enzymes used to make food products. Prosecutors estimated the intellectual property loss between $7 million and $20 million.[62] Huang pleaded guilty and was sentenced to eighty-seven months in prison and three years of supervised release.[63]

Huang Leping "Nicole"
(arrested 2010, suspended sentence 2010)

Huang Leping, a Chinese national and a businesswoman, attempted to transfer restricted defense technology to a research institute affiliated with a Chinese state-owned firm, the China Electronics Technology Group Corporation (CETC). Huang and her husband, Chang York-Yuan, were co-owners of General Technology Systems Integration, Inc. (GTSI), based in Ontario, California. In 2009 GTSI entered into contracts with the Sichuan Institute of Solid-State Circuits—also known as the CETC Twenty-fourth Research Institute—to design and export two kinds of high-performance analog-to-digital converters. Under Huang and Chang's direction, GTSI hired two engineers to work on this project. Huang and Chang both separately lied to federal agents, telling them that this project had been cancelled after the two engineers were contacted by federal authorities in relation to the legality of the project, which would have required valid export licenses because the converters have national security applications.[64] According to U.S. Commerce Department documents, Huang also advised the hired engineers and other GTSI employees on ways to communicate discreetly about the project, such as using personal rather than work email addresses as well as code words for the converters and the client.[65] Also, see Chang York-Yuan.

Huang Zhenyu (indicted 2014)

Huang Zhenyu (黄振宇) is one of the five members of the Chinese signals intelligence unit (Unit 61398) indicted by the U.S. Department of Justice in May 2014. Huang registered and managed domain accounts that other officers of Unit 61398 used to hack into U.S. companies. The unit also assigned him to create a database for intelligence on the iron and steel industries, including information taken from U.S. companies.[66] Also see Gu Chunhui, Sun Kailiang, Wang Dong, and Wen Xinyu.

Jiang, Qingchang "Frank" (arrested 2003, convicted 2005)

Qingchang "Frank" Jiang was president of EHI Group USA Inc./Araj Electronics and attempted to export microwave amplifiers to the Fifty-fourth Research Institute, also known as the Communication, Telemetry, and Telecontrol Research Institute.[67] This institute is affiliated with the China Electronics Technology Group (中国电子科技集团公司) and is involved primarily with missile-, signals intelligence–, and telecommunications-related technologies, according to the institute's website.[68] In spring 2002 Jiang purchased nine microwave amplifiers and shipped four to the Hebei Far-East Harris Company, which shared an address with the Fifty-fourth Research Institute. In 2005 Jiang was acquitted of export control violations—the government could not prove he knowingly circumvented export regulations—but was convicted on making false statements.[69]

Jin Hanjuan (arrested 2007, convicted 2012)

Jin Hanjuan was a naturalized U.S. citizen and software engineer at Motorola who attempted to start her own company in China with stolen company intellectual property. Jin was arrested at Chicago O'Hare International Airport in February 2007 with a one-way ticket to China, $31,000 in cash, and hundreds of Motorola documents stored electronically. Jin had worked at Motorola for nine years. Before her planned departure from the United

States, she had been working for the Chinese telecommunications firm Sun Kaisens, which develops some products for the People's Liberation Army (PLA).[70] In 2006 and 2007 Jin was on prolonged medical leave from Motorola and spent a great of time in China, where she started working with Sun Kaisens on projects for the PLA.[71] Also in Jin's possession was a set of PLA documents describing requirements for future telecommunications projects.[72] She was sentenced to four years in prison, and the sentence was upheld on appeal.[73]

Karabasevic, Dejan (arrested 2011, convicted 2011)

Dejan Karabasevic was an engineer at the American Superconductor Corporation (AMSC) who helped the company's Chinese customer, Sinovel, steal its software for operating wind turbines. Two Sinovel employees, Su Liying and Zhao Haichun, recruited Karabasevic in spring 2011 to provide AMSC's proprietary software in exchange for a six-year, $1.7 million contract and promises of "all the human contact" he could want.[74] The theft of AMSC's software was discovered when its employees working on malfunctioning Sinovel wind turbines discovered they were running on outdated and pirated AMSC software.[75] In 2011 Karabasevic was sentenced to one year in jail and two years' probation.

Kuok Chi-Tong (arrested 2009, convicted 2010)

Kuok Chi-Tong of Macau is a businessman who attempted to acquire global positioning system (GPS) devices used by the North Atlantic Treaty Organization and the U.S. military as well as military communications–related equipment. Kuok told investigators, according to *Wired*, that he had been "acting at the direction of officials for the People's Republic of China."[76] Beginning in 2006 Kuok started contacting individuals in and around U.S. defense industries, and a tip from a British company raised Kuok's profile with U.S. law enforcement.[77] The items Kuok sought ranged from GPS devices with anti-spoofing features to software used to secure satellite communications from military aircraft to encryption technology developed under contract to the U.S. National Security Agency. He also specifically sought encryption devices that enable communications with the U.S. Department of Defense's classified networks, such as the Secret

Internet Protocol Router Network.[78] Kuok was arrested at Hartsfield-Jackson International Airport in Atlanta in 2009 while transiting to a supposed meeting in Panama with undercover agents. He was convicted in 2010 in a jury trial, but two of the four counts on which he was convicted were overturned in 2012 by the Ninth Circuit Court of Appeals, which accepted Kuok's defense that he committed these export violations under duress.[79] After starting a company in 2000, Kuok met and assisted a Chinese cultural official, "Zheng Kung-Pen," in acquiring items from abroad that could not normally be purchased in China. The opinion recorded Kuok's counsel stating that "what started out as a friendly relationship turned serious at one business dinner, when Zheng—after encouraging Kuok to drink to excess—pressured Kuok into signing a note promising to locate and purchase certain items that could not be obtained in China." Kuok later tried to back out, but Zheng implied threats against Kuok's family and regularly provided Kuok with surveillance photos of Kuok with his family. In 2002 Zheng explained that others were being asked to do what Kuok was doing and told him that his family would be thrown in a "black jail"—an off-the-books detention facility—if he stopped cooperating. In 2005 Kuok asked Zheng to let him off after he learned he could be violating U.S. export laws, and in 2007 Kuok asked again because he developed a tumor. Each time Zheng refused, keeping the pressure on Kuok to acquire technology overseas illegally.[80]

Lau Hing-Shing "Victor" (indicted 2009, pleaded guilty 2012)

Lau Hing-Shing is a Hong Kong resident who attempted to ship export-controlled thermal-imaging devices from the United States to Hong Kong. Specifically, Lau tried to purchase twelve infrared thermal-imaging devices for export to China and Hong Kong and transferred nearly $40,000 to the United States in partial payment. These thermal imagers had a variety of potential military uses, such as unmanned vehicle payloads, weapon sights, and security and surveillance products. Lau was arrested at Toronto International Airport in 2009 when he traveled to take possession of the imagers and was later extradited to the United States. He was sentenced to ten months in prison followed by two years of supervised release.[81]

Lee, Charles Yu-Hsu (arrested 2008, pleaded guilty 2010)

Charles Yu-Hsu Lee was a naturalized U.S. citizen from Taiwan who shipped ten thermal-imaging cameras illegally to Shanghai between 2002 and 2007. Charles Lee purchased the $9,500 cameras and provided them to his uncle, Sam Ching-Sheng Lee, for shipment to China. Lee was informed at the time of purchase that these thermal-imaging cameras could not be exported without a license. In 2010 Charles Lee was sentenced to six days in prison and fined $3,000.[82]

Lee Lan (arrested 2006, acquitted 2009)

Lee Lan (also known as Li Lan) was a U.S. citizen and engineer at NetLogic Microsystems who stole proprietary chip technology to set up a business in China with Ge Yuefei. The two stole chip designs from NetLogic and Taiwan's Semiconductor Manufacturing Company to start a business backed by a firm, Beijing Electronic Development Company, with links to the Chinese military.[83] Lee and Ge also reportedly planned to acquire funding dispersed through the 863 Program.[84] The federal jury deadlocked on the charges that the two stole trade secrets from NetLogic and acquitted them on charges of stealing from Semiconductor Manufacturing Company in 2009.[85] Also, see Ge Yuefei.

Lee, Peter (arrested 1997, pleaded guilty 1997)

Peter Lee was a naturalized Taiwanese and U.S. citizen who revealed classified information about nuclear weapon design to Chinese scientists in 1985 and about submarine detection in 1997 while on trips to China. During the 1980s and 1990s, Dr. Lee first worked at the Los Alamos National Laboratory and then at defense contractor TRW. He first came to the FBI's attention in 1982, and the Los Angeles Field Office opened a second case on him in 1991.[86] In 1985 Lee met with a Chinese scientist in his Beijing hotel room and answered questions about a diagram related to nuclear weapon design. The next day, Lee was taken to a conference where for at least two hours he spoke and responded to questions related to similar diagrams and his own design work. In 1997 Dr. Lee traveled to China at the invitation and expense of the Institute of Applied Physics and Computational Mathematics, one of China's leading defense labs. He delivered two presentations for Chinese scientists on his classified U.S. Navy work related to submarine detection. Because of his work for TRW and his top secret clearance, he was required to file a travel report and fill out a post-travel questionnaire. During follow-up interviews with the FBI in August 1997, Lee admitted that he provided classified information to Chinese scientists in 1985 and lied on his travel forms about his Chinese contacts, his activities in China, and who paid for the trip. A federal court sentenced Lee to 1 year in a halfway house, 3 years of probation, 3,000 hours of community service, and a $20,000 fine after he pleaded guilty.[87]

Lee, Sam Ching-Sheng
(arrested 2008, pleaded guilty 2010)

Sam Ching-Sheng Lee was a naturalized U.S. citizen who shipped ten thermal-imaging cameras illegally to Shanghai between 2002 and 2007. He was part owner and chief operations manager of Multimillion Business Associate Corporation, through which the cameras were shipped abroad. Lee was assisted by his nephew Charles Lee. While his nephew purchased the $9,500 cameras, Sam Lee found customers in Shanghai and arranged the shipments. At least one alleged Chinese customer had plans to bring their own thermal-imaging and night vision equipment to market, suggesting the customer intended to reverse engineer the camera that the Lees provided. In 2011 Sam Lee was sentenced to twelve months in prison and fined $10,000.[88]

Li Li "Lea" (arrested 2010, pleaded guilty 2011)

Li Li, the vice president of Beijing Starcreates Space Science and Technology Development Company Limited, attempted to export computer chips that were classified as defense articles on the U.S. Munitions List. Under the U.S. arms embargo placed on China in 1990, such articles cannot be exported to China. Li and her boss, Xian Hongwei, were arrested in Hungary in 2010 and extradited to the United States in spring 2011. The two attempted to acquire radiation-hardened programmable read-only memory microchips (PROMs), which store the initial start-up program for a computer system and are built to withstand the conditions present in outer space. Li and Xian intended to order thousands of these PROMs, suggesting production-level quantities, and planned to break up the purchases into smaller shipments to multiple countries to disguise the conspiracy. The intended end user was the China Aerospace Science and Technology Corporation, a state-owned company that develops and produces a range of missile-related technologies, launch vehicles, and spacecraft among other industrial products. Li was sentenced to twenty-four months in prison and spent seven months jailed in Hungary awaiting extradition.[89]

Li Qing (charged 2007, pleaded guilty 2008)

Li Qing was a Chinese national and U.S. permanent resident who attempted to acquire piezoresistive accelerometers for "a special agency, a scientific research institute in China."[90] Along with an unidentified coconspirator in China, Li attempted to purchase thirty 7270A-200K accelerometers from Endevco. These devices measure massive shocks, such as those caused by nuclear and chemical explosions, and have many military applications, including precision-guidance systems for bombs and missiles.[91] Li contacted Endevco about purchasing the accelerometers, but company representatives demurred. Suspicious that Li might attempt to export the devices, Endevco contacted federal law enforcement, and they launched a sting operation to draw out Li and her coconspirator. The coconspirator promised that if the first thirty accelerometers worked out, the undercover agents should expect more and larger orders.[92] Li pleaded guilty in 2008 and was sentenced to one year and one day in prison, three years of supervised release, and a fine of $7,500.[93]

Li Shaoming (stopped 2012)

Li Shaoming was the chief operating officer or the chief executive officer of the Kings Nower Seed Company, a subsidiary of Beijing Dabeinong Technology Group.[94] Li was stopped and searched alongside his colleague and coconspirator Ye Jian in 2012, and U.S. authorities seized dozens of corn seed packets hidden in microwave popcorn packets. Neither man was arrested to preserve the continuing investigation into corn seed theft and Hailong "Robert" Mo.

Li, Terry Teng Fang (arrested 2004, pleaded guilty 2006)

Terry Teng Fang Li, a naturalized U.S. citizen from Taiwan and the president of Universal Technologies, Inc., sold electronic components to Chinese arms manufacturers.[95] Li was sentenced to one year of probation, and the court ordered Universal Technologies to cease its operations.[96]

Li Yuan (pleaded guilty 2012)

Li Yuan was a Chinese national working as a research chemist in the U.S. headquarters of the French pharmaceutical company Sanofi-Aventis who stole data on compounds for the benefit of a Chinese company. Li stole Sanofi-Aventis trade secrets, including research data that had not yet been patented, to sell on the website of Abby Pharmatech, a U.S.-based unit of Xiamen KAK Science and Technology Company. She had a 50 percent share in Abby Pharmatech. Li was sentenced to eighteen months in prison and ordered to pay $131,000 in restitution.[97]

Liang, Jason Jian (indicted 2010, pleaded guilty 2011)

Jason Jian Liang, a naturalized U.S. citizen and the owner of Sanwave International Corporation, exported more than sixty thermal-imaging cameras to China and Hong Kong. At least seven of the cameras were exported illegally, because low-light vision devices are considered defense articles and are banned for export to China. The cameras Liang exported illegally were manufactured by L-3 Communications Infrared Products. He was sentenced to forty-six months in prison and three years of supervised release in 2011.[98]

Liang Xiuwen "Jennifer" (arrested 2003, pleaded guilty 2003)

Liang Xiuwen, a co-owner of Maytone International, conspired with the help of her husband Zhuang Jinghua to export components for U.S. military aircraft and missiles. Specifically, Liang and Zhuang attempted to export F-14 Tomcat parts as well as components for the HAWK surface-to-air missile, TOW anti-tank missile, and AIM-9 Sidewinder air-to-air missile. At least one of the Chinese purchasers was believed to be in Shenyang.[99]

The two were caught in 2003 as part of lengthy undercover investigation into U.S. companies that offer defense articles over the Internet to foreign buyers. In 2005 Liang was sentenced to thirty months in prison and fined $6,000.[100]

Liew, Christina (indicted 2011)

Christina Liew (also known as Qiao Hong) and her husband Walter Liew were co-owners of USA Performance Technology Inc. She actively participated in her husband's attempt to sell DuPont trade secrets related to processing chloride-route titanium dioxide to the Chinese state-owned enterprise Pangang Group.[101] Also see Liew, Walter.

Liew, Walter (indicted 2011, convicted 2014)

Walter Liew (also known as Liu Xuanxuan) was the co-owner and president of USA Performance Technology Inc. who stole DuPont trade secrets for the Chinese state-owned enterprise Pangang Group and its subsidiaries. Liew and his coconspirators—his wife Christina Liew, Robert Maegerle, and Hou Shengdong, as well as Chao Tze—succeeded in part in transferring DuPont's proprietary information on processing chloride-route titanium dioxide ($TiO2$), which is widely used as a white pigment. Mr. Liew discovered Beijing's interest in $TiO2$ during meetings with government officials in China during the early 1990s. He subsequently began assembling a group of former DuPont employees to acquire and eventually sell $TiO2$-related trade secrets to Chinese firms. A federal jury found Lieu guilty of violations of the Economic Espionage Act, tax evasion, bankruptcy fraud, and obstruction of justice in 2014, and he was sentenced to fifteen years in prison, forfeiture of $27.8 million in profits, and $511,667.82 in fines.[102]

Lin Hai (arrested 2001, fled abroad 2004)

Lin Hai was a Chinese national and U.S. permanent resident who conspired with Xu Kai and Cheng Yongqing to steal proprietary software from his employer, Lucent Technologies. Specifically, Cheng and his coconspirators attempted to acquire switching software associated with Lucent's PathStar Access Server. The three men were starting their own company,

ComTriad Technologies, in partnership with Datang Telecommunication Technology Industry Group, and they received between $500,000 and $1.2 million in startup capital from their Chinese partner. Cheng, Lin, and Xu originally sought venture capital financing in the United States but approached Datang after their U.S. interlocutors asked to see the product specifications based on the stolen Lucent software. In April 2001 the three transferred their modifications on the Lucent PathStar software to China electronically, presumably to Datang.[103] Sometime in 2004 while free on bail, Lin Hai fled the United States to avoid facing charges or prison time but lost out on the plea deal as a result.[104]

Lin Yong (indicted 2013)

Lin Yong was a Chinese national and a researcher for the Kings Nower Seed Company, a subsidiary of Beijing Dabeinong Technology Group. The FBI recorded a conversation with coconspirator Ye Jian in which both made statements that demonstrated they understood the theft of seeds was illegal and that they intended to smuggle the seeds past U.S. customs.[105] Also see Mo, Hailong "Robert."

Liu Sixing "Steve" (convicted 2012)

Liu Sixing was a Chinese national working at L-3 Communications, Space, and Navigation Division in New Jersey. Liu stole thousands of files from his employer that detailed the performance and design of guidance systems for missiles, rockets, target locators, and unmanned aerial vehicles. He intended to position himself for future employment in China, and he traveled there to deliver presentations at several universities, the Chinese Academy of Sciences, and government-organized conferences. L-3 trained Liu about U.S. export control laws and indicated that most company products were covered by those laws. Federal agents searched Liu's personal computer upon his return from a November 2010 trip to China and found the stolen files. In a follow-up interview, he lied to federal authorities about the nature of his defense work. A jury convicted Liu on arms control and economic espionage violations as well as lying to federal agents, and he was sentenced to seventy months in jail and three years of supervised release.[106]

Liu Wenchyu (arrested 2006, convicted 2011)

Liu Wenchyu (also known as David Liou) was a retired Dow Chemical Company research scientist who attempted to sell the company's trade secrets in China. Following Liu's retirement from Dow Chemical in 1992 after twenty-five years, he founded his own chemical company to manufacture and sell products similar to those of Dow. For example, Liu worked on the development and manufacture of elastomers, including Dow's widely used Tyrin chlorinated polyethylene (CPE), and he attempted to build the capacity to produce Tyrin CPE and other proprietary Dow compounds within his own company. To do so, he paid a Dow employee $50,000 for the company's production manual and other information about CPE manufacture. Dow's CPE compounds are used in automotive and industrial hoses, vinyl siding, and electrical cable jackets.[107] Liu recruited at least three other current and former Dow employees to assist him with acquiring proprietary CPE information, including relating to the establishment of a CPE manufacturing facility in China. He was sentenced to five years in prison, two years of supervised released, the forfeiture of $600,000, and a fine of $25,000 for perjuring himself in depositions and conspiracy to commit trade theft.[108]

Long Yu (arrested 2014, sentenced 2017)

Long Yu, a Chinese national with U.S. permanent residency and a senior engineer at the United Technologies Research Center, attempted to take the company's proprietary documents related to advanced titanium used in U.S. military aircraft. Long worked at the defense contractor from 2008 to May 2014, when he was let go because of a federal investigation into his activities. After he left United Technologies, Long went to China. On his return from China in August 2014, federal authorities searched his luggage at John F. Kennedy International Airport. They found registration documents for a new corporation in China and a mostly completed application for a job at a state-controlled aerospace research center.[109] The application form highlighted Long's experience with the F119 and F135 engines used in the F-22 and F-35, respectively. United Technologies is the parent company of Pratt and Whitney, which manufactures the F119 and F135 engines. When Long attempted to make a subsequent trip to China in November, his luggage contained the proprietary documents related to United Technologies' titanium processes. The documents bore warning markings that indicated they were proprietary and export controlled.[110] Yu was sentenced to two and a half years in prison after pleading guilty.

Lu Fu-Tain (arrested 2010, pleaded guilty 2011)

Lu Fu-Tain, the owner of Fushine Technology in Cupertino, California, sold microwave amplifiers to a Chinese company without proper export licenses. When Lu sold a microwave amplifier to Everjet Science and Technology Corporation in 2004, Fushine maintained a sales representative relationship with Miteq Components, which manufactures microwave and satellite communications components and subsystems. Later, Lu agreed to forfeit thirty-six additional microwave amplifiers that may have been intended for China. Company emails indicated that Lu and his subordinates knowingly obfuscated the recipients of these products and the need for an export license. In 2012 Lu was sentenced to fifteen months in prison, three years of supervised release, and a $5,000 fine.[111]

Maegerle, Robert (arrested 2012, convicted 2014)

Robert Maegerle worked as an engineer at DuPont from 1956 to 1991 and participated in Walter Liew's conspiracy to sell DuPont trade secrets related to processing chloride-route titanium dioxide (TiO2) to the Chinese state-owned enterprise Pangang Group.[112] He possessed detailed knowledge of TiO2-related technologies and setting up production lines, which he provided the Pangang Group alongside specific information about DuPont's TiO2 facility in Taiwan.[113] Also see Walter Liew.

Man, Wenxia "Wency" (arrested 2015, convicted 2016)

Wenxia "Wency" Man was a naturalized U.S. citizen and vice president of California-based AFM Microelectronics Corporation who attempted to acquire and export fighter jet engines and other defense articles. AFM Microelectronics had a Shenzhen office and reportedly had links to Xifei Aviation Components Company, an independent company that provided support to the People's Liberation Army's (PLA's) General Staff Department and General Armaments Department and the PLA Air Force.[114] Man conspired with Zhang Xinsheng, whom she described as a "technology spy" for the PLA who acquired foreign defense technology for domestic Chinese production. According to the U.S. Justice Department, Man and Zhang attempted to acquire and export the following defense articles and related technical data: Pratt and Whitney F135-PW-100 engines used in the F-35 Joint Strike Fighter; Pratt and Whitney F119-PW-100 turbofan engines used in the F-22 Raptor fighter jet; General Electric F110-GE-132 engines designed for the F-16 fighter jet; and the General Atomics MQ-9 Reaper/Predator B unmanned aerial vehicle.[115] The two thought to use either South Korea, Israel, or Hong Kong as the channel through which to disguise China as the ultimate end user.[116] In 2016 Man was sentenced to roughly four years in prison.[117] Also see Zhang Xinsheng.

Meng Hong (indicted 2009, pleaded guilty 2010)

Meng Hong was a Chinese national with U.S. permanent residency and former DuPont research scientist who attempted to steal the company's proprietary data to commercialize several projects with Beijing University (北京大学). Specifically, Meng stole files relating to organic light emitting diode (OLED) research, to which he had extensive access during his employment at DuPont beginning in 2002. Meng requested some of the files through official channels when offered his resignation in 2009. He told DuPont that he intended to take a job with DuPont China and that he needed the OLED files for background. The company denied him access. In a search of Meng's company-issued laptop, DuPont found that he copied roughly six hundred files onto an external storage device. The company also discovered that Meng had accepted a position with Beijing University's college of engineering without informing DuPont as he was obligated to do.[118] A federal court sentenced Meng to fourteen months in prison after he pleaded guilty in 2010.

Meng, Xiaodong "Sheldon" (charged 2006, pleaded guilty 2007)

Xiaodong "Sheldon" Meng was a software engineer at Quantum3D who stole sensitive motion simulation software to sell to the Chinese military as well as the Malaysian and Thai militaries. He was a naturalized Canadian citizen working for Quantum3D until spring 2003. The most important program, Mantis, simulated real-world motion, such as flight, for military training purposes, and Quantum3D executives described the program as the "crown jewel" of their company. This program and others stolen by Meng allow precision night training for fighter pilots.[119] Without authorization, Meng installed demo software at a PLA Navy research center. Meng was the first to be prosecuted under the Economic Espionage Act for providing assistance to a foreign government.[120]

Mo, Hailong "Robert" (arrested 2014, pleaded guilty 2016)

Hailong "Robert" Mo was a Chinese national with U.S. permanent residency who, alongside five associates, dug up corn seeds from an Iowa farm to send back to China. Mo, Wang Lei, and four other associates visited test plots owned by Pioneer, Monsanto, and LG Seeds across Illinois and Iowa to steal seeds. All but one of the men worked for Beijing Dabeinong Technology Group (or its subsidiaries), where Mo worked as director of international business. Mo and Wang were caught collecting seeds in Iowa in May 2011 by a Pioneer security guard and came to the attention of law enforcement.[121] Mo was arrested later at his home in Boca Raton, Florida.[122] In 2016 Mo pleaded guilty to conspiracy to steal agricultural trade secrets for breaching the intellectual property rights of Monsanto and DuPont.[123] He was sentenced to three years in prison and three years of supervised release and was ordered to forfeit some of his property. Also see Li Shaoming, Wang Lei, and Ye Jian.

Mo Yun (arrested 2014, charges dropped)

Mo Yun is the sister of Hailong "Robert" Mo and the spouse of Shao Genhuo, chief executive officer of the Beijing Dabeinong Technology Group. She was arrested in July 2014 and held with her brother under de facto house arrest in Des Moines, Iowa.[124] In 2007–8 Mo led a research division at Dabeinong, and her text messages around this time brought her into the conspiracy, but charges were ultimately dropped when the judge disallowed her text messages to be used as evidence.[125]

Moo, Ko-Suen "Bill"
(arrested 2005, pleaded guilty 2006)

Ko-Suen "Bill" Moo was a South Korean–born Taiwanese businessman who attempted to smuggle a variety of military, primarily aerospace, equipment to China along with Frenchman Maurice Serge Voros. They had attempted to acquire UH-60 Blackhawk engines, the AGM-129 cruise missile, the AIM-120 air-to-air missile, and the F110-GE-129 afterburning turbofan engine for the F-16.

Park, Kwonhwan "Howard" (arrested 2004)

Kwonhwan "Howard" Park was a South Korean who attempted to sell military hardware to China. Specifically, Park along with Sung-Ryul "Roger" Chun sought to purchase two helicopter engines from an unnamed Connecticut company and helmet-mounted night vision equipment. The latter was found in Park's luggage as he prepared to fly to China. He also attempted to falsify the end user certificates to suggest the Malaysian military was the purchaser, but the company from which he purchased the engines discovered no record of a transaction and alerted federal authorities.[126]

Piquet, Joseph (indicted 2008, sentenced 2009)

Joseph Piquet, the owner and president of AlphaTronX, attempted to purchase and illegally ship military electronic components to Hong Kong and China. AlphaTronX was a Florida-based company that produced electronic components, and it was initially named in the indictment before a court dismissed the charges against the company. Piquet conspired to purchase electronics, including power amplifiers used in early warning radar and missile target acquisition systems, from Northrop Grumman Corporation and export them to unknown Chinese end users. One customer or middleman was Thompson Tam, a director of the China-based Ontime Electronics Technology, who also was indicted. Piquet was convicted of seven export violations and sentenced to five years in prison followed by two years of supervised release.[127] Also see Tam, Thompson.

Qi Xiaoguang (arrested 2012, pleaded guilty 2013)

Qi Xiaoguang was an employee at Ningbo Oriental Crafts Ltd. who conspired with his boss, Huang Jili, to steal cellular glass insulation. Qi and Huang attempted to purchase the formulas and manufacturing processes for FoamGlas from an employee at Pittsburg Corning for $100,000. The court ruled that the potential loss to Pittsburg Corning was more than $7 million, including the research, development, and protection of the proprietary information related to FoamGlas. The person whom Qi and Huang attempted to pay to break in to Pittsburg Corning's engineering department and steal this information was cooperating with federal authorities. After an agreement was reached and the three met for a second time to exchange money and documents, the FBI arrested Qi and Huang. Qi was sentenced to time served and was fined $20,000.[128] Also see Huang Jili.

Qin Yu (indicted 2010, convicted 2012)

Qin Yu and his wife Du Shanshan were co-owners of Millennium Technology International, and they attempted to sell proprietary General Motors (GM) information to China-based Chery Automobile. Between 2003 and 2006, Du removed roughly $40 million worth of GM documentation on hybrid vehicles. Qin then approached Chery to sell GM's hybrid vehicle research and designs, and they pitched Chery on a joint venture to build hybrid cars.[129] Like his wife, Qin was convicted on unauthorized possession of trade secrets and conspiracy for the same. The court also convicted him on wire fraud and obstruction of justice, resulting in a three-year prison sentence.[130] Also see Du Shanshan.

Roth, John Reece (charged 2008, convicted 2008)

Dr. John Reece Roth was a professor emeritus at the University of Tennessee who illegally exported technologies and data related to unmanned aerial vehicles (UAVs). In addition to selling technical data relating to UAV-related plasma technology, Roth took controlled U.S. military data with him to China and emailed other related files to an individual in China. He also exported similar data to Iran. In 2009 a federal court sentenced Roth to four years in prison, two years of supervised release, and a $1,700 fine.[131]

Semiconductor Manufacturing International Corporation
(中芯国际集成电路制造有限公司)

The Shanghai-based Semiconductor Manufacturing International Corporation (SMIC) is one of the leading semiconductor foundries in the world, and the company is listed on both the Hong Kong and New York stock exchanges. In the 2000s Taiwan Semiconductor Manufacturing Company (TMSC) twice took SMIC to court in the United States for the theft of trade secrets. In 2004 TMSC filed a lawsuit in a California state court alleging SMIC stole trade secrets. The lawsuit alleged that "by January 2003, SMIC had hired away more than 100 TSMC employees who collectively had knowledge of virtually all of TSMC's proprietary technology and business trade secrets."[132] SMIC settled the lawsuit in January 2005 for $175 million payable over six years and a cross-licensing agreement through 2010 on SMIC and TSMC patents.[133] SMIC also settled a second lawsuit for theft of trade secrets and nonpayment of the previous settlement with TSMC in 2009. SMIC moved to settle the case after a California court found the company guilty of stealing trade secrets but before the court established damages. The settlement meant SMIC would pay $200 million and offer TSMC stock and warrants worth approximately $90 million.[134]

Shan Yanming (arrested 2002, convicted 2004)

Shan Yanming was an employee of Daqing Oil Field, a division of PetroChina, who attempted to steal software from 3DGEO Development Inc. The Mountain View, California–based company writes seismic imaging software for the oil and natural gas industries. The FBI arrested Shan at San Francisco International Airport in October 2002 as he prepared to leave the country.[135] On his laptop, Shan had a password cracking program that he had used on the 3DGEO's networks to help him access parts of the network from which he was kept. The company maintained a close eye on Shan because another PetroChina employee had attempted to access the network to steal software two years prior.[136] He was convicted in 2004 for illegally accessing 3DGEO's computer network and copying the company's proprietary source code.[137] A federal court sentenced Shan to two years in prison.[138]

Shen Huisheng "Charlie" (pleaded guilty 2014)

Shen Huisheng was a Taiwanese national who attempted to export crystal methamphetamine from Taiwan to the United States and subsequently asked undercover FBI agents about the possibility of acquiring sensitive defense technology on behalf of a Chinese intelligence service. Shen's partner in this endeavor was Chang Huanling. In a series of conversations beginning in 2012, Shen and Chang sought to acquire information on the E-2 Hawkeye reconnaissance aircraft, the stealth technology used in the F-22, missile engine technology, and unmanned aerial vehicles. The two sent the undercover agents a code book to protect their communications and set up a Hong Kong bank account to handle these transactions. In 2015 Shen was sentenced to forty-nine months in prison and a $200 special assessment.[139] Also see Chang Huanling.

Shih, Martin (indicted 2004, deceased before trial)

Martin Shih was owner of Night Vision Technology based in Cupertino, California. The company manufactured thermal-imaging and infrared devices for use in military-grade night vision equipment. In 2001 and 2002 Shih and Philip Cheng attempted to export the equipment illegally to China via a separate company, SPCTEK, that Cheng established to hide their activities.[140] Cheng also intended the company to begin manufacturing night vision technology equipment in China. An informant tipped off U.S. authorities and reported Cheng and Shih would use false end user documents claiming Taiwan as the destination while night vision cameras would be diverted to China. The two were indicted in 2004, but Shih died of cancer before trial, and Cheng received two years of jail time and a $50,000 fine.[141] Also see Philip Cheng.

Shu Quansheng (arrested 2008, pleaded guilty 2008)

Shu Quansheng was a naturalized U.S. citizen and the president, secretary, and treasurer of AMAC International, Inc., who provided defense-related assistance to the Chinese military and the China Academy of Launch Vehicle Technology (CALVT, 中国运载火箭技术研究院). Specifically, Shu assisted in the design and development of a cryogenic fueling system for heavy payload launch vehicles and provided controlled U.S. military technical data on liquid hydrogen tanks and various cryogenic pumps, valves, filters, and instruments. He also attempted to bribe three Chinese officials by offering percentages on approved contracts. Shu also consulted for other firms and represented them in contract negotiations with Chinese entities, such as CALVT. He arranged for delegations of Chinese officials and scientists to tour European space launch facilities.[142] His company, AMAC, was based in Newport News, Virginia, with offices in Beijing, and at least part of the company's research was funded through grants by the Small Business Research Program run by the U.S. Department of Energy and the National Aeronautics and Space Administration. Dr. Shu was sentenced to fifty-one months in prison and forfeited at least $386,740 to the federal government.[143]

Shull, Donald (arrested 2005, pleaded guilty 2005)

Donald Shull was a U.S. citizen who assisted Howard Hsy in exporting night vision equipment to China via an intermediary in Taiwan.[144] Specifically, they exported plastic optical filters suitable for night vision lighting; night vision goggles with helmet mounts for fixed-wing and rotary aircraft; and liquid crystal displays that can be integrated into avionics.[145] Shull and Hsy used forged documents to purchase night vision equipment that was shipped to an Auburn, Washington–based company that one of them owned before being transferred to China via Taiwan. The two men may have believed that the Taiwan connection was the end user.[146] In February 2006 Shull was sentenced to two years of probation and fined $10,000.[147]

Song Jiang (indicted 2011, fled to China)

Song Jiang was a Chinese national and associate of Yuan Wanli who assisted in the latter's effort to acquire controlled programmable logic devices while impersonating a U.S. company. Song Jiang used the alias Jason Jiang and, according to the indictment, Song also occasionally pretended to be Yuan in English-language meetings and discussions.[148] Also see Yuan Wanli.

State Administration of Foreign Experts Affairs
(国家外国专家局)

The State Administration of Foreign Experts Affairs's (SAFEA's) mission, according to a statement no longer on its website, is "to facilitate the 'introduction of advanced technology and make Chinese more competitive internationally' by managing the recruitment of skilled persons from abroad and sending [Chinese] overseas for training."[149] The SAFEA's recruitment of foreign experts includes any area of endeavor that Beijing designates as a strategic interest. In recent years, the SAFEA and its subordinate talent-spotting organizations have attempted to draw foreign expertise to support the following research areas: social stability risk assessment; domestic surveillance and intelligence-led policing systems;[150] public administration; agriculture and animal husbandry;[151] as well as software and integrated circuits.[152] The administration runs a broad range of local and national programs to attract foreign talent, such as working with provincial and municipal governments to create recruitment programs to support local initiatives and organizing the annual Conference on International Exchange of Professions, an international and state-level talent exchange fair.[153] In 2011 SAFEA introduced a national recruitment drive, known as the 1,000 Talent Program, for five hundred to one thousand foreign experts in key industries. Those experts would commit to three years in China, and Beijing would provide them with a 1 million RMB (roughly $148,000) annual salary and, for those doing scientific research, an addition 3 to 5 million RMB (roughly $440,000–740,000) for research.[154] Although its work is largely public, SAFEA has been involved in the illegal acquisition of technology, such as the Noshir Gowadia case, and knowledgeable observers believe SAFEA also provides talent spotting for other actors to secretly approach foreign experts.[155] In addition to its provincial- and local-level offices, SAFEA also oversees the related work by the China Association for International Exchange of Personnel (中国国际人才交流协会) and China International Talent Exchange Foundation (中国国际人才交流基金会). These two organizations' leadership largely overlaps with SAFEA, suggesting they provide a nongovernmental fig leaf in cases where Beijing's direct role in SAFEA would be a hindrance.

Su Liying (indicted 2013)

Su Liying was the deputy director of Sinovel's research and development department who was indicted for his role in recruiting American Semiconductor Corporation (AMSC) engineer Dejan Karabasevic to steal trade secrets for Sinovel.[156] Su and Zhao Haichun recruited Karabasevic to steal AMSC source code for operating wind turbines so that Sinovel could produce and retrofit wind turbines without paying AMSC roughly $800 million for previously delivered goods and services. Also see Karabasevic, Dejan.

Sun Kailiang (indicted 2014)

Sun Kailiang (孙凯亮) is one of the five members of the Chinese signals intelligence unit (Unit 61398) indicted by the U.S. Department of Justice in May 2014. Specifically, Sun allegedly hacked into the networks of Westinghouse, U.S. Steel, and Alcoa on behalf of Chinese state-owned enterprises. In the case of Westinghouse, he took proprietary technical and design specifications related to the AP1000 nuclear plant as well as proprietary, nonpublic emails belonging to company executives responsible for managing the relationship and negotiations with the Chinese firm. In the case of U.S. Steel, Sun and Wang Dong used a spear-phishing attack to gain access to U.S. Steel employees' emails involved in litigation with a Chinese company. In the case of Alcoa, Sun stole thousands of emails related to the company's relationship with a Chinese state-owned enterprise in 2008.[157] Also see Gu Chunhui, Huang Zhenyu, Wang Dong, and Wen Xinyu.

Tam, Thompson (indicted 2008)

Thompson Tam, a director of the China-based Ontime Electronics Technology, was indicted for his involvement in Joseph Piquet's efforts to export controlled electronic components to Hong Kong and China. Among the components sought by Piquet and Tam were power amplifiers used in early warning radar and missile target acquisition systems and low noise amplifiers that have both commercial and military applications. As of 2016, Tam remained at large.[158] Also see Piquet, Joseph.

Tsu Chi-Wai "William" (indicted 2009, pleaded guilty 2009)

Tsu Chi-Wai was a resident of Beijing and vice president of Cheerway Trading, based in Hacienda Heights, California, who illegally shipped four hundred integrated circuits to China. These circuits have a variety of applications including military communications and sensors. Prosecutors alleged Cheerway served as a front for Tsu to hide the shipment of integrated circuits and possibly other defense-related articles to his Beijing-based firm Dimagit Science and Technology Company Ltd. Dimagit is a Chinese defense company and includes among its clients the 704 Research Institute (also known as the Aerospace Long March Rocket Technology Company)—a subsidiary of state-owned China Aerospace Science and Technology Corporation (CASC). Tsu was arrested in January 2009 and pleaded guilty in March of that year; he was sentenced to forty months in prison.[159]

Universal Technologies, Inc.

Universal Technologies, Inc., of Mount Laurel, New Jersey, was a company run by Terry Teng Fang Li, who established it, according to court filings, "for the purpose of acquiring national security-controlled technology for the People's Republic of China and its military factories."[160] A federal court ordered the company to cease operations after Li pleaded guilty to export violations in 2006.[161]

Wang Dong (indicted 2014)

Wang Dong (王东) is one of the five members of the Chinese signals intelligence unit (Unit 61398) indicted by the U.S. Department of Justice in May 2014. Wang and Sun Kailiang used a spear-phishing attack to gain access to U.S. Steel employees' emails involved in litigation with a Chinese company.[162] Also see Gu Chunhui, Huang Zhenyu, Sun Kailiang, and Wen Xinyu.

Wang Hongwei (stopped 2012, indicted 2013)

Wang Hongwei was one of the alleged coconspirators in the effort to steal corn seed from Pioneer, Monsanto, and LG Seeds centered around

Hailong "Robert" Mo. According to the indictment, the FBI believes Wang to be a dual Chinese and Canadian citizen but did not link him to Beijing Dabeinong Technology Group or its subsidiary, Kings Nower Seed Company. Wang was stopped in 2012 on the same day as Li Shaoming and Ye Jian at the U.S.-Canadian border in Vermont, and U.S. authorities seized forty-four bags of seed in his vehicle and luggage.[163] Also see Mo, Hailong "Robert."

Wang Lei

Wang Lei was one of Hailong "Robert" Mo's coconspirators in stealing corn seeds from Pioneer, Monsanto, and LG Seeds.[164] Wang is a Chinese national and vice chairman of the Kings Nower Seed Company, a subsidiary of Beijing Dabeinong Technology Group.[165] Also see Mo, Hailong "Robert."

WaveLab, Inc. (charged 2008, pleaded guilty 2008)

WaveLab, Inc., based in Reston, Virginia, purchased hundreds of microcircuit power amplifiers in 2006 and exported them to an unnamed entity in China. Wavelab assured the manufacturing company, TriQuint Semiconductor, that the power amplifiers were for domestic sale. Power amplifiers like the ones WaveLab purchased have a variety of military applications in communications and electronic warfare. When confronted by federal authorities, WaveLab chief executive officer Walter Zheng arranged a plea agreement that penalized the company but exempted him from criminal charges personally.[166] In 2008 WaveLab was sentenced to one year of supervised probation, a fine of $15,000, forfeiture of $85,000, and a loss of export privileges for five years.[167]

Wei Yufeng "Annie" (convicted 2010)

Wei Yufeng (sometimes known as Annie Wei) ran the Waltham, Massachusetts, office of Chitron Electronics Company Limited (Chitron-U.S.) and channeled the company's purchases of U.S. export-controlled technology through Chitron's Hong Kong office to China without obtaining proper export licenses. Wei is the ex-wife of Chitron founder Wu Zhenzhou. Chitron-U.S. first would purchase controlled electronics components and have them shipped to Waltham. Wu explicitly instructed his employees and Wei to never mention to U.S. companies that these parts would be shipped overseas. Chitron-U.S. would then ship the components, without having obtained export licenses, to Hong Kong, where freight forwarders would move the products to the Shenzhen office. Chitron sold electronic components to a wide variety of military-related customers—including factories, research institutes, and subsidiary units of the China Electronics Technology Group Corporation—that worked on electronic warfare, military radar, fire control, military guidance and control equipment, missile systems, and satellite communications. In addition to the export control violations, Wei was convicted on immigration fraud for having knowingly provided false information on her application for U.S. permanent residency status. Wei was sentenced to twenty-three months in prison and two years of supervised release; she also was subject to deportation.[168] Also see Wu Zhenzhou "Alex."

Wen Xinyu (indicted 2014)

Wen Xinyu (文新宇) is one of the five members of the Chinese signals intelligence unit (Unit 61398) indicted by the U.S. Department of Justice in May 2014. Specifically, Wen allegedly hacked into the networks of SolarWorld AG, Allied Industrial and Service Workers International Union (USW), and Allegheny Technologies Inc. (ATI). In the case of SolarWorld, Wen and an unidentified fellow officer stole information related to, among other things, the company's cash flow, manufacturing metrics, production line, and privileged communications related to ongoing litigation. In the case of USW, Wen stole emails from senior union employees containing nonpublic information about USW strategies related to pending trade disputes over Chinese trade practices in at least two industries. Finally, in the case of ATI, Wen stole the network credentials for almost every ATI employee after the company became embroiled in a trade dispute with a Chinese state-owned enterprise.[169] Also see Gu Chunhui, Huang Zhenyu, Sun Kailiang, and Wang Dong.

Wu Zhenzhou "Alex" (charged 2009, convicted 2010)

Wu Zhenzhou (sometimes known as Alex Wu) founded and controlled Chitron Electronics Company Limited, a Shenzhen-based company with subsidiaries in Hong Kong and Waltham, Massachusetts, and sold U.S. export-controlled technology to Chinese defense companies without obtaining proper export licenses. Wu received assistance from his now ex-wife Wei Yufeng, who also ran the Waltham office (Chitron-U.S.). Chitron-U.S. first would purchase controlled electronics components and have them shipped to Waltham. Wu explicitly instructed his employees and Wei to never mention to U.S. companies that these parts would be shipped overseas. Chitron-U.S. would then ship the components, without having obtained export licenses, to Hong Kong, where freight forwarders would move the products to the Shenzhen office. Chitron sold electronic components to a wide variety of military-related customers—including factories, research institutes, and subsidiary units of the China Electronics Technology Group Corporation—that worked on electronic warfare, military radar, fire control, military guidance and control equipment, missile systems, and satellite communications. A federal court sentenced Wu to seven years in prison, fined him $15,000, and made him subject to deportation; the sentence was upheld on appeal.[170] Also see Wei Yufeng "Annie."

Xian Hongwei (arrested 2010, pleaded guilty 2011)

Xian Hongwei, also known as Harry Zan, was the president of Beijing Starcreates Space Science and Technology Development Company Limited who attempted to export computer chips that were classified as defense articles on the U.S. Munitions List. Under the U.S. arms embargo placed on China in 1990, such articles cannot be exported to China. Xian along his coconspirator, Li Li, were arrested in Hungary in 2010 and extradited to the United States in spring 2011. The two attempted to acquire radiation-hardened programmable read-only memory microchips (PROMs), which store the initial start-up program for a computer system and are built to withstand the conditions present in outer space. Xian and Li intended to order thousands of these PROMs, suggesting production-level quantities, and planned to break up the purchases into smaller shipments to multiple countries to disguise the conspiracy. The intended end user was the China Aerospace Science and Technology Corporation, which is a state-owned company that develops and produces a wide range of missile-related technologies, launch vehicles, and spacecraft, among other industrial products. Xian was sentenced to twenty-four months in prison and spent seven months jailed in Hungary awaiting extradition.[171] Also see Li "Lea."

Xu Bing (charged 2007, pleaded guilty 2009)

Xu Bing was a Chinese national and a manager at Everbright Science and Technology Ltd. who attempted to acquire night vision equipment for export to China. The F-1600 night vision technology that Xu attempted to acquire included image intensifiers that are on the U.S. Munitions List and require export licenses. In meeting with an undercover law enforcement agent, Xu asked the agent to remove the serial numbers and other identifiable information from night vision equipment.[172] Everbright applied for export licenses prior to the illegal effort but was denied because of the U.S. government ban on exporting defense articles to China. Xu was sentenced to twenty-two months in prison and two years of supervised release in 2009.[173]

Xu Kai (arrested 2001, pleaded guilty 2005)

Xu Kai was a Chinese national and U.S. permanent resident who conspired with Lin Hai and Cheng Yongqing to steal proprietary software from his employer, Lucent Technologies. Specifically, Cheng and his coconspirators attempted to acquire switching software associated with Lucent's PathStar Access Server. The three men were starting their own company, ComTriad Technologies, in partnership with Datang Telecommunication Technology Industry Group, and they received between $500,000 and $1.2 million in startup capital from their Chinese partner. Cheng, Lin, and Xu originally sought venture capital financing in the United States but approached Datang after their U.S. interlocutors asked to see the product specifications based on the stolen Lucent software. In April 2001 the three transferred their modifications on the Lucent PathStar software to China electronically, presumably to Datang.[174] Xu and Cheng Yongqing avoided prison time as part of their plea agreement in 2005, but ComTriad paid a $250,000 fine.[175] Also see Cheng Yongqing and Lin Hai.

Xu Weibo "Kevin" (arrested 2004, pleaded guilty 2005)

Xu Weibo was a naturalized U.S. citizen and the president of Manten Electronics, a New Jersey company that shipped approximately $400,000 in export-controlled equipment to banned Chinese end users between 2003 and 2004. He is also the husband of Chen Xiuling. The electronic components shipped to Chinese research institutes played important roles within a wide variety of defense systems, ranging from electronic warfare to missiles. In addition to falsifying end user certificates and using Hong Kong as a transshipment point, Xu also created at least one shell company, GMC, that was identified as the end user for some exports to China. GMC probably was created with the complicity of Manten vice president Chen Haoli and his wife Chan Kwan-chun, because the shell company was registered at their home address.[176] Xu was sentenced to forty-four months in prison followed by two years of supervised release. Manten also forfeited the revenue from the illegal sales.[177] Also see Chen Xiuling.

Yan Wengui (arrested 2014)

Yan Wengui was a naturalized U.S. citizen and Arkansas-based research geneticist at the U.S. Department of Agriculture who was accused of stealing seed strains for the China Academy of Agricultural Science and the Crop Research Institute. Yan along with Zhang Weiqiang hosted a delegation from the Chinese institutes to Ventria and U.S. Department of Agriculture facilities in 2012 following a trip to China to discuss cooperation. Investigators found proprietary seed strains in the luggage of the delegation as they were departing the United States and in the homes of Zhang and Yan.[178] The motivations of Zhang and his coconspirator are unclear. Also see Zhang Weiqiang.

Yang Bin (arrested 2012, pleaded guilty 2013)

Yang Bin, a Chinese national and businessman with the Changsha Harsay Industry Company, attempted to illegally export accelerometers to China. The Endevco 7270–200K accelerometers Yang attempted to acquire can be used for, among other things, "smart" munitions, bunker-busting bombs, military aircraft, and measuring nuclear and chemical explosions. In 2010 he posted a request on an Internet business forum that he was looking to acquire accelerometers made by Honeywell. An undercover U.S. Immigration and Customs Enforcement agent responded positively, and they arranged for a meeting in Bulgaria where the agent could deliver two accelerometers in person. Bulgarian authorities arrested Yang at Washington's request, and he was extradited to the United States in May 2012. In 2013 Yang was sentenced to twenty-seven months in prison and three years of supervised release.[179]

Yang Chunlai (arrested 2011, pleaded guilty 2012)

Yang Chunlai was a naturalized U.S. citizen and senior software engineer at the CME Group who downloaded company source code to start his own business in China. Yang along with two unnamed business associates planned to use the CME Group's global trading platform and related software to establish a China-based mercantile exchange. They also intended to sell their software derived from CME Group's products to speed up the Zhangjiagang chemical electronic trading market. He pleaded guilty to two counts of trade secret theft for stealing more than 10,000 files that CME estimated were worth $50 million.[180] Yang avoided jail time, receiving four years of probation.[181]

Yang Feng (arrested 2007, pleaded guilty 2007)

Yang Feng (also known as Yang Fung) was the president of Excellence Engineering Electronics, Inc., who exported controlled electronics to China. Specifically, Yang sold microwave integrated circuits to unknown end users.[182]

Yang Fung (charged 2007, pleaded guilty 2007)

Yang, the president of Excellence Engineering Electronics, Inc., pleaded guilty to charges of illegally exporting controlled microwave integrated circuits to China without Department of Commerce authorization.

Yang Lian (arrested 2010, pleaded guilty 2011)

Yang Lian was a former software engineer at Microsoft who attempted to buy computer chips classified as defense articles on the U.S. Munitions List for an unnamed partner in China. He attempted to export three hundred radiation-hardened programmable semiconductors that are primarily used in satellites or other aerospace products. According to the FBI, Yang also considered creating a company to conceal the fact that the intended end user was in China as well as planning to falsify purchase orders to suggest the parts could be legally exported. One of the people Yang contacted to pursue the acquisition of these semiconductors cooperated with the FBI and helped engineer the bureau's sting operation. Yang wired $60,000 to an FBI account and was prepared to make another payment of $20,000 as part of the $700,000 total for the semiconductors. Yang's motive presumably was financial, and he described his interlocutors in China as "old school friends."[183] He was sentenced to eighteen months in prison in 2011.[184]

Yang Su (arrested 2008)

Yang Su attempted to purchase and illegally export amplifiers that are export-controlled for military purposes. The amplifiers in this case are used for digital radios and wireless area networks. Yang and his colleague Ding Zhengxing were arrested in Saipan, where they planned to take possession of the purchased amplifiers. A third person, Peter Zhu of Shanghai Meuro Electronics Company, was not caught. As of October 2016 no further information was available on the disposition of this case.[185]

Yang, Tzu-Wei "David" (arrested 2001 sentenced 2002)

Tzu-Wei "David" Yang was a Taiwanese national with U.S. permanent residency who ran a freight forwarding company to be used in a plot to smuggle encryption devices to China. Yang along with You-Tsai "Eugene" Hsu planned to purchase and ship the KIV-7HS encryption device made by Mykotronx to China via an intermediary in Singapore. Hsu was the one who contacted Mykotronx and made the arrangements.[186] Yang received two concurrent thirty-month prison sentences for his role in the conspiracy.[187] Also see Hu, You-Tsai "Eugene."

Ye Fei (arrested 2001, pleaded guilty 2006)

Ye Fei is a naturalized U.S. citizen and engineer at Transmeta who was arrested with Zhong Ming at San Francisco International Airport attempting to leave the country with proprietary information from Sun Microsystems, NEC Electronics Corporation, and Transmeta, among others. Ye previously worked at Sun.[188] At the time of his arrest, Ye had the proprietary documents in his possession. The two individuals were the first two prosecuted successfully under the Economic Espionage Act passed in 1996. Zhong and Ye intended to establish their company in China manufacturing integrated circuits, and they sought 863 Program funding and assistance from the Hangzhou municipal government to support their new endeavor.[189] According to the prosecuting attorney, the two engineers appear motivated by greed rather than any desire to assist the Chinese government.[190] Also see Zhong Ming.

Ye Jian (stopped 2012)

Ye Jian was the research manager of the Kings Nower Seed Company, a subsidiary of Beijing Dabeinong Technology Group.[191] Ye was stopped and searched alongside his colleague and coconspirator Li Shaoming, and U.S. authorities seized dozens of corn seed packets hidden in microwave popcorn packets. Neither man was arrested to preserve the continuing investigation into corn seed theft and Hailong "Robert" Mo.

Yu Xiangdong "Mike" (arrested 2009)

Yu Xiangdong of Beijing was a product engineer at Ford Motor Company from 1997 to 2007 who attempted to carry four thousand sensitive company documents, including designs, to China in 2009. When U.S. authorities arrested Yu at Chicago O'Hare International Airport, he was carrying an external hard drive with the company documents. In 2005 he began talks with Shenzhen-based Foxconn PCE Industry Inc. about future employment and may have begun providing Ford designs in those meetings.

Yuan Wanli (indicted 2011, fled to China)

Yuan Wanli was a Chinese national and businessman who attempted to acquire controlled programmable logic devices while impersonating an employee of an unnamed U.S. company. He worked for the China Wingwish Group, which procured dual-use electronics for sale in China, and was assisted by Song Jiang. Yuan falsely claimed to be Nicholas Bush

and an employee of the impersonated U.S. company. As part of the decep-
tion, Yuan created a fake website and email addresses for the U.S. company
and misrepresented the address of a freight forwarder as being associated
with this company.[192] Yuan and Song attempted to purchase programmable logic devices manufactured by the Lattice Semiconductor Corporation.
The devices were designed to operate at extreme temperatures and were
of sufficient quality for military applications, such as in missiles or radar
systems. The U.S. government seized $414,000 transferred into U.S. banks
as a part of the down payment for the programmable logic devices.[193] Also
see Song Jiang.

Zhang Bo (arrested 2012, pleaded guilty 2013)

Zhang Bo was a contractor doing computer programming for the Federal
Reserve Bank of New York who stole software code that cost the U.S.
Treasury Department $9.8 million to develop. He copied the code onto an
external hard drive and told fellow employees that he had lost the hard drive.
Investigators started looking into Zhang after a coworker complained to a
supervisor that he had lost that hard drive. Although Zhang told authorities that he stole the code for private use in case he lost his job, there was
never any clear motive for the theft. The software code he stole related to the
Government-wide Accounting and Reporting Program, which tracks U.S.
government expenditures and provides government agencies with their
operating balance. Zhang was charged with stealing government property
rather than trade secret theft, which carries a much more serious penalty.
The court sentenced Zhang to six months of house arrest.[194]

Zhang, Michael Ming
(indicted January 2009, pleaded guilty 2009)

Michael Ming Zhang was the owner and president of J. J. Electronics, based
in Rancho Cucamonga, California, who exported controlled dual-use electronic components to China and imported counterfeit computer chips.
Among the dual-use components were electronic systems used in U.S.
tanks made by Vetronix Research Corporation. Zhang shipped these parts
abroad through both the Shenzhen office of J. J. Electronics and Fangyuan
Electronics Limited, a transshipment point company in China and Hong

Kong.[195] Zhang also trafficked roughly 4,300 counterfeit Cisco chips in 25 separate transactions with an estimated value of $3.3 million. In 2010 a court sentenced Zhang to eighteen months in prison and three years of supervised release and forced him to pay the companies whose parts had been counterfeited.[196]

Zhang Mingsuan (arrested 2012, pleaded guilty 2013)

Zhang Mingsuan was a Chinese national who attempted to acquire military-grade carbon fiber. Although Zhang claimed to be acquiring the material for sports equipment, he stated to an undercover U.S. Department of Commerce investigator that he needed the carbon fiber in connection with upcoming flight tests of a Chinese fighter plane.[197] At the time, the specific carbon fiber, Toray-type M60JB-3000-50B, cost roughly $1,000 per pound, and prosecutors alleged Zhang was prepared to spend $4 million and was looking for a steady supply.[198] One report claimed Zhang was acting on behalf of China North Industries Corporation. He pleaded guilty to violating the International Emergency Economic Powers Act and was sentenced to nearly five years in prison.[199]

Zhang Weiqiang (arrested 2014)

Zhang Weiqiang, a rice breeder at Ventria Bioscience in Manhattan, Kansas, was accused of stealing seed strains for the China Academy of Agricultural Science and the Crop Research Institute. Zhang, a U.S. permanent resident, along with Yan Wengui hosted a delegation from the Chinese institutes to Ventria and U.S. Department of Agriculture facilities in 2012 following a trip to China to discuss cooperation. Investigators found proprietary seed strains in the luggage of the delegation as they were departing the United States and in the homes of Zhang and Yan.[200] The motivations of Zhang and his coconspirator are unclear. Also see Yan Wengui.

Zhang Xinsheng (indicted 2015)

Zhang Xinsheng is a Chinese national who was indicted in connection with Wenxia "Wency" Man's efforts to acquire U.S. fighter jet engines. Man described Zhang's position as a "technology spy" who worked on behalf of the PLA to acquire or copy foreign defense technology for domestic production.[201] According to the U.S. Justice Department, Man and Zhang attempted to acquire and export the following defense articles and related technical data: Pratt and Whitney F135-PW-100 engines used in the F-35 Joint Strike Fighter; Pratt & Whitney F119-PW-100 turbofan engines used in the F-22 Raptor fighter jet; General Electric F110-GE-132 engines designed for the F-16 fighter jet; and the General Atomics MQ-9 Reaper/Predator B unmanned aerial vehicle.[202] The two thought to use either South Korea, Israel, or Hong Kong as the channel through which to disguise China as the ultimate end user.[203] Also see Man, Wenxia "Wency."

Zhang, Zhaowei "Kevin" (arrested 2012)

Zhaowei "Kevin" Zhang was a naturalized Canadian citizen who conspired to export defense articles without a license. Specifically, Zhang attempted to acquire gyroscopes used in unmanned aerial vehicles and missile guidance systems. He sought U.S. intermediaries who could ship the equipment to his Calgary home, where he would then repackage the gyroscopes for shipping to China. Neither the ultimate end user nor Zhang's compensation were named in the court documents.[204]

Zhao Haichun (indicted 2013)

Zhao Haichun was a technology manager at Sinovel who was indicted for his role in recruiting American Semiconductor Corporation (AMSC) engineer Dejan Karabasevic to steal trade secrets for Sinovel.[205] Zhao and Su Liying recruited Karabasevic to steal AMSC source code for operating wind turbines, so that Sinovel could produce and retrofit wind turbines without paying AMSC roughly $800 million for previously delivered goods and services. Also see Dejan Karabasevic.

Zhao Huajun (arrested 2013)

Zhao Huajun, a researcher at the Medical College of Wisconsin, stole samples of a possible cancer-fighting compound that he intended to pass to Zhejiang University. He was captured on security footage entering and leaving the laboratory at the time the sample vials went missing.[206]

Zhejiang Hongchen Irrigation Equipment Company (indicted 2012, pleaded guilty 2014)

Zhejiang Hongchen Irrigation Equipment Company, with the aid of Janice Kuang Capener, stole trade secrets from the Utah-based Orbit Irrigation Products. Capener, who worked at Orbit's China manufacturing facility, stole sales and pricing information from that company, and she provided that information to Zhejiang Hongchen as a part of a coordinated effort to undermine Orbit's market position. Zhejiang Hongchen pleaded guilty to stealing trade secrets and related crimes. The company was sentenced to three years of probation, fined $100,000, and forced to pay $300,000 in restitution to Orbit Irrigation Products.[207]

Zhong Ming (arrested 2001, pleaded guilty 2006)

Zhong Ming is a Chinese citizen with U.S. permanent residency and an engineer at Transmeta who was arrested with Ye Fei at San Francisco International Airport attempting to leave the country with proprietary information from Sun Microsystems, NEC Electronics Corporation, and Transmeta, among others. The two individuals were the first two prosecuted successfully under the Economic Espionage Act passed in 1996. As part of the plea agreement, Zhong assisted in the investigation of Lee Lan and Ge Yuefei.[208] Zhong and Ye intended to establish their company in China manufacturing integrated circuits, and they sought 863 Program funding and assistance from the Hangzhou municipal government to support their new endeavor.[209] Also see Ye Fei.

Zhu, Peter (indicted 2007)

Peter Zhu of Shanghai Meuro Electronics Company was a third defendant in Ding Zhengxing and Yang Su's plot to purchase and illegally export amplifiers that are export-controlled for military purposes. The indictment was unsealed in December 2007, and no further information could be found about Zhu's identity.[210] Also see Ding Zhengxing and Yang Su.

Zhu Zhaoxin (pleaded guilty 2004)

Zhu Zhaoxin was a Chinese national who attempted to purchase controlled satellite and radar technologies for export to China. In his effort to acquire the equipment, he came in contact with federal law enforcement who controlled the attempted transaction and lured Zhu to a U.S. jurisdiction. Zhu was sentenced to two years in prison and three years of supervised release.[211]

Zhuang Jinghua (arrested 2003, pleaded guilty 2003)

Zhuang Jinghua was a co-owner of Maytone International who conspired with his wife, Liang Xiuwen, to export components for U.S. military aircraft and missiles. Zhuang previously had been an international sales manager for Harris Corporation, a Fortune 500 company specializing in communications equipment. Specifically, Zhuang and Liang attempted to export F-14 Tomcat parts as well as components for the HAWK surface-to-air missile, TOW anti-tank missile, and AIM-9 Sidewinder air-to-air missile. At least one of the Chinese purchasers was believed to be in Shenyang. The two were caught in 2003 as part of lengthy undercover investigation into U.S. companies that offer defense articles over the Internet to foreign buyers. In 2003 Zhuang was sentenced to thirty months in prison and fined $6,000.[212] Also see Liang Xiuwen "Jennifer."

♦ FIVE ♦

Espionage during the Revolution and the Early People's Republic

A fter the death of Mao Zedong in 1976, the party allowed more open discussion of recent history and current events. A "literature of the wounded" developed that critically portrayed the impact of the Cultural Revolution on ordinary people. Authorities allowed historians to write in more detail, beyond the previous focus on Mao's role. They published biographies, diaries, and "annals" or "chronicles" (年谱, *nianpu*) recording the experiences of other key figures such as Zhou Enlai, Ye Jianying, Luo Ruiqing, and Yang Shangkun.[1] These included works on CCP intelligence figures of note and other mostly fragmented descriptions of working-level activity. Though selective in their treatment of events, these accounts opened a window on how espionage, signal intercept, and other intelligence disciplines assisted the 1949 Chinese Communist victory. However, with rare exceptions, they are mum about operations after 1949.

PRC sources, especially the popular accounts, tend to stress the heroic and the terrible, who should be lauded, and who was responsible. The times of the revolution were awful indeed: both main Chinese parties, Nationalist and Communist, and the invading Japanese regularly displayed behavior as ruthless in intelligence and security work as did soldiers on the conventional battlefield. Writers tended to ignore their own party's reprehensible acts and stress evidence against the evil other. With the communists, in the spirit of "making the past serve the present," peasants are always brave, as are communist soldiers and CCP intelligence figures, while landlords, KMT spies, and others are venal and cruel. Imperialists are devious and despicable, and China's problems are the fault of foreigners and traitors,

195

not of her loyal leaders—except for the ones who were less loyal or responsible for ideological "deviations."

This focus on heroics and crimes, defining enemies and friends, continues in accounts up to the present. It is part of a "script" that avoids tarnishing more than a few moments in Chinese Communist Party history. Those spoiled bits are blamed on a selection of villains—the latest including Bo Xilai, Zhou Yongkang, and numerous others netted in Xi Jinping's anticorruption campaign, waged to fight graft but also to achieve political supremacy.

In China, biographies of intelligence and security leaders and accounts of operations are edited with particular care. They are always sensitive because of what they might reveal about intelligence sources and methods and the party's strategy, planning, and priorities. This chapter employs both those accounts and unapproved works. We attempt to go beyond the CCP's script for an unvarnished look at operations, the warts as well as the wonders, from the early days until the near present.

Boursicot, Bernard (伯纳德 · 布尔西科, Bai na de—Bu er xi ke, 1944–)

See Shi Peipu.

Classified Materials Theft, 1966–67

By August 1966 the violent phase of the Chinese Cultural Revolution was under way. In Beijing, marauding Red Guard groups began searching for "black materials" (黑资料, *hei ziliao*) to implicate those they considered enemies of Mao Zedong. As Red Guard militants laid hands on these materials, they often published them verbatim in homegrown newspapers and pamphlets.[2]

The mounting chaos was fed by encouragement from Mao himself and the Cultural Revolution Group (CRG, 中央文化大革命小组, *Zhongyang wenhua da geming xiaozu*), headed by the chairman's wife, Jiang Qing (江青). In this rapidly deteriorating situation, even the secure areas of the CCP's foreign intelligence organization, the Central Investigation Department, came under threat. In early August, the CID director Kong Yuan appealed to Tong Xiaopeng, the confidential secretary of premier

Zhou Enlai, for help in repelling members of the Red Guard rebel faction (造反派, *zaofan pai*) that had surrounded his building. They demanded entry to look for black materials.[3]

Zhou was alarmed but did not directly respond—a sign that his position vis-à-vis the CRG was perilous. Instead, between August 16 and 31, Zhou sent an official of the Central Committee Confidential Office, Li Zhizong, to persuade the rebels to cease their action. They briefly detained Li, but he succeeded in postponing Red Guard efforts to enter the CID. The situation temporarily assuaged, Zhou had Tong draft a Central Committee memorandum (中央文件, *Zhongyang wenjian*) ordering the protection of secret materials and forbidding their theft.[4]

In response, Jiang Qing accused Zhou Enlai of engaging in "eclecticism" and creating a "firefighting unit" to prevent Red Guards from finding black materials. She then accused Xu Ming, the spouse of Kong Yuan, of spying for disgraced Beijing mayor Peng Zhen. (Xu Ming was herself a veteran intelligence officer from the revolution and a longtime member of Zhou's staff. According to Tong, she had made an enemy of Jiang a decade before while serving under her in the propaganda department film section.) Ultimately, Zhou's memorandum to protect classified materials was vetoed by Mao.[5]

The situation further deteriorated as a troubled capital contemplated the new year. Kong Yuan and his deputy Zou Dapeng were arrested and tortured in late 1966, subjected in subsequent months to struggle meetings (斗争会, *douzheng hui*) by radical Red Guards, where they suffered from exhausting verbal invective and physical abuse. Eventually they were sent to labor for years in remote regions. Xu Ming committed suicide on December 31, 1966, depressed at being suspected of disloyalty by Mao, and Kong himself might have tried but failed to kill himself at the same time. Xu Ming left a note saying that she and her family were loyal and innocent of wrongdoing.[6] Rebel faction Red Guard groups in Beijing grew powerful enough to negotiate "opportunities for inspection" (检查的机会, *jiancha de jihui*) into the National Defense Science and Technology Commission (国防科委, *Guofang kewei*) and the National Defense Industry Office (国防公办所, *Guofang gongban suo*).[7]

In early 1967 the two Red Guard factions inside of the CID began fighting each other. On March 18, Mao approved Zhou's suggestion that military officers take charge of the CID in order to secure its materials and return the workplace to normal.[8]

In the spreading chaos, the CID was not the only organ to be taken over in this fashion. That same month, the Posts and Telecommunications, Railways, and Communications ministries were placed under military control, as was the CCP Central Organization Department, and the famous Daqing oilfield. The entire Tibet Autonomous Region was placed under military control in May.[9]

Dalbank (Dal'bank, Dal'niyvostochnyi Bank, The Far Eastern Bank in Harbin, 1923–34)

Dalbank's name came from the Russian phrase *Dalniy Vostok*, or Far East. Based in Harbin, it handled genuine trade and investment in Manchuria but worked elsewhere in China on behalf of the Comintern and the GRU (Soviet military intelligence) to conduct financial operations supporting clandestine Soviet networks in China. The GRU's mission was to keep track of Japanese and Chinese Nationalist military developments.[10]

Dalbank worked with other Soviet-owned businesses including Sovtorgflot, a GRU-controlled trading company and shipping business in Harbin, and the Chinese Eastern Railway, used by the Russians as a cover for collecting intelligence about cross-border movements of bandits and White Russian remnants.

On February 28, 1927, forces of the Chinese warlord Zhang Zuolin (张作霖, Chang Tso-lin) seized documents aboard the Soviet vessel *Pamiat Lenina* while anchored off Nanjing that incriminated Russian organizations in propaganda activities disallowed by bilateral agreement. On April 6–7, Peking police, controlled by Zhang's forces, raided Dalbank, other Soviet businesses, and the Soviet embassy. They seized documents showing that the Russians were interested not only in assisting the Nationalist Chinese revolution but also in preparing for a communist uprising.

Zhang Zuolin published a Chinese translation of the documents in a book that discredited Soviet efforts in China, and may have influenced Chiang Kai-shek to turn against the Chinese Communists in the April

12 coup d'état that marked the end of the Nationalist-Communist First United Front.[11] After the CCP's Guangzhou uprising in December, the Chinese Central Government severed relations with the Soviet Union, and Dalbank's representatives were forced to flee areas controlled by the Nationalists.[12]

No evidence to date indicates that the CCP received any direct help from Dalbank, but their example of clandestine financial operations may have been noted by Mao Zedong's brother, Mao Zemin (毛泽民), who led the CCP's first national bank, which was founded in 1932. An official account of the exploits of Mao's younger brother claims that the bank helped break the enemy's blockade and assisted in the underground movement, assertions that require additional research.[13]

Downey-Fecteau Case

John Downey and Richard Fecteau were CIA paramilitary officers, referred to officially by the Chinese as *wuzhuang tewu* (武装特务, armed special agents). They were shot down and captured in the Changbai mountains district of Jilin province on the night of November 29, 1952, while on a mission to collect a courier. He was a member of an ethnic Chinese Staroma team inserted by the CIA, meant to link up with local guerrilla forces, collect intelligence, and look for opportunities to engage in sabotage and psychological warfare. The agency's analysts later determined that the entire Staroma team had been captured and compromised and that their request for the courier's exfiltration was a trap. Richard Fecteau and John Downey were held until 1971 and 1973, respectively. Their mission and ordeal of captivity are described in the video *Extraordinary Fidelity*.[14]

Hong Kong (香港, *Xianggang*): Overview

Hong Kong has attracted Chinese and foreign intelligence operations since before the start of the Chinese Communist movement in 1921. Like Macau (see subsequent entry), Hong Kong has a majority Chinese population, albeit with a significant foreign element. However, Hong Kong has a larger population, a more dynamic economy with vigorous international trade, a larger territory, and a more varied and abundant foreign presence. This is true today as it was throughout the Chinese Revolution. It may have made related CCP espionage activities such as front organizations, intelligence stations, safe houses, smuggling and couriering, high-technology diversion, and agent recruiting easier to conduct and keep secret than in Macau. Hong Kong was and remains a base for foreign intelligence organizations to "watch" China. Hong Kong's utility to espionage may not survive Chinese attempts under Xi Jinping to change the nature of the territory, now a PRC special administrative region.

Early CCP Operations

A year after the CCP was founded in Shanghai, it supported the 1922 seaman's strike in Hong Kong but did not have sufficient resources in south China to have any impact. However, in 1925–26 during the Guangzhou–Hong Kong strike and boycott, the CCP and the Chinese Socialist Youth League together grew tenfold to more than seven thousand members, and the communists were active enough to influence at least two key unions. The economic damage caused by the strike and boycott and the April 1927 CCP–KMT split led to British suppression of unions in general and the CCP in particular, especially in the wake of the disastrous Canton (Guangzhou) uprising that December. For the next ten years, Hong Kong authorities cooperated with the KMT to suppress communist activity. Among those nabbed by the British in 1929 was the father of future PRC prime minister Li Peng, whom they deported to the KMT in Guangdong for quick execution.[15]

To facilitate communication with the leadership in Shanghai, the CCP established a clandestine radio in Kowloon, which began transmitting in January 1930. It was set up by Li Qiang, the future PRC trade minister. Already a veteran of VIP protection operations, Li was the new head of the Fourth Section (communications) of the party's nascent intelligence body, the Special Services Section (see chapter 1). The operators used a cipher designed by Zhou Enlai, nicknamed *Haomi* (the Hao code) after Zhou's clandestine work name, Wu Hao.[16]

Other early CCP intelligence operations in Hong Kong are described in the entries on Deng Fa (chapter 2) and Gong Changrong (chapter 3).

Hong Kong and CCP Intelligence during the Anti-Japanese War

CCP intelligence ran two broad efforts in the Pearl River Delta, including Hong Kong, adjacent areas, and Macau from 1938 to 1945: commando and military intelligence under the organization consolidated in 1942 and named the East River Column, and an urban agent network directly controlled by Pan Hannian (chapter 3) from the Eighth Route Army Liaison Office in Hong Kong, headed by Liao Chengzhi. Concerning his intelligence duties, Pan reported directly to Yan'an after February 1939, when the Social Affairs Department was established under Kang Sheng (chapter 2).

Zhou Enlai chose Liao for this task in October 1937. Mao gave the network three priorities: publicize to the outside world the anti-Japanese stand of the CCP and its forces, prompt overseas Chinese and sympathetic foreigners to contribute money and matériel to the cause, and compile information on the latest developments in international affairs.[17] The team included Zhang Weiyi, an older and more experienced cadre picked a year later by Pan Hannian to run the SAD intelligence network in Hong Kong.[18] Liao arrived in Hong Kong in January 1938 after Zhou Enlai's negotiations with the British to establish the office. The British wanted it to stay clandestine to avoid attention from the Japanese and KMT, while the CCP wanted the most open operation possible. The two sides compromised by agreeing on a semi-open arrangement (see *Ban gongkai huodong* in the web-based glossary). The CCP's outpost would be hidden from public view, albeit in a busy part of Hong Kong at 18 Queensway, Central.[19] The establishment later adopted the business name of Yue Hwa, which survives today as the famous department store chain specializing in mainland goods.

In 1938–39 Liao fostered "Return to Hometown Service Teams" in Hong Kong and nearby localities in Guangdong, with the object of gathering as many people of military age as possible to join the anti-Japanese effort. In the months leading to the Pacific War in 1941, these teams were consolidated into the Hong Kong and Kowloon Independent Brigade, with a main detachment, a marine unit, a logistics unit, couriers, and an intelligence organization. The last two had a higher percentage of women than did the combat elements. The intelligence workers were unarmed agents stationed around the New Territories and Kowloon, some of whom were passive observers sending reports of enemy activity, while others sought opportunities to work among the Japanese army and puppet forces. The East River People's Anti-Japanese Guerrilla Column (东江人民抗日游击 纵队, *Dongjiang renmin kangri youji zongdui*) was founded from these organizations in February 1942.[20]

At the start of the Pacific War, Yan'an passed instructions to the East River Column to establish an underground evacuation route to remove Chinese friends of the CCP under the united front policy. They assisted left wing personages such as the writer Mao Dun and some KMT officials, British government officials who remained at large under occupation, some escaped prisoners from the Japanese internment camps, and Allied flyers shot down in the area. They developed intelligence on Japanese army units and ship movements and pursued limited guerrilla attacks against Japanese transport links and isolated units.[21] Just as Japanese forces in other parts of China were stretched thin and could not cover every square mile of occupied territory, so in this region Japan could only secure Hong Kong Island and urban Kowloon. Parts of Kowloon and virtually all of the Crown Colony's New Territories were frequently visited or controlled by CCP or Nationalist guerrillas, especially at night.[22] By 1944 the East River Column had established a network of intelligence stations and subordinate intelligence points, as the CCP had done in northern China, gathering information that was passed on to the CCP and at times to the British to generate targeting data for Allied bombing raids. This activity was the product of cooperation between the British Army Assistance Group (BAAG) and the CCP and was fostered by Zhou Enlai in his discussions with the British ambassador in Chongqing. While approved in Yan'an (and the subject of much consternation among KMT officials), the cooperation was driven in part by the enthusiasm of Zeng Sheng and his cadre in Hong Kong on the one hand, and BAAG on the other, to pursue common goals such as tying down Japanese troops who might have been used elsewhere.[23] BAAG officers observed that East River Column guerrillas were superior in skill if not numbers to nearby KMT units and more adept at infiltrating Japanese units to gather intelligence useful for the eventual Allied liberation.[24]

Yan'an ordered Liao to withdraw in December 1941, and he established a remote headquarters about 150 kilometers to the north, probably intending to remain in the region while staying mobile in order to avoid capture.[25] However, three KMT agents apprehended Liao on May 30, 1942.[26] Until that time, the orders of Yan'an seemed to have been strictly followed: when East River Column guerrillas retreated from the KMT in the face of overwhelming force in 1939, Yan'an ordered them to move back toward Hong Kong, and they complied in spite of the danger. However, Liao's capture left the East River Column without a representative from the party center. General Zeng Sheng led them for the rest of the war. He was a more locally oriented CCP leader who appears to have been less closely tied to Yan'an than was Liao.[27] Now on his own, Zeng operated with combat utility uppermost, completely unaffected by the Yan'an Rectification and Salvation campaigns of 1942–44; writings we reviewed about the East River Column do not mention struggle sessions or anyone being recalled to Yan'an to face criticism.

Jin Wudai (金无怠, 1922–86)

Jin Wudai of Beijing was known in the United States as Larry Wu-Tai Chin. A student in Yenching University beginning in 1940, Jin studied English. He left for Fujian province in the south during World War II, obtaining employment with British and American forces. Jin returned to Beijing after the Japanese surrender, finished his degree in 1947, and landed a job the following year at the U.S. consulate in Shanghai. With the communist victory looming in 1949, Jin moved to Hong Kong with the consulate staff and remained a U.S. government employee for the rest of his career. Probably about the time of his 1947 graduation or beforehand, he was recruited by the CCP, most likely the Social Affairs Department, which then had numerous resources in the cities and on university campuses.

Jin was among the most damaging spies in U.S. history. Though he became an employee of a CIA sideline activity, the Foreign Broadcast Information Service (FBIS), Jin was occasionally requested to evaluate documents for the CIA, and he met officers from its China program. Jin helped interview captured Chinese soldiers during the Korean War and revealed their identities in his reports for Beijing. He also revealed that the newly inaugurated Nixon administration (1969–74) was interested in a rapprochement with China.

While based in Okinawa at Kadena Air Force Base with FBIS, Jin left his first wife, Doris, in 1959 for Cathy Zhou Jinyu (周谨予), whom he married in 1962 just after the FBIS moved him to Santa Rosa, California. Tod Hoffman relates an FBI interview where Jin revealed that Doris complained after the divorce about the small settlement she received from him, considering the "millions" China paid him to spy.[28]

By contrast, Cathy claimed that she was ignorant of Jin's spying, saying that "everything I knew was from the newspapers, magazines, television, and the court" after his arrest. In her memoir, Cathy complained of false rumors that she had turned in her husband. In spite of the situation after his November 1985 arrest, she wrote that they wholeheartedly supported each other. Jin urged her to seek solace in Buddhism and asked that she contact Deng Xiaoping, for whom Jin had helped interpret in 1979 during the Chinese leader's American visit. Jin held out hope for assistance from China, and Cathy also wrote letters to members of Congress, but to no avail: the Chinese side denied any connection to him. He despaired before committing suicide in February 1986, after his conviction on espionage charges but before sentencing.[29]

Jin's downfall came not from his own conduct or anyone's mistake, but from a CIA agent within the new Ministry of State Security (MSS), Yu Qiangsheng (俞强声, also known as Yu Zhensan). Yu did not reveal Jin's name to his American handlers but gave them some travel details of a Chinese agent inside the CIA. The FBI was able to tie these details to Jin after he retired in 1983 and built a case against him over subsequent months.[30]

Kashmir Princess Bombing Case (克什米尔公主号飞机 被炸案, *Keshenmi'er Gongzhu Hao bei zha an*)

This case is an exception to the rule that Chinese mainland sources avoid discussing post-1949 espionage cases. However, accounts from the mainland contain inconsistencies.

On April 11, 1955, the Indian airliner Kashmir Princess, Air India flight 300 from Hong Kong to Jakarta, crashed in Indonesian waters five hours after departure. Three crewmembers survived, but the other eleven persons onboard, including Chinese officials and journalists from the

PRC, Vietnam, and Europe, were killed. The crash was caused by a time bomb planted by a KMT agent while the aircraft was on the tarmac at Kai Tak Airport in Hong Kong, then a British colony.[31]

The original target of the bomb plot was PRC premier Zhou Enlai, who with his senior entourage was scheduled to take the flight to the Nonaligned Conference in Bandung. However, Zhou and senior colleagues rescheduled their travel four days beforehand, and a party of junior officials and journalists took their place on the manifest.[32]

Some aspects of the case appear clear, confirmed by both British and PRC accounts:

- there was a KMT plot to bomb Zhou's flight
- more than forty Nationalist Chinese agents in Hong Kong were involved, working on behalf of the KMT Intelligence Bureau (情报局, Qingbao ju)
- they recruited a single individual already employed as a ground crew member by Kai Tak airport, Zhou Ju (周驹, also known as Zhou Ziming, 周梓铭; Cantonese: Chow Keoi, also known as Chow Chi-ming), promising him sanctuary in Taiwan and 600,000 Hong Kong dollars
- all of these agents including the perpetrator either escaped or were deported by the British from Hong Kong to Taiwan, breaking up a large Nationalist spy ring in in the colony.[33]

However, a sensitive controversy remains. Though vigorously contested by Li (2015) and by a Xinhua account (2004), the most internally consistent hypothesis comes from Tsang (1994).[34] It is more specific than other accounts on the KMT's motives for planting the bomb, what Zhou Enlai and PRC intelligence knew and when they knew it, why the flight was not cancelled or diverted, and what roles the British, the Hong Kong government, and U.S. intelligence played.

In early 1955 the truce ending the Korean War, in which the British fought on the side of the United Nations against China, was less than two years old. Zhou Enlai succeeded in upgrading Sino-British relations with an exchange of chargés d'affaires in London and Beijing. This step toward normal diplomatic relations alarmed Generalissimo Chiang Kai-shek, leader of the Republic of China's Nationalist government on Taiwan. Chiang feared that British recognition of Beijing might lead to the PRC's admission to the United Nations, displacing Taiwan (which did not occur until political circumstances changed over a decade later). The Taiwan government likely decided to disrupt relations between Britain and mainland China, as Chiang considered Zhou's diplomacy and the Nonaligned Conference itself, scheduled for April 1955 in Bandung, to be a threat to his regime. Therefore, even when Zhou Enlai changed his travel plans on April 7, avoiding Air India flight 300, the KMT allowed the bomb plot to go ahead as it might disrupt the conference and damage Sino-British relations.[35]

British archives indicate that in the wake of the bombing, the Hong Kong authorities played a balancing act to survive between China, Taiwan, and the United States, and that they found only circumstantial evidence that the United States was involved. After apprehending forty-four of the perpetrators, the British concluded the best outcome would be successful convictions, but the worst would be putting them on trial and losing the case. Deportation was a middling option that carried the advantage of being under the full control of the British. However, a critical player eluded justice. On May 18 Zhou Ju was secretly smuggled out by the KMT intelligence bureau aboard a civil air transport flight operated by the Central Intelligence Agency—raising the possibility that the United States was either negligent or involved in the plot after all.[36]

Tsang argues that the CCP came out on top in the end, ridding Hong Kong of at least forty-four Nationalist spies, winning a propaganda battle, and testing how far the British could be pushed to go against the United States and Taiwan.[37] However, to win these gains, did Zhou, now regarded as an almost saintly figure in the CCP pantheon, use CCP intelligence and the foreign ministry to sacrifice innocent Xinhua and foreign journalists?

These ideas may seem fantastic and have caused outrage in China, but PRC efforts to refute them have met with only limited success and contain two critical contradictions. The 2004 Ministry of Foreign Affairs document release and the 2015 article by Li Hong, a former PRC intelligence officer working at the time under Luo Qingchang (chapter 2), assert that CCP intelligence issued a report on April 9 that the KMT intended to plant a time bomb aboard Air India flight 300, departing Hong Kong two days later. This led to a démarche from the Chinese Ministry of Foreign Affairs to the British representative in Beijing on the morning of April 10. While the British archives record that démarche, they say that the warning was not specific or even particularly urgent: it was about a threat to the passengers, not a time bomb. Moreover, the Xinhua and Li Hong accounts do not address an even more central question: If Zhou Enlai knew on or before April 9 that the threat against the flight was a time bomb, why did he not cancel or delay the flight or reroute the passengers to another mode of transport?

Though the hypothesis that Zhou sacrificed loyal citizens and foreign journalists is as intriguing to some as it is maddening to others, another possibility is apparent. At the moment when these questions arose in Beijing, the Chinese Communist Party was in crisis, as were its intelligence organs under Li Kenong. Mao Zedong's confidence in his senior colleagues had been badly shaken by the 1954 Gao Gang–Rao Shushi affair, which led the chairman to suspect a broad antiparty conspiracy between senior communists and the KMT enemy, and in March 1955 he remained concerned by the "rampant influence" of "domestic counterrevolutionary remnants."[38] Moreover, Mao Zedong decided on April 2, 1955, to arrest Pan Hannian under suspicion of being a KMT agent. Pan was a highly respected contemporary of Li Kenong in CCP intelligence during the revolution and in 1955 was a vice mayor of Shanghai. His arrest on April 3 was followed by a purge of CCP intelligence officers. Five days later, Mao Zedong approved Li Kenong's recommendation for an intelligence reorganization and the creation of the Central Investigation Department.[39]

Under these circumstances, rescheduling or rerouting Air India flight 300 might have either been overtaken by the events of the moment or required a decision by Mao Zedong under circumstances of great tension. Li Hong does not mention these events, though in his position he would have been aware of them. Future research in currently unavailable archives may eventually reveal if confusion, inertia, or fear contributed to the tragedy of Air India flight 300.

Intelligence during the Early PRC
Details about CCP intelligence operations in Hong Kong from 1949 onward, especially during the multi-agency interim period through 1955,

are scant. However, there is some information on Pan Jing'an, who was the CID station chief there under the guise of a Bank of China official from 1958 to 1982 (see chapter 3). During the Cultural Revolution, Zhou Enlai apparently resisted pressure to bring Pan back to Beijing, and the CID station chief stayed on post. However, it is unclear how his station was affected by the turmoil of 1967.

There may have been a division of effort between the CID and the Ministry of Public Security in Hong Kong during these years, with the presence of Pan's CID station and a separate MPS effort to recruit large numbers of bellhops, hotel cleaners, taxi drivers, postmen, and others to gather information on foreign visitors.[40]

In the 1970s and 1980s Hong Kong was an occasional meeting place between the CID's agent inside the CIA, Larry Wu-tai Chin, and his handlers from Beijing, showing the Crown Colony's continuing utility as a spot for clandestine operations. In the run-up to the 1997 handover of Hong Kong to China, British officials made efforts to strengthen Hong Kong's export controls in order to maintain the "free world status" of the territory for U.S. shipments of controlled technology. However, the growing number of mainland-controlled businesses during this time and the burgeoning cross-border trade probably made easier the smuggling of sensitive dual-use technology from Hong Kong to the Chinese military.

The Kowloon Walled City (九龙寨城, Jiulong Zhaicheng)

After the 1842 cession of Hong Kong to Great Britain under the Treaty of Nanjing, Chinese efforts to monitor British activities may have been based in the Walled City, which Beijing maintained as a government installation in the territory abutting Hong Kong that remained Chinese. However, the British desired an expansion of Hong Kong. In 1898 they initiated negotiations with Beijing's envoy, Viceroy Li Hongzhang, to lease what became the New Territories, allowing the colony better defense and more arable land. The Walled City lay within that area, and Beijing insisted on retaining sovereignty over it during the negotiations for the ninety-nine-year New Territories lease (1898–97).[41]

Such a place seems ideal as a base for espionage, and indeed the area became "a special area administratively distinct from the rest of the colony."[42] However, Qing Dynasty efforts after 1899 and subsequent

Nationalist Chinese actions regarding the Walled City seem confined to retaining sovereignty in name rather than in fact. After the founding of the PRC in 1949, communist officials consistently objected to British efforts to evict residents, demolish old structures, and so on, citing violations of Chinese sovereignty. This echoed the pragmatic stance of previous Chinese governments by opposing colonial authority inside the Walled City without pushing the envelope by trying to establish an official presence there. Meanwhile, the British ran regular police patrols inside the enclave to stop violent crime. By contrast, unlicensed physicians and dentists, gambling, prostitution, and drug use were more common than in other Hong Kong neighborhoods.[43]

At some point, CCP intelligence may have gained a foothold within the Walled City. In his memoir, the novelist Frederick Forsyth wrote that a friend employed by the Secret Intelligence Service took him to a restaurant in the Walled City in the 1980s, claiming that the establishment was run by CCP intelligence, serving as both a meeting place for British and Chinese intelligence officials and an operational base.[44] No additional source has surfaced to confirm this claim; one Western former intelligence officer with experience in Hong Kong commented that the CCP could just as easily have rented office space downtown and that the Hong Kong station chief of CCP intelligence probably sat in the old Bank of China building, now demolished. Indeed, Pan Jing'an, the CID station chief in Hong Kong, had the cover of chief auditor in the bank.[45] If the Walled City was used by CCP intelligence, it was probably to hold clandestine meetings and hide assets, not to serve as any sort of operational headquarters.

In 1987 with the agreement of the PRC government, the British took full control of the settlement and prepared it for demolition, which was carried out in 1993. The site is now a park, where traces of the Qing-era imperial residence are the only preserved remnants.[46]

Macau (Macao, 澳门, Aomen)

Long before it was the "Vegas of Asia," Macau was a Portuguese-administered *porto de abrigo*, or haven, for political activists. Secret societies dedicated to overthrowing the Manchu (Qing) dynasty were based there in the 1870s. The father of modern China, Sun Yat-sen, resided in the enclave at different times in the 1890s, and he founded the *Tongmenghui* (*Liga Unida*, or Unity League) in Macau in 1905.[47]

With the collapse of China's last dynasty in 1911–12 and the Bolshevik victory in Russia in 1918, Macau became an increasingly attractive haven for another activity: espionage. The Portuguese rounded up Chinese communist cells in 1927 and 1929 and in the 1930s. While Ho Chi Minh briefly lived in Macau, the Indochinese communist party held an early congress in the Hotel Cantão (Canton Hotel) on March 27–31, 1935. In 1937 a Russian NKVD "illegal" agent posing as a Frenchman was discovered operating a restaurant.[48] These are just the publicly known cases.

As they prepared to invade China, the Japanese made investments in Macau, posting intelligence officers under commercial cover.[49] In May 1935 news reports circulated that Tokyo had offered Lisbon U.S. $100 million to buy Macau, apparently as a military base.[50] When Tokyo's forces swept across the mainland and reached south China in mid-1938, Macau had become "a center for Japanese espionage and in turn one for Chinese counter-espionage," according a Portuguese report, which urged neutrality to preserve Lisbon's control.[51] Japanese soldiers patronized Macau hotels, restaurants, and gambling houses without paying, the Kempeitai (Japanese army secret police) maintained a strong presence, and Japanese forces controlled movement in and out. However, Japan mostly respected Macau's neutrality (as Germany respected that of Portugal): the British consulate stayed in place, the Portuguese administration remained intact, and Macau absorbed hundreds of thousands of refugees.[52]

Though the environment remained hostile to the Chinese communists, their urban agents and rural guerrillas found opportunities to expand operations. Pan Hannian, who ran all communist espionage operations in Japanese-occupied China, directed Dr. Ke Lin, a veteran secret agent, to move from Hong Kong to Macau in 1935 and establish a medical clinic. The mission: befriend and re-recruit General Ye Ting (who had taken refuge in Macau) to the communist cause. Ke was successful and continued clandestine operations in the Portuguese enclave for sixteen years. Most important for the long term, Ke cultivated and recruited Macau business figures such as Ho Yin and Ma Man-kei.[53]

When the Japanese army arrived in 1938, Chinese Communist East River Column guerrillas began operating in the region. They maintained three clandestine radio stations: in the Hong Kong New Territories, on Landau Island, and in downtown Macau. The Macau station operated without interruption from the Salesian School (Escola Salesiana—today's Instituto Salesiano) on Rua Central (Central Street). The Japanese tried but failed to locate the Macau station, which stayed on the air, undetected, until the end of the war.[54]

With Japan's surrender in August 1945, the Chinese Nationalists surrounded Macau, as had the Japanese before them, and placed operatives among "class associations" of herbalists, barbers, hotel employees, and factory workers.[55] In the midst of regular Nationalist bombings and shootings against communists in Macau, Ho Yin appealed to the Portuguese for protection. Lisbon's representatives tolerated secret operations of both the Nationalists and Communists as long as they did not disturb public order.

The Nam Kwong Company, founded in August 1949, became Beijing's unofficial office in Macau through 1987—when Xinhua, the New China News Agency, assumed that role as it had in Hong Kong.[56] Ho Yin and Ma Man-kei founded educational and business associations to counter the continuing strong presence of the exiled Nationalists on Taiwan, who were tolerated by the Portuguese due to the anticommunist stance of the Salazar government in Lisbon. Ho Yin became the chief intermediary between Beijing and Macau's Portuguese governor and ran some of Macau's lucrative gold smuggling operations—enriching himself and bringing $27 million a month into China after the People's Republic was declared in 1949.[57] Portuguese officials largely turned a blind eye to these re-exports, which during the Korean War also included petroleum, tires, and medicines destined for the Chinese People's Volunteers in Korea.

The balance of power in Macau dramatically shifted in 1966. After a string of Nationalist bombings and assassination attempts, including a grenade thrown at a car carrying Ho Yin on May 8 and the advent of the Cultural Revolution on the mainland that month, Beijing's agents in Macau prepared to move.[58] Portuguese mishandling of an unlicensed communist school on Taipa Island triggered demonstrations beginning December 3, which became known as the "12–3 (*Um dois três*) incident." Portuguese authorities were forced to close or expel Taiwan's overt and clandestine organizations.[59] While leaving Portuguese administrators in charge of day-to-day operations, Chinese representatives now had the final say in important matters, allowing Beijing's organizations to freely operate. In 1989, when a Portuguese police official was asked about possible re-exports of U.S. dual-use technology from Macau into the PRC, he said, "This is their country. We must respect their wishes."[60]

In recent times, PRC-appointed authorities have allowed those who would be suppressed as religious dissidents on the mainland to operate in Macau but have pursued a vigorous counterintelligence program—tightening up on organized crime and examining cases such as the perceived use of at least one American casino by the CIA to spot and recruit corrupt Chinese officials.[61] This is at least one indication that the role of Macau as a haven for international intrigue is not yet over.

Number Stations

Number stations refer to high-frequency (shortwave) transmissions of number groups with no explanation. Though they originated in the early twentieth century, these broadcasts can still be heard around the world. At least some probably carry enciphered messages from intelligence agencies for clandestine agents in the field abroad. During the Cold War, number station transmissions originated from Russia, its Warsaw Pact allies, Cuba, China, North Korea,[62] the United Kingdom, Australia, and some U.S. possessions. Such broadcasts continue today, including some in the Chinese language that carry a PRC signature.

Chinese number station broadcasts appear to send messages that probably originate as plaintext Chinese characters, converted into the publicly available four-digit standard telegraphic code (STC, 标准编码, *biaozhun bianma*).[63] The STC code groups can be encrypted using a one-time pad (OTP, 一次性密码本, *yi ci xing mima ben*), virtually guaranteeing security absent procedural errors. The agent at the receiving end, if equipped with the same OTP, can decipher the message at leisure after copying it by listening with an ordinary shortwave radio.

The four-digit enciphered groups are usually read by a woman in clearly spoken Mandarin (*Putonghua*) and seem tightly scripted. Broadcasts begin with a station identifier, such as "This is Zhuhai" (我是珠海, *Wo shi Zhuhai*), followed by an alert to have pen and paper ready (现在有报, *xianzai youbao*). Each four-digit group is spoken twice, yielding a transmission rate of roughly one Chinese character every five seconds.

This may seem like an oddly slow method, especially compared to messaging by computer and mobile phone. However, it is far more secure for the highly vulnerable "illegal" agent in the field, who lacks diplomatic immunity and cherishes obscurity. An OTP is easy to hide and simple to destroy, and a shortwave radio can be locally procured. Also, unlike dead drops, the post, mobile phones, or computers, the radio receiver leaves no trace of user identity or location. There are no Internet protocol addresses, cookies, or nearby base stations recording a personal unlocking key or other cell phone equipment number. The clandestine agent copying an encrypted message can be anywhere and is unlocatable by direction finding or other technology.

The Conet Project, Enigma 2000, and others have posted recordings on YouTube and at the Internet Archive of Chinese and other number stations and maintain lists of active broadcasts. While number stations may seem like a relic of the Cold War, they continue to operate today because their effectiveness and security are unmatched by the alternatives.

In popular culture, number station transmissions are depicted in the television series *The Americans*.[64]

Shi Peipu (时佩璞, 1938–2009)

In late 1964 the MPS exploited a forbidden sexual relationship between the Beijing opera star Shi Beipu and a French diplomat, Bernard Boursicot. The MPS may simply have taken advantage of the opportunity to blackmail Boursicot rather than create it. Perhaps not coincidentally, on September 3 of that year, Zhou Enlai received a briefing of current operations from MPS minister Xie Fuzhi. In postbriefing comments, Zhou advised him, "When carrying out investigations, we must resolutely oppose the use of the 'honey trap' [美人计, *meiren ji*]."[65]

Boursicot was just twenty and on his first tour overseas in 1964, assigned to an administrative role at the French embassy in Beijing. He reportedly was out of his intellectual and social depth with other French officers and was a newly realized bisexual. He fell in love with a local person, Shi Peipu (时佩璞). As a local Chinese allowed to associate with foreigners and give language lessons, Shi was probably coopted by the Beijing Public Security Bureau (see Ying Ruocheng, chapter 3). Shi convinced Boursicot that he was really a woman maintaining the disguise of a man for personal and family reasons. He maintained this ruse through manipulation and guile and eventually introduced Boursicot to an MPS officer who took control, soliciting documents and other information. Altogether, Boursicot handed over about 150 classified documents during this and subsequent tours in French overseas missions.

Chinese officers continued to control Boursicot in his subsequent assignments in Mongolia, Beijing, and Southeast Asia. The pair were arrested in 1983, and it was only then that Boursicot learned that his lover was a man. Four years later both men were pardoned by the French government in a bid to reduce tensions with Beijing. Shi continued to perform Chinese opera for a number of years afterward and died in 2009. Boursicot has spent his later years in China and France.[66]

Three Heroes of the Dragon's Lair
(龙潭三杰, *Longtan sanjie*)

The Three Heroes name primarily refers to a CCP intelligence network that operated from December 1929 to April 1931. The network is depicted as an unqualified intelligence success, although two of its three members did not survive for long.

The spy ring was the first CCP "intelligence small group" (情报小组, *qingbao xiaozu*) inside a KMT security service.[67] Their operation began after Qian Zhuangfei (钱壮飞) and Hu Di (胡底), both already active CCP members, moved to Shanghai in late 1927 in the wake of the April 12 Nationalist-Communist split. After a winter of surviving on odd jobs, Qian joined a Nationalist-run radio technology class in mid-1928, which was secretly sponsored by the newly established KMT Investigations Branch (调查科, *Diaocha ke*), charged with hunting down CCP members.[68]

Qian strived to be perceived as a good student of Sun Yat-sen's Three People's Principles, the KMT's orthodoxy. In the autumn of 1928 he brought himself to the attention of the KMT wireless bureau director U. T. Hsu

(徐恩增, Xu Enzeng), employing to advantage their shared dialect from Huzhou county, Zhejiang.[69] Unfortunately for Hsu, he placed undue trust in Qian, hiring him as a confidential secretary in April 1929. Though Hsu had no previous intelligence experience, in December 1929 he replaced Chen Lifu as head of the investigations bureau. Qian Zhuangfei accompanied him to the secret organization and, in Hsu's words, became "one of the most capable workers . . . taking care of our top-secret files."[70]

That same month, after connecting with Qian, Li Kenong successfully sat for examinations to enter the wireless bureau and was appointed as a news editor. Qian introduced Hu Di to a connection in Shanghai, and Hu began work in the municipal wireless management bureau. With all three placed inside the Nationalist government, they became a network controlled by Li Kenong, reporting to Special Services Section (SSS) intelligence branch chief Chen Geng. Qian, increasingly trusted by Hsu, took charge of the communications room at the investigations bureau's headquarters in Nanjing. Li Kenong in Shanghai and Hu Di in Tianjin also were inducted into the investigations bureau, with cover jobs in wireless management.[71]

Though the efforts of the Three Heroes did not fully immunize the CCP from its enemies, their infiltration of the KMT investigations branch and the work of other SSS groups under Chen Geng kept arrests lower than they might have been. However, the defection in April 1931 of Chen's boss, SSS director Gu Shunzhang, exposed the Three Heroes network and compromised hundreds of other communists and their havens across the country.

Even before Gu's 1931 defection, KMT pressure was on the rise. On January 3 two Central Committee members, Luo Yiyuan (罗绮园) and Yang Baoan (杨匏安), were arrested after betrayal by the husband of a young female communist forced to live with Luo as his spouse for cover purposes.[72]

U. T. Hsu called Gu Shunzhang "a genius in secret service work" and "a living encyclopedia of communist underground activities," but unfortunately for the KMT, they moved too slowly to exploit the situation.[73] When apprehended in Wuhan on April 25, Gu decided to cooperate to avoid torture and eventual death, but he would not reveal vital information without a personal meeting with Chiang Kai-shek, who was hundreds of miles away in Nanjing. After some indecision about how to transport Gu to Nanjing, he was put on a military aircraft on April 27 and arrived in Nanjing that day. Meanwhile in Nanjing, Qian Zhuangfei spotted the first reporting telegram on April 25. He intercepted and decrypted the messages and sent a courier to warn Li Kenong in Shanghai and alert the CCP Central Committee.[74] As a result, senior communists knew about Gu's defection before the Nationalist command in Nanjing. Without this lucky break and Qian's diligence, the CCP Central Committee might have been destroyed, eliminating leaders such as Zhou Enlai and leaving the party in the hands of Zhu De and Mao Zedong with the Red Army in Jiangxi.

Their network compromised, Li, Qian, and Hu fled for Mao's headquarters. Many other communists also survived.[75] Li Kenong went on to a distinguished intelligence career, but both Qian Zhuangfei and Hu Di were killed during the Long March: Qian in an aerial bombardment, and Hu in a "mistaken" purge—not an unfamiliar circumstance for the party under Mao.[76] In this sense, the fates of the Three Heroes are a microcosm of the high risks taken by CCP intelligence operatives in the Chinese communist revolution.

Tibet (བོད *Bod*, 西藏, *Xizang*)

To CCP leaders in Beijing, control of Tibet is of vital importance for geopolitical reasons. It is the origin of several major rivers in Asia, and it borders the province of Sichuan, a vital Chinese agricultural region that is also the southwestern corner of China's core area. Due to a recent history of foreign influence—Indian, British, and arguably American—and because Tibetans throughout history have strived for independence when China is weak, Beijing's leaders are focused on securing Tibet from outside forces.

Chinese concerns about foreign infiltration of Tibet are not without reason. As U.S. and Taiwan agent insertions declined and failed in northern, eastern, and southern China after 1949, the Americans decided in 1957 to step up efforts to support local resistance in Tibet. Tibet was considered a dangerous assignment for CCP cadre in those days, as illustrated by the April 1958 murder of a PLA officer in Lhasa whose duties included "investigation and research and operational work targeting Tibetan elite and religious circles."[77]

When the Dalai Lama and his advisors fled Lhasa on horseback for India in March 1959, they were met and accompanied by a CIA-trained Tibetan radio team that had been on the ground for almost two years. The Dwight D. Eisenhower White House closely tracked reports from the agents, Athar and Lotse, describing the Dalai's exodus. India gave the group refuge, and they settled in Dharamsala, India, now a center of pilgrimage. These events contributed to an indelible perception among the CCP leadership that, given the chance, India and the United States would employ Tibetans to split the PRC and that some Tibetans would take the chance, if offered, to exit toward independence.[78]

U.S. espionage and paramilitary operations in Tibet ended in 1968 and were buried for good with the Sino-U.S. rapprochement in 1972, but Beijing continues to perceive a threat in Tibet from foreign agents.[79] Consequently, the CCP devotes considerable resources to ascertain whether Western forces are infiltrating Tibet and to keep tabs on Tibetans in exile, particularly the Dalai Lama.

Yellow Crane Pavilion Incident
(黄鹤楼事件, *Huanghe lou shijian*)

This event in the annals of Chinese VIP protection operations showed that the developing personality cult of Mao Zedong could actually endanger his safety and those of others. It caused a significant shift, albeit not the last one, in how the chairman was protected.

Mao visited Wuhan in February 1953 accompanied by MPS minister Luo Ruiqing (罗瑞卿), Hubei party secretary Li Xiannian (李先念), Yang Shangkun (杨尚昆) of the party central office, and Wang Dongxing (汪东兴), director of the central guards bureau (中央保卫局, *zhongyang baowei ju*). Wang later became an MPS vice minister and was in charge of the program to protect the CCP leadership.[80]

On the fifth day after lunar new year, Mao expressed a desire to visit Hanyang (汉阳), a district in Wuhan. Wang Renzhong (王任重), the vice mayor, urged the chairman not to go, saying the district's "social order is unstable." Mao insisted, forcing Wang and Li to admit that they had recently been to Hanyang—so why should the chairman avoid it? After crossing the Yangtze River to Hanyang, Mao decided to attend a fair at the Yellow Crane Pavilion. Upon arrival, Mao stopped to buy fried bean curd from a hawker. Two small girls recognized him and cried out, drawing a crowd. As more people gathered, Luo and Yang suggested that the chairman change his coat and put on a hat and sunglasses. He did so but it was too late: more and more people gathered around, eager to see Mao, whose height (five feet eleven inches), heavy build, and familiar face made him stand out in any crowd.[81]

The situation began to grow chaotic as people crowded the small party, shouting, "Long live Chairman Mao! Long live the Chinese Communist Party!" and trying to touch him. Mao, seldom wanting for personal courage, removed his hat and sunglasses and began waving to the masses. Li Yinqiao (李银桥), the officer in charge of his protection detail, and his men struggled to place Mao and the other VIPs back into their vehicles. They headed toward the river, a kilometer away, and boarded a ferry. As the boat embarked, people all around seemed to know of Mao's presence. The air was filled with chants of "Long live Chairman Mao," leaving no prospect of safely returning to shore. Luo, Yang, and Li discussed what to do next. They were worried, not unreasonably, that "counterrevolutionary elements" might realize Mao was in the area and try to harm him.

Arriving at the western shore of the Yangzi where a vehicle was waiting, Li and three other junior personnel attempted to distract the crowds by announcing that Mao had left Wuhan—but no one believed it. A persistent worker who wanted to see Mao impulsively stripped off his clothes to show he carried no weapon, begging to lay eyes upon the chairman. Meanwhile Mao was still onboard the ferry, which continued along the shore, seeking a river wharf without hazardous crowds. Luo picked one that appeared safe and summoned cars to the spot, but by the time they alighted, more crowds appeared. Nonetheless, Mao's security detail managed to push through and escape.

The group returned to the chairman's temporary quarters, nervous as if they had just been in a battle, with "eyes staring wide" (眼睛还瞪的大大的,

yanjing hai dengde da da de).[82] Luo, humiliated, engaged in a spontaneous self-examination, first to Mao and later before the entire Politburo. Mao downplayed the incident, saying it was not Luo's fault: "I must really stay within the Summer Palace, not go to places like the Yellow Crane Pavilion" (真是出不了的颐和园, 下不了的黄鹤楼呀, *Zhen shi chubuliao de Yiheyuan, xiabuliao Huanghe lou ya*).[83]

In the face of the growing personality cult, it was a lesson in the need to more carefully plan Mao's public appearances. Luo Ruiqing and Wang Dongxing worked together to increase the chairman's security. By 1956 Mao's bodyguards and other entourage on the road totaled more than two hundred people. When he flew, all air traffic in China was grounded, and his food was tested for poison. However, Mao began to complain that year about the increased security. He felt his staff was unduly copying the Soviets; he believed the masses loved him and wished him no harm; and he valued his privacy, believing that Luo Ruiqing and Wang Dongxing reported what they knew to others in the party leadership. In 1957 Mao's travel entourage was reduced to less than one-tenth of the previous number.[84]

In the Cultural Revolution (1966–76), Mao's security was again increased, though in 1967 the chairman had to order "Rebel" Red Guards under the influence of Wang Dongxing, chief of his security detail, to cease political attacks against the leadership.[85]

◆ SIX ◆

Espionage during China's Rise

Far more espionage cases are available for examination after 1989. This genuine upsurge of activity seems driven by a growing foreign presence in China and increasing opportunities for the PRC services (and probably tasking from the CCP) to gather intelligence abroad. While there are more cases to examine, the details are less available than for the historic set (see chapter 5). Intelligence officials from China and elsewhere strive to protect sources and methods from each other and wish to avoid upsetting commercial and diplomatic relations between an economically vibrant China and its trading partners.

The cases in chapters 4, 5, and 6 show significant continuity in Chinese espionage methods, which are largely similar to those used by other professional intelligence services. For example, these cases indicate that PRC intelligence services seek opportunities stemming from personal compromises by targeted individuals, be they sexual or otherwise; that Chinese intelligence professionals do not limit themselves to recruiting Chinese alone; and that there is significant interest in acquiring not only national secrets but also foreign technology and intellectual property of value to China's economy and national defense. The latter includes both dual-use technology and other critical data to assist Chinese planners in fulfilling PRC Five-Year Plan goals.[1] Therefore, not only national leaders but also business executives should understand the risk of losing competitive advantage to CCP-sponsored technology acquisition operations.

This traditional spying has not gone away (and never will), though today's headlines are dominated by cyber theft. Even on the computer screen, there is a link to the past. Network intrusions by the famous former PLA Third Department Unit 61398 (61398 部队, *budui*) targeted information reminiscent of that sought by spies of earlier eras: biographical data on persons of interest, classified material, and technology useful to military modernization. So much espionage activity has shifted to the digital world because that is where the information resides. CCP intelligence operations during the Anti-Japanese War (1937–45) focused on China's largest cities because that was where the Japanese and the Nationalists had their headquarters and kept their secrets. So too do 61398, Shady RAT, and their brethren concentrate on the overseas computer networks where the information Beijing desires is stored in quantities unimaginable during the predigital age. Not only are the amounts of data vast, but also the operational sophistication of China's hackers continues to grow.

The most notable aspect of China's recent intelligence operations is the integration of traditional human agent operations with capabilities in cyberspace. At nearly every phase of intelligence collection, the Ministry of State Security and military intelligence are capable of using computer network exploitation to supplement traditional human intelligence and vice versa. Previously, Chinese intelligence relentlessly gathered dossiers on potential targets by interviewing retired foreign government officials, their friends, and their families. Building this database of names enabled the rapid identification of potential targets for recruitment as they traveled to and from China. These means, however, have been supplemented by the hacking of foreign databases to acquire personal data en masse. The MSS theft of data from Taiwanese residential databases and the U.S. Office of Personnel Management are only the examples that are publicly known. Criminal indictments issued by the U.S. Department of Justice in September and October 2018 show intelligence officers from the Jiangsu State Security Department ran a network of human sources and hackers to acquire foreign aviation technology. The corporate insiders recruited by this MSS department both facilitated access to foreign networks and helped cover up MSS activity on the internal networks. It is this combination of human and technical means that demonstrates China's intelligence activities have achieved world-class status.

Anonymous German Member of Parliament (pitched summer 2016)

An unnamed member of parliament (MP) received a message through the social networking site LinkedIn from a Chinese manager named "Jason Wang." Wang sought to engage the MP in a consulting agreement for analysis of German foreign policy and domestic politics. After exchanging several messages, Wang offered €30,000 as the beginning payment for responses to a set of questions. The Federal Office for the Protection of the Constitution intervened prior to any payment being made to the MP but reportedly not before he provided the Ministry of State Security (MSS) with some initial thoughts on German policy and politics.[2]

Anonymous Japanese Communicator (pitched 2003–4)

An unnamed Japanese code clerk based at the consulate in Shanghai committed suicide in May 2004 after being pressured by the Shanghai State Security Bureau (SSSB) to provide information on his colleagues and consular communications. The SSSB exploited the clerk's affair with a woman working at a karaoke bar by approaching her in 2003 and then pressuring him to provide personal details on his colleagues, the consulate's Chinese contacts, and the schedule for diplomatic pouches sent back to Tokyo.[3]

Anonymous U.S. Academic Researcher (pitched 2011–12)

A U.S. academic researcher with a senior fellow position with a Washington, DC–based think tank received an approach from a provincial state security department following a lecture in the provincial capital. The MSS officer was covered as a research fellow at the provincial academy of social sciences. Over the weeks following the lecture, the officer reached out via phone and email to arrange a meeting in person where the U.S. scholar was based. At this meeting, the officer offered him several thousand Chinese yuan as a down payment on a consulting arrangement. The scholar would write analytic papers based on his contacts and interviews with colleagues and contacts in Washington, DC, in response to prompts from the officer. He rejected the pitch.[4]

Bergersen, Gregg (arrested 2008, pleaded guilty 2008)

Gregg Bergersen worked for the Defense Security Cooperation Agency (DSCA) on its East Asia portfolio, including Taiwan. He became involved with Chinese intelligence through Kuo Tai-shen. The first recorded meeting between the two was in early 2007. Kuo presented himself as a businessman looking to get involved in U.S. military sales to Taiwan. He led Bergersen to believe that he worked for Taiwan's ministry of national defense (though a PRC official based in Guangzhou was Kuo's real controller) and held out a job offer with a six-figure salary for when Bergersen retired from the Department of Defense. The relationship was cemented with a paid trip to Las Vegas and cash payments. Bergersen provided classified data on U.S. defense systems and policy, and the two conspired to form a company to transfer U.S.-made command, control, communications, computers, intelligence, surveillance, and reconnaissance systems to Taiwan. Shortly after his arrest, Gregg Bergersen pleaded guilty and was sentenced to five years in prison.[5]

Bishop, Benjamin Pierce (sentenced 2014)

Lt. Col. Benjamin Bishop, USA (Ret.), met Claudia He, a PRC national, at an international military conference in Hawaii. The two began a romantic relationship in 2011, and Bishop began communicating classified information by email and phone to her. Claudia He was a PhD student at Tsinghua University and in the United States was a visiting fellow researching international relations and military strategy. Unbeknownst to Bishop, she was also in contact with the MSS when she visited Beijing. The MSS paid her several thousand dollars to write interview-based papers on U.S. defense partnerships, nuclear issues, and Asia-Pacific strategy, based in part on her contact with Bishop. Bishop pleaded guilty to communicating classified national defense information to an unauthorized person and unlawfully retaining classified national defense papers. A federal court sentenced him to seven years in prison.[6]

Chang Chih-hsin (張祉鑫; recruited 2010, arrested 2012)

Commander Chang Chih-hsin of the Taiwan navy was the chief political warfare officer at the naval meteorology and oceanography office when he was recruited by Chien Ching-kuo and Lu Chun-chun in 2010 or 2011. That year Chien and Lu took Chang on a trip to Cebu in the Philippines where he was introduced to Chinese intelligence officers. Chang's materials for his handlers is unknown, but he did have access to a broad set of data related to meteorological and oceanographic battle environments that he may have passed. He also agreed to assist Chinese intelligence in spotting and recruiting other active-duty military officers. Following his retirement in 2012, Chang met with Chinese intelligence officers in Fuzhou and Xiamen while on tours to China. Taiwan's supreme court upheld his fifteen-year prison sentence in 2014.[7]

Chen Chu-fan (陳築藩; recruited after 2004, convicted 2013, overturned 2016)

Lieutenant General Chen Chu-fan was the deputy commander of Taiwan's military police command and a high-ranking Kuomintang official who spied for the Shanghai State Security Bureau (SSSB). Chen was influential in Kuomintang political and military circles, having served as the ministry of national defense legislative liaison and deputy director of the Kuomintang's Taipei City chapter. After his retirement in 2004, he began traveling to China and sometime thereafter came into contact with the SSSB. He agreed to assist the SSSB in recruiting a spy network inside Taiwan and introduced former Military Intelligence Bureau officer Chen Shu-lung to the SSSB. The two Chens sold documents to Chinese intelligence related to military troop deployments and planning, military exercises, election analysis, and Falun Gong activities in Taiwan. Taiwanese courts sentenced Chen to twenty months in prison in 2013 and upheld the sentence on appeal in 2014, but the sentence was overturned in 2016.[8]

Chen Shu-lung (陳蜀龍; recruited 2006, convicted 2013)

Chen Shu-lung was a retired Taiwanese army major who worked for the Military Intelligence Bureau. In 2006, Chen was approached by retired Lieutenant General Chen Chu-fan on behalf of the SSSB, and he began spying for China. It is unclear whether Chen actually met SSSB officers or whether General Chen was his sole point of contact. The two Chens sold Chinese intelligence documents related to military troop deployments and planning, military exercises, election analysis, and Falun Gong activities in Taiwan.[9] Chen Shu-lung also sold the identities of Military Intelligence Bureau and National Security Bureau officers. He tricked one such officer into visiting Shanghai, where the officer was detained and interrogated by the MSS for three days in 2007. In 2013 a Taiwanese court sentenced Chen to eight years in prison but reduced the sentence to five years on appeal in 2014.[10]

Chen Wen-jen (陳文仁; recruited 1990s, arrested 2012)

Chen Wen-jen was discharged from the Taiwan air force as a lieutenant in 1992 and moved to China sometime thereafter. He went into business and married a Chinese citizen before he was recruited by 2PLA. Chen reconnected with an active-duty air force colleague, Yuan Hsiao-feng, in 2001. The two sold classified data to 2PLA, conveyed in flash drives, until 2007. Taiwanese authorities began investigating Chen and Yuan in 2011 after they attempted to recruit two junior officers. Chen was rumored to have recruited another officer who provided data on Taiwanese combat aircraft. In 2013 a Taiwan court sentenced Chen to twenty years in prison because his espionage occurred after he retired from the air force.[11]

Chien Ching-kuo (錢經國; recruited 2009, sentenced 2013)

Following his retirement from the Taiwan navy in 2009, former lieutenant Chien Ching-kuo was recruited by Lu Chun-chun and introduced to Chinese intelligence on an all-expenses-paid trip to Bali, Indonesia. Chien operated a barbecue restaurant in Taipei after his retirement, which he used for meetings with potential Taiwanese sources. He provided classified information to China relating to Taiwanese plans to send naval vessels to the Horn of Africa for antipiracy missions. The plans ultimately did not come to fruition. In addition, he assisted Chinese intelligence in spotting and recruiting other Taiwanese security officials. Chinese intelligence treated him to overseas trips. They also arranged formal CCP status for Chien in 2011. He joined Lu on some of these trips, where he assisted Chinese intelligence in recruiting other sources, such as Chang Chih-hsin. A Taiwanese court sentenced him to three years in prison.[12]

Chou Chih-li (周自立; arrested 2015)

Taiwan air force colonel Chou Chih-li was arrested as part of Zhen Xiaojiang's spy ring in 2015 alongside three other current or former military officers. There is no evidence that Chou spied while he was in uniform. He contacted serving Taiwanese military officers on behalf of Zhen and attempted to acquire classified defense information.[13]

Chun, Kun Shan (recruited 2011, sentenced 2017)

Kun Shan Chun was a naturalized U.S. citizen working as an electronic technician for the FBI. Chun began working for the FBI New York field office as a technician in 1997 and received a top-secret clearance the following year in connection with his work. In 2006 Chun and his family developed contacts with businesspeople associated with Zhuhai Kolion Technology Company Ltd. (Kolion), possibly because some of Chun's family members invested in the company. Kolion repeatedly asked Chun between 2006 and 2010 to perform consulting tasks in exchange for payment or international trips. In 2011 Kolion representatives introduced Chun to a Chinese official, who is unidentified in public documents, while Chun was on a trip to France and Italy partly financed by Kolion. The official, who appears to have been an intelligence officer, tasked Chun with providing details on the FBI's internal organization, how to identify traveling FBI agents, and the FBI's surveillance technology. This official only met Chun outside the United States.[14] Chun was sentenced two years in prison in 2017 after pleading guilty to acting as unregistered agent of a foreign power.[15]

Claiborne, Candice (contacted 2003–5, arrested 2017)

Candice Claiborne was an office management specialist at the U.S. Department of State recruited by the SSSB. The criminal affidavit suggests Claiborne met the SSSB officers in Shanghai while she was posted there from 2003 to 2005 and assigned to the consul general. The SSSB arguably did not recruit her in the normal sense but acquired leverage through supporting her son (identified in the affidavit as coconspirator A). Most of the support (cash, personal electronics, meals, international travel and vacations, tuition at a Chinese fashion school, a furnished apartment, and a monthly stipend) went to Claiborne's son. As she apparently balked at the tasking given to her by the SSSB and tried to warn her son away from the SSSB officers, their relationship and her son's presence in Shanghai kept her connected. Claiborne may have been a reluctant participant near her arrest in 2017, but her earlier diary entries suggested someone enticed by the promise of making an additional $20,000 per year and happy with the smaller payments she already earned.[16] She pleaded not guilty in 2017 and is awaiting trial as of this writing.

Co-optee (Cut-out)

Counterintelligence officials in several countries have noticed frequent Chinese use of civilian collaborators to enable foreign intelligence operations. The FBI defines them as "mutually trusted person[s] or mechanism[s] used to create a compartment between members of an operation to enable them to pass material and/or messages securely. A cut-out or co-optee can operate under a variety of covers, posing as diplomats, journalists, academics, or business people both at home and abroad. These individuals are tasked with spotting, assessing, targeting, collecting, and running sources."[17] Examples may include Zhen Xiaojiang and Zhou Hongxu.

Doumitt, Paul (pitched 1988)

Paul Doumitt was a married, forty-five-year-old U.S. Embassy communications officer based in Beijing who was pitched by the MSS. Doumitt began a long-term romantic relationship with a young Chinese shopkeeper while his wife was in France taking care of her sick mother. MSS officers confronted Doumitt in a shop across the street from that of his mistress. They threatened to expose graphic details of the affair to his wife and embassy colleagues, demanding that he identify U.S. intelligence officers serving at the embassy. Doumitt claimed he identified diplomatic security officers serving openly in the regional security office—who manage the embassy's overall security arrangements and threats to U.S. government personnel abroad—as potential intelligence officers. He reported the meeting to the regional security office, and then-Ambassador Winston Lord sent him home.[18]

Fondren, James (recruited 1999, convicted 2009)

Col. James Fondren, USA (Ret.), worked as an independent consultant after his retirement. At the time of his arrest, he was deputy director of the Washington, DC, liaison office of U.S. Pacific Command (PACOM). Fondren served in this position from 2001 to 2008 and was convicted of passing defense secrets between 2004 and 2008. He was recruited by Kuo Tai-shen in the 1990s. Kuo introduced Fondren to his case officer, Lin Hong, in 1999, giving Fondren no doubt that a Chinese official received the consulting reports he wrote for Kuo. Kuo and Fondren hid their espionage relationship in a consulting business, but Kuo was the latter's only customer. Fondren typically sold his opinion papers to Kuo for $350 to $800 apiece. While employed by PACOM, he routinely shared classified and unclassified documents with Kuo, including drafts of the annual Pentagon report on Chinese military power. In 2010 Fondren was sentenced to three years in prison after being convicted in a five-day trial in 2009.[19]

Gao Xiaoming "Helen" (detained 2010, not prosecuted)

Gao Xiaoming, a contract translator for the U.S. Department of State between 2010 and 2014, confessed to providing information on her colleagues and their activities. A person whom she believed to be an intelligence officer approached her in China in 2007, asking her to provide information on her social contacts in the United States. She was given a one-time payment of $6,000 at the time and claimed she was wired $5,000 in January 2010. She later lived "briefly for free" with an architect who possessed a top-secret clearance for his work designing U.S. embassy facilities for the State Department. That employee admitted to discussing his work on U.S. facilities and his State Department colleagues by name. During her background check for her State Department contract and her U.S. naturalization paperwork, Gao concealed her relationship with the Chinese intelligence officer. For unknown reasons, U.S. authorities declined to prosecute the case either on charges related to being an unregistered agent or related to lying on immigration and security paperwork.[20]

Gyantsan, Dorjee (recruited by 2015, convicted 2018)

Dorjee Gyantsan was a pro-Tibetan radio station worker living in Sweden who provided Chinese intelligence with information on other Tibetan exiles. The circumstances of Gyantsan's recruitment are unknown, but he did receive small payments (the highest reportedly was $6,000) and had his expenses reimbursed. Gyantsan provided personal information about Tibetans living abroad, such as where they lived, their family ties, and their political activities, when he met with his Chinese case officer in Poland. The Swedish authorities claimed two case officers handled Gyantsan, including a diplomat attached to the Chinese embassy in Poland and a Sweden-based journalist for the official paper *China Daily*.[21] A Swedish court sentenced him to twenty-two months in jail.[22]

Hansen, Ron Rockwell (arrested 2018)

Ron Hansen was a former intelligence officer with the U.S. Army and a case officer for the Defense Intelligence Agency (DIA). After his retirement from active duty in 2006, Hansen became a member of H-11 Digital Forensics Company and H-11 Digital Forensics Services. As part of his Asia-related business, he maintained an office and an apartment in China. One of his office partners, going by the name "Robert," maintained connection with China's intelligence services. Although he was employed in the private sector, Hansen continued as an intelligence contractor involved in human intelligence operations for DIA until 2011. Hansen began trying to rejoin the DIA in early 2012, contacting a string of former colleagues and congressional staff through 2016. The FBI began investigating him in 2014, and he agreed to nine voluntary meetings with the bureau. He told them in early 2014 that two MSS officers began meeting with him in Beijing and that his partner "Robert" made the arrangements. A third MSS officer, "Max Tong," made the introduction after serving as an MSS contact since 2011. In their pitch, the two MSS officers offered $300,000 per year for "consulting services" and began overpaying Hansen for computer forensics products. After this meeting, "Robert" no longer served as an intermediary. The officers gave Hansen a preprogrammed cell phone for him to use inside China to arrange meetings with his handlers. Hansen and his MSS handlers also refined their method of transferring money. Previously he had received cash, but he had been caught by U.S. Customs for not declaring currency in excess of $10,000. In 2016 they began processing payments to a Visa merchant account related to a company Hansen owned. The MSS handled roughly $200,000 in payments this way until Hansen's arrest in 2018. He provided the MSS with information on his former colleagues, analytic products based on classified materials, and export-controlled computer forensics equipment. In June 2018 Hansen was arrested and charged with fifteen counts related to espionage, money laundering, and export control violations.[23]

He, Claudia (not prosecuted)

Claudia He was a PhD student at a Chinese university researching international security issues. The MSS paid He to write papers on U.S. defense issues and strategy toward China based on her contacts while she was in the United States as a visiting fellow at the University of Maryland and sleeping with defense contractor Benjamin Bishop.[24] See Benjamin Pierce Bishop.

Ho Chih-chiang (何志強; recruited 2007, arrested 2010)

Ho Chih-chiang was a China-based Taiwanese businessman who was recruited in 2007 to assist Chinese intelligence in spotting and recruiting other Taiwanese sources. Chinese intelligence paid Ho and offered other unspecified privileges for his business inside China. During a trip to Taiwan, Ho made a failed recruitment of a National Security Bureau (NSB) officer in which he offered $20,000, expensive liquor, and promise of regular pay higher than an NSB pension. Ho asked the NSB officer for information relating to the service's overseas deployments, satellite communications, and Taipei's policies toward Falun Gong, Tibetan independence, and Japan.[25]

Hsieh Chia-kang (謝嘉康; recruited 2009–10, arrested 2017)

Major General Hsieh Chia-kang was the deputy commander of the Matsu defense command at the time of his arrest. When the investigation into his spying began, Hsieh was moved from his position as commander of the missile defense command, where he had access to technical details for the U.S.-made MIM-104F Patriot missile and the domestically developed

Tien-Kung III and Hsiung-Feng 2E cruise missiles. Retired Taiwan army colonel Hsin Peng-sheng allegedly brought Hsieh into contact with Chinese intelligence, who recruited the general in 2009 or 2010. Hsieh met his handlers in Malaysia and Thailand. Taiwanese investigators were not clear whether Hsieh had been paid in exchange for providing classified defense information and helping recruit other Taiwanese military officers. A fellow military officer told security officials about the connection between Hsieh and someone recruited by Chinese intelligence.[27]

Hsin Peng-sheng (辛澎生; recruited 2016, arrested 2017)

Retired Taiwan army colonel Hsin Peng-sheng worked in the travel industry, and Chinese intelligence recruited him in 2016 while he was leading a Taiwanese tour group to China. Hsin agreed to assist Chinese intelligence in finding and recruiting other Taiwanese sources and recruited Major General Hsieh Chia-kang, with whom he had previously served. Unspecified sources told the Ministry of Justice Investigation Bureau in 2016 that Hsin had been recruited, prompting the investigation that led to Hsin and Hsieh.[26]

Hsu Nai-chuan (許乃權; arrested 2015)

Taiwan army major general Hsu Nai-chuan was the highest-ranking officer implicated in the Zhen Xiaojiang spy ring. He served as the commander of both the Kinmen and Matsu defense commands and commander of the Kaohsiung military academy. He also had been a candidate for Kinmen magistrate. He was sentenced to three years in prison, which was reduced by two months on appeal. The high court ruled that his efforts to build Zhen's spy network only qualified as "attempts at" rather than acts of espionage.[28]

Jiangsu State Security Department

The Jiangsu State Security Department (JSSD) is the Jiangsu provincial-level department of the MSS. In September and October 2018 the U.S. Department of Justice released criminal complaints and indictments related to the JSSD's worldwide efforts from 2010 to 2015 to acquire the underlying technology related to a turbofan engine used for U.S.- and

European-made commercial aircraft. The JSSD operation involved Chinese intelligence officers using a combination of human agents recruited inside foreign aerospace manufacturing companies and outside hackers to gain access to the targeted companies' networks. JSSD officers also employed a Chinese graduate student in the United States to run background checks on potential recruitment targets and may have directed him to join the U.S. Army Reserves. The United States lured Xu Yanjun, a JSSD deputy division director involved in the operation, to Belgium, where he was arrested and extradited. Xu had presented himself as a representative of the Jiangsu Science and Technology Promotion Association to bring foreign experts and employees of the targeted companies to China. While in China, the JSSD would attempt to acquire documents or other pertinent technical information from the visitors in exchange for travel expenses and modest honoraria. The JSSD officers, like Xu, maintained close contact with researchers from the Nanjing University of Aeronautics and Astronomics (南京航空航天大学) about aviation technology and even accompanied university staff on travel.[29]

Ko Cheng-sheng (柯政盛; recruited 1998, arrested 2013)

Vice Admiral Ko Cheng-sheng served as deputy commander of Taiwan's navy from 2000 to 2003. Australian-Taiwanese businessman Shen Ping-kang recruited Ko on behalf of Chinese intelligence in 1998. To hide the relationship, Shen paid for Ko and his family to travel to Australia. From there, Ko and Shen would travel to China together to meet with their handlers. It is unclear whether military intelligence or the United Front Work Department recruited the pair. Taiwanese authorities could not provide a clear accounting of what Ko betrayed to China. After Ko's retirement in 2003, he attempted to recruit several younger officers. A Taiwanese court sentenced him to fourteen months in prison in 2014, possibly taking into account Ko's age and cooperation.[30]

Ko Chi-hsien (葛季賢; indicted 2015, convicted 2017)

Retired Taiwan air force officer Ko Chi-hsien was one of several air force officers implicated in the Zhen Xiaojiang spy ring. He previously served as deputy commander of the air force academy flight training command.[31] In

1990 Ko was one of four F-104G pilots involved in a tense confrontation over the Taiwan Strait when Chinese fighters intercepted two Taiwanese RF-104G reconnaissance planes. He was regarded as a hero for his role in getting the Chinese interceptors to back off the reconnaissance planes.[32] A Taiwanese court sentenced Ko to three to ten years in prison.

Kuo Tai-shen (arrested 2008, pleaded guilty 2008)

Kuo Tai-shen was a Louisiana-based furniture importer and naturalized Taiwanese American who served as the principal agent between the 2PLA and his sources James Fondren and Gregg Bergersen. As Kuo began doing business in China in the early 1990s, a Chinese friend introduced him to Lin Hong of the Guangzhou Friendship Association as "someone [Kuo] needed to know to do business in China."[33] No public information is available on how the relationship subsequently developed. They used Kuo's mistress, Kang Rixin, as an intermediary and met in her Beijing apartment rented by Kuo. In 2007 Kuo and Lin began using commercial encryption to communicate via email.[34] Initially, Kuo's intelligence value was his marriage to an old Kuomintang family in Taiwan. In 1996 he met Fondren, a retired U.S. Air Force lieutenant colonel. Two years later, Kuo began paying Fondren for consulting services. He also introduced Fondren to Lin in 1999. Fondren's reports became more valuable in 2001 when he became the deputy director of the U.S. Pacific Command liaison office in Washington, DC. Kuo continued to handle Fondren until his arrest, and, as part of his own plea, he testified against Fondren in his 2009 trial.[35] Kuo also developed Bergersen, another Defense Department source, who worked on Asian issues for the Defense Security Cooperation Agency (DSCA). Although Kuo's case officer never seemed enthusiastic about Bergersen, Kuo sought to use Bergersen to get a contract for transferring U.S. technology to Taiwan in support of the Po Sheng program. He acted as Bergersen's case officer, wining and dining him as well as treating him to a gambling trip in Las Vegas in 2007. In return, Bergersen gave him access to DSCA documents, some of which were classified, on U.S.-Taiwan military cooperation. After his arrest in 2008, Kuo pleaded guilty and was sentenced to more than fifteen years in prison.[36]

Lee, Jerry Chun Shing (arrested 2018)

Jerry Chun Shing Lee is a former CIA case officer who retired in 2007 and was recruited by the MSS's Guangdong State Security Department in 2010. According to the affidavit, two MSS officers approached Lee in Shenzhen to offer $100,000. They told him they knew his background and "were in the same line of work" before offering to take care of him for life. Less than a month later, the MSS officers began tasking Lee to collect CIA and national defense information. During a trip to the United States in 2012, U.S. investigators searched Lee's belongings to find notebooks containing classified information about agents recruited by the CIA, agency operational facilities, meeting locations, and operational phone numbers. Lee also provided information about another retired case officer, and the MSS appears to have used that information to approach the case officer in 2013. Lee and his MSS handlers communicated through a series of separate email accounts and phone numbers as well as one of Lee's business associates. The FBI arrested Lee in January 2018.[37]

Leung, Katrina (recruited 1984, arrested 2003)

Katrina Leung is a Chinese American businesswoman and civic leader recruited by FBI agent James J. Smith in 1982 to report on her contacts and conversations in China. Between 1982 and 2000, the FBI paid Leung $1.7 million for her reporting on Chinese politics, military, and efforts to influence U.S. elections. Her reporting was eventually disseminated directly to policymakers at the White House and the National Security Council.[38] She first came to the FBI's attention in 1981 due to her proximity and relationship to several subjects of a bureau investigation into illicit technology transfers. The FBI attempted to run Leung as a double agent, and in 1984 the MSS recruited her during one of her frequent trips to China. Her case officer Mao Guohua directed her to open a separate post office box for their communications. The full extent of her relationship to the MSS is unknown, but the first documented instance of passing classified information to the ministry without approval occurred in 1990 when the FBI received a report that Leung alerted the MSS to sensitive technical and counterintelligence operations. This was the first of several incidents that suggested Leung had turned on the FBI, and the bureau allowed her handler J. J. Smith to address the issues himself. Problematically, Leung and Smith began sleeping together in 1983 and continued to do so up until their arrests in 2003. Sometime in the 1990s, Smith started sharing operational details with Leung and consulting her on other U.S. intelligence community operations. During their liaisons she examined and copied classified documents from Smith's briefcase for the MSS. Consequently, Leung probably betrayed nearly every U.S. operation and investigation of which the FBI's Los Angeles field office was aware. The FBI received a report in 2000 that identified Smith, who would soon retire, as the likely source of the problems.[39] The subsequent investigation began slowly, and the FBI arrested the pair in 2003. A federal court dismissed all charges against Leung in 2005, because the judge believed the U.S. government had "irreversibly prejudiced" Leung's ability to mount a defense in its plea agreement with Smith.[40]

Li Zhihao (李志豪; arrested 1999)

Dubbed the most famous communist double agent ever to infiltrate Taiwan's military intelligence bureau, Li betrayed at least three of the bureau's agents on the Chinese mainland before being apprehended in 1999. Li staged an escape by swimming to Hong Kong in the late 1980s, apparently at the direction of the Guangdong State Security Bureau. He was eventually recruited by Taiwan intelligence, which did not discover Li's true loyalties for a decade. In 1999 a Taiwan court sentenced him to life in prison. In 2015 Taipei appeared to trade Li back to Beijing in exchange for the release of two military intelligence bureau officers, Chu Kung-hsun and Hsu Chang-kuo, whom Chinese intelligence kidnapped from Vietnam in 2006. Taiwanese authorities, however, denied there was an explicit trade. Shortly afterward on November 7, 2015, CCP leader Xi Jinping and KMT leader Ma Ying-jeou conducted a scheduled meeting in Singapore.[41]

Liu Chi-ju (劉其儒; indicted 2015)

Liu Chi-ju is a retired Taiwan air force officer who was connected to the Zhen Xiaojiang ring. He served as an intermediary between Zhen and two other sources, Ko Chi-hsien and Lou Wen-ching, whom he had been instrumental in recruiting. Although Liu was indicted, his whereabouts are unknown, and he presumably stayed in China where he has business interests.[42]

Lo Hsien-che (羅賢哲; recruited 2004, sentenced 2011)

Brigadier General Lo Hsien-che was serving as the chief of Taiwan army electronic information when Taiwanese authorities arrested him in February 2011 for spying for China. Lo was recruited by 2PLA while he served as a defense attaché in Thailand. According to Taiwanese sources, the recruiting officer was a 2PLA secret line officer who had served in Washington, DC, covered as a commercial officer in the embassy.[43] Lo's primary handler was a female Chinese intelligence officer who lived in Thailand and possessed Australian citizenship. This woman traveled frequently between Thailand, Australia, China, and the United States and maintained contact with Lo over the Internet after he returned to Taiwan in 2005. Some reports suggest she acted as a honey trap (see *meiren ji* in the web-based glossary). Lo was paid by 2PLA $100,000 to $200,000 per delivery of classified information.[44]

U.S. intelligence confronted Lo during a visit to the United States in August 2010. Lo claimed that he was forced to confess his activities on video and that the Americans turned the file over to Taiwan authorities after he refused to act as a double agent. Because of his confession, Lo was sentenced in 2011 to life in prison rather than execution.[45]

Lu Chun-chun (盧俊均; recruited before 2009, arrested 2014)

Lu Chun-chun was a Taiwanese officer whose last military post was at the missile command center in 2005. Following his retirement, Lu joined friends in a China-based business venture where his contacts in the Xiamen municipal government introduced him to Chinese intelligence officers. Lu also recruited Chien Ching-kuo in 2009 with cash gifts and an all-expenses paid trip to Bali, Indonesia, where Chien was introduced to Chinese intelligence officers. Lu and Chien together recruited Chang Chih-hsin and introduced him to Chinese intelligence in Cebu, Philippines. The pair attempted to recruit at least three other Taiwanese officials in this way. It is unclear what other information or services Lu provided to Chinese intelligence. Lu received a three-year suspended sentence because he did not have a criminal record.[46]

Maihesuti, Baibur (recruited 2008, convicted 2010)

Baibur Maihesuti was a naturalized Swedish citizen of Uighur descent who reported personal details, contact information, travels, and political leanings of other Uighurs primarily in Europe. Maihesuti joined the World Uighur Congress to spy on its membership, and he also reported on other Chinese exiles of interest to Beijing. The two MSS officers who recruited and handled him worked from the Chinese embassy in Stockholm under journalistic and diplomatic cover. The MSS paid Maihesuti in both cash and unspecified services. They used a covert telephonic system to communicate with Maihesuti. In 2010 Swedish authorities sentenced him to sixteen months in prison.[47] This is one of the few cases known to have been conducted completely outside China.

Mak, Chi (麦大志; convicted 2007)

Chi Mak was a naturalized American citizen who came to the United States via Hong Kong. From his emigration in the 1960s to the British colony, Mak maintained a relationship with military intelligence, probably 2PLA. In Hong Kong, he reportedly kept logs of U.S. and other naval vessels docking in the harbor. Mak came to the United States in 1978 and was naturalized as a citizen in 1985. During the years between arriving in the United States and acquiring a security clearance in 1996, his intelligence activities are not clear. In 1987 a relative of Mak's wife working for the ministry of aviation asked Mak to serve as a conduit for Greg Dongfan Chung (chapter 4) to send information back to China, because the Mak channel was safer than others.[48] After Mak acquired a secret clearance while working for L-3 subsidiary Power Paragon on U.S. Navy projects, he began providing a wide range of export-controlled, but not necessarily classified, technical information to Chinese military intelligence. Among the files were data on submarine electronics, the quiet electric drive for the Virginia-class submarine, an electromagnetic aircraft launch system for aircraft carriers, and the Aegis combat system with its associated command and control systems. Mak used his family members, most notably his brother Tai Mak, as couriers. The Maks appeared to be ideologically motivated, and the only direct compensation was that Mak's case officer looked after Tai Mak's mother-in-law. Tai Mak and his wife were arrested at Los Angeles International Airport in late 2005 as they prepared to leave for Hong Kong in possession of CDs with encrypted data intended for the PLA. Mak was arrested shortly thereafter. In 2008 a federal court sentenced Mak to twenty-four years for export control violations, being an agent of a foreign power, and lying to federal agents.[49]

Mak Tai-wang (sentenced 2008)

Tai Mak, as he is usually known, is the younger brother of Chi Mak and acted as the latter's courier to 2PLA. He came to the United States via Hong Kong in 2001, and he worked as a broadcast engineer for Phoenix Television, which is closely connected to the Chinese party-state. According to some reports, Tai Mak also was a PLA officer or had another formal affiliation with the military.[50] The FBI arrested Tai Mak and his wife at Los Angeles International Airport in late 2005 as they attempted to fly to Hong Kong with CDs containing technical data collected by Chi Mak and encrypted by his son Billy Mak. In 2008 a federal court sentenced Tai Mak to ten years in prison for his role in supporting his brother's espionage.

Mallory, Kevin (recruited 2017, convicted 2018)

Kevin Mallory was a defense contractor and former CIA operations officer who sold classified documents to the SSSB. He met with the SSSB in China under the guise of academic exchange with the Shanghai Academy of Social Sciences. During meetings in March and April 2017, Mallory sold eight classified documents for $25,000. He also wrote two white papers on U.S. policy at the request of his handlers. The SSSB officers provided him with a cell phone with an encrypted messaging app installed for communication and transferring files as well as SD cards. Mr. Mallory had a long career with the U.S. government, including stints in the Army (1981–86), the State Department Diplomatic Security Service (1987–90), and several active-duty assignments as a reservist, holding an active security clearance through 2012. He was found guilty in June 2018 for lying to investigators and providing defense information to aid a foreign government.[51]

Shanghai State Security Bureau

The SSSB is the MSS element responsible for intelligence and counterintelligence operations in Shanghai municipality. Unlike many of the provincial and local MSS units, the SSSB runs clandestine agent operations against foreign countries inside and outside China. It is known for being one of the most active units operating against the United States. The SSSB was created no later than 1985, but it was not part of the original MSS organization created in 1983. Many of the cover organizations used in SSSB operations are throwaway corporate outfits, such as the Shanghai Pacific and International Strategy Consulting Company used to approach Nate Thayer, but it does use the Shanghai Academy of Social Sciences to provide operational cover for its officers and hide the operational purpose behind a source's travel to China.[52] See Anonymous Japanese Communicator; Claiborne, Candice; Mallory, Kevin; Shriver, Glenn Duffie; Thayer, Nate.

Shen Ping-kang (沈秉康; recruited 1998, arrested 2013)

Shen Ping-kang is a Taiwanese businessman with Australian citizenship who served as a go-between for Chinese military intelligence and Admiral Ko Cheng-sheng. Because of his cross-strait business, Shen came into contact with the 2PLA and the PLA's political warfare officers. Shen's Chinese contacts learned of his relationship to Admiral Ko and recruited him as a pathway to Ko. Between 1998 and 2007 Shen paid for several all-expense paid trips for Ko and his family to Australia, from where Shen and Ko would then would travel to China. News reports were unclear whether it was military intelligence or the United Front Work Department that recruited Shen. He was sentenced to twelve months in prison in 2014.[53]

Shriver, Glenn Duffie (recruited 2004, pleaded guilty 2010)

Glenn Duffie Shriver was a recent college graduate when the SSSB recruited him in 2004. He responded to a call for papers on U.S.-China relations, and the SSSB officers followed up with him because of his supposedly prize-winning paper. Between 2005 and 2010, Shriver attempted to join the Department of State as a foreign service officer and the CIA as a case officer. The SSSB paid him $70,000 for his efforts. Throughout this time period, Shriver was in communication with his primary SSSB handler on a monthly basis, and one of his handlers offered to meet him in Hong Kong if coming to Shanghai was too risky. According to one account, CIA and FBI officials knew about Shriver's recruitment by the SSSB, and the final stages of the background investigation were a sham to prepare for prosecution. In October 2010 Shriver pleaded guilty to conspiring to steal classified information, and he received a four-year prison sentence.[54]

Smith, James J. "J. J." (arrested 2003)

FBI special agent J. J. Smith was the primary handler of Katrina Leung from 1982 through 2001 as well as Leung's primary source of information within the FBI. Within a year of recruiting Leung, the two began a romantic relationship. Smith's handling of Leung and the intelligence reporting she provided made him a key figure in the FBI's China operations. He won a U.S. Intelligence community "collector of the year" award in the early 1990s.[55] The successes and plaudits allowed Smith to handle Leung with minimal oversight, even when problems emerged. Sometime after Leung was recruited by the MSS in 1984 as part of the bureau's double agent operation, Leung gained access to information about the FBI's operations. First, Smith consulted Leung about ongoing investigations and operations, including those involving other intelligence agencies. Second, Leung started copying classified documents from Smith's briefcase that he brought to their trysts. Smith also compromised sensitive technical operations against Chinese targets.

Thayer, Nate (pitched 2014)

Veteran U.S. journalist Nate Thayer was approached via email by the SSSB to provide short interview-based reports on U.S. policy in Asia. Two men, both claiming to work for the Shanghai Pacific and International Strategy Consulting Company (SPISCC), sent Thayer emails offering to pay him for short reports on a variety of policy topics based on his contacts across U.S. and foreign governments. The SPISCC claimed their focus was on "U.S. policies toward Asian countries, U.S. interactions with them, and [the] implications [for] China and Chinese enterprises." For the first papers suggested to Thayer, they wanted to know about the Burmese Kyaukpyu Port project and U.S.-Cambodia talks on how to manage tensions in the

South China Sea. SPISCC offered to pay $500 to $1,500 per five- to seven-page paper completed on a one- to two-week timeline. The SSSB officers offered to meet him inside or outside China, including Singapore.[56] The case ultimately went nowhere as Thayer declined to take the SPISCC consulting offer.

Wang Hung-ju (Wang Hongru, 王鴻儒; arrested 2017)

Wang Hung-ju is a former Taiwan National Security Bureau (NSB) officer who ended his career as a bodyguard for vice president Annette Lu (2002–3). He went into business after his retirement, traveling back and forth to China or living there for extended periods. In 2009 the SSSB or a Shanghai-based military intelligence unit recruited Wang to work alongside Taiwanese businessman Ho Chih-chiang in building an espionage ring in Taiwan. It is not clear, however, why Taiwanese authorities arrested Ho in 2010 while waiting seven more years to arrest Wang. One possibility is that they did not see arrestable behavior until Wang pitched a former NSB colleague who was working at the military police command. Wang offered his former coworker a sum "several times his pension" and a trip to Singapore where he would meet a Chinese intelligence officer. The former colleague rejected the approach and reported Wang to security officials. According to a ministry of national defense spokesman, no active-duty military officers worked in Wang's spy ring.[57]

Yuan Hsiao-feng (袁曉風; recruited 2001, arrested 2012)

Yuan Hsiao-feng was a Taiwan air force lieutenant colonel recruited by 2PLA agent Chen Wen-jen in 2001. On at least twelve occasions while on active duty between 2001 and 2007 he used flash drives to pass defense secrets relating to his position as an air traffic controller. Yuan was reportedly paid roughly $269,000 by 2PLA. Taiwanese counterintelligence began an investigation into Yuan and Chen after the pair failed to recruit two junior officers in August 2011. Following his conviction on twelve counts of espionage, a Taiwanese court sentenced Yuan to twelve life sentences.[58]

Zhen Xiaojiang (鎮小江; arrested 2015)

Zhen Xiaojiang is a former PLA army captain who recruited a spy ring of at least four military officers and a Kaohsiung nightclub owner. Zhen, by some accounts, joined a military intelligence service after his retirement from active duty, but he may also have been a co-optee acting as a go-between for military intelligence. In 2005 he acquired a Hong Kong residency permit and started traveling regularly to and from Taiwan. The Taiwanese prosecuted for their activities on Zhen's behalf include Major General Hsu Nai-chuan, air force Colonel Chou Chih-li, air force pilot Sung Chia-lu, civilian air force official Yang Jung-hua, and nightclub operator Lee Huan-yu. Zhen acquired classified information on Taiwan's French-made Mirage 2000 fighters, the ultra-high-frequency radar at Leshan, and other advanced Taiwanese military technology. He provided free trips to Southeast Asia for Taiwanese military officers and sometimes arranged for meetings with Chinese intelligence during the travel. He was sentenced to four years in prison in 2016.[59]

Zhou Hongxu (周泓旭; arrested 2017)

Taiwanese authorities detained Chinese national Zhou Hongxu in March 2017 for spying after he pitched a junior foreign ministry official. Zhou promised to pay the diplomat in cash or overseas travel in exchange for classified documents. Zhou himself would not take possession of the documents, but the diplomat would have personally delivered them to another Chinese contact arranged by Zhou on an all-expenses-paid trip to Japan. Zhou first came to Taiwan in 2009 to study at Tamkang University on an exchange program. He returned to Taiwan in 2012 to earn a master's degree in business at National Cheng-chi University and returned to China after completing the degree in 2016. Zhou came again to Taiwan in February on an investment visa but was arrested in March after his failed pitch of the foreign ministry official. Taiwanese investigators told journalists that Zhou was an active networker and had tried to develop other students and officials during his time as a student.[60]

• SEVEN •

Intelligence and Surveillance
in China, Then and Now

Chinese Intelligence, 1927–Present

Books on international espionage generally feature a yawning China gap, with that nation missing from the text and index or mentioned in only a trivial way. Only a few authors writing in English have discussed the subject in detail in recent years.[1]

Meanwhile, documentaries, television dramas, and movies about espionage during the Chinese Communist Revolution ending in 1949 have become a virtual industry in the People's Republic of China (PRC). They were preceded by numerous written histories and especially biographies of revolutionary heroes. There is no shortage of material published in Chinese on the mainland, and there is a reasonable selection from Hong Kong and Taiwan. The problem for the foreign observer is sorting the wheat from the chaff—the actual history from the official story with its often-inflated narrative.

Although our understanding is neither ideal nor complete, we have tried to fill the gap by showing the activities of intelligence operations behind the scenes in modern Chinese history. As secret matters and decisions about them are connected with major events, previously unimagined cause and effect are uncovered. The following overview is meant to complement other sections of this volume.

In the aftermath of the violent April 1927 split with the Chinese Nationalists, the CCP quickly moved to improve its nascent intelligence and security structure, remedying a nearly fatal ignorance of enemy capabilities and intentions.[2] However, they took several years to achieve major successes. Among the first was the 1929–30 infiltration of Nationalist

245

intelligence via a spy ring led by Li Kenong. His trio was nicknamed the Three Heroes of the Dragon's Lair.[3] Just as the Brécourt Manor assault of June 6, 1944, led by the late Richard Winters, is taught at West Point, so the Three Heroes case is taught to trainees entering the PRC Ministry of State Security (MSS) and other relevant civilian and military organs.

Almost exactly four years later, in April 1931, the party faced another desperate struggle after the defection of its own intelligence chief, Special Services Section (SSS) director Gu Shunzhang.[4] In an act of revenge and to set an example, Zhou Enlai arranged the murder of Gu's wife and family. Fortunately for the CCP, the Three Heroes ring was in place to provide early warning—although Gu betrayed them. All three, and many others, had to flee for their lives to the Red Army base in Jiangxi, commanded by Mao Zedong and Zhu De.[5] In the aftermath of this disaster, the party's highly clandestine habits contributed to the ability of members to cycle in and out of CCP intelligence: some temporarily, such as Chen Yun and Li Qiang, and some who remained in long-term service, such as Pan Hannian, Kong Yuan, and Li Kenong.

Though depicted in CCP-approved sources as a period of brave struggles by clever operatives, the next four years were increasingly hopeless. The party was forced to evacuate the cities—first its political leadership and then most of its clandestine operatives, including future CCP intelligence leader Kang Sheng. They lost contact with the urban proletariat that in Marxist theory was vital to advancing socialist revolution. This contributed to the CCP's focus on the peasantry as the engine to overthrow the old order. The vociferous and violent efforts of the CCP to hold on in the cities testify, among other things, to their willingness to follow doctrinaire orders from Moscow and a determination to stay among China's small proletariat.

As the urban fight ended in a bloody defeat (1933–34), the last of the CCP center relocated to the Red Army base in Ruijin, Jiangxi—itself under siege by the superior Nationalist army. The SSS (1927–35), now almost irrelevant, would soon be abolished. Its intelligence officers, including Li Kenong and Pan Hannian, were reassigned to military intelligence or other duties in the Red Army's Political Protection Bureau (PPB), though a few clandestine agents remained inside the Nationalist central government and army. One of them, Mo Xiong, was on Generalissimo Chiang Kai-shek's staff and uncovered details of his "Fifth Encirclement" that aimed to destroy the Red Army. Mo warned the CCP, enabling its escape in October 1934 to embark on the epic Long March.

Countless intelligence officers must have perished on the journey; of the 86,000 soldiers and other communists who began the march in Jiangxi, only 20,000 made it as far as Sichuan in May 1935. When the march ended in northern Shaanxi that October, only five thousand remained in the columns led by Mao Zedong and Zhu De, though others under Zhang Guotao joined in 1936. Deng Fa, who started the march as head of CCP intelligence, ended it displaced by Li Kenong.[6]

In November 1937 Stalin ordered CCP intelligence veteran Kang Sheng to return from Moscow to China and the party's new base in Yan'an, accompanied by Chen Yun and the more senior (but soon to be insignificant) Wang Ming. One or more Russian advisors may also have flown in with them. Kang took over the PPB and in February 1939 formed the Social Affairs Department (SAD), a reorganized intelligence organ of elevated status directly subordinate to the CCP Central Committee.[7]

A powerful dynamic took hold of the CCP leadership during this time: widespread fear of enemy agents among the untested bourgeois urban youth who flocked to Yan'an at the beginning of the Anti-Japanese War (1937–45). As Mao consolidated his authority and shunted aside a challenge from Wang Ming, he and Kang pursued an increasingly extreme hunt for spies, starting with junior party members. In this he had the agreement of other prominent communists, including future victims Chen Yun and Liu Shaoqi.[8] By late 1943 their campaigns were aimed at Mao's perceived rivals at the top of the party, including Zhou Enlai. Though devastating to party unity, the campaigns created a toxic environment that was difficult for Chinese Nationalist or Japanese intelligence to penetrate. At this time, Mao Thought was first proposed as a guideline for the party,[9] and he famously declared that in Yan'an, "Spies are as thick as hemp."[10]

Under a December 1943 rebuke from Moscow and widespread dissatisfaction in the ranks, Mao was forced to wind down his purge and publicly apologize for its excesses a year later.[11] In 1946–47, Mao replaced Kang with the senior deputy in SAD, Li Kenong—the lone survivor of the Three Heroes ring.[12] Li refocused intelligence on the party's external enemies, which contributed to the 1949 victory and establishment of the PRC. However, Kang Sheng was not purged: Mao kept his loyal acolyte in reserve, albeit outside the newly established PRC Intelligence Services. Li Kenong was the better man for, among other things, negotiating an agreement with Moscow on cooperation between the Chinese and Soviet intelligence services.

The CCP's enemies did not relent after being forced from the Chinese mainland, and U.S. efforts to contain China during and after the Korean War (1950–53) led the CCP to send "illegal" agents (sans diplomatic cover) overseas to the nations of China's periphery and probably beyond.[13] Probes by the Nationalist enemy, now exiled on Taiwan, and their American backers gave Mao and his security apparatus numerous reasons to pursue vigorous counterintelligence measures. To an extent, they rebuilt the hypervigilant environment of Yan'an throughout society, pursuing mobilization and suppression campaigns to enhance political control and eliminate perceived enemies. In his mounting paranoia, Mao overreacted to a mistake by one of his wartime master spies, Pan Hannian, leading to the 1955 purge of Pan and punishment of between eight hundred and one thousand other intelligence professionals. In those same months Mao approved the creation of the PRC's first foreign spy agency, the Central Investigation Department (CID), headed by Li Kenong.[14]

For the rest of the 1950s, the CID and other agencies, notably PLA military intelligence, the Ministry of Public Security (MPS), and the CCP Inspection Bureau, established interagency coordination and common standards to further national intelligence goals.[15] Successful U.S. and Taiwan agent insertions in northern, eastern, and southern China declined in the 1950s as the CCP's bureaucratic control over the majority Han society increased, but in Tibet the Americans stepped up efforts as local resistance mounted.[16] Relations between Chinese and Soviet intelligence frayed, and Soviet advisors inside the security services departed a year in advance of the 1960 Sino-Soviet split.[17]

The sidelining of CID director Li Kenong in 1957 by declining health before his death in 1962 left able deputies including Kong Yuan in charge, and secrecy was the CID's hallmark.[18] Normal operations continued until the Cultural Revolution began in 1966. The chaos that began that year threw both foreign intelligence and domestic counterintelligence operations into disarray. Li Kenong's old and still militant boss, Kang Sheng, returned to take political control of intelligence and security, and MPS minister Xie Fuzhi fully supported Mao's program and notoriously denounced former patrons including Deng Xiaoping. The existing foreign intelligence leadership was almost entirely swept aside into labor reform or worse. In April 1967 Red Guard factions fighting inside the CID led Mao and Zhou to place it under PLA control, at least in part to prevent disclosure of classified materials to Red Guard newspapers. Perhaps the only senior survivor from previous decades was Luo Qingchang, who was appointed head of the CID after it was released from military control.[19]

In spite of his support for Mao's radical program, Luo stayed in office after the chairman's 1976 death and subsequent arrest of his wife, Jiang Qing, and other radical Gang of Four leaders. During the rise of Deng Xiaoping beginning in 1979, Luo's survival stood in sharp contrast with the fates of Xie Fuzhi and Kang Sheng, who were posthumously condemned and expelled from the CCP.

The end of the Cultural Revolution reversed the prominence of radical left policies and led to a massive rehabilitation of those previously condemned. Thousands of CCP intelligence cadres who had been denounced and imprisoned were among them. However, their cases were handled slowly, perhaps to protect the intelligence methods they practiced but certainly owing to the political sensitivity of correcting the mistakes of Mao Zedong. Chen Yun, a CCP intelligence veteran and now the party's economic czar, led efforts to clear the names of these cadres one by one, with careful investigations that took months or years. Prominent among them were Pan Hannian (1906–77), posthumously rehabilitated in August 1982, and Yang Fan (1912–99), released in 1978 and cleared in December 1983.[20]

In a major reorganization, the MMS founded in 1983 replaced the CID. Only then did Deng Xiaoping force Luo Qingchang to retire, and other Cultural Revolution beneficiaries may have exited with him.[21] They had irritated Deng Xiaoping by resisting his July 1979 suggestion that the CID cease using diplomatic posts as cover positions for officers overseas.[22] If the departures were significant in number, it would have been the third time after 1955 and 1966 that an exodus of experienced officers, whatever their politics, reduced the ranks of Chinese Communist foreign intelligence professionals.

The post-1983 era has been characterized by a constraint on MSS operations overseas and increasingly aggressive foreign operations by PLA intelligence, both in human intelligence and in its highly successful cyber collection. The June 4, 1989, Tian'anmen incident injected a seemingly permanent level of mutual suspicion into Sino-American relations. Chinese concerns about spying by its major trading partners, especially the United States, Japan, Britain, and Taiwan have steadily increased, as did these nations' concerns about Chinese espionage.[23]

Surveillance in China Today

Most PRC citizens, especially members of the Han majority, do not draw the focused attention of the security and surveillance apparatus unless they challenge authority. But others are more readily perceived as threats to the status quo. Non-Han minorities such as Tibetans and Uighurs, if suspected of "separatism" (favoring independence from China), attract instant scrutiny. Others, such as democracy and human rights activists, the attorneys who defend them, and unsanctioned religious practitioners also attract official surveillance.

Foreigners entering China automatically attract higher than average official and unofficial attention, but this is not monolithic or absolute. Those with jobs of interest to the security services—diplomats, journalists, representatives of nongovernmental organizations, and those working for foreign businesses of interest—receive the most scrutiny. The last category includes foreigners working in "sensitive units" (敏感的单位, *min gan de danwei*), such as large corporations that have the firm support of their home governments and those bringing desired technology into China.[24] By contrast, other business people, visitors, and students have a lower profile. They make up the vast majority of the roughly 600,000 resident foreigners in China and the tens of thousands of tourists who visit each month.

For all people, Chinese and foreign, there is a baseline of programs that accomplish a routine surveillance serving the administrative requirements of the Chinese state. Local police, working from municipal or county Public Security Bureaus (PSBs; see the Ministry of Public Security [MPS]), keep in view all PRC citizens within their jurisdiction via the national identification (ID) card (身份证, *shenfen zheng*) system that records each resident's home and place of work. Though not everyone strives to comply, especially those who move for a new job, this system is probably more effective than ever because of advancing technology and the CCP's determination to improve, and preserve, itself. Police maintain a large database that links each citizen's ID card number with his or her name and date of birth, ethnicity, sex, and address, with links to other data of interest such as the person's residence permit (户口, *hukou*) and the *dang'an* (档案) file containing work-related information. This can be termed a "baseline of surveillance" because it is applied to every PRC citizen, tracking the routine details of life, allowing authorities to detect the unexpected and decide whether to investigate it.

Foreigners are a less permanent fixture than PRC citizens but are nonetheless tracked with the same baseline goals in mind. Those living semipermanently in China, typically on employment or marriage visas, must register with the local PSB in their place of residence and, if employed, must also report their presence in the police district where they work. Some foreigners manage to avoid this but risk expulsion. Foreign visitors on business, exchange students, and tourists are not exempted, even if they visit the home of a friend. At hotels, every foreigner submits his or her passport to the front desk, where staff copies the important pages and sends them to the local public security bureau. If the foreigner is a student reporting for classes at a university, the school must similarly comply.

Just as Chinese must always carry their national ID cards, foreigners are required by law to carry their passports. These steps enable PSBs to more easily account for every resident and *every visiting foreigner* in their jurisdiction. While this may seem extreme to foreigners, place yourself in the shoes of a local PSB commander: if a person, be s/he foreigner or Chinese, in your district goes missing or commits a crime, the CCP will hold *you* accountable: you had better be able to provide full information on demand for higher-ups. PRC authorities view this system more as accountability than surveillance. Beijing's mindset about baseline surveillance helps explain why the CCP views universal human rights like privacy and freedom of expression and religion as canards intended to subvert its rule.

Lately joining these baseline programs is the "social credit" system (社会信用体系, *shehui xinyong tixi*), scheduled to fully roll out by 2020. The system is enabled in significant measure by Alibaba (阿里巴巴), the highly successful online sales platform. It runs Alipay, which allows users to buy a wide range of products, even vegetables in a farmer's market, with just a mobile phone. Alipay also offers users entry into Zhima (芝麻), or Sesame, Credit. The company is assembling a "social integrity system" that has already integrated into Zhima Credit a government database of six million people who have defaulted on court fines. According to Lucy Peng, chief executive officer of Ant Financial Services (the online finance arm of Alibaba Group), Zhima Credit will "ensure that the bad people in society don't have a place to go, while good people can move freely and without obstruction."[25] Alibaba will probably work closely with the CCP to meet its goals of societal control. The company not only has 2,094 party members among its employees; it also upgraded its internal CCP organ to a Group Party Committee (集团党委, *Jituan dang wei*) at the same time in 2012 as it hired its first chief risk officer (首席险官, *shouxi xianguan*). He is Shao Xiaofeng (邵晓锋), an award-winning twenty-year veteran of the MPS.[26] Shao's high post within his firm's hierarchy is the envy of most corporate security executives outside of China, who occasionally rise to that level but are normally relegated to a much lower rung on the ladder.

Beyond baseline surveillance lie the tools used by most nations to monitor criminal activity. Drug trafficking, an increasingly serious problem, and other offenses such as suspected espionage attract intense surveillance. Though putting an exact number to these efforts is difficult, the MPS and the MSS appear to employ thousands of people to run six basic efforts:

- foot and vehicle surveillance
- observation via the expansive urban closed-circuit television camera networks
- landline and mobile telephone recording and position tracking
- electronic monitoring of email and all other online activity

- interviews with people in contact with the subject
- data from the use of credit cards and automatic teller machines.[27]

These methods are not unlike those used in other countries, including Thailand; the difference lies in the priority given to surveillance by the CCP, its technological sophistication, the numbers of people doing the watching, and the lack of procedural guarantees of privacy.[28] No warrant issued by a judge is needed to initiate intense surveillance on a person or organization.

What kind of activity prompts focused security attention and an investigation? Like anywhere else, these capabilities are employed if someone is suspected of committing a crime or becomes the object of security or intelligence interest. A crucial difference for China is that the country hosts very few foreigners by percentage of population compared to other lands, and officials are suspicious of them as a group for historical reasons. One former Western intelligence officer with long experience in China put it this way: "Because there are few foreigners in relation to the Chinese population, a foreigner in China creates a 'wake,' like a ship, wherever he travels, particularly when off the regular expat and tourist tracks. Chinese have excellent memories for the unusual in their lives, and seeing a foreigner where none has been before is an event that the average Chinese will remember, even if he is not enthusiastic about reporting it immediately."[29]

The last time there was such a historic peak of foreigners in China was the troubled 1920s and 1930s, when China chafed under foreign occupation and expanding Japanese conquest. While there are many differences between then and now, modern-day Chinese security officials, if of a conservative mindset, know this and could easily see danger in the mounting number of foreigners. To keep this problem in perspective, we can recall that modern China is not a country build on immigrants—instead, it is a country with a relatively static ethnic balance that has occasionally isolated itself, even up to the twentieth century.

Activities by foreign guests considered suspicious that attract surveillance include, but are not limited to, contact with known dissidents or other persons already targeted for surveillance; diplomats or journalists who visit university campuses or minority areas; religious proselytizing; straying too close to closed areas or military zones; and possessing a former foreign government affiliation, particularly an intelligence or military tie. So, for example, if you live in China and attend a church, and that fact is not registered with the State Administration for Religious Affairs (国家宗教事务局, *Guojia zongjiao shiwu ju*), that could be of interest. If the church's youth group decides to leaflet the local bar area, local authorities will notice and possibly take unanticipated action.

The antispy campaign that began secretly in early 2014 and was only publicized in 2016 intensified security service attention to foreigners, especially people from Australia, New Zealand, Britain, Canada, Japan, Taiwan, and the United States.[30] Unlike counterspies and police in, for example, Russia and Burma, Chinese agents tracking foreigners tend to be subtle and professional, not blatant—with some exceptions, such as locally contracted thugs who carry out intimidation on behalf of authorities. In short, unless a well-trained surveillance team wants you to know they're watching or you have experience and relevant training, you probably won't detect them.

Though some groups such as diplomats and journalists may receive priority, the security services cannot watch every foreigner all the time. In the end, Chinese security forces operating in the PRC might be roughly compared to the U.S. Navy on the high seas: they can't be everywhere at once, but they go where they want and dominate the area once in place.

◆ Note on Web-Based Glossary ◆
of Chinese Espionage
and Security Terms

The vocabulary used by the PRC intelligence services and the Ministry of Public Security for tradecraft skills, tasks, types of operations, categories of people, and so on reveals parallels and contrasts with Western practices. A Marxist-Leninist-Stalinist-Mao-thought worldview is one distinguishing factor (for example, *chanchu hanjian*, traitor weeding; *shenmi zhuyi*, mysticism; *sanci da de zuoqing*, three big left deviations). Another is the long history of Chinese operations before modern times (*jiandie*, spy; *meiren ji*, "beautiful person plan," or honey trap). The conspiratorial and secret origins of the Chinese Communist Party and the help provided by the Soviet Union in its early years also stand out: *dixia*, underground; *danxian*, single line control; *neixian*, "inner line" or penetration agent; and the *san qin*, or "three diligences" for a secret agent.

Because of its size and the probability that regular updates are required, we have placed this glossary online at ccpintelterms.com. We welcome comments and suggestions—especially when backed by evidence—on ways to improve the online glossary and the rest of our work.

✦ Notes ✦

Preface

1. See the bibliography for the works of Michael Dutton, Michael Schoenhals, Scot Tanner, Frederic Wakeman, Miles Maochun Yu, and William Hannas, James Mulvenon, and Anna Puglisi to expand on this text. Theirs are among the better-quality works about Chinese clandestine operations. The forthcoming work by David Chambers will also be of interest for its in-depth treatment of CCP intelligence in the Chinese Revolution.

2. "The Elephant and the Blind Men," https://www.jainworld.com/literature /story25.htm.

Introduction

1. Chinese definitions of intelligence resemble those of other countries but have their own precision. For example, a PRC dictionary defines intelligence (情报, *qingbao*) as "investigative and other methods to collect confidential information on military, political, economic, diplomatic, scientific, and various aspects of the other side." A Taiwan military textbook defines intelligence as "specific reports that use secret, open, and semi-open methods to compile information on an adversary, including military preparation and development, intent, and future battle area layout." Li Zengqun, ed., *Shiyong Gong'an Xiao cidian* [A Practical Public Security Mini-Dictionary] (Harbin: Heilongjiang Renmin Chubanshe, 1987), 345, 363; Hu Wenlin, ed., *Qingbao Xue* [The Study of Intelligence] (Taipei: Zhongyang Junshi Yuanxiao, 1989), 1–2, 5–6.

2. See the web-based glossary of Chinese espionage and security terms for further definitions of *qingbao* [intelligence], *anquan* [security], *gong'an* [public security], *baowei* [protection], and other related ideas. As we will see in subsequent chapters, the term *tewu* [special operations] is a catch-all that includes *qingbao* [intelligence] and *baowei* [protection], with its subset of

assassination work, and *zhencha* ["detection" or scouting, which seems to be a combination of tactical intelligence and counterintelligence field work], while *gong'an* [public security] included both *jingcha* [policing] and *chan-chu hanjian* [digging out or "weeding" traitors to the Han Chinese—people who illegitimately assist foreigners]. Hao Zaijin, *Zhongguo mimi zhan— zhonggong qingbao, baowei gongzuo jishi* [China's Secret War—The Record of Chinese Communist Intelligence and Protection Work] (Beijing: Zuojia Chubanshe, 2005), 3. An American definition of security, the "establishment and maintenance of protective measures which are intended to ensure a state of inviolability from hostile acts or influences," seems to include Chinese ideas of *baowei* [protection of important persons] and *gong'an* [public security]. Leo D. Carl, *CIA Insider's Dictionary of U.S. and Foreign Intelligence, Counterintelligence, and Tradecraft* (Washington, DC: NIBC Press, 1996), 566.

3. Chen Yung-fa, *Zhongguo Gongchandang Qishi Nian* [Seventy Years of the Chinese Communist Party] (Taipei: Linking Books, 1998), 221; Feng Xiaomei, ed., *1921–1933: Zhonggong Zhongyang zai Shanghai* (Shanghai: Zhonggong Dangshi Chubanshe, 2006), 368.

4. Hao, *Zhongguo mimi zhan*, 1, 6–8; Mu Xin, *Yinbi zhanxian tongshuai Zhou Enlai* [Zhou Enlai, Guru of the Hidden Battlefront] (Beijing: Zhongguo Qingnian Chubanshe, 2002), 8–9, 14–15, 133–34; Chen, *Zhongguo Gongchandang Qishi Nian*, 109–10; U. T. Hsu, *The Invisible Conflict* (Hong Kong: China Viewpoints, 1958), 10; Xue Yu, "Guanyu zhonggong zhongyang teke nuogan wenti de tantao" [An Investigation into Certain Issues Regarding the CCP Central Committee Special Branch], *Zhonggong Dangshi Yanjiu* [The Study of Chinese Communist History], no. 3 (1999), 2–3.

5. Because he was a traitor, some PRC accounts avoid admitting Gu was in charge of the SSS, but authoritative sources there and from Taiwan make clear that Gu had "actual responsibility" for the whole organ "in the long term" until his capture. Hsu, *The Invisible Conflict*, 56–57; Hao, *Zhongguo mimi zhan*, 5, 8; Chang Jun-mei, ed., *Chinese Communist Who's Who*, vol. 2 (Taipei: Institute of International Relations, 1970), 435; Liu Wusheng, ed., *Zhou Enlai Da Cidian* [The Dictionary of Zhou Enlai] (Nanchang: Jiangxi Renmin Chubanshe, 1998), 31.

6. Zhao Yongtian, *Huxue Shuxun* [*In the Lair of the Tiger*] (Beijing: Junshi Kexue Chubanshe, 1994), 3.

7. Frederick C. Teiwes, *Politics and Purges in China: Rectification and the Decline of Party Norms, 1950–65* (Armonk, NY: M. E. Sharpe, 1979), 159.

8. A similar hazard was faced by cadres who had conducted dangerous "underground" work in enemy areas for the CCP organization and propaganda departments. The most prominent in this last category was former PRC president Liu Shaoqi, who suffered and died in prison during the Cultural Revolution.

9. An ideal that was at its height in the Cultural Revolution (1966–76) but has roots in the pre-1949 revolution. For brief explanations, see Frederick C. Teiwes and Warren Sun, *The End of the Maoist Era: Chinese Politics During the Twilight of the Cultural Revolution* (Armonk, NY: M. E. Sharpe, 2007), 329, 390n17; Alexander V. Pantsov and Steven I. Levin, *Mao: The Real Story* (New York: Simon and Schuster, 2012), 555–56; Andrew G. Walder, *China Under Mao: A Revolution Derailed* (Cambridge: Harvard University Press, 2015), 336–37.

10. Central Intelligence Agency, "Beijing Institute for International Strategic Studies Established," December 14, 1979, CIA Electronic Reading Room, https://www.cia.gov/library/readingroom/docs/DOC_0001257059.pdf.

11. Peter Mattis, "Assessing the Foreign Policy Influence of the Ministry of State Security," *China Brief*, January 14, 2011, https://jamestown.org/program /assessing-the-foreign-policy-influence-of-the-ministry-of-state-security/.

12. Lu Ning, "The Central Leadership, Supraministry Coordinating Bodies, State Council Ministries, and Party Departments," in *The Making of Chinese Foreign and Security Policy in the Era of Reform, 1978–2000*, ed. David Lampton (Stanford, CA: Stanford University Press, 2001), 50, 414.

13. Kan Zhongguo, "Intelligence Agencies Exist in Great Numbers, Spies Are Present Everywhere; China's Major Intelligence Departments Fully Exposed," *Chien Shao* (Hong Kong), January 1, 2006.

14. "Leadership Changes at the Fourteenth Party Congress," in *China Review 1993*, ed. Maurice Brosseau and Joseph Cheng Yu-shek (Hong Kong: Chinese University Press, 1993), 2.23.

15. Willy Wo-Lap Lam, "Surprise Elevation for Conservative Patriarch's Protégé Given Security Post," *South China Morning Post*, March 17, 1998.

16. "Renwu Ku: Chen Wenqing, 人物库: 陈文清 [Personalities Database. Chen Wenqing]," Xinhua, February 28, 2013, http://news.xinhuanet.com /rwk/2013-02/28/c_124400603.htm.

17. Dean Cheng, "Chinese Lessons from the Gulf Wars," in *Chinese Lessons from Other Peoples' Wars*, ed. Andrew Scobell, David Lai, and Roy Kamphausen (Carlisle, PA: U.S. Army War College Strategic Studies Institute, 2011), 153–200.

18. Kai Cheng, *Li Kenong, Zhonggong yinbi zhanxian de zhuoyue lingdao ren* [Li Kenong: Outstanding Leader of the CCP's Hidden Battlefront] (Beijing: Zhongguo Youyi Chubanshe, 1996), 430–32.

19. Peter Mattis, "Modernizing Military Intelligence: Realigning Organizations to Match Concepts," in *China's Evolving Military Strategy*, ed. Joe McReynolds (Washington, DC: The Jamestown Foundation, 2016), 308–33.

20. Peter Mattis, "PLA Personnel Shifts Highlight Intelligence's Growing Military Role," *China Brief*, November 5, 2012, https://jamestown.org/program /pla-personnel-shifts-highlight-intelligences-growing-military-role/.

21. Authors' interview, Beijing, August 2017.

22. The following paragraphs draw from Peter Mattis, "China Reorients Strategic Military Intelligence," *Jane's Intelligence Review*, March 3, 2017.

23. Nathan Thornburgh, "Inside the Chinese Hack Attack," *Time*, August 25, 2005, http://content.time.com/time/nation/article/0,8599,1098371,00.html; Richard Norton-Taylor, "Titan Rain—How Chinese Hackers Targeted Whitehall," *The Guardian*, September 4, 2007, https://www.theguardian.com /technology/2007/sep/04/news.internet.

24. See https://citizenlab.ca/2009/03/tracking-ghostnet-investigating-a-cyber-espi onage-network.

25. Ellen Nakashima, "Report on 'Operation Shady RAT' Identifies Widespread Cyber-spying," *Washington Post*, August 3, 2011, https://www.washington post.com/national/national-security/report-identifies-widespread-cyber -spying/2011/07/29/gIQAoTUmqI_story.html?utm_term=.dea6a5a91ff3; Kim Zetter, "Google Hack Attack Was Ultra Sophisticated, New Details Show," *Wired*, January 14, 2010, https://www.wired.com/2010/01/operation -aurora/.

26. Ellen Nakashima, "Chinese Hackers Who Breached Google Gained Access to Sensitive Data, U.S. Officials Say," *Washington Post*, May 20, 2013, https://www.washingtonpost.com/world/national-security/chinese -hackers-who-breached-google-gained-access-to-sensitive-data-us-offi cials-say/2013/05/20/51330428-be34–11e2–89c9–3be8095fe767_story .html?utm_term=.5623b53c1113.

27. Brian Bennett and W. J. Hennigan, "China and Russia Are Using Hacked Data to Target U.S. Spies, Officials Say," *Los Angeles Times*, August 31, 2015, http://www.latimes.com/nation/la-na-cyber-spy-20150831-story.html.

28. "APT1: Exposing One of China's Cyber Espionage Units," Mandiant, February 19, 2013, https://www.fireeye.com/content/dam/fireeye-www/services /pdfs/mandiant-apt1-report.pdf.

29. Insikt Group, "Recorded Future Research Concludes Chinese Ministry of State Security Behind APT3," Recorded Future, May 17, 2017, https://www.recordedfuture.com/chinese-mss-behind-apt3/.

30. See entry for Geng Huichang in chapter 2 of this book.

31. Mark Mazzetti et al., "Killing C.I.A. Informants, China Crippled U.S. Spying Operations," *New York Times*, May 20, 2017, https://www.nytimes.com/2017/05/20/world/asia/china-cia-spies-espionage.html. This account is bolstered by the authors' interviews with several U.S. and allied intelligence officers throughout 2017.

32. Winston Lord to Henry Kissinger, "Memcon of Your Conversations with Chou En-lai," Office of the President, National Security Council, July 29, 1971, Digital National Security Archive, https://nsarchive2.gwu.edu/NSAEBB/NSAEBB66/.

33. Ernest May, "Conclusions: Capabilities and Proclivities," in *Knowing One's Enemies: Intelligence Assessment before the Two World Wars*, ed. Ernest May (Princeton: Princeton University Press, 1986), 532–33.

34. For example, Peter Mattis, "New Law Reshapes Chinese Counterterrorism Policy and Operations," *China Brief*, January 25, 2016, https://jamestown.org/program/new-law-reshapes-chinese-counterterrorism-policy-and-operations/.

35. Authors' interview, Washington, DC, July 2012.

Chapter 1. Chinese Communist Intelligence Organizations

1. For example, Zhang Shaohong and Xu Wenlong, *Hongse guoji tegong* [Red International Agents] (Haerbin: Haerbin Chubanshe, 2005); Yu Tianming, *Hongse jiandie—daihao Bashan* [Red Spy—Code Name Bashan] (Beijing: Zuojia Chubanshe, 1993).

2. Mark Kelton, "Putin's Bold Attempt to Deny Skripal Attack," *The Cipher Brief*, September 19, 2018, https://www.thecipherbrief.com/putins-bold-attempt-to-deny-skripal-attack.

3. Yu, *Hongse jiandie—daihao Bashan*; Shen Xueming, ed., *Zhonggong diyi jie zhi diwu jie Zhongyang weiyuan* [Central Committee Members from the First CCP Congress to the Fifteenth] (Beijing: Zhongyang Wenxian Chubanshe, 2001), 621; Mu Xin, *Chen Geng tongzhi zai Shanghai* [Comrade Chen Geng in Shanghai] (Beijing: Wenshi Zike Chubanshe, 1980), 6–8.

4. Mu, *Yinbi zhanxian tongshuai Zhou Enlai*, 6–9.

5. Hao, *Zhongguo mimi zhan*, 2.

6. Hao, 2; Mu, *Yinbi zhanxian tongshuai Zhou Enlai*, 7.

7. Xue, "Guanyu zhonggong zhongyang teke," 2.

8. Different PRC sources provide varying accounts of the earliest days of CCP intelligence, but the most convincing and rigorously analytical account is by Xue, "Guanyu Zhonggong Zhongyang Teke."

9. Xue, 2–4; *Zhou Enlai nianpu 1898–1949* [Annals of Zhou Enlai, 1898–1949] (Beijing: Zhongyang Wenxian Chubanshe, 1989), 128.

10. Xue, "Guanyu zhonggong zhongyang teke," 3–4.

11. Most sources admit that Gu was at least the de facto head of the SSS: "the actual head" (*shiji fuze ren*) in Hao, *Zhongguo mimi zhan*, 5; the "leader" (*bu zhang*) in *Zhongguo gongchandang lingdao jigou yange he chengyuan minglu* [Directory of Organizations and Personnel of the Communist Party of China During the Revolution] (Beijing: Zhonggong Dangshi Chubanshe, 2000), 117. See also Chang, *Chinese Communist Who's Who*, v. 2, 435; Frederic Wakeman Jr., *Policing Shanghai, 1927–1937* (Berkeley: University of California Press, 1995), 138–39.

12. Hao, *Zhongguo mimi zhan*, 9; Maochun Yu, *OSS in China: Prelude to Cold War* (New Haven, CT: Yale University Press, 1996), 34–35; Barbara Barnouin and Yu Changgen, *Zhou Enlai, A Political Life* (Hong Kong: Chinese University of Hong Kong, 2006), 45–46; Mu, *Chen Geng tongzhi zai Shanghai*, 34–40.

13. Mu, *Yinbi zhanxian tongshuai Zhou Enlai*, 12.

14. In Ruijin from 1932 to 1934, Li Kenong was simultaneously the head of the Enforcement Department of the PPB (*Zhengzhi baoweiju zhixingbu buzhang*) and of the PPB in the First Front Army. "Li Kenong," *News of the Communist Party of China*, http://cpc.people.com.cn/GB/34136/2543750.html, and http://www.xwwb.com/web/wb2008/wb2008news.php?db=15&thisid=95528.

15. Zhao Shaojing, "Suqu 'Guojia zhengzhi baoweiju' yu sufan kuodahua went banzheng" [The Soviet Area State Political Protection Bureau and the Question of Enlarging the Purge of Counter-revolutionaries], http://www.scuphilosophy.org/research_display.asp?cat_id=94&art_id=7873, Sichuan University Institute for Philosophy, 9 May 2009.

16. January 1931 (Hao, *Zhongguo mimi zhan*, 15) or May that year (Xu Zehao, *Wang Jiaxiang nianpu* [Annals of Wang Jiaxiang] (Beijing: Zhongyang Wenxian Chubanshe, 2001), 56–57).

17. Tan Zhenlin, Li Yimang, Li Yutang, Wu Lie, Hai Jinglin, and Ma Zhulin were also noted in leadership positions for the new bureau. Hao, *Zhongguo mimi zhan*, 13; Shen, *Zhongyang weiyuan*, 322.

18. Hao, *Zhongguo mimi zhan*, 10; Shen, *Zhongyang weiyuan*, 99; He Jinzhou, *Deng Fa Zhuan* [A Biography of Deng Fa] (Beijing: Zhonggong Dangshi Chubanshe, 2008), 70–71.

19. As already noted, while in Ruijin, Li was simultaneously the head of the Enforcement Department of the PPB and of the PPB in the First Front Army.

20. Warren Kuo, *Analytical History of the Chinese Communist Party*, vol. 3 (Taipei: Institute of International Relations, 1970), 6.

21. Kuo; "Zhang Shunqing," *Baidu Encyclopedia* online, http://baike.baidu.com /view/2710205.htm. Zhang was also on the army political officer career track. He attained a party committee position in Guangdong in 1942 but was captured and killed there by the KMT in 1944.

22. Kuo, *Analytical History*, 7.

23. Mu, *Yinbi zhanxian tongshuai Zhou Enlai*, 463–64, 466; interview with Taiwan academic, 2016. Available organization directories are not specific about Qian's duties.

24. Yang Shilan, "Deng Fa," in *Zhonggong Dangshi Renwu Zhuan* [Biographies of Personalities in Chinese Communist Party History], vol. 1 (Xi'an: Xi'an Renmin Chubanshe, 1980), 359.

25. Interview, 2016.

26. Hao, *Zhongguo mimi zhan*, 19–20.

27. Edgar Snow, *Red Star Over China* (London: Victor Gollancz Ltd., 1938), 431; Edgar Snow, *Random Notes on Red China (1936–1945)* (Cambridge, MA: Harvard University Press, 1957), 42, 43, 46.

28. Hao, *Zhongguo mimi zhan*, 54.

29. Kang Sheng ran all party intelligence by August 1938. Zhong Kan, *Kang Sheng Pingzhuan* [A Critical Biography of Kang Sheng] (Beijing: Hongqi Chubanshe, 1982), 77. The third predecessor absorbed into the SAD was the Guard Division (保卫处, *Baowei chu*), Mao's protection unit in Yan'an.

30. Donald W. Klein and Anne B. Clark, *Biographic Dictionary of Chinese Communism, 1921–1965*, vol. 1 (Cambridge, MA: Harvard University Press, 1971), 425; interview with party historian, 2016.

31. Kuo's writings were the only publicly available, comprehensive information in English about CCP intelligence from 1968–71 until the 1980s, and they remain useful today. When Kuo died in August 1985, *qian'gu* floral wreath inscriptions were written for him by Chiang Ching-kuo and Lee Teng-hui. Interview, Taipei archivist, 2008, and extract of unclassified collection on Warren Kuo viewed in 2008.

32. CCP Secretariat, "Guanyu chengli shehui bu de jueding" [Concerning the Decision to Establish the Central Social Department], February 18, 1939, in *Kangzhan shiqi chubao wenjian* [Documents on Digging Out Traitors and Protection in the Anti-Japanese War], December 1948.

33. Warren Kuo, *Analytical History of the Communist Party of China*, vol. 4 (Taipei: Institute of International Relations, 1971), 374–35.

34. One of the SAD's public names was the Enemy Area Work Commission. Li Kenong became a deputy director in March 1941, when he also became a SAD deputy director. *Zhongguo Gongchandang zuzhi shi ziliao, 4, 1945.8– 1949.9* [Materials on CCP Organizational History, vol. 4, August 1945–1949] (Beijing: Zhonggong Dangshi Chubanshe, 2000), 549; Hao, *Zhongguo mimi zhan*, 54, 59.

35. Kai, *Li Kenong*, 364; Hao, *Zhongguo mimi zhan*, 105.

36. *Zhongguo Gongchandang zuzhi shi ziliao*, vol. 4, 549.

37. Xu Aihua, "Zhongguo de Fu'er Mosi, yuan Gongan buzhang Zhao Cangbi de Yan'an baowei gongzuo" [China's Sherlock Holmes: Former MPS Minister Zhao Cangbi's Protection Work in Yan'an], *Renminwang*, November 12, 2009, http://dangshi.people.com.cn/GB/85038/10366238 .html; Hao, *Zhongguo mimi zhan*, 137.

38. Yan'an Anti-Japanese University (延安抗大, *Yan'an Kangda*), North Shaanxi Public School (陕北公学, *Shaanbei Gongxue*), the Marx-Lenin Institute (马列学院, *Malie Xueyuan*). Yin Qi, *Pan Hannian de qingbao shengya* [The Intelligence Career of Pan Hannian] (Beijing: Renmin Chubanshe, 1996), 83–88, 125–27.

39. Yin, 83–88.

40. Definitions of "illegal" agents: Norman Polmar and Thomas B. Allen, *The Encyclopedia of Espionage* (New York: Gramercy Books, 1997), 277; Carl, *CIA Insider's Dictionary*, 271–72; Ilya Dzhirkvelov, *Secret Servant: My Life with the KGB and the Soviet Elite* (London: Collins, 1987), 106–8, 178; Robert Whymant, *Stalin's Spy: Richard Sorge and the Tokyo Espionage Ring* (New York: St. Martin's Press, 1996) 26–39; Ruth Werner, *Sonya's Report* (London: Chatto and Windus, 1991), 42–46, 98–111.

41. Frederic Wakeman Jr., *Spymaster: Dai Li and the Chinese Secret Service* (Berkeley: University of California Press, 2003), 341, 523.

42. Ji Chaozhu, *The Man on Mao's Right* (New York: Random House, 2008), 19–22, 32–34.

43. Wakeman, *Spymaster*, 523; Kai, *Li Kenong*, 285, 287.

44. Kuo, *Analytical History*, vol. 4, 148.

45. Michael Dutton, *Policing Chinese Politics* (Durham and London: Duke University Press, 2005), 106–7.

46. Frederick C. Teiwes and Warren Sun, "From a Leninist to a Charismatic Party: The CCP's Changing Leadership, 1937–1945," in *New Perspectives on the Chinese Communist Revolution*, ed. Tony Saich and Hans Van de Ven (Armonk, NY: M. E. Sharpe, 1995), 346–47.

47. He, *Deng Fa Zhuan*, 165; Hao, *Zhongguo mimi zhan*, 189; Jin Chongji, ed., *Chen Yun zhuan* [The Biography of Chen Yun] (Beijing: Zhongyang Wenxian Chubanshe, 2005), 335.

48. *Suimengqu Gonganshi changbian* [A Public Security History of Suiyuan and Inner Mongolia in Draft] (Hohhot: Neimenggu Gongan Ting Gongan Shi Yanjiu Shi, 1986), 122–23.

49. Gao, *Hong taiyang zenyang shengqi de*, 465–66; Gao Wenqian, *Wannian Zhou Enlai* [Zhou Enlai's Later Years] (Hong Kong: Mirror Books, 2003), 82; Peter Vladimirov, *The Vladimirov Diaries, Yenan, China: 1942-1945* (New York: Doubleday and Company, 1975), 136, 190–94.

50. Chen Yung-fa, "Suspect History and the Mass Line: Another Yan'an Way," in *Twentieth Century China: New Approaches*, ed. Jeffrey S. Wasserstrom (London: Routledge, 2003), 182–83; Lin Qingshan, *Kang Sheng Zhuan* (Jilin: Jilin Renmin Chubanshe, 1996), 112; Hao, *Zhongguo mimi zhan*, 318–321; Jin, *Mao Zedong Zhuan*, 655.

51. Kai, *Li Kenong*, 266–68; Yin, *Pan Hannian de qingbo Shengya*, 185–87.

52. Kai, *Li Kenong*, 279.

53. See State Council of the People's Republic of China, http://english.gov.cn/state_council/2014/09/09/content_281474986284154.htm.

54. Gu Chunwang, *Jianguo Yilai Gong'an Gongzuo Da Shi Yaolan* [Major Highlights in Police Work Since the Founding of the Nation] (Beijing: Qunzhong Chubanshe, 2003), 2–3; Shu Yun, *Luo Ruiqing Dajiang* [General Luo Ruiqing] (Beijing: Jiefangjun Wenyi Chubanshe, second ed., 2011), 258–59; *Zhou Enlai nianpu 1949–1976* [Annals of Zhou Enlai, 1949–1976], 3 vols. (Beijing: Zhongyang Wenxian Chubanshe, 1997), 6; Michael Schoenhals, *Spying for the People: Mao's Secret Agents, 1949–1967* (New York: Cambridge University Press, 2013), 27; Kai, *Li Kenong*, 364–65; Guo Xuezhi, *China's Security State, Philosophy, Evolution, and Politics* (Cambridge: Cambridge University Press, 2012), 73–74, 355; Dutton, *Policing Chinese Politics*, 139, 157.

55. Shu, *Luo Ruiqing Dajiang*, 258–59.

56. Public Security Police Station Organization Regulations (December 1954), http://www.npc.gov.cn/wxzl/wxzl/2000-12/10/content_4274.htm.

57. Børge Bakken, "Transition, Age, and Inequality: Core Causes of Chinese Crime," delivered at the 20th International Conference of the Hong Kong Sociological Association, Chinese University of Hong Kong, December 1, 2018; Shu, *Luo Ruiqing Dajiang*, 259–61; Wakeman, *Spymaster*, 361.

58. Shu Guang Zhang, *Deterrence and Strategic Culture: Chinese-American Confrontations, 1949–1958* (Ithaca: Cornell University Press, 1992), 66; Gu, *Gong'an Gongzuo*, 19.

59. Maury Allen, *China Spy: The Story of Hugh Francis Redmond* (New York: Gazette Press, 1998), 108–9, 178; "Ben DeFelice Dies," *Washington Post*, April 9, 2004; Gu, *Gong'an Gongzuo*, 53; Nicholas Dujmovic, "Two CIA Prisoners in China, 1952–1973: Extraordinary Fidelity," *Studies in Intelligence* 50, no. 4 (2006).

60. Dutton, *Policing Chinese Politics*, 147.

61. Dutton, 167–68, 175.

62. David Ian Chambers, "Edging in from the Cold: The Past and Present State of Chinese Intelligence Historiography," *Studies in Intelligence* 56, no. 3 (September 2012): 34, https://www.cia.gov/library/center-for-the-study-of-intelligence/csi-publications/csi-studies/studies/vol.-56-no.-3/pdfs/Chambers-Chinese%20Intel%20Historiography.pdf; Zhang Yun, *Pan Hannian Zhuan* [Biography of Pan Hannian] (Shanghai: Shanghai Renmin Chubanshe, 1996), 317; Kai, *Li Kenong*, 406; Guo, *China's Security State*, 72–75, 345–48; Gu, *Gong'an Gongzuo*, 82–83; Dutton, *Policing Chinese Politics*, 176–78.

63. Guo, *China's Security State*, 72–75; Dutton, *Policing Chinese Politics*, 172–73.

64. "身份证意识将代替户口意识" [Substituting the national ID card for the *hukou* in people's consciousness], *Fazhi Ribao*, December 26, 2002, http://www.people.com.cn/GB/14576/28320/28321/28332/1926520.html; authors' interviews with Public Security officers in 2008 and 2015; interviews with PRC citizens in 2018.

65. Andrew Nathan and Andrew Scobell, *China's Search for Security* (New York: Columbia University Press, 2012), 295.

66. BBC News, "In Your Face: China's All-seeing State," December 10, 2017, https://www.bbc.com/news/av/world-asia-china-42248056/in-your-face-china-s-all-seeing-state.

67. ZDNet, "Chinese Company Leaves Muslim-tracking Facial Recognition Database Exposed Online," February 14, 2019, https://www.zdnet.com/article/chinese-company-leaves-muslim-tracking-facial-recognition-database-exposed-online/.

68. Nathan and Scobell, *China's Search for Security*, 295; Yao Gen, "姚艮在与苏联专家工作的日子里" [In the days of working with Soviet advisors], 公安史话 [Public Security History], http://www.mps.gov.cn/n2254860/n2254883/n2254884/c3590085/content.html.

69. Schoenhals, *Spying for the People*, 24.

70. Schoenhals, 25.

71. Tsering Shakya, *The Dragon in the Land of Snows* (New York: Columbia University Press, 1999) 170–84, 282–86, 358–60; James Lilley and Jeffrey

Lilley, *China Hands: Nine Decades of Adventure, Espionage, and Diplomacy in Asia* (New York: Public Affairs, 2004), 136–37.

72. Gu, *Gong'an Gongzuo*, 304, 307, 317; Dutton, *Policing Chinese Politics*, 224–26; Roderick MacFarquhar and Michael Schoenhals, *Mao's Last Revolution* (Cambridge, MA: Harvard University Press, 2006), 97–98, 225; Guo, *China's Security State*, 79–83; Schoenhals, *Spying for the People*, 26–28; Yang Shengqun, *Deng Xiaoping nianpu 1904–1974*, v. 2 [Annals of Deng Xiaoping, 1904–1974] (Beijing: Zhongyang Wenxian Chubanshe, 2009), 1930.

73. Shen, *Zhonggong diyi*, 304; Li Haiwen, "Hua Guofeng feng Zhou Enlai zhiming diaocha Li Zhen shijian" [Hua Guofeng and Zhou Enlai Investigate the Li Zhen incident], Zhongguo Gongchandang Xinwen Wang [Chinese Communist Party News Network], http://dangshi.people.com.cn/n/2013/12 16/c85037-23851428.html. Within a year Kang Sheng, his mentor, would become inactive due to illness.

74. *Zhou Enlai nianpu 1949–1976*, vol. 3, 629, 174–80; Lilley and Lilley, *China Hands*, 181–84.

75. Lilley and Lilley, *China Hands*, 162–66, 177–78, 180.

76. Gu, *Gong'an Gongzuo*, 358.

77. Gu, entries at the end of each year (see especially 1959–62 and 1970–81); Dutton, *Policing Chinese Politics*, 239, 257–58.

78. Gu, *Gong'an Gongzuo*, 362; CIA, "Soviet Diplomats Expelled from China on Espionage Charges," January 19, 1974, https://www.cia.gov/library/reading room/docs/CIA-RDP78S01932A000100010083-6.pdf.

79. Dutton, *Policing Chinese Politics*, 237.

80. Dutton, 270–71.

81. Ding Zhaoshen, *Duan wei Yang Fan* [The Broken Mast, Yang Fan] (Beijing: Qunzhong Chubanshe, 2001), 6; Kai, *Li Kenong*, 409; Chambers, "Edging in from the Cold," 34.

82. *Washington Post*, July 7, 1983.

83. CIA Directorate of Intelligence, "China: Reorganization of Security Organs" (Washington, DC: Central Intelligence Agency, August 1, 1983, declassified copy, U.S. Library of Congress); Peter Mattis, "The Analytic Challenge of Understanding Chinese Intelligence Services," *Studies in Intelligence* 56, no. 3 (September 2012), https://www.cia.gov/library/center-for-the-study-of-intelligence/csi-publications/csi-studies/studies/vol.-56-no.-3/pdfs/Mattis-Understanding%20Chinese%20Intel.pdf.

84. Author interview with municipal PSB official, 2009.

85. "Mou shi ming gan danweiqingbao" [The weak password of the intelligence platform of a sensitive unit in a certain city] (Bao'an District Government,

Shenzhen), April-May 2015, https://wooyun.shuimugan.com/bug/view?bug_no=107569.

86. Gu, *Gong'an Gongzuo*, 828 (line 5), 834 (list of concerns in 1991 summary).

87. Sarah Cook and Leeshai Lemish, "The 610 Office: Policing the Chinese Spirit," *China Brief* 11, issue 17 (September 16, 2011), https://jamestown.org/program/the-610-office-policing-the-chinese-spirit/.

88. Gu, *Gong'an Gongzuo*, 1087.

89. Gu, 1320.

90. Confidential interviews.

91. Bing Lin, "Tiqu dianzi shuju ye xu quanzhaogongmin yinsi" [Extraction of electronic data requires attention to citizen privacy], *Beijing Shibao*, September 22, 2016; "China: New Rules on Electronic Data Collection Take Effect," *Duihua Human Rights Journal*, October 11, 2016, duihuahrjournal.org; State Council Document 692, "Zhonghua Renmin Gongheguo Fan Jiandie Fa Shishi Xize" [PRC Counterespionage Law Detailed Regulations], December 6, 2017, http://www.gov.cn/zhengce/content/2017–12/06/content_5244819.htm.

92. *Operation Mekong*, Bona Film Group, China, Thailand, 2016.

93. "One organ, two name plates" (一个机构, 两块牌子, *Yige jigou, lian kuai paizi*); Kai, *Li Kenong*, 364; Hao, *Zhongguo mimi zhan*, 105, 411.

94. Schoenhals, "A Brief History of the CID of the CCP."

95. The full agency name was 中共中央军事委员会总参谋部情报部, *Zhonggong Zhongyang Junshi Weiyuanhui Zongcanmou bu Qingbao bu*.

96. Hao, *Zhongguo mimi zhan*, 411; Kai, *Li Kenong*, 343.

97. Robert J. Alexander, *International Maoism in the Developing World* (Westport, CT: Praeger Publishers, 1999), 280–82; Andrew Hall Wedeman, *The East Wind Subsides: Chinese Foreign Policy and the Origins of the Chinese Cultural Revolution* (Washington, DC: The Washington Institute Press, 1987), 184–87; Schoenhals, "Brief History of the CID of the CCP," 269–70.

98. Hao, *Zhongguo mimi zhan*, 375–76; Kai, *Li Kenong*, 344–45.

99. Joyce Wadler, *Liaison: The Real Story of the Affair that Inspired M. Butterfly* (New York: Bantam, 1994); see also Joyce Wadler, "The True Story of M. Butterfly," *New York Times*, August 15, 1993, https://www.nytimes.com/1993/08/15/magazine/the-true-story-of-m-butterfly-the-spy-who-fell-in-love-with-a-shadow.html; Robert David Booth, *State Department Counterintelligence: Leaks, Spies, and Lies* (Dallas, TX: Brown Books Pub. Group, 2014), 108–9; C. S. Trahair, *Encyclopedia of Cold War Espionage, Spies, and Secret Operations* (Westport, CT: Greenwood Press, 2004), 165–66.

100. Schoenhals, "Brief History of the CID of the CCP," 270.

101. Schoenhals.

102. Schoenhals.

103. Shen Zhihua, *Mao Zedong, Shidalin yu Chaoxian zhanzheng* [Mao Zedong, Stalin and the Korean War] (Guangzhou: Guangdong Renmin Chubanshe, 2003), 465–66. Mao probably learned of Stalin's death a few hours after telling Li Kenong to take sick leave. *Zhou Enlai nianpu 1949–1976*, vol. 1, 288.

104. Schoenhals, "Brief History of the CID of the CCP," 270–71.

105. A military intelligence department remained in the CMC.

106. Schoenhals, "Brief History of the CID of the CCP"; Yang Shangkun, *Yang Shangkun Riji, Shang* [The Diary of Yang Shangkun, 2 vols.] (Beijing: Zhongyang Wenxian Chubanshe, 2001), 161, 165, 169, 185 (separate military intelligence from the CMC: "决定把军情由军委分开, 在党内成为一调查部, 由克农兼部长," 169). Confidential document.

107. Even in 1969, a classified CIA report referred to the SAD and did not note the existence of the CID. See Central Intelligence Agency, "Communist China: The Political Security Apparatus," POLO 35, February 20, 1969 (declassified), ii-iv, 10–16, 22–25, 29, 31, 33–35, 65, 70–71.

108. Schoenhals, "Brief History of the CID of the CCP," 15–16; Yang, *Yang Shangkun Riji*, vol. 1, 1, 185, 359, vol. 2, 226.

109. The MSS Intelligence History and Research Division (情报室研究处, *Qingbao shi yanjiu chu*) conducts such prepublication vetting. Chambers, "Edging in from the Cold," 37.

110. Gu, *Gong'an Gongzuo*, 82–84, entries for March 21 to April 11, 1955.

111. Gu, 89, entry for August 25, 1955.

112. Andrew G. Walder, *China Under Mao: A Revolution Derailed* (Cambridge, MA: Harvard University Press, 2015), 135.

113. Kai, *Li Kenong*, 406–9.

114. Kai, 406–8; Gu, *Gong'an Gongzuo*, 82; Chambers, "Edging in from the Cold," 34.

115. Kai, *Li Kenong*, 405–8; Zhu Zi'an, "Chuanqi Jiangjun Li Kenong" [Legendary General Li Kenong], in *Dangshi Zonglan* [Party History Survey], no. 9 (2009): 7.

116. For a colorful account of such operations, see Frank Holober, *Raiders of the China Coast: CIA Covert Operations During the Korean War* (Annapolis, MD: Naval Institute Press, 1999).

117. Schoenhals, "Brief History of the CID of the CCP."

118. PRC Ministry of Foreign Affairs, "The Second Upsurge in the Establishment of Diplomatic Relations," http://www.fmprc.gov.cn/mfa_eng/ziliao _665539/3602_665543/3604_665547/t18056.shtml.

119. Confidential document.
120. Schoenhals, "Brief History of the CID of the CCP," 15.
121. Gu, *Gong'an Gongzuo*, 93–94.
122. China eventually supported national liberation movements and governments confronting the PRC's opponents in Southeast Asia and elsewhere. Alexander, *International Maoism in the Developing World*, 280–82; Wedeman, *The East Wind Subsides*, 184–87; C. C. Chin and Karl Hack, *Dialogues with Chin Peng: New Light on the Malayan Communist Party* (Singapore: Singapore University Press, 2004).
123. Schoenhals, "Brief History of the CID of the CCP."
124. The Nam Kwong Company, founded in August 1949, became the CCP's unofficial office in Macau through 1987, when Xinhua, the New China News Agency, assumed that role. Geoffrey C. Gunn, *Encountering Macau: A Portuguese City-State on the Periphery of China, 1557–1999* (Boulder, CO: Westview Press, 1996), 174.
125. Schoenhals, "Brief History of the CID of the CCP"; Yang, *Yang Shangkun Riji*, v. 1, 337, 352, 359–60, v. 2, 79.
126. Schoenhals, "Brief History of the CID of the CCP," 10; Klein and Clark, *Biographic Dictionary*, vol. 1, 511; Kai, *Li Kenong*, 418–20.
127. Yang, *Yang Shangkun Riji*, v. 2, 216–32.
128. *Zhonggong Diyi*, 513.
129. Obituary, "Luo Qingchang: cengren Zhongyang Diaocha Bu buzhang Zhou Zongli linzhong qian zhaojian" [Luo Qingchang: the former Central Investigation Department Director whom Zhou Enlai summoned on his deathbed], dangshi.people.com.cn, April 21, 2014.
130. Yang Shengqun, ed., *Deng Xiaoping nianpu, 1940–1974, Xia* [The Annals of Deng Xiaoping, 1940–1974, vol. 3] (Beijing: Zhongyang Wenxian Chubanshe, 2009), 1930.
131. Tong Xiaopeng, *Fengyu sishinian* [Forty years of trial and hardships] (Beijing: Zhongyang Wenxian Chubanshe, 1997), 403–6; MacFarquhar and Schoenhals, *Mao's Last Revolution*, 98.
132. Confidential document.
133. MacFarquhar and Schoenhals, *Mao's Last Revolution*, 98.
134. Guo, *China's Security State*, 359, 361; Obituary, "Luo Qingchang: cengren" puts the revival date at 1973, while Shen, *Zhongyang weiyuan*, 513, says the date was 1975.
135. Zhonggong Zhongyang Wenxian Yanjiushi, *Deng Xiaoping nianpu, 1904–1974, Xia* [The Annals of Deng Xiaoping, 1904–1974, vol. 3] (Beijing: Zhongyang Wenxian Chubanshe, 2009), 1972; Office of the Historian, U.S.

Department of State, *Foreign Relations of the United States, 1969–1976*, vol. 18, *China, January 1973–May 1973*, "Kissinger's Visits to Beijing and the Establishment of the Liaison Offices, January 1973–May 1973," https://hist ory.state.gov/historicaldocuments/frus1969-76v18/ch1; Guo, *China's Security State*, 361–62.

136. MacFarquhar and Schoenhals, *Mao's Last Revolution*, 415; obituary, "Luo Qingchang: cengren," April 21, 2014.

137. William C. Hannas, James Mulvenon, and Anna B. Puglisi, *Chinese Industrial Espionage: Technology Acquisition and Military Modernization* (New York: Routledge, 2013), 20–23.

138. Roderick MacFarquhar, "Succession to Mao and the End of Maoism," in *The Politics of China: Sixty Years of the People's Republic of China*, 3rd ed., ed. Roderick MacFarquhar (Cambridge: Cambridge University Press, 2011), 314.

139. Confidential document.

140. Jonathan D. Pollack, "The Opening to America," in *Cambridge History of China*, vol. 15 (Cambridge: Cambridge University Press, 1991), 458–60.

141. Maurice Meisner, *Mao's China and After: A History of the People's Republic* (New York: The Free Press, 1999), 453–66.

142. Meisner, 483–84, 486–87; Richard Baum, "The Road to Tiananmen," in MacFarquhar, *The Politics of China*, 350–54; Orville Schell and John Delury, *Wealth and Power: China's Long March to the Twenty-First Century* (New York: Random House, 2013), 281–82.

143. Maurice Meisner, *Mao's China and After*, 461–66.

144. Mark Stokes and Ian Easton, "The Chinese People's Liberation Army General Staff Department: Evolving Organization and Missions," in *The People's Liberation Army as Organization 2.0*, ed. Kevin Pollpeter and Kenneth W. Allen (Vienna, VA: DGI Inc., 2015), 146–47.

145. The U.S. sting operation in 1987 against a 2PLA military attaché in Washington, Hou Desheng, is the only publicly discussed example of a Chinese military attaché engaged in clandestine human intelligence operations. James Mann and Ronald Ostrow, "U.S. Ousts Two Chinese Envoys for Espionage," *Los Angeles Times*, December 31, 1987.

146. Depending which sources are relied upon, the PLA also possessed a Seventh Bureau, variously described as belonging to the 2PLA technical system or as a fourth analytic bureau. Nicholas Eftimiades, *Chinese Intelligence Operations* (Annapolis, MD: Naval Institute Press, 1994), 78–84, 86; Kan Zhongguo, "Intelligence Agencies Exist in Great Numbers, Spies Are Present Everywhere; China's Major Intelligence Departments Fully Exposed," *Chien*

Shao (Hong Kong), January 1, 2006; Howard DeVore, *China's Intelligence and Internal Security Forces* (Coulsdon, UK: Jane's Information Group, 1999), sec. 4–2.

147. These geographic areas of responsibility are the best available information, even if they appear outdated and insufficient for Beijing's likely intelligence needs. This is an area where circular reporting is difficult if not impossible to identify.

148. "Character and Aim," China Institute for International Strategic Studies, undated, http://www.ciiss.org.cn/xzyzz.

149. Bates Gill and James Mulvenon, "Chinese Military-Related Think Tanks and Research Institutes," *The China Quarterly*, no. 171 (September 2002): 619.

150. Gill and Mulvenon, 621–62. CFISS was a major partner in an effort centered at the Carnegie Endowment for International Peace on crisis management in U.S.-China relations; see *Managing Sino-American Crises: Cast Studies and Analysis*, ed. Michael D. Swaine, Zhang Tuosheng, and Danielle F. S. Cohen (Washington, DC: Brookings Institution Press, 2006).

151. Elsa Kania and Peter Mattis, "Modernizing Military Intelligence: Playing Catchup (Part Two)," *China Brief* 16, issue 9 (December 21, 2016), https://jamestown.org/program/modernizing-military-intelligence-playing-catchup-part-two/.

152. Authors' interviews, August 2017.

153. "China Names Head of New Security Ministry," Associated Press, June 21, 1983; "Functions of New Ministry of State Security," Xinhua, June 20, 1983.

154. "Inaugural Meeting of the Ministry of State Security," Xinhua, July 1, 1983.

155. "Vice Minister of Public Security Ling Yun Discusses Counter-revolutionary Offenses," Xinhua, June 30, 1979.

156. According to one former senior intelligence official, even minister Xu Yongyue's princeling status in the security services and decade-long service as personal secretary to Chen Yun was insufficient for acceptance by MSS headquarters elite. Authors' interview, November 2013.

157. Zhao Xiangru, "Ministry of State Security Holds First Meeting," *People's Daily*, July 2, 1983.

158. Jane Li, "China to Prosecute Former Spy Chief for Corruption," *South China Morning Post*, December 30, 2016, http://www.scmp.com/news/china/policies-politics/article/2058244/china-prosecute-ex-deputy-spy-chief-corruption.

159. "Chen Xitong resigns from office, Beijing takes more intensive action against corruption," *Ming Pao*, April 28, 1995.

160. The latter, however, somehow managed to survive, resurfacing after his successor in charge of counterespionage went down. Peter Mattis, "The Dragon's Eyes and Ears: Chinese Intelligence at the Crossroads," *The National Interest*, January 20, 2015, https://nationalinterest.org/feature/the-dragons-eyes-ears-chinese-intelligence-the-crossroads-12062.
161. These dates are estimated based upon provincial-level personnel appointments and news reports of espionage arrests inside China.
162. Samantha Hoffman and Peter Mattis, "Managing the Power Within: China's Central State Security Commission," *War on the Rocks*, July 18, 2016, https://warontherocks.com/2016/07/managing-the-power-within-chinas-state-security-commission/.
163. Authors' interviews, July 2012, March 2015, September 2017, November 2017; Institute on Global Conflict and Cooperation, "China and Cybersecurity: Political, Economic, and Strategic Dimensions," Report from Workshops held at the University of California, San Diego, April 2012, 6; "Taiwan Unveils Chinese Spy Master," *The Straits Times*, December 7, 2000; "Guo'an bu die bao renyuan 10 wan ren: guowai 4 wan duo guonei 5 wan duo" [Ministry of State Security espionage personnel number 100,000 with more than 40,000 abroad and 50,000 at home], *China Digital Times*, June 1, 2015, https://chinadigitaltimes.net/chinese/2015/06/; Ding Ke, "Tegong-minyun-Falungong: yi ge shengming de zhenshi gushi [Secret Agent—Democracy Movement—Falungong: The True Story of a Life (Part I)]," Ming Hui Net, September 12, 2003, http://www.minghui.org/mh/articles/2003/9/12/57232.html; Jon R. Lindsay, Tai-ming Cheung, and Derek S. Reveron, *China and Cybersecurity: Espionage, Strategy, and Politics in the Digital Domain* (New York: Oxford University Press, 2015), 32.

Chapter 2. Chinese Communist Intelligence Leaders

1. Jin, *Chen Yun Zhuan*, 105.
2. Hao, *Zhongguo mimi zhan*, 13.
3. Mu Xin, "Chen Geng," in *Zhonggong dangshi renwu zhuan*, vol. 3, 2.
4. Donald W. Klein and Anne B. Clark, *Biographic Dictionary of Chinese Communism, 1921–1965*, vol. 2 (Cambridge, MA: Harvard University Press, 1971), 190–92; Shen, *Zhongyang weiyuan*, 460–61.
5. He Lin, ed., *Chen Geng Zhuan* [Biography of Chen Geng] (Beijing: Dangdai Zhongguo Chubanshe, 2007), 16; Mu, "Chen Geng," 3–4.
6. He, *Chen Geng Zhuan*, 19; Mu, "Chen Geng," 5–6. Chen saving Chiang Kai-shek is also recorded in Howard L. Boorman, *Biographic Dictionary of Republican China*, vol. 1 (New York: Columbia University Press, 1970), 190,

and in other mainland sources, but not in Jay Taylor, *The Generalissimo: Chiang Kai-shek and the Struggle for Modern China* (Cambridge, MA: Belknap Press, 2009). On the wider campaign see C. Martin Wilbur, "The Nationalist Revolution: From Canton to Nanking, 1923–28," in *Cambridge History of China*, vol. 12, ed. John K. Fairbank (Cambridge: Cambridge University Press, 1983), 555.

7. Mu Xin, *Chen Geng tongzhi zai Shanghai*, 4–6; Mu, "Chen Geng," 6–8.

8. Mu, *Chen Geng tongzhi zai Shanghai*, 6.

9. Warren Kuo, *Analytical History of the Chinese Communist Party*, vol. 2 (Taipei: Institute of International Relations, 1968), 55, 92nn18–19.

10. He, *Chen Geng Zhuan*, 45. For more details, see the entry on Ke Lin.

11. He, 40–41; Mu, *Chen Geng tongzhi zai Shanghai*, 34–40; Yin, *Pan Hannian de qingbao shengya*, 9–10, 14–16; Quan Yanchi, *Zhongguo miwen neimu* [Secrets and Insider Stories of China] (Lanzhou: Gansu wenhua chubanshe, 2004), 44; Kuo, *Analytical History*, vol. 2, 285–87; Yu, *OSS in China*, 34–35; Hao, *Zhongguo mimi zhan*, 9.

12. He, *Chen Geng Zhuan*, 41.

13. Mu, *Chen Geng tongzhi zai Shanghai*, 23–24.

14. Mu, 25.

15. Robert Bickers, "Changing Shanghai's 'Mind': Publicity, Reform, and the British in Shanghai, 1928–1931," China Society Occasional Papers no. 26, 1992, 8–9.

16. Hao, *Zhongguo mimi zhan*, 6.

17. He, *Chen Geng Zhuan*, 41–42.

18. He, 48–51; Mu, "Chen Geng," 13–15.

19. Mu, "Chen Geng," 16–18.

20. Li Songde, *Liao Chengzhi* (Singapore: Yongsheng Books, 1992), 431–32; Wang Junyan, *Liao Chengzhi Zhuan* [The Biography of Liao Chengzhi] (Beijing: Renmin Chubanshe, 2006), 3, 33–34, 678.

21. Mu, "Chen Geng," 19–22; Snow, *Random Notes on Red China*, 92–99.

22. Mu, "Chen Geng," 22–25, 68–78, 83–85; Chen Jian, *Mao's China and the Cold War* (Chapel Hill: University of North Carolina Press, 2001), 127.

23. Mu, "Chen Geng," 85–88.

24. "陈文清任国家安全部部长　耿惠昌不再担任 [Chen Wenqing becomes minister of state security as Geng Huichang steps down]," *China Economic News* via 163.com, November 7, 2016, http://news.163.com/16/1107/10/C58 T707V000187V8.html.

25. "陈小工：全国人大外事委员会委员、中将 [Chen Xiaogong: National People's Congress Foreign Affairs Committee Member, Lieutenant General],"

环球网 [*Global Times Online*], November 21, 2013, http://world.huanqiu.com /hot/2013-11/4588673.html.

26. Mattis, "PLA Personnel Shifts Highlight Intelligence's Growing Military Role."

27. "陈小工 [Chen Xiaogong]."

28. James Mulvenon, "Chen Xiaogong: A Political Biography," *China Leadership Monitor* no. 22 (Fall 2007).

29. Mulvenon; Ray Cheung, "Knives Being Sharpened Behind Sino-U.S. Smiles," *South China Morning Post*, October 26, 2003; Kevin Pollpeter, "U.S.-China Security Management: Assessing the Military-to-Military Relationship" (Santa Monica, CA: RAND, 2004), 26.

30. Mulvenon, "Chen Xiaogong," 3-4.

31. Kenneth W. Allen et al., "China's Defense Minister and Ministry of National Defense," in Pollpeter and Allen, *The PLA as Organization 2.0*, 111, 117.

32. "Central Asia Expert to Head PLA Intelligence," *South China Morning Post*, January 12, 2012, http://www.scmp.com/article/989896/central-asia-expert-head-pla-intelligence.

33. Yang Shilan, "Deng Fa," in *Zhonggong dangshi renwu zhuan*, vol. 1, 347-48.

34. Yang, 348-55.

35. Hao, *Zhongguo mimi zhan*, 12, 14-15; Yang, "Deng Fa," 356-57; Jiang Liuqing, *Zhonggong Chanchu Baowei Shiji* [A History of Chinese Communist Weeding and Protection] (Beijing: Jiefangjun Chubanshe, 2014), 63-65; Stephen C. Averill, "The Origins of the Futian Incident," in *New Perspectives on the Chinese Communist Revolution*, ed. Tony Saich and Hans Van de Ven (Armonk, NY: M. E. Sharpe, 1995), 85-86, 91.

36. Hao, *Zhongguo mimi zhan*, 13-15; Xu, *Wang Jiaxiang Nianpu*, 56-57; Jiang Guansheng, *Zhonggong zai Xianggang, Shang* [The Chinese Communists in Hong Kong, vol. 1] (Hong Kong: Cosmos Books, Inc., 2011), 118-19; Shen, *Zhongyang weiyuan*, 322.

37. Yang, "Deng Fa," 356-57; Teiwes and Sun, "From a Leninist to a Charismatic Party," 370, 387n140.

38. "Yifen juemi qingbao cushi hongjun tiaoshang changzhenglu" [Secret Intelligence Prompted Red Army to Embark on Long March], *Zhongguo Gongchandang xinwenwang*, April 8, 2009, http://dangshi.people.com.cn /GB/144956/9090941.html.

39. "Order of battle" is the military term for the details about a military force.

40. *Zhonggong dangshi renwu zhuan*, vol. 31, 357-58.

41. Yang, "Deng Fa," 359; *Zhou Enlai nianpu 1898-1949*, 293; Warren Kuo, *Analytical History of the Chinese Communist Party*, vol. 3 (Taipei: Institute of International Relations, 1970), 133.

42. He Jinzhou, *Deng Fa zhuan* [Biography of Deng Fa] (Beijing: Zhonggong Dangshi Chubanshe, 2008), 123–27; Yang, "Deng Fa," 359; Snow, *Red Star Over China*, 52–53.

43. Teiwes and Sun, "From a Leninist to a Charismatic Party," 387n140; Otto Braun, *A Comintern Agent in China 1932–1939* (St. Lucia: University of Queensland Press, 1982), 31, 152; Dieter Heinzig, *The Soviet Union and Communist China 1945–1950* (Armonk, NY: M. E. Sharpe, 1998), 26; Yang, "Deng Fa," 360–62.

44. He, *Deng Fa zhuan*, 127; Shen, *Zhongyang weiyuan*, 99.

45. Shen, *Zhongyang weiyuan*, 99; Yang, "Deng Fa," 361–63; He, *Deng Fa zhuan*, 144.

46. Yang, "Deng Fa," 363.

47. Vladimirov, *The Vladimirov Diaries,* 130–31; Gao Hua, *Hong taiyang shi zeyang shengqi de* [How Did the Red Sun Rise Over Yan'an: A History of the Rectification Movement] (Hong Kong: Chinese University Press, 2000), 508–9.

48. Teiwes and Sun, "From a Leninist to a Charismatic Party," 374.

49. Mayumi Itoh, *The Making of China's War with Japan: Zhou Enlai and Zhang Xueliang* (New York: Palgrave, 2016), 212.

50. "人物名片：耿惠昌 [Personality Card: Geng Huichang]," Xinhua, March 17, 2013 http://news.xinhuanet.com/rwk/2013-03/17/c_124468635.htm; "Chen Wenqing becomes minister of state security as Geng Huichang steps down."

51. Chi Hsiao-hua, "Scholar Minister Who Is Low-Profiled and Withdrawn," *Sing Tao Jih Pao*, August 31, 2007.

52. 刘之根 [Liu Zhigen], 耿惠昌 [Geng Huichang], "一九八四年美国大选形势展望 [Forecasting the 1984 U.S. Presidential Election]," 现代国际关系 [*Contemporary International Relations*], no. 6 (1984): 7–10, 62.

53. "The Five Fresh Faces in the Political Reshuffle," *South China Morning Post*, August 31, 2007; Chi, "Scholar Minister Who Is Low-Profiled and Withdrawn."

54. "Geng Huichang," China Vitae, http://www.chinavitae.com/biography/Geng_Huichang/career.

55. Shen, *Zhongyang weiyuan*, 621.

56. Mu, *Chen Geng tongzhi zai Shanghai*, 4–6; Mu, "Chen Geng," 6–8.

57. Wang Jianying, ed., *Zhongguo gongchandang zuzhi shi ziliao huibian,* vol. 2 [A Compilation of Chinese Communist Party Organizational History, vol. 2] (Beijing: Zhonggong Zhongyang Dangxiao Chubanshe, 1995), 35.

58. Hao, *Zhongguo mimi zhan*, 5–7.

59. The Eyuwan soviet base area (鄂豫皖根据地, *Eyuwan genjudi*) was in the border areas of Hunan, Anhui, and Henan, about five hundred miles west of Shanghai. The closest nearby city was Wuhan.

60. Wakeman, *Spymaster*, 42–45; Hsu Kai-yu, *Chou En-lai, China's Gray Eminence* (New York: Doubleday, 1968), 128.

61. Liu, *Zhou Enlai da cidian* 31–32; Hao, *Zhongguo mimi zhan*, 8–9; Barnouin and Yu, *Zhou Enlai*, 45–48.

62. Jin, *Chen Yun Zhuan,* 104; Hao, *Zhongguo mimi zhan*, 9–10.

63. Jin, *Chen Yun Zhuan*, 104; Liu, *Zhou Enlai da cidian*, 31–32; *Zhou Enlai nianpu 1898–1949*, 210–11.

64. Wakeman, *Spymaster*, 178; Li Tien-min, *Chou En-lai* (Taipei: Institute of International Relations, 1970), 152–53; *Wu Hao: Blood Soaked Secrets in the Dark Shadows of History,* in *Dangshi Wencong*, no. 88 (2003) describes the murder of Gu's entire family in a matter-of-fact style.

65. Stuart Schram, Stephen C. Averill, and Nancy Hodes, *Mao's Road to Power: Revolutionary Writings 1912–1949,* vol. 4 (Armonk, NY: M. E. Sharpe, 1992), 163–65, has the translated text of "Order the Arrest of Gu Shunzhang, a Traitor to the Revolution, A General Order Issued by the Council of People's Commissars of the Provisional Central Soviet Government, 10 Dec 1931."

66. Wakeman, *Spymaster*, 466; Hsu, *The Invisible Conflict*, 62–63.

67. Little information is available on Hua's parents. An underground circular written in 1977 by supporters of Deng Xiaoping claimed that Hua's mother had many lovers, including Kang Sheng, who protected him. Robert Weatherly, *Mao's Forgotten Successor: The Political Career of Hua Guofeng* (New York: Palgrave Macmillan, 2010), 23–26.

68. Wang Yongjun and Liu Jianbai, eds., *Zhongguo Xiandaishi Renwu Zhuan* [Biographies of Personalities in Modern Chinese History] (Chengdu: Sichuan Renmin Chubanshe, 1986). Hua is absent in this account. See also Shen, *Zhongyang weiyuan*, 183–84.

69. Weatherly, *Mao's Forgotten Successor,* 30–33.

70. Weatherly, 36–38, 69.

71. Weatherly, 70, 75, 83, 90.

72. Weatherly, 4–6, 78; Shen, *Zhongyang weiyuan*, 183.

73. Weatherly, *Mao's Forgotten Successor,* 84–89, 94–96. The other four provinces Mao viewed favorably were Hebei, Hubei, Zhejiang, and Henan.

74. Weatherly, *Mao's Forgotten Successor,* 100–10; Shen, *Zhongyang weiyuan*, 183.

75. Teiwes and Sun, *The End of the Maoist Era*, 36–37, 270; Weatherly, *Mao's Forgotten Successor*, 114–16.

76. *Zhou Enlai nianpu 1949–1976*, vol. 3, 629.

77. Teiwes and Sun, *The End of the Maoist Era*, 119.

78. *Zhou Enlai nianpu 1949–1976*, vol. 3, 629, 694; Teiwes and Sun, *The End of the Maoist Era*, 443–45, 448–56, 492–98.

79. Teiwes and Sun, *The End of the Maoist Era*, 496–98; Shen, *Zhongyang weiyuan*, 183; MacFarquhar and Schoenhals, *Mao's Last Revolution*, 419–20.

80. Teiwes and Sun, *The End of the Maoist Era*, 158, 206, 208, 327–31, 383–87.

81. Teiwes and Sun, 574–81; MacFarquhar and Schoenhals, *Mao's Last Revolution*, 443–49.

82. Hannas, Mulvenon, and Puglisi, *Chinese Industrial Espionage*, 20–23.

83. MacFarquhar, "Succession to Mao and the End of Maoism," 314.

84. The authors are grateful to Frederick Teiwes for this observation.

85. Shen, *Zhongyang weiyuan*, 183.

86. "中国人民解放军总参谋部有多少位将军 [The Chinese PLA General Staff Department Has How Many Generals]," 铁血网 [Iron and Blood Online Forums], October 29, 2008, http://bbs.tiexue.net/post2_3140644_1 .html.

87. "第七届欧中论坛在乌克兰成功举行 [Seventh Europe-China Forum Successfully Held in Ukraine]," Embassy of the People's Republic of China in Ukraine, September 20, 2008, http://ua.china-embassy.org/chn/dsxxpd/dwhd /t513763.htm; "500 Representatives to Attend the Sixth Xiangshan Forum," China Military Online, October 13, 2015, http://english.chinamil.com.cn /news-channels/china-military-news/2015–10/13/content_6721282.htm.

88. Willy Wo-Lap Lam, "Meeting Endorses New Leadership for Army; Seal of Approval for New Military Lineup," *South China Morning Post*, October 19, 1992.

89. Authors' interview, July 2016.

90. Roberto Suro, "Not Chinese Agent, Says Chung," *Washington Post*, May 12, 1999.

91. This entry is adapted from Mattis, "Assessing the Foreign Policy Influence of the Ministry of State Security."

92. "贾春旺同志简历 [Biographical Notes on Comrade Jia Chunwang]," 人民 网领导人资料库 [People's Net Leadership Database], November 27, 2002, http://www.people.com.cn/GB/shizheng/252/9667/9683/20021127/875910 .html.

93. Cheng Li, *China's Leaders: The New Generation* (Lanham, MD: Rowman and Littlefield Publishers, 2001), 89–90, 104–6; Long Hua, "How China Developed the 'Jiang-Zhu Structure,'" *Hong Kong Economic Journal*, March 23, 1998.

94. "Chen Xitong resigns from office, Beijing takes more intensive action against corruption," *Ming Pao*, April 28, 1995.
95. Willy Wo-Lap Lam, "Security Boss Tipped to Leap Forward," *South China Morning Post*, May 29, 1997.
96. Kai, *Li Kenong*, 430–32.
97. Willy Wo-Lap Lam, "Jiang and Li Grasp Control of Security; Proteges of President and Premier Moved Up," *South China Morning Post*, March 2, 1998; Willy Wo-Lap Lam, "Zhu Cabinet a Blend of Four Generations; Leaders Have Say in Achieving Factional Balance," *South China Morning Post*, March 19, 1998.
98. In spite of his many name changes, we will use Kang Sheng throughout. Sources disagree on Kang's birth year and date for joining the CCP, but the official records document 1898 and 1925, respectively. Shen, *Zhongyang weiyuan*, 701; Wang and Liu, *Zhongguo Xiandaishi Renwu Zhuan*, 733.
99. John Byron and Robert Pack, *The Claws of the Dragon: Kang Sheng—The Evil Genius Behind Mao and His Legacy of Terror in the People's Republic of China* (New York: Simon and Schuster, 1992), 42–44.
100. Shen, *Zhongyang weiyuan*, 701; Zhong, *Kang Sheng Pingzhuan*, 25. Though based on party records and insider accounts, the bitter and accusatory style of *Kang Sheng Pingzhuan*, released to justify Kang's expulsion from the CCP, make it reliable only when confirmed by other sources.
101. Zhong, *Kang Sheng Pingzhuan*, 36; Shen, *Zhongyang weiyuan*, 701.
102. Mu, *Yinbi zhanxian tongshuai Zhou Enlai*, 377; Yin, *Pan Hannian de qingbao shengya*, 30–31.
103. Hao, *Zhongguo mimi zhan*, 56; Shen, *Zhongyang weiyuan*, 701.
104. Wang Qun, "Kang Sheng Zai Zhongyang Shehuibu" [Kang Sheng in the Central Social Affairs Department], *Bainian Chao* [Hundred Year Tide], May 2003, http://mall.cnki.net/magazine/Article/BNCH200305004.htm; Hao, *Zhongguo mimi zhan*, 56; Shen, *Zhongyang weiyuan*, 701.
105. Wang and Liu, 734.
106. Robert Conquest, *Inside Stalin's Secret Police: NKVD Politics 1936–1939* (London: MacMillan Press Ltd., 1985), 1; Robert Conquest, *The Great Terror: A Reassessment* (New York: Oxford University Press, 1991), 33–35.
107. Interview with party historian, 2016; Chen, "Suspect History and the Mass Line," 243.
108. Including Li Lisan and Ho Chi Minh, both later released. William J. Duiker, *Ho Chi Minh: A Life* (New York: Hyperion, 2000), 211–14.
109. Zhong, *Kang Sheng Pingzhuan*, 57–60.

110. Sophie Quinn-Judge, *Ho Chi Minh, The Missing Years* (Berkeley: University of California Press, 2002), 202, 207–8; Duiker, *Ho Chi Minh*, 213; Pantsov and Levine, *Mao: The Real Story*, 271.

111. Kuo, *Analytical History*, vol. 3, 340–41, 392–93.

112. Pantsov and Levine, *Mao: The Real Story*, 328–29; Teiwes and Sun, "From a Leninist to a Charismatic Party," 343–45, 371; Zhong, *Kang Sheng Pingzhuan*, 75–77.

113. Pantsov and Levine, *Mao: The Real Story*, 333–34.

114. Spies as thick as fur: "特务如麻" (*tewu ru ma*); Zhong, *Kang Sheng Pingzhuan*, 54–55; Wang and Liu, *Zhongguo Xiandaishi Renwu Zhuan*, 734–35; Wang, "Kang Sheng Zai Zhongyang Shehuibu"; Hao, *Zhongguo mimi zhan*, 287.

115. Gao, *Hong taiyang zenyang shengqi de*, 465.

116. Gao, *Wannian Zhou Enlai*, 82; Gao, *Hong taiyang zenyang shengqi de*, 465; Roger Faligot, *Les Services Secrets Chinois de Mao aux Jo* [The Chinese Secret Services of Mao and Zhou] (Paris: Nouveau Monde, 2008), 81–82.

117. Schoenhals, "A Brief History of the CID of the CCP," 4; Kai, *Li Kenong*, 279–80.

118. Wang and Liu, *Zhongguo Xiandaishi Renwu Zhuan*, 735; Roderick MacFarquhar, *The Origins of the Cultural Revolution*, vol. 2: *Contradictions Among the People, 1956–1957* (New York: Columbia University Press, 1974), 148–49, 359–60.

119. Wang and Liu, *Zhongguo Xiandaishi Renwu Zhuan*, 735.

120. The handover from Deng to Kang occurred during the Eleventh Plenum of the Eighth Central Committee, led by Lin Biao, held August 13–23, 1966. Yang Shengqun, ed., *Deng Xiaoping nianpu 1904–1974* [The Annals of Deng Xiaoping], vol. 2 (Beijing: Zhongyang Wenxian Chubanshe, 2012), 1930.

121. An Ziwen and Lu Dingyi, respectively. MacFarquhar and Schoenhals, *Mao's Last Revolution*, 96–98.

122. Kang Sheng claiming to be able to tell a spy simply by looking (我看你就像特务, *Wo kan ni jiu xiang tewu*). Hao, *Zhongguo mimi zhan*, 280–81. For a definition of "mysticism" specific to security work, see Li Zengqun, ed., *Shiyong Gong'an xiao cidian* [A Practical Public Security Mini-Dictionary] (Harbin: Heilongjiang Renmin Chubanshe, 1987), 345.

123. Li Zhisui, *The Private Life of Chairman Mao: The Memoirs of Mao's Personal Physician* (London: Chatto and Windus, 1994), 549; Wang and Liu, *Zhongguo Xiandaishi Renwu Zhuan*, 737.

124. Deng remained silent on Kang Sheng even as Kang was posthumously expelled from the CCP. Teiwes and Sun, *The End of the Maoist Era*, 14–15, 366–67.

125. Interview, Frederick Teiwes, citing a CCP historian, 2017.

126. MacFarquhar and Schoenhals, *Mao's Last Revolution*, 33.

127. Originally named Chen Kaiyuan, Kong used a number of aliases including Tian Fu, Chen Tiezheng and Shi Xin.

128. Shen, *Zhongyang weiyuan*,111–12. See also Tian Changlie, ed., *Zhonggong Jilinshi dangshi renwu* [Personalities in Party History in Jilin Municipality] (Jilin: Dongbei Shida Chubanshe, 1999).

129. *Who's Who in Communist China* (Hong Kong: Union Research Institute, 1966), 312.

130. Mao Zedong later described this development one of as the "14 great events" in his "Report on an Investigation of the Peasant Movement in Hunan" (March 28, 1927). See Tony Saich, ed., *The Rise to Power of the Chinese Communist Party* (Armonk, NY: M. E. Sharpe, 1996), 205–6.

131. Shen, *Zhongyang weiyuan*; Tian, *Zhonggong Jilinshi dangshi renwu*.

132. See "Mosike Dongfang Daxue: Peiyangle yi pi Zhongguo geming de zhongjian" [Moscow University of the East: training the backbone of the Chinese revolution], http://dangshi.people.com.cn/GB/16079450.html.

133. Wang Jianying, ed., *Zhongguo Gongchandang zuzhi shi ziliao huibian* [Compilation of Materials on CCP Organizational History], vol. 2 (Beijing: Hongqi Chubanshe, 1983), 172.

134. See http://www.cqvip.com/read/read.aspx?id=1000063937.

135. According to a Chinese researcher, the details on training are less available in the PRC and in Chinese records than they might be if Russian archives were available. Interview, 2016.

136. Kong served as SAD deputy for eighteen months before being replaced by Li Kenong. *Gongan Shi Zhishi Wenda* [Public security knowledge questions and answers] (Beijing: Zhongguo Jingcha Xuehui Qunzhong Chubanshe, 1994), 21; "Kong Yuan," biography, on *Zhongguo zhengfu wang* (official web site of the PRC central government), http://www.gov.cn/gjjg/2008-10/16/content_1122294.htm; "Kong Yuan jianli jieshao, Kong Yuan Xu Ming de guanxi" [A brief introduction to Kong Yuan, the Kong Yuan and Xu Ming relationship], Lishi shang de Jintian [Today on History], April 6, 2017, http://www.todayonhistory.com/people/201704/25081.html.

137. *The Communist* no. 1 (October 1939), cited in Warren Kuo, *Analytical History of the Chinese Communist Party*, vol. 4 (Taipei: Institute of International Relations, 1971), 124–25, 382. For other expressions of concern about agents and undesirables among the 100,000 people who arrived in Yan'an after July 1937, see "Zhongyang guanyu shencha ganbu wenti de zhishi" [Central Committee Instruction Concerning the Question of Investigating

Cadres], August 1, 1940, in *Zhonggong zhongyang wenjian xuanji*, vol. 12 [Selected Documents of the CCP Central Committee] (Beijing: Zhonggong zhongyang dangxiao chubanshe, 1992), 444–47; Lyman Van Slyke, "The Chinese Communist Movement During the Sino-Japanese War," in Fairbank, *Cambridge History of China*, vol. 13, 620–21, 634–35.

138. "Kong Yuan," http://www.jlsds.cn/yanjiu/renwu/kongyuan.html.

139. Yu, *Hongse jiandie—daohao bashan*, 242–43, 555–57.

140. Van Slyke, "The Chinese Communist Movement During the Sino-Japanese War," 718.

141. Though Deng Xiaoping also lost office during the Cultural Revolution, he was relatively immune from harm because his background was "totally clear": he had never worked in enemy areas and was a partisan of Mao, a 毛泽东的人 (*Mao Zedong de ren*). Interview with party historian, 2016.

142. See http://www.cqvip.com/read/read.aspx?id=1000063937.

143. The CCP Central Committee Finance Commission (Zhonggong Zhongyang Caijing Weiyuanhui) and the Government Administration Council Finance and Economic Commission (Zhengwuyuan Caizheng Jingji Weiyuanhui). Shen, *Zhongyang weiyuan*, 111.

144. "Kong Yuan, 1906–1990," *Jilin Dangshi Renwu* [Personalities in Jilin party history], http://www.jldsyjs.org/news_view.aspx?id=724.

145. "Kong Yuan, 1906–1990"; Shen, *Zhongyang weiyuan*, 111.

146. Shen.

147. Kai, *Li Kenong*, 417–18.

148. CCP-approved books by Hao Zaijin, Kai Cheng, and Li Li describe Li Kenong's life and times. See also http://dangshi.people.com.cn/GB/17 0835/175363/10479349.html.

149. Michael Schoenhals, "The Central Case Examination Group, 1966–1979," *China Quarterly*, no. 145 (March 1996): 97.

150. "Kong Yuan," http://www.jlsds.cn/yanjiu/renwu/kongyuan.html.

151. Shen, *Zhongyang weiyuan*, 112.

152. Kai, *Li Kenong*, 1–2.

153. Kai, 6–7; Shen, *Zhongyang weiyuan*, 322; Klein and Clark, *Biographic Dictionary of Chinese Communism, 1921–1965*, vol. 1, 509.

154. Kai, *Li Kenong*, 7–11; Faligot, *Les Services Secrets Chinois de Mao aux Jo*, 51–52; Chang Jun-mei, ed., *Chinese Communist Who's Who*, vol. 2 (Taipei: Institute for International Relations, 1970), 438; Mu, *Chen Geng tongzhi zai Shanghai*, 34–40; Barnouin and Yu, *Zhou Enlai*, 45–46; Yu, *OSS in China*, 34–35; Hao, *Zhongguo mimi zhan*, 9; Kuo, *Analytical History*, vol. 2, 55, 92nn18–19; "Yifen juemi qingbao cushi hongjun tiaoshang changzhenglu."

155. Hao, *Zhongguo mimi zhan*, 11–12. The "Order the Arrest of Gu Shunzhang" was issued in Ruijin on December 10, 1931, about when Zhou Enlai arrived there. Schram, Averill, and Hodes, *Mao's Road to Power*, vol. 4, 163–65.

156. Hao, *Zhongguo mimi zhan*, 10, 13–15; Xu, *Wang Jiaxiang Nianpu*, 56–57; Shen, *Zhongyang weiyuan*, 99, 322; He, *Deng Fa Zhuan*, 70–71.

157. Hao, *Zhongguo mimi zhan*, 20; Kai, *Li Kenong*, 74–80.

158. Wang Fang, *Wang Fang Huiyi Lu* [The Memoirs of Wang Fang] (Hangzhou: Zhejiang Renmin Chubanshe, 2006), 14.

159. Snow, *Red Star Over China*, 69. While in Ruijin, Li Kenong was simultaneously the head of the PPB Enforcement Department (*Zhixingbu buzhang*) and of the PPB in the First Front Army. See http://cpc.people.com.cn /GB/34136/2543750.html.

160. Kai, *Li Kenong*, 374, 396, 406; Fan Shuo, *Ye Jianying zai guanjian shike* [Ye Jianying in Crucial Moments] (Shenyang: Liaoning Renmin Chubanshe, 2001), 197–200; Chang, *Chinese Communist Who's Who*, vol. 2, 439.

161. Hao, *Zhongguo mimi zhan*, 54, 59; Kai, *Li Kenong*, 232.

162. Kai, 232; *Ba lu jun huiyi shiliao* [Eighth Route Army Memoirs and Historical Materials] 3 (Beijing: Jiefangjun Chubanshe, 1991), 18, 19, 21; Fang Ke, *Zhonggong Qingbao Shou Nao, Li Kenong* [Chinese Communist Intelligence Chief, Li Kenong] (Beijing: Zhongguo Shehui Kexue Chubanshe, 1996), 304–6.

163. Kai, *Li Kenong*, 127.

164. Kai, 127–29; Yin, *Pan Hannian de qingbao shengya*, 92; *Zhou Enlai nianpu 1949–1976*, vol. 3, 341–71; *Ba lu jun huiyi shiliao*, 19.

165. Wakeman, *Spymaster*, 341, 523.

166. Wakeman, 523.

167. Gao, *Hong taiyang shi zeyang shengqi de*, 509; "Zhongyang guanyu shencha ganbu de jueding" [Central Committee Decision Concerning Cadre Examination], August 15, 1943, in *Zhonggong zhongyang wenjian xuanji*, vol. 14, 89–96.

168. Vladimirov, *The Vladimirov Diaries*, 100, 154, 218.

169. Chen Yung-fa, "The Blooming Poppy Under the Red Sun: The Yan'an Way and the Opium Trade," in Saich and Van de Ven, *New Perspectives on the Chinese Communist Revolution*, 273–75.

170. Gao, *Hong taiyang shi zeyang shengqi de*, 465.

171. David D. Barrett, *Dixie Mission: The United States Army Observer Group in Yenan, 1944* (Berkeley: University of California Center for Chinese Studies, 1970), 34.

172. Teiwes and Sun, *The Formation of the Maoist Leadership*, 374; Zeng Qing-ghong, ed., *Zhongguo gongchandang zuzhishi ziliao,* vol. 4, no. 1 [Materials on Chinese Communist Organizational History] (Beijing: Zhongguo gongchandang zuzhishi ziliao bianshen weiyuanhui, 2000), 41; Kai, *Li Kenong,* 279–80, 295–96, 364; Schoenhals, "A Brief History of the CID of the CCP," 4.

173. Kai, *Li Kenong,* 266–67.

174. Chambers, "Edging in from the Cold," cf. 266n62.

175. Schoenhals, "A Brief History of the CID of the CCP," 7.

176. "Pan Hannian Yang Fan sheng si lian: yuanyu yi zuo 24 nian" [Pan Hannian and Yang Fan's life and death: a 24-year miscarriage of justice], Xinwen Wu Bao, December 4, 2005.

177. Kai, *Li Kenong,* 406–8.

178. Kai, 405–8; Zhu Zi'an, "Chuanqi Jiangjun Li Kenong" [Legendary General Li Kenong], *Dangshi Zonglan* [Party History Survey], no. 9 (2009): 7.

179. Schoenhals, "A Brief History of the CID of the CCP," 10; Kai, *Li Kenong,* 417–18.

180. Kai, 418–20.

181. Schoenhals, "A Brief History of the CID of the CCP," 26; Kai, *Li Kenong,* 412.

182. Major General: *Shaojiang* (少将), appointed 1955. Li Haiwen, "Hua Guofeng feng Zhou Enlai zhiming diaocha Li Zhen shijian" [Hua Guofeng and Zhou Enlai Investigate the Li Zhen incident], Zhongguo Gongchandang Xinwen Wang [Chinese Communist Party News Network], http://dangshi.people.com.cn/n/2013/1216/c85037-23851428.html.

183. Shen, *Zhongyang weiyuan,* 304; Li, "Hua Guofeng feng Zhou Enlai zhiming diaocha Li Zhen shijian."

184. Teiwes and Sun, *The End of the Maoist Era*, 119, 119n26.

185. No relation to Liu Fuzhi. The two men were both ministers of public security but at different times: Xie Fuzhi from 1959 to 1972, and Liu Fuzhi from 1983 to 1985.

186. Shen, *Zhongyang weiyuan,* 304; more detail in Li, "Hua Guofeng feng Zhou Enlai."

187. Shen, 304; Li, "Hua Guofeng feng Zhou Enlai."

188. Teiwes and Sun, *The End of the Maoist Era*, 93–94.

189. Telephone interviews, Jan Wong and Norman Shulman, April 2016. See http://www.janwong.ca/redchinablues.html.

190. Lilley and Lilley, *China Hands*, 174–84.

191. MacFarquhar and Schoenhals, *Mao's Last Revolution*, 228–29, 233–39; Ma Jisen, *The Cultural Revolution in the Foreign Ministry of China* (Hong Kong: The Chinese University Press, 2004), 267–84.

192. Li Haiwen notes that Li's family life and career were both satisfactory.

193. Sidney Rittenberg and Amanda Bennett, *The Man Who Stayed Behind* (New York: Simon and Schuster, 1993), 170–72; Byron and Pack, *The Claws of the Dragon*, 189.

194. Byron and Pack, *The Claws of the Dragon*, 334–35.

195. Ye Maozhi and Liu Ziwei, *Zhongguo guo'an wei* [China's National Security Commission] (New York and Hong Kong: Leader Press and Mirror Books, 2014), 79–80.

196. Hao, *Zhongguo mimi zhan*, 10.

197. "凌云同志逝世 [Comrade Ling Yun Passes Away]," Xinhua, http://www.xin huanet.com/politics/2018–03/21/c_1122569805.htm.

198. "解密：中国解放军最神秘的部门—总参谋部 [Decoded: Chinese People's Liberation Army's Most Secretive Department, the General Staff Department]," 看历史 [Reading History Online], January 30, 2015, http://www.read lishi.com/ysmw/20150130/2201.html.

199. Hao, *Zhongguo mimi zhan*, 91.

200. Hao; Shen, *Zhongyang weiyuan*, 513; obituary, "Luo Qingchang"; Hu Jie, *Zhongguo Xibu mimi zhan* [Western China's Secret War] (Beijing: Jincheng Chubanshe, 2015), 343–46.

201. Shen, *Zhongyang weiyuan*, 513.

202. Obituary, "Luo Qingchang."

203. MacFarquhar and Schoenhals, *Mao's Last Revolution*, 98.

204. Xuezhi Guo, *China's Security State: Philosophy, Evolution, and Politics* (Cambridge: Cambridge University Press, 2012), 359, 361.

205. Obituary, "Luo Qingchang," puts the revival date at 1973, while Shen, *Zhongyang weiyuan*, 513, says the date was 1975.

206. Yang, *Deng Xiaoping nianpu 1904–1974*, vol. 3, 1972; Office of the Historian, U.S. Department of State, *Foreign Relations of the United States, 1969–1976*, vol. 18, *China, January 1973–May 1973*, "Kissinger's Visits to Beijing and the Establishment of the Liaison Offices, January 1973–May 1973"; Xuezhi, *China's Security State*, 361–62.

207. MacFarquhar and Schoenhals, *Mao's Last Revolution*, 415; obituary, "Luo Qingchang."

208. MacFarquhar and Schoenhals, 413–30, 446–49.

209. Alexander V. Pantsov and Steven I. Levine, *Deng Xiaoping: A Revolutionary Life* (New York: Oxford University Press, 2015), 345–57; Vogel, *Deng Xiaoping*, 266–93.

210. Confidential document.
211. Confidential document.
212. Ezra F. Vogel, *Deng Xiaoping and the Transformation of China* (Cambridge, MA: Harvard University Press, 2013), 373–79.
213. Shen, *Zhongyang weiyuan*, 513.
214. Dutton, *Policing Chinese Politics*, 218–21, 227–30; MacFarquhar and Schoenhals, *Mao's Last Revolution*, 98–99.
215. Shu, *Luo Ruiqing dajiang*, 126–27.
216. Klein and Clark, *Biographic Dictionary of Chinese Communism, 1921–1965*, vol. 2, 642.
217. Schoenhals, *Spying for the People*, 27; Huang Lei, "Luo Ruiqing: zhi xiang shang qianxian de xin Zhongguo di yi ren Gong'an bu zhang" [Luo Ruiqing: the first Minister of Public Security for New China who only wanted to go to the front lines], http://cpc.people.com.cn/GB/64162/64172/85037/85038/65 80245.html.
218. Gu, *Jianguo yilai Gong'an gongzuo da shi yaolan*, 4, 5, 7; Yu Yongbo and Xu Caihou, eds., *Chen Yi Zhuan* [Biography of Chen Yi] (Beijing: Dangdai Zhongguo Chubanshe, 1997), 463; Shu, *Deterrence and Strategic Culture*, 66.
219. Dutton, *Policing Chinese Politics*, 146–47.
220. Gu, *Jianguo yilai Gong'an gongzuo da shi yaolan*, 53–56; Pantsov and Levine, *Mao: The Real Story*, 392–93.
221. Gu, *Jianguo yilai Gong'an gongzuo da shi yaolan*, 76.
222. Dutton, *Policing Chinese Politics*, 205–8.
223. MacFarquhar, *The Origins of the Cultural Revolution*, vol. 2, 242–43.
224. Dutton, *Policing Chinese Politics*, 218.
225. Dutton, 219–22.
226. Qiu Jin, *The Culture of Power: The Lin Biao Incident in the Cultural Revolution* (Stanford, CA: Stanford University Press, 1999), 206.
227. Hao, *Zhongguo mimi zhan*, 378.
228. Shu, *Luo Ruiqing dajiang*, 388–89.
229. Wang Yongjun, ed., *Zhongguo Xiandai Shi Renwu Zhuan* [Biographies of Modern Chinese Historical Figures] (Chengdu: Sichuan Renmin Chubanshe, 1986), 806–7; Shen, *Zhongyang weiyuan*, 759–60.
230. Teiwes and Sun, *The End of the Maoist Era*, 15–16n41.
231. Wang, *Zhongguo Xiandai Shi Renwu Zhuan*, 808; Shen, *Zhongyang weiyuan*, 759–60; MacFarquhar and Schoenhals, *Mao's Last Revolution*, 474–75.
232. Schoenhals, *Spying for the People*, 171.
233. Guo Jian, Yongyi Song, and Yuan Zhou, *Historical Dictionary of the Chinese Cultural Revolution* (Lanham, MD: The Scarecrow Press, 2006), 328–29; Teiwes and Sun, *The End of the Maoist Era*, 15–16.

234. Agents were reinstated after statements by Zhou Enlai and Ye Jianying. Schoenhals, *Spying for the People*, 1–5.

235. MacFarquhar and Schoenhals, *Mao's Last Revolution*, 207–10.

236. Shen, *Zhongyang weiyuan*, 760.

237. Cheng, *China's Leaders*, 222–23.

238. "Minister of State Security Xu Yongyue," China News Service, March 17, 2003; "许永跃简历 [Xu Yongyue's Resume]," Xinhua; Kung Shuang-yin, "Special Dispatch: New Minister of State Security Xu Yongyue on Handling Internal Contradictions," *Ta Kung Pao*, March 19, 1998.

239. Lam, "Surprise Elevation for Conservative Patriarch's Protégé Given Security Post."

240. "耿惠昌任国家安全部部长 [Geng Huichang Becomes Minister of State Security]," Xinhua, August 30, 2007, http://news.xinhuanet.com/newscen ter/2007–08/30/content_6634183.htm; Bill Savadove, "Beijing Surprises with Five New Ministers," *South China Morning Post*, August 31, 2007, http:// www.scmp.com/article/606160/beijing-surprises-five-new-ministers.

241. Mattis, "Assessing the Foreign Policy Influence of the Ministry of State Security."

242. Authors' interview, November 2013.

243. Kung, "Special Dispatch."

244. "港媒统计称解放军新晋升18名中将 凸显科技强军 [Hong Kong Media State 18 Promotions Will Highlight S&T-strengthened Army]," 中国新闻网 [China News Service], http://www.chinanews.com/hb/2013/08–06/5126903 .shtml.

245. [Yue Huairang], "杨晖、顾祥兵、孙和荣、王平出任东部战区领导 [Yang Hui, Gu Xiangbing, Sun Herong, Wang Ping Become the Leadership of the Eastern Theater Command]," 澎拜 [The Paper], February 4, 2016, http://www .thepaper.cn/newsDetail_forward_1429364.

246. "Intelligence Chief under the Spotlight in U.S.," *China Daily*, May 20, 2011, http://usa.chinadaily.com.cn/epaper/2011–05/20/content_12547895.htm; 杨晖 [Yang Hui], "杨晖、顾祥兵、孙和荣、王平出任东部战区领导 [Gu Xiangbing, Sun Herong, Wang Ping Become the Leadership of the Eastern Theater Command]," 澎拜 [The Paper], February 4, 2016.

247. 杨晖 [Yang Hui], "中俄军事安全合作概述 [Outline of Sino-Russian Military Security Cooperation]," 俄罗斯中亚东欧研究 [East European, Russian, and Central Asian Studies], no. 1 (2005), 87–88.

248. *Zhou Enlai nianpu 1898–1949*, 31, 33–35, 37–38, 40; Chae-Jin Lee, *Zhou Enlai: The Early Years* (Stanford, CA: Stanford University Press, 1994), 141–49.

249. In 1985 Zhou's affiliation with the CCP officially starts in "Spring 1921." *Zhou Enlai nianpu 1898–1949*, 47.

250. Liu, *Zhou Enlai da cidian*, 18.

251. Li, *Chou En-lai*, 84–85, 150–51; Chang, *Chinese Communist Who's Who*, vol. 1, 435.

252. "Nie Rongzhen," in Shen, *Zhongyang weiyuan*, 612–13.

253. Jin, *Chen Yun Zhuan*, 105; Hao, *Zhongguo mimi zhan*, 2–3.

254. Klein and Clark, *Biographic Dictionary*, vol. 1, 207.

255. Xue, "Guanyu zhonggong zhongyang teke nuogan wenti de tantao," 3.

256. *Zhou Enlai nianpu 1898–1949*, 128; Xue, "Guanyu zhonggong zhongyang teke nuogan wenti de tantao," 4.

257. Xue, "Guanyu zhonggong zhongyang teke nuogan wenti de tantao," 4.

258. Hao, *Zhongguo mimi zhan*, 5.

259. Mu, *Yinbi zhanxian tongshuai Zhou Enlai*, 14; Hao, *Zhongguo mimi zhan*, 7–8.

260. Hao, *Zhongguo mimi zhan*, 8; Jin, *Chen Yun Zhuan*, 103; Kai-yu Hsu, *Chou En-lai, China's Gray Eminence* 94; Shen, *Zhongyang weiyuan*, 621.

261. On August 24, 1928, the KMT raided an address on Hsin Chai Road in Shanghai based on information supplied by Bai Xin. They arrested CCP CMC director Yang Yin, CMC member Yan Changyi, Jiangsu CMC cadre Xing Shizhen, and CCP member Zhang Jichun. See Mu, *Yinbi zhanxian tongshi Zhou Enlai*, 187. Yang Yin was also an early CCP member (1922) and a major figure in the Guangdong CCP. He became a member of the CCP Central Committee in 1928. In October 1933 the CCP renamed the Chinese Soviet Republic No. 1 Red Army Infantry School after Peng and Yang. Shen, *Zhongyang weiyuan*, 68–269; Kuo, *Analytical History*, vol. 2, 92, 312.

262. Mu, *Yinbi zhanxian tongshuai Zhou Enlai*, 194; Hao, *Zhongguo mimi zhan*, 6–7.

263. Mu, *Yinbi zhanxian tongshuai Zhou Enlai*, 195; Liu, *Zhou Enlai da cidian*, 8–29.

264. Kuo, *Analytical History*, vol. 2, 292.

265. Mu, *Yinbi zhanxian tongshuai Zhou Enlai*, 97–198.

266. Mu, 200.

267. Mu, 212–14; *Zhou Enlai nianpu 1898–1949*, 166–67; Kuo, *Analytical History*, vol. 2, 93–294.

268. Liu, *Zhou Enlai da cidian*, 1–32; *Zhou Enlai nianpu 1898–1949*, 166–67, 210–11.

269. Wakeman, *Spymaster*, 178; *Wu Hao: Blood Soaked Secrets*; Li, *Chou En-lai*, 52–53.

270. The number murdered in Gu's family was between four and twenty-four. Gao Wenqian, *Zhou Enlai: The Last Perfect Revolutionary* (New York: Public Affairs, 2007), 168; Kai-yu Hsu, *Chou En-lai: China's Gray Eminence*, 94–97; Dick Wilson, *Chou, The Story of Zhou Enlai, 1898–1976* (London: Hutchinson and Co., 1984), 110–12.

271. Zhou departed Shanghai in December 1931. Shen, *Zhongyang weiyuan*, 540; Liu, *Zhou Enlai da cidian*, 32.

272. Averill, "The Origins of the Futian Incident," 81–83, 107–9; Chang, *Chinese Communist Who's Who*, vol. 2, 104, vol. 1, 171; Pantsov and Levine, *Mao: The Real Story*, 264.

273. Hao, *Zhongguo mimi zhan*, 13.

274. He, *Deng Fa zhuan*, 70–71.

275. Pantsov and Levine, *Mao: The Real Story*, 27–81.

276. Pantsov and Levine, 95–96.

277. Kai, *Li Kenong*, 74, 396, 406; Fan, *Ye Jianying zai guanjian shike*, 97–200; Chang, *Chinese Communist Who's Who*, vol. 2, 439.

278. Teiwes and Sun, *The Formation of the Maoist Leadership*, 342–44.

279. *Zhou Enlai nianpu 1898–1949*, 394.

280. Jin, *Chen Yun Zhuan*, 231; Kuo, *Analytical History*, vol. 3, 336–40.

281. Wang Ming, Chen Yun, and Kang Sheng were appointed to the Secretariat, and the top nine members of the Central Committee were Zhang Wentian, Mao Zedong, Wang Ming, Chen Yun, Zhou Enlai, Zhang Guotao, Bo Gu, and Xiang Ying. Jin, *Chen Yun Zhuan*, 231. For the analysis on Zhou Enlai's predicament during this period, see Teiwes and Sun, "From a Leninist to a Charismatic Party," 363–65.

282. Kuo, *Analytical History*, vol. 3, 341.

283. Yu, *OSS in China*, 3–44; Feng Kaiwen, "Zhang Luping," in *Zhonggong dangshi renwu zhuan*, vol. 27, 196.

284. His story is fascinating. See Rittenberg and Bennett, *The Man Who Stayed Behind*.

285. Barnouin and Yu, *Zhou Enlai*, 89–90; Chae-Jin Lee, *Zhou Enlai: The Early Years*, 1.

286. Gao, *Hong taiyang shi zeyang shengqi de*, 465.

287. Teiwes and Sun, "The Formation of the Maoist Leadership," 374; Roderick MacFarquhar, *The Origins of the Cultural Revolution*, vol. 3: *The Coming of the Cataclysm 1961–1966* (New York: Columbia University Press, 1997), 292–93; Zeng, *Zhongguo gongchandang zuzhishi ziliao*, vol. 4, no. 1, 41; Vladimirov, *The Vladimirov Diaries*, 486, 488, 514, 517; Byron and Pack, *Claws of the Dragon*, 89, 192; Kai, *Li Kenong*, 295–96, 364.

288. Schoenhals, "A Brief History of the CID of the CCP," 3; Chang, *Chinese Communist Who's Who*, vol. 1, 172.

289. Schoenhals, "A Brief History of the CID of the CCP," 3.

290. "Kang Sheng," in *Zhongguo Xiandaishi Renwu Zhuan*, 734.

291. In 1947, Xiong warned of a planned Nationalist attack on Yan'an. John Gittings, "Xiong Xianghui" (obituary), *The Guardian*, September 25, 2005, https://www.theguardian.com/news/2005/sep/26/guardianobituaries.china. Kissinger held few illusions, writing to Nixon that the Chinese were "tough ideologues who totally disagree with us on where the world is going. At the same time, they are hard realists who calculate they need us because of a threatening Soviet Union, a resurgent Japan, and a potentially independent Taiwan." "Kissinger's Second Visit to China, October 1971," from *Xin Zhongguo waijiao fengyun* [The Diplomacy of New China], vol. 3, 9–70, https://nsarchive2.gwu.edu//NSAEBB/NSAEBB70/doc21.pdf.

292. MacFarquhar and Schoenhals, *Mao's Last Revolution*, 415; obituary, "Luo Qingchang."

Chapter 3. Notable Spies of the Chinese Revolution and the Early PRC

1. John N. Hart, *The Making of an Army "Old China Hand": A Memoir of Colonel David D. Barrett* (Berkeley: University of California Institute of East Asian Studies, 1985).

2. "Zhonggong Taiwan shuji Cai Xiaogan panbian, Taiwan dixia zuzhi quan jun fumo" [The defection of the CCP Taiwan secretary Cai Xiaogan sinks the entire Taiwan underground organization], *Sohu News*, May 26, 2014, http://history.sohu.com/20140526/n400044379.shtml.

3. Taylor, *The Generalissimo*, 370–71; "Zhonggong Taiwan shuji Cai Xiaogan panbian."

4. "Zhonggong Taiwan shuji Cai Xiaogan panbian."

5. "Zhonggong Taiwan shuji Cai Xiaogan panbian."

6. Ian Easton, *The Chinese Invasion Threat: Taiwan's Defense and America's Strategy in Asia* (Arlington, VA: Project 2019 Institute, 2017), 48–52.

7. John Earl Haynes and Harvey Klehr, *Venona: Decoding Soviet Espionage in America* (New Haven: Yale University Press, 1999), 129.

8. James C. Van Hook, review of R. Bruce Craig, *Treasonable Doubt: the Harry Dexter White Spy Case* (Lawrence: University Press of Kansas, 2004), in *Intelligence in Recent Public Literature*, April 2007.

9. Haynes and Klehr, *Venona*, 139–40, 143–45.

10. Anne-Marie Brady, *Making the Foreign Serve China: Managing Foreigners in the People's Republic* (Lanham, MD: Rowman and Littlefield, 2003), 195.

11. Edgar A. Porter, *The People's Doctor: George Hatem and China's Revolution* (Honolulu: University of Hawaii Press, 1997), 249, 268; Ji Chaozhu, *The Man on Mao's Right* (New York: Random House, 2008), 267.

12. John Pomfret, *The Beautiful Country and the Middle Kingdom* (New York: Henry Holt, 2016), 346–47, 644; Richard Trahair, *Encyclopedia of Cold War Espionage, Spies, and Secret Operations* (Westport, CT: Greenwood Press, 2004), 298; Frank Coe [柯弗兰], "Mao Zedong shi dangdai zui weida de Ma Kesi zhuyi zhe" (Mao Zedong Is the Greatest Marxist of the Modern Era), *Renmin Ribao* (*People's Daily*), December 28, 1976, http://blog.sina.com .cn/s/blog_ec9c21c00102vlco.html.

13. Mao and Jiang married on November 20, 1938. Pei Yiran, *Hongse shenghuo shi: geming suiyue nei xie shi, 1921–1949* [Red Life: Those Years of Revolution, 1921–1949] (Taipei: Showwe Information Co. Ltd., 2015), 349. See also "Yang Yinlu's Secret: Mao and Jiang's Marriage Was Not a Failure of Choice," March 3, 2013.

14. Zhou Hui, "Dong Jianwu," in *Zhonggong dangshi renwu zhuan*, vol. 68, 323; Dong Xiafei and Dong Yunfei, *Shenmi de Hongse Mushi, Dong Jianwu* [The Mysterious Red Pastor, Dong Jianwu] (Beijing: Beijing Chubanshe, 2001), 1–2; Snow, *Red Star Over China*, 56.

15. Zhang Yiyu, ed., *Shanghai Yinglie Zhuan Qi Zhuan* [Biographies of Shanghai's Brave Martyrs, vol. 7] (Shanghai: Zhonggong Shanghai Shiwei Dangshi Yanjiushi, and Shanghai Shi Minzheng Ju, 1991), 149–50.

16. Zhang, *Shanghai Yinglie Zhuan Qi Zhuan*, 150; Hong Kong Police Force, "Provisional List, Hong Kong Police Deaths in the Course of Duty, 1841–1941," https://www.police.gov.hk/offbeat/788/eng/n10.htm; Chan Lau Kit-ching, *From Nothing to Nothing: The Chinese Communist Movement in Hong Kong, 1921–1936* (New York: St. Martin's Press, 1999), 179.

17. Zhang, *Shanghai Yinglie Zhuan Qi Zhuan*, 151.

18. Zhang, 151–52.

19. Zhang, 154–56.

20. Pomfret, *The Beautiful Country and the Middle Kingdom*, 346–47, 644; Trahair, *Encyclopedia of Cold War Espionage, Spies, and Secret Operations*, 298.

21. Haynes and Klehr, *Venona*, 140.

22. Kai-yu Hsu, *Chou En-lai: China's Grey Eminence*, 27, 45; Shinkichi Eto, "China's International Relations, 1911–1931," in Fairbank, *Cambridge History of China*, vol. 13, 109–10; Boorman, *Biographical Dictionary of Republican China*, 293–97; Josephine Fowler, *Japanese and Chinese Immigrant Activists: Organizing in American and International Communist Movements* (New Brunswick, NJ: Rutgers University Press, 2007), 51.

23. The account herein draws both on sources cited below and the hagiographic documentary "History Legend Dr. Ke Lin," featured on China Central Television, August 12, 2016.

24. Xiao Zhihao, *Zhonggong Tegong* [Chinese Communist Special Operations] (Beijing: Shidai Wenxian Chubanshe, 2010), 205–6. Thanks to Dr. David Chambers for this reference.

25. Mu, *Chen Geng Tongzhi zai Shanghai*, 54–55, 58–59; Xiao, *Zhonggong Tegong*, 205.

26. Per these references, the former Fan Zhengbo residence is at the modern-day 淮海中路五二六弄, 43号 [No. 43, Lane 526, Huaihai Zhong Road].

27. Mu, *Chen Geng Tongzhi zai Shanghai*, 59–65; Mu Xin, *Yinbi zhanxian tongshuai Zhou Enlai* [Zhou Enlai, Guru of the Hidden Battlefront] (Beijing: Zhongguo Qingnian Chubanshe, 2002), 212–14; *Zhou Enlai nianpu 1898–1949*, 166–67; Kuo, *Analytical History*, vol. 2, 293–94; Xiao, *Zhonggong Tegong*, 205–6.

28. Xiao, *Zhonggong Tegong*, 204, 206; Hui Guisong, "Aomen Zhonggong dixia dang ren Ke Lin" [Ke Lin of the Macau CCP Underground Party], *Guangxi Shenji*, no. 5 (1999): 34.

29. Hui, "Aomen Zhonggong dixia dang ren Ke Lin," 34–35.

30. Geoffrey C. Gunn, *Encountering Macau: A Portuguese City-State on the Periphery of China, 1557–1999* (Boulder, CO: Westview Press, 1996), 128–29.

31. Gunn, 153–55.

32. Vasco Silverio Marques and Anibal Mesquita Borges, *O Ouro no Eixo Hong Kong Macau, 1946–1973* [The Gold on the Axis of Hong Kong and Macau, 1946–1973] (Macau: Instituto Português do Oriente, 2012), 183, 217, 237, 246, 488; Gunn, *Encountering Macau*, 145–46.

33. Xiao, *Zhonggong Tegong*, 206–7. Thanks to Macau historian João Guedes for his comments on this entry.

34. Ding Jizhong, "Li Qiang," in *Zhonggong dangshi renwu zhuan*, vol. 72, 230–33.

35. Ding, 234–36.

36. Ding, 235–36.

37. Mu, *Yinbi zhanxian tongshuai Zhou Enlai*, 8–9.

38. Ding, "Li Qiang," 237–38.

39. Ding, 238; Hao, *Zhongguo mimi zhan*, 2.

40. According to references on the web, the house is located at the modern address of Number 9, Alley 420, Yan'an West Road, Shanghai (中共中央第一个秘密电台旧址: 延安西路420弄 (原大西路福康里) 9号.

41. Ding, "Li Qiang," 238–39.

42. Ding, 239–40; Hao, *Zhongguo mimi zhan*, 7.

43. Mu, *Yinbi zhanxian tongshuai Zhou Enlai*, 197–98.

44. Kuo, *Analytical History*, vol. 2, 292, 312; Mu, *Yinbi zhanxian tongshuai Zhou Enlai*, 187, 194–95; Liu, *Zhou Enlai da cidian*, 28–29; Hao, *Zhongguo mimi zhan*, 6–7; Shen, *Zhongyang weiyuan*, 100, 268–69.

45. Ding, "Li Qiang," 240–41.

46. Ding, 241–43.

47. Ding, 241–44.

48. Ding, 244, 250.

49. Ding, 252–56.

50. Yibin Xinwen Wang [Yibin Sichuan, News Network]: Liu Ding, http://www.ybxww.com/content/2011–6/13/2011613190904_2.htm.

51. Yibin Xinwen Wang.

52. Intelligence training during Russian study tours was often included for some CCP cadre during this period. Interview with party historian, 2016.

53. Tong, *Fengyu sishinian*, vol. 1, 19–20.

54. Hao, *Zhongguo mimi zhan*, 6.

55. Yibin Xinwen Wang.

56. Hao, *Zhongguo mimi zhan*, 24–25; Kai, *Li Kenong*, 113–15; *Zhou Enlai nianpu 1898–1949*, 300–2 (entries for February 20 and March 5, 1936); Hans Van de Ven, *War and Nationalism in China, 1925–1945* (New York: Routledge, 2003), 170, 177–89; Wu Dianyao, "Liu Ding," in *Zhonggong dangshi renwu zhuan*, vol. 43, 303. Thanks to Dr. David Chambers for drawing this reference to our attention.

57. *Henan Guangbo Dianshi Daxue Xuebao* [Journal of the Henan Radio and Television University], no. 3, 2005, http://baike.baidu.com/subview/1590 34/9278390.htm.

58. North University of China, http://new.nuc.edu.cn/xxgk/lrxz.htm.

59. Yibin Xinwen Wang.

60. Yibin Xinwen Wang.

61. Yibin Xinwen Wang.

62. Chang, *Chinese Communist Who's Who*, vol. 2, 111–12.

63. Wilbur, "The Nationalist Revolution," in Fairbank, *Cambridge History of China*, vol. 12, 694; Chang, *Chinese Communist Who's Who*, vol. 2, 112; "Song juemi qingbao de qiren qigong Mo Xiong" [The Exceptional Talent and Rare Service of Mo Xiong], *Renmin Wang*, August 2013, http://dangshi.people.com.cn/n/2013/0815/c85037–22572055.html.

64. "Yifen juemi qingbao cushi hongjun tiaoshang changzhenglu" [Secret Intelligence Prompted Red Army to Embark on Long March].

65. Zhonggong Fujian Shengwei Xuanchuan Bu [Fujian CCP Committee Propaganda Department, ed.], *Changzheng, Changzheng: Cong Min Xibei dao Shaanbei* [Long March, Long March: From Northwest Fujian to Northern Shaanxi] (Fuzhou: Fujian Jiaoyu Chubanshe, 2006), 390–91.

66. Chang, *Chinese Communist Who's Who*, vol. 2, 112.

67. "Nie Rongzhen," in Shen, *Zhongyang weiyuan*, 612–13.

68. Timothy Cheek, "The Honorable Vocation: Intellectual Service in CCP Propaganda Institutions in Jin-Cha-Ji, 1937–1945," in Saich and Van de Ven, *New Perspectives on the Chinese Communist Revolution*, 255–57; Vladimirov, *The Vladimirov Diaries*, 164.

69. "Nie Rongzhen," in Klein and Clark, *Biographic Dictionary of Chinese Communism*, 2, 696–701; Xiaobing Li, *China at War: An Encyclopedia* (Santa Barbara, CA: ABC CLIO, 2012), 322–23.

70. Liu, *Zhou Enlai da cidian*, 32; Larry Wortzel and Robin Higham, *Dictionary of Contemporary Chinese Military History* (Santa Barbara, CA: ABC CLIO, 1999), 188–89; "Yi kaiguo yuanshuai ceng zai Zhonggong Teke zuo tegong bei Mao Zedong xicheng wei Lu Zhishen" [Marshal of the nation's founding was a special agent and nicknamed Lu Zhishen by Mao Zedong], January 25, 2016, http://mil.news.sina.com.cn/history/2016–01–25/doc-ifxnurxn9928426.shtml.

71. David Chambers is the author of a forthcoming biography of Pan Hannian and generously assisted the authors.

72. Chen Xiuliang, "Pan Hannian," in *Zhonggong dangshi renwu zhuan*, vol. 25, 24.

73. Chen, 25.

74. Shu-mei Shih, *The Lure of the Modern: Writing Modernism in Semicolonial China, 1917–1937* (Berkeley: University of California Press, 2001), 239, 256; Yin, *Pan Hannian de qingbao shengya*, 8, 14–15; Chen Xiulang, "Pan Hannian," 26–28.

75. Yin, *Pan Hannian de qingbao shengya*, 8–9, 14–15; Chen, "Pan Hannian," 31.

76. Yin, *Pan Hannian de qingbao shengya*, 73–77; Chen, "Pan Hannian," 31–32.

77. Chen, "Pan Hannian," 31–33.

78. Yin, *Pan Hannian de qingbao shengya*, 8, 14–15, 71–72; Van de Ven, *War and Nationalism in China 1925–1945*, 149, 164.

79. Chen, "Pan Hannian," 34–35.

80. Wang Junyan, *Liao Chengzhi zhuan* [The Biography of Liao Chengzhi] (Beijing: Renmin Chubanshe, 2006), 48; Van de Ven, *War and Nationalism in China*, 181; Yin, *Pan Hannian de qingbao shengya*, 79–80.

81. Wang Junyan, *Liao Chengzhi zhuan*, 44; Yin, *Pan Hannian de qingbao shengya*, 90–92, 126–27; Hao, *Zhongguo mimi zhan*, 59–60; Chen, "Pan Hannian," 35.

82. The KMT Juntong's Research Institute on International Questions (*Juntong Guoji Wenti Yanjiusuo*).

83. The security training included basic points such as: don't be photographed except for office business; don't write letters to family or friends; and don't discuss this work with anyone. Yin, *Pan Hannian de qingbao shengya*, 90, 92–94.

84. Kai, *Li Kenong*, 430.

85. Yin, *Pan Hannian de qingbao shengya*, 131–35, 139.

86. Li Shiqun requested that a family friend, Hu Xiufeng, be used for this work. She was already deployed elsewhere, but Pan discovered that her sister, Hu Xiumei was available.

87. Chen Xiuliang, "Pan Hannian," in *Zhonggong dangshi renwu zhuan*, vol. 25, 41.

88. Kai, *Li Kenong*, 428–33; Yin, *Pan Hannian de qingbao shengya*, 158–60.

89. Yin, *Pan Hannian de qingbao shengya*, 185; Chen, "Pan Hannian," 43.

90. John Burns, "The Structure of Communist Party Control in Hong Kong," *Asian Survey* 30, no. 8 (August 1990), 749; Chen, "Pan Hannian," 43–44.

91. Yin Qi, *Pan Hannian Zhuan* [The Biography of Pan Hannian] (Beijing: Zhongguo Renmin Gong'an Daxue Chubanshe, 1996), 283–84, 416–17.

92. Liu Shufa, ed., *Chen Yi nianpu* [The Annals of Chen Yi], vol. 2 (Beijing: Renmin Chubanshe, 1995), 672–73. This account of the period between the CCP National Conference (March 21-31, 1955) and the Fifth Plenum of the Seventh Central Committee, which began on April 4, omits Chen's fatal encounters with Pan Hannian and Mao Zedong on April 1-2.

93. Mao Zedong, opening speech, National Conference of the Communist Party of China, March 21, 1955, https://www.marxists.org/reference/archive/mao /selected-works/volume-5/mswv5_41.htm.

94. Yin, *Pan Hannian Zhuan*, 344–45; Mao, opening speech.

95. Yin, *Pan Hannian Zhuan*, 344–45.

96. Yin, 346–48.

97. Gu, *Gong'an Gongzuo*, 82–83; Zhang Yun, *Pan Hannian Zhuan* [Biography of Pan Hannian] (Shanghai: Shanghai Renmin Chubanshe, 1996), 317; Kai, *Li Kenong*, 406; Xuezhi, *China's Security State*, 345–48; Yin, *Pan Hannian de qingbao shengya*, 348.

98. Gu, *Gong'an Gongzuo*, 83.

99. Yin, *Pan Hannian de qingbao shengya*, 220.

100. Kai, *Li Kenong*, 406–8.

101. Chambers, "Edging in from the Cold," 34; Teiwes, *Politics and Purges in China*, 140–41.

102. Frederick Teiwes, *Politics at Mao's Court: Gao Gang and Party Factionalism in the Early 1950s* (Armonk, NY: M. E. Sharpe, 1990), 131–34.

103. Kai, *Li Kenong*, 408.

104. Kai, 408–9.

105. Chen Jingtan, *Xie gei Xianggang ren de Zhongguo xiandai shi* [Modern History of China for Hong Kong People] (Hong Kong: Zhonghua Shu ju youxian gongsi, 2014), 198–200; Luo Linhu, "Pan Jing'an," *Renmin Wang*, May 2, 2012, http://blog.people.com.cn/article/1335940968010.html; Hong Kong Apple Daily video, "Pan Jing'an Xianggang Jishi" (Chronicle of Pan Jing'an in Hong Kong), September 8, 2013, https://www.youtube.com/watch?v=kr7xTz65GwE.

106. Jiang Hongbin, "Song Qingling," in *Zhonggong dangshi renwu zhuan*, vol. 28, 8–11.

107. "China: Whispers of Woe," *Time Magazine*, May 30, 1927.

108. Located at the present-day address of 7 Xiangshan Road (香山路7号). Jiang, "Song Qingling," 13; Baruch Hirson, Arthur Knodel, and Gregor Benton, *Reporting the Chinese Revolution: The Letters of Rayna Prohme* (Ann Arbor, MI: Pluto Press, 2007), 77–81.

109. Jiang, "Song Qingling," 12–13.

110. Hirson, Knodel, and Benton, *Reporting the Chinese Revolution*, 12–13, 88–92, 96.

111. Jonathan Spence, *The Search for Modern China* (New York: W. W. Norton and Co., 1999), 343–44. Meiling's sister, Ailing, married H. H. Kung (孔祥熙, Kong Xiangxi), the banker who later held ministerial posts and became the republic's premier. Their brother, Paul T. V. Soong, (Song Ziwen, 宋子文) became the KMT Central Government's finance minister and minister of foreign affairs. Daniel H. Bays, *A New History of Christianity in China* (Malden, MA: Wiley-Blackwell, 2012), 124–25.

112. Jiang, "Song Qingling," 14; Kenneth R. Whiting, *The Soviet Union Today: A Concise Handbook* (New York: Praeger, 1966), 134, 155.

113. Jiang, "Song Qingling," 15.

114. Jiang, "Song Qingling," 18; Wakeman, *Spymaster*, 175–77.

115. Wakeman, *Spymaster*, 153, 449n110.

116. Wang, *Liao Chengzhi Zhuan*, 33–34, 678; Klein and Clark, *Biographic Dictionary of Chinese Communism, 1921-1965*, vol. 2, 783–84; Jiang, "Song Qingling," 21.

117. *Zhou Enlai nianpu 1898–1949*, 301.

118. Jiang, "Song Qingling," 28–29.

119. Snow, *Red Star Over China*, 16–17, 21–24, 42–43; Schram, *Mao's Road to Power*, 152–53.

120. Jiang, "Song Qingling," 41.

121. Jiang, 43.

122. Alexander V. Pantsov and Steven I. Levine, *Deng Xiaoping: A Revolutionary Life* (New York: Oxford University Press, 2015), 138.

123. Jiang, "Song Qingling," 69–70; MacFarquhar and Schoenhals, *Mao's Last Revolution*, 576n3.

124. Soong Ch'ing-ling, "Women's Liberation in China," *Peking Review*, February 11, 1972, https://www.marxists.org/subject/china/peking-review/1972/PR 1972-06a.htm.

125. Hu, *Zhongguo Xibu mimi zhan*, 341–42.

126. Hu, 343–45.

127. Hu, 344–46; Hu Jie and Sun Guoda, "Wo Dang qingbao shishang de yici da jienan" [A catastrophe in the history of our party's intelligence services], *Beijing Ribao* [Beijing Daily], August 31, 2009, http://theory.people.com.cn /GB/9953216.htm; Hao Zaijin, "Gongchandang de qingbao gongzuo yizhi bi Guomindang gaoming" [The Communist Party's Intelligence Works has Always Been Brilliant Compared to the KMT], June 8, 2015, https://www .boxun.com/news/gb/z_special/2015/06/201506081843.shtml.

128. Confidential document.

129. *Nu Jiaotong Yuan* [The Woman Courier] (Changchun: Changchun dianying zhipian chang, 1977), https://www.youtube.com/watch?v=OH1nfXaOGqY. Although Wang was a courier in World War II, the film was set a few years later during the Chinese civil war.

130. *Dianying "Nu Jiaotong Yuan" yuanxing Wang Xirong jinri lishi* [Inspiration for the film "The Woman Courier" Wang Xirong passed away today], November 4, 2011, http://dlguodj.blog.163.com/blog/static/46 8443332011104104245168/.

131. Author interviews with Madame Wang Xirong, August 2008, arranged courtesy of the Dalian Municipal Government.

132. Author interviews; film, https://www.youtube.com/watch?v=OH1nfXa OGqY.

133. Author interviews.

134. Author interviews; CRI Online, "Nu Jiaotong Yuan," http://gb.cri.cn/38 21/2005/07/05/1545@608488.htm.

135. Ying Ruocheng and Claire Conceison, *Voices Carry: Behind Bars and Back-stage During China's Cultural Revolution* (Lanham, MD: Rowman and Littlefield, 2009).

136. Schoenhals, *Spying for the People*, 150–51, 225.

137. Some sources date Zeng's entry into the Hong Kong Police as 1947 and some as 1948. "Zao zhu chujing Xianggang di yi jiandie Zeng Zhaoke qushi" [Zeng Zhaoke, Hong Kong's first spy who was expelled, dies], Apple Nextmedia, December 29, 2014, http://hk.apple.nextmedia.com/news /art/20141229/18984529; Gene Gleason, *Hong Kong* (New York: John Day Company, 1963), 109.

138. Steve Tsang, "Target Zhou Enlai: The 'Kashmir Princess' Incident of 1955," *The China Quarterly* no. 139 (September 1994): 775.

139. Gleason, *Hong Kong*, 109.

140. "High profile funeral for 'James Bond'," *The Standard* (Hong Kong), December 30, 2014, http://www.thestandard.com.hk/section-news.php?id =152765&story_id=43611882&d_str=20141230&sid=4.

141. "Zao zhu chujing Xianggang di yi jiandie Zeng Zhaoke qushi"; Gleason, *Hong Kong*, 109. The courier was rumored to have been carrying instructions from a controller in Macau. There may be more to this story since carrying a lot of cash would not seem unusual for someone arriving from Macau, a gambling haven.

142. Wen Hui Po (Wenhui Bao), December 26, 2006, http://paper.wenweipo .com/2006/12/26/CH0612260002.htm.

143. Wen Hui Po.

144. Interview with a Western diplomat based in China during the 1980s and 1990s.

145. Guan Qingning, "Wo suo zhidaode Zeng Zhaoke xiansheng" [Zeng Zhaoke as I knew him], *Ming Pao*, January 19, 2015, https://news.mingpao.com.

146. MacFarquhar, *The Origins of the Cultural Revolution*, vol. 3, 205–6; Gleason, *Hong Kong*, 110–11.

147. Maochun Yu, *OSS in China*, 43–44; Feng Kaiwen, "Zhang Luping," in *Zhonggong dangshi renwu zhuan*, vol. 27, 196–97, 199–202, 206–7.

Chapter 4. Economic Espionage Cases

1. Christopher Andrew and Vasili Mitrokhin, *The Sword and the Shield: The Mitrokhin Archive and the Secret History of the KGB* (New York: Basic Books, 1999), 219–20.

2. Hannas, Mulvenon, and Puglisi, *Chinese Industrial Espionage*, 13–14, 189–90.

3. Grant Rodgers, "FBI: Plot to Steal Seed Corn a National Security Threat," *Des Moines Register*, March 29, 2015, https://www.desmoinesregister.com/story/news/crime-and-courts/2015/03/29/seed-corn-theft-plot-national-security-fbi/70643462.

4. "DBN Biotech," www.dbnbc.com/en/nlist.asp?ncid=15&c=2&stl=0.

5. Immigration and Customs Enforcement, "Chinese National Pleads Guilty to Conspiring to Violate Arms Export Control Act," December 15, 2014, https://www.ice.gov/news/releases/chinese-national-pleads-guilty-conspiring-violate-arms-export-control-act.

6. Department of Justice, "Chinese Nationals Sentenced in New Mexico for Conspiring to Violate Arms Export Control Act," April 23, 2015, https://www.justice.gov/opa/pr/chinese-nationals-sentenced-new-mexico-conspiring-violate-arms-export-control-act.

7. "Chinese Nationals Sentenced."

8. "Chinese Nationals Sentenced."

9. U.S. District Court for the District of New Jersey, 2012, United States of America v. Hui Sheng Shen and Huan Ling Chang—Amended Complaint, https://www.justice.gov/archive/usao/nj/Press/files/pdffiles/2012/Shen,%20Hui%20Sheng%20and%20Chang,%20Ling%20Huan%20amended%20Complaint.pdf.

10. Department of Justice, "Summary of Major U.S. Export Enforcement, Economic Espionage, Trade Secret and Embargo-Related Criminal Cases (January 2009 to the Present: Updated May 13, 2015)," May 2015, https://www.justice.gov/file/438491/download.

11. Federal Bureau of Investigation, "California Couple Charged with Conspiring to Export Sensitive Technology to People's Republic of China," October 15, 2010, https://www.fbi.gov/losangeles/press-releases/2010/la101510-1.htm.

12. "Summary of Major U.S. Cases (January 2009 to the Present)."

13. Federal Bureau of Investigation, "Chinese Man Found Guilty of Illegally Exporting Sensitive Thermal-Imaging Technology to China," https://www.fbi.gov/losangeles/press-releases/2009/la022309usa.htm; Federal Bureau of Investigation, "Three Sentenced to Federal Prison for Illegally Exporting Highly Sensitive U.S. Technology to China," https://www.fbi.gov/losangeles/press-releases/2009/la080409.htm.

14. Federal Bureau of Investigation, "Chinese Man Found Guilty of Illegally Exporting Sensitive Thermal-Imaging Technology to China"; Federal Bureau of Investigation, "Three Sentenced to Federal Prison for Illegally Exporting Highly Sensitive U.S. Technology to China."

15. Eileen M. Albanese, U.S. Department of Commerce, "Order Denying Export Privileges," November 27, 2007. https://efoia.bis.doc.gov/index.php/documents/export-violations/412-e2020/file.

16. Robert E. Kessler, "N.Y. Man Charged with Illegal Export of Military Parts—Equipment Headed for China in Shipment of Scrap," *Seattle Times*, January 6, 1998, http://community.seattletimes.nwsource.com/archive/?date=19980106&slug=2727275.

17. Kessler.

18. Andrew Backover, "Feds: Trio Stole Lucent's Trade Secrets," *USA Today*, May 3, 2001, http://usatoday30.usatoday.com/tech/news/2001–05–03-lucent-scientists-china.htm; "New Indictment Expands Charges Against Former Lucent Scientists Accused of Passing Trade Secrets to Chinese Company," April 11, 2002, https://www.justice.gov/archive/criminal/cybercrime/press-releases/2002/lucentSupIndict.htm.

19. Jeffrey Gold, "Firm Guilty of Stealing Lucent Information," *The Record*, March 18, 2005.

20. "集团介绍–中国电子科技集团公司," http://www.cetc.com.cn/zgdzkj/_300891/_300895/index.html.

21. U.S. Department of Commerce, Bureau of Industry and Security, "Entity List: Supplement No. 4 to Part 744 of the Export Administration Regulations," September 20, 2016, https://www.bis.doc.gov/index.php/policy-guidance/lists-of-parties-of-concern/entity-list.

22. "U.S. Nuclear Engineer, China General Nuclear Power Company and Energy Technology International Indicted in Nuclear Power Conspiracy against the United States," https://www.justice.gov/opa/pr/us-nuclear-engineer-china-general-nuclear-power-company-and-energy-technology-international. https://www.justice.gov/opa/pr/us-nuclear-engineer-pleads-guilty-violating-atomic-energy-act.

23. Department of Justice, "Former Boeing Engineer Charged with Economic Espionage in Theft of Space Shuttle Secrets for China," February 11, 2008, https://www.justice.gov/archive/opa/pr/2008/February/08_nsd_106.html.

24. Rob Davies, "Espionage Arrest of Nuclear Engineer Fuels U.S. Suspicions of Chinese Tactics," *The Guardian*, August 11, 2016, https://www.theguardian.com/technology/2016/aug/11/espionage-arrest-of-nuclear-engineer-fuels-us-suspicions-of-chinese-tactics.

25. John R. Wilke, "Two Silicon Valley Cases Raise Fears of Chinese Espionage—Authorities Suspect Alleged Trade-Secret Thefts Tied to Government-Controlled Companies," *Wall Street Journal*, January 15, 2003.

26. Department of Justice, "Major U.S. Export Enforcement Prosecutions During the Past Two Years," October 28, 2008, https://www.justice.gov/archive/opa/pr/2008/October/08-nsd-959.html.

27. "Major U.S. Export Enforcement Prosecutions."

28. Troy Graham, "Camden Firm Pleads Guilty to Missile-Parts Export State Metal Industries Sold the Scrap, Officials Said, to a Company with Ties to China," *Philadelphia Inquirer*, June 15, 2006.

29. Cleopatra Andreadis, "Couple Charged: Sold GM Secrets to China?" *ABC News*, July 23, 2010, http://abcnews.go.com/TheLaw/Business/michigan-couple-charged-corporate-espionage/story?id=11236400.

30. Jonathan Stempel, "Former GM Engineer, Husband Sentenced in Trade Secret Theft Case," *Reuters*, May 1, 2013, http://www.reuters.com/article/generalmotors-tradesecrets-sentencing-idUSL2N0DI25Z20130501.

31. "Major U.S. Export Enforcement Prosecutions."

32. "Summary of Major U.S. Cases (January 2009 to the Present)."

33. Josh Gerstein, "Spy Charges In High-Stakes Microchip Race," *The New York Sun*, June 19, 2006, http://www.nysun.com/national/spy-charges-in-high-stakes-microchip-race/34620/.

34. Howard Mintz, "Silicon Valley Espionage Case Only Second of Kind in Nation to Go to Trial," *San Jose Mercury News*, October 18, 2009, http://www.mercurynews.com/2009/10/18/silicon-valley-espionage-case-only-second-of-kind-in-nation-to-go-to-trial/.

35. Howard Mintz, "Federal Jury Deadlocks on Most of Espionage Case against Two Silicon Valley Engineers," *San Jose Mercury News*, November 20, 2009, http://www.mercurynews.com/2009/11/20/federal-jury-deadlocks-on-most-of-espionage-case-against-two-silicon-valley-engineers/.

36. Mintz; "North Wales Man Sentenced For Illegally Exporting Goods," January 17, 2013, https://www.justice.gov/usao-edpa/pr/north-wales-man-sentenced-illegally-exporting-goods.

37. Peter Boylan, "Secrets Sold: 'I Did It for the Money'," *Honolulu Advertiser*, October 28, 2005.

38. Mark A. Kellner, "Engineer Pleads Not Guilty in Espionage Case," *Air Force Times*, November 27, 2006, 44.

39. "Hawaii Man Sentenced to 32 Years in Prison for Providing Defense Information and Services to People's Republic of China," *U.S. Federal News Service*, January 25, 2011, http://search.proquest.com/docview/847323491/citation/77C368FB08EB4D70PQ/2.

40. "Hawaii Man Sentenced."

41. "Chinese Man Found Guilty."

42. "Three Sentenced to Federal Prison."

43. Mortimer, "Maryland Woman Charged with ITAR Offences."

44. Burnett, "U.S. Export Enforcement Examples." Undated.

45. U.S. Department of Commerce, Bureau of Industry and Security, "Order Relating to Yaming Nina Qi Hanson," July 15, 2013, https://efoia.bis.doc.gov /index.php/component/docman/doc_view/868-e2332?Itemid=.

46. "Summary of Major U.S. Export Enforcement, Economic Espionage, Trade Secret and Embargo-Related Criminal Cases (January 2009 to the Present: Updated May 13, 2015)."

47. John Shiffman and Duff Wilson, "Special Report: How China's Weapon Snatchers Are Penetrating U.S. Defenses," *Reuters*, December 17, 2013, http://www.reuters.com/article/breakout-sting-idUSL2N0JV1UV20131217.

48. "Summary of Major U.S. Cases (January 2009 to the Present)."

49. Rob Davies, "Who Is the U.S. Engineer Accused of Nuclear Espionage?" *The Guardian*, August 11, 2016, https://www.theguardian.com/business/2016 /aug/11/nuclear-consultant-accused-espionage-china-us-szuhsiung-al len-ho; Maria L. La Ganga, "Nuclear Espionage Charge for China Firm with One-Third Stake in UK's Hinkley Point," *The Guardian*, August 10, 2016, https://www.theguardian.com/uk-news/2016/aug/11/nuclear-espionage- charge-for-china-firm-with-one-third-stake-in-hinkley-point.

50. "U.S. Nuclear Engineer, China General Nuclear Power Company and Energy Technology International Indicted in Nuclear Power Conspiracy against the United States," https://www.justice.gov/opa/pr/us-nuclear-engineer-china- general-nuclear-power-company-and-energy-technology-international.

51. Department of Justice, "U.S. and Chinese Defendants Charged with Eco- nomic Espionage and Theft of Trade Secrets in Connection with Conspir- acy to Sell Trade Secrets to Chinese Companies," https://www.justice.gov /opa/pr/us-and-chinese-defendants-charged-economic-espionage-and- theft-trade-secrets-connection.

52. Christopher Marquis, "2 Arrested in Case on Selling Encryption Device," *New York Times*, August 30, 2001, http://www.nytimes.com/2001/08/30 /us/2-arrested-in-case-on-selling-encryption-device.html.

53. Gail Gibson, "Chinese Nationals Held in Attempted Export of Encryption Devices," *Baltimore Sun*, August 30, 2001, http://articles.baltimoresun.com /2001–08–30/news/0108300163_1_encryption-hsu-undercover-agents.

54. "Two Are Sentenced for Trying to Export Encryption Device," *Associated Press*, October 20, 2002.

55. Paul Shukovsky, "Charge against Bellevue Man Linked to Spy Case," *Seat- tle Post-Intelligencer*, March 7, 2005, http://www.seattlepi.com/local/article /Charge-against-Bellevue-man-linked-to-spy-case-1168039.php.

56. U.S. Immigration and Customs Enforcement, "Select ICE Arms and Strategic Technology Investigations," November 2006, http://fas.org/asmp/ice asti.htm.

57. "Eastside News: Guilty Plea for Illegal Exports," *The Seattle Times*, http://old .seattletimes.com/html/eastsidenews/2002669960_hsy07e.html.

58. U.S. Attorney's Office for the Western District of Washington, "Bellevue Man Sentenced for Violating Arms Export Act: Illegally Exported Night Vision Goggles to Taiwan—Co-Conspirator Sent Them to China," March 23, 2006, https://www.justice.gov/archive/usao/waw/press/2006/mar/hsy.html.

59. "Summary of Major U.S. Cases (January 2009 to the Present)."

60. Department of Justice, "Chinese Business Owner, Employee Plead Guilty, Sentenced for Stealing Trade Secrets from Sedalia Plant," https://www.jus tice.gov/usao-wdmo/pr/chinese-business-owner-employee-plead-guilty-sentenced-stealing-trade-secrets-sedalia.

61. Christopher Drew, "New Breed of Spy Steals Employer's Secrets U.S. Companies at Risk of Spying by Own Workers," *New York Times*, October 17, 2010, http://www.nytimes.com/2010/10/18/business/global/18espionage.html.

62. Jeremy Pelofsky, "Chinese Man Pleads Guilty for U.S. Trade Secret Theft," *Reuters*, October 18, 2011, http://www.reuters.com/article/us-crime-china-theft-idUSTRE79H78R20111018.

63. Department of Justice, "Chinese National Sentenced to 87 Months in Prison for Economic Espionage and Theft of Trade Secrets," https://www.justice. gov/opa/pr/chinese-national-sentenced-87-months-prison-economic-espi onage-and-theft-trade-secrets.

64. "California Couple Charged."

65. U.S. Department of Commerce, Bureau of Industry and Security, "Order Relating to Leping Huang, A.K.A. Nicole Huang, A.K.A. Nicola Huang," June 12, 2012, https://efoia.bis.doc.gov/index.php/component/docman /doc_view/782-e2272?Itemid=.

66. "Chinese National Sentenced."

67. Matt Richtel, "Handful of Indictments Over Technology," *New York Times*, January 15, 2003, http://www.nytimes.com/2003/01/15/business/handful -of-indictments-over-technology.html.

68. "About Us_CETC 54," http://en.cti.ac.cn/About_Us/.

69. Laurie J. Flynn, "Chinese Businessman Acquitted of Illegal High-Technology Exports," *New York Times*, May 10, 2005, http://query.nytimes.com/gst/full page.html.

70. Jason Keyser, "Motorola Trade Secrets Thief Gets 4-Year Term," *Associated Press*, August 29, 2012, http://www.usatoday.com/money/industries/tech nology/story/2012-08-29/motorola-trade-secrets-thief/57409376/1.

71. Richard Posner, *United States of America v. Hanjuan Jin*, Dissent U.S. Court of Appeals for Seventh Circuit, 2013.

72. "Summary of Major U.S. Cases (January 2009 to the Present)."

73. Keyser, "Motorola Trade Secrets Thief Gets 4-Year Term"; Posner, *United States of America v. Hanjuan Jin.*

74. Erin Ailworth, "Files Trace Betrayal of a Prized China-Mass. Partnership," *Boston Globe*, July 10, 2013, https://www.bostonglobe.com/bus iness/2013/07/09/global-chase-cracked-corporate-espionage-case/8HC7 wKBJezDkNFNSWB5dFO/story.html.

75. Michael Riley and Ashlee Vance, "Inside the Chinese Boom in Corporate Espionage," *Bloomberg.com*, March 15, 2012, http://www.bloomberg.com /news/articles/2012–03–15/inside-the-chinese-boom-in-corporate-espio nage.

76. Kevin Poulsen, "Chinese Spying Claimed in Purchases of NSA Crypto Gear," *Wired*, July 9, 2009, https://www.wired.com/2009/07/export/.

77. Jeremy Pelofsky, "Chinese Man Convicted on U.S. Smuggling Charges," *Reuters*, May 12, 2010, http://www.reuters.com/article/us-usa-security-smuggling-idUSTRE64B61V20100512.

78. Poulsen, "Chinese Spying Claimed in Purchases of NSA Crypto Gear."

79. Pelofsky, "Chinese Man Convicted on U.S. Smuggling Charges."

80. United States Court of Appeals, Ninth Circuit, *United States v. Chi Tong Kuok,* http://caselaw.findlaw.com/us-9th-circuit/1591353.html.

81. Federal Bureau of Investigation, "Chinese Man Indicted for Attempting to Illegally Export Thermal Imaging Cameras," https://www.fbi.gov/cincinnati /press-releases/2009/ci061009.htm; "Summary of Major U.S. Cases (January 2009 to the Present)."

82. Department of Justice, "Summary of Major U.S. Export Enforcement, Economic Espionage, Trade Secret, and Embargo-Related Criminal Cases (January 2010 to the Present: Updated June 27, 2016)," June 28, 2016, https://www .justice.gov/nsd/files/export_case_list_june_2016_2.pdf/download.

83. Gerstein, "Spy Charges in High-Stakes Microchip Race."

84. Mintz, "Silicon Valley Espionage Case Only Second of Kind in Nation to Go to Trial."

85. Mintz, "Federal Jury Deadlocks on Most of Espionage Case against Two Silicon Valley Engineers."

86. Some former U.S. officials believe Dr. Lee was involved with the Chinese intelligence services; however, no public information corroborated these assertions. Therefore, the Lee case appears in this chapter rather those involving the intelligence services.

87. *The Peter Lee Case: Hearings before the Subcommittee on Administrative Oversight and the Courts of the Committee on the Judiciary*, Senate 106th Cong. 2 (2000).

88. "Summary of Major U.S. Export Enforcement, Economic Espionage, Trade Secret, and Embargo-Related Criminal Cases (January 2010 to the Present: Updated June 27, 2016)."

89. U.S. Attorney's Office for the Eastern District of Virginia, "Chinese Nationals Sentenced 24 Months for Illegally Attempting to Export Radiation-Hardened Microchips to the PRC," https://www.justice.gov/archive/usao/vae/news/2011/09/20110930Chinesenr.html; "Two Chinese Nationals Charged with Illegally Attempting to Export Military Satellite Components to the PRC," https://www.justice.gov/opa/pr/two-chinese-nationals-charged-illegally-attempting-export-military-satellite-components-prc.

90. "Woman Charged in Effort to Smuggle O.C. Sensors," *Associated Press*, October 18, 2007, http://www.ocregister.com/articles/company-78962-china-san.html.

91. Department of Justice, "Woman Charged in Plot to Illegally Export Military Accelerometers to China," October 18, 2007, https://www.justice.gov/archive/opa/pr/2007/October/07_nsd_833.html.

92. "Woman Charged in Effort to Smuggle O.C. Sensors."

93. "Summary of Major U.S. Cases (January 2009 to the Present)."

94. David Martin, "Unraveling the Great Chinese Corn Seed Spy Ring," *Al-Jazeera America*, October 6, 2014, http://america.aljazeera.com/watch/shows/america-tonight/articles/2014/10/6/unraveling-the-greatchinesecornseedspyring.html.

95. "Couple Charged in Export Fraud," *Courier Post*, July 30, 2004.

96. Graham, "Camden Firm Pleads Guilty."

97. "Summary of Major U.S. Cases (January 2009 to the Present)"; David Voreacos, "Former Sanofi Chemist Gets 18 Months for Trade Secrets Theft," *Bloomberg.com*, May 7, 2012, http://www.bloomberg.com/news/articles/2012-05-07/former-sanofi-chemist-gets-18-months-for-trade-secrets-theft-1-.

98. "Summary of Major U.S. Cases (January 2009 to the Present); R. Scott Moxley, "Huntington Beach Businessman Nailed for Exporting Thermal Imaging Cameras to China," *OC Weekly*, April 25, 2012, http://www.ocweekly.com/news/huntington-beach-businessman-nailed-for-exporting-thermal-imaging-cameras-to-china-6464727.

99. Steve Chawkins, "Thousand Oaks Arms Exporter Is Sentenced," *Los Angeles Times*, December 16, 2003, http://articles.latimes.com/2003/dec/16/local/me-vnexport16.

100. "Select ICE Arms and Strategic Technology Investigations."
101. "U.S. and Chinese Defendants Charged."
102. Federal Bureau of Investigation, "Walter Liew Sentenced to 15 Years in Prison for Economic Espionage," https://www.fbi.gov/contact-us/field-offices/san francisco/news/press-releases/walter-liew-sentenced-to-15-years-in-prison-for-economic-espionage.
103. Backover, "Feds: Trio Stole Lucent's Trade Secrets"; Department of Justice, "New Indictment Expands Charges Against Former Lucent Scientists Accused of Passing Trade Secrets to Chinese Company," April 11, 2002, https://www.justice.gov/archive/criminal/cybercrime/press-releases/2002/lucentSupIndict.htm.
104. Gold, "Firm Guilty of Stealing Lucent Information."
105. Gold.
106. Federal Bureau of Investigation, "Former Employee of New Jersey Defense Contractor Sentenced to 70 Months in Prison for Exporting Sensitive Military Technology to China," https://www.fbi.gov/newark/press-releases/2013/for mer-employee-of-new-jersey-defense-contractor-sentenced-to-70-months-in-prison-for-exporting-sensitive-military-technology-to-china.
107. Bill Singer, "Industrial Espionage at Dow Chemical," *Forbes*, February 8, 2011, http://www.forbes.com/sites/billsinger/2011/02/08/industrial-espio nage-dow/.
108. Department of Justice, "Former Dow Research Scientist Sentenced to 60 Months in Prison for Stealing Trade Secrets and Perjury," January 13, 2012, https://www.justice.gov/opa/pr/former-dow-research-scientist-sentenced-60-months-prison-stealing-trade-secrets-and-perjury.
109. Federal Bureau of Investigation, "Former Connecticut Resident Charged with Attempting to Travel to China with Stolen U.S. Military Program Documents," December 9, 2014, https://www.fbi.gov/contact-us/field-offices /newhaven/news/press-releases/former-connecticut-resident-charged-with-attempting-to-travel-to-china-with-stolen-u.s.-military-program-docu ments.
110. "Summary of Major U.S. Cases (January 2009 to the Present)."
111. "Summary of Major U.S. Cases (January 2009 to the Present)."
112. "U.S. and Chinese Defendants Charged."
113. Department of Justice, "Two Individuals and Company Found Guilty of Conspiracy to Sell Trade Secrets to Chinese Companies," https://www.jus tice.gov/opa/pr/two-individuals-and-company-found-guilty-conspiracy-sell-trade-secrets-chinese-companies.

114. Wendell Minnick, "Chinese National Convicted of Export Violations," *Defense News*, June 10, 2016, http://www.defensenews.com/story/defense /international/2016/06/10/chinese-national-convicted-export-viola tions/85695920/.

115. Department of Justice, "California Resident Convicted of Conspiring to Illegally Export Fighter Jet Engines and Unmanned Aerial Vehicle to China," https://www.justice.gov/opa/pr/california-resident-convicted-conspiring-illegally-export-fighter-jet-engines-and-unmanned.

116. Wendell Minnick, "China Accused of Trying to Acquire Fighter Engines, UAV," *Defense News*, October 27, 2015, http://www.defensenews.com/story /defense/policy-budget/industry/2015/10/27/china-accused-trying-acquire-fighter-engines-uav/74676946/.

117. Associated Press, "California Woman Sentenced for Conspiring to Send China Military Gear," *The Guardian*, August 20, 2016, https://www.the guardian.com/us-news/2016/aug/20/us-military-equipment-export-china-wenxia-man-sentencing.

118. Jaikumar Vijayan, "Former DuPont Researcher Hit with Federal Data Theft Charges," *Reuters*, October 7, 2009, http://www.reuters.com/article/urnidgn s852573c40069388000257647006e70d-idUS416454660020091007.

119. Randy Boswell, "Canadian in Silicon Valley Charged with Spying, Theft: Technology Worker Accused of Trying to Sell Stolen Flight Simulation Software," *Vancouver Sun*, December 15, 2006; Connie Skipitares, "Cupertino Man Charged in Alleged Theft of Trade Secrets," *San Jose Mercury News*, December 14, 2006.

120. Howard Mintz, "Silicon Valley Engineer Sentenced for Economic Espionage," *The Mercury News*, June 18, 2008, http://www.mercurynews .com/2008/06/18/silicon-valley-engineer-sentenced-for-economic-espio nage/.

121. Martin, "Unraveling the Great Chinese Corn Seed Spy Ring."

122. John Eligon and Patrick Zuo, "U.S. Suspects Chinese in Theft of Seed Research," *New York Times*, February 6, 2014.

123. Davies, "Espionage Arrest of Nuclear Engineer Fuels U.S. Suspicions of Chinese Tactics."

124. Davies.

125. Grant Rodgers, "FBI: Plot to Steal Seed Corn a National Security Threat," *Des Moines Register*, March 30, 2015, http://www.desmoinesregister.com/story /news/crime-and-courts/2015/03/29/seed-corn-theft-plot-national-secu rity-fbi/70643462/.

126. "Two S. Koreans Charged with Arms Export to China," *Washington Times*, http://www.washingtontimes.com/news/2004/may/10/20040510-113348-1076r/.

127. "Summary of Major U.S. Cases (January 2009 to the Present)."

128. "Summary of Major U.S. Cases (January 2009 to the Present)."

129. Andreadis, "Couple Charged."

130. Stempel, "Former GM Engineer, Husband Sentenced in Trade Secret Theft Case."

131. "Summary of Major U.S. Cases (January 2009 to the Present)."

132. Marius Meland, "TSMC Refiles Trade-Secret Suit vs. Mainland Foundry," *Law360*, July 28, 2004, http://www.law360.com/articles/1857/tsmc-refiles-trade-secret-suit-vs-mainland-foundry.

133. Marius Meland, "Asian Chip Makers Settle Trade-Secrets, Patent Suit in $175M Deal," *Law360*, January 31, 2005, http://www.law360.com/articles/2941/asian-chip-makers-settle-trade-secrets-patent-suit-in-175m-deal.

134. Dan Nystedt, "TSMC in US$290M Settlement with China's Biggest Chip Maker," *PCWorld*, November 10, 2009, http://www.pcworld.com/article/181803/article.html.

135. Richtel, "Handful of Indictments Over Technology."

136. Wilke, "Two Silicon Valley Cases Raise Fears of Chinese Espionage."

137. K. Oanh Ha, "Stealing a Head Start: Trade Secrets Lost to Students, Businessmen, Researchers," *San Jose Mercury News*, September 28, 2006.

138. Jay Solomon, "Phantom Menace: FBI Sees Big Threat from Chinese Spies; Businesses Wonder; Bureau Adds Manpower, Builds Technology-Theft Cases; Charges of Racial Profiling; Mixed Feelings at 3DGeo," *Wall Street Journal*, August 10, 2005.

139. "Summary of Major U.S. Cases (January 2009 to the Present)."

140. "San Jose Company Indicted for Illegal Exports," *Silicon Valley Business Journal*, May 31, 2004, http://www.bizjournals.com/sanjose/stories/2004/05/31/daily34.html.

141. Henry K. Lee, "Cupertino Man Gets 2 Years for Exporting Military Technology to China," *SFGate*, December 5, 2007, http://www.sfgate.com/bayarea/article/Cupertino-man-gets-2-years-for-exporting-military-3235173.php.

142. Department of Justice, "Virginia Physicist Arrested for Illegally Exporting Space Launch Data to China and Offering Bribes to Chinese Officials," September 24, 2008, https://www.justice.gov/archive/opa/pr/2008/September/08-nsd-851.html.

143. Department of Justice, "Virginia Physicist Sentenced to 51 Months in Prison for Illegally Exporting Space Launch Data to China and Offering

Bribes to Chinese Officials," April 7, 2009, https://www.justice.gov/opa/pr/virginia-physicist-sentenced-51-months-prison-illegally-exporting-space-launch-data-china-and.

144. "Guilty Plea for Illegal Exports."
145. "Select ICE Arms and Strategic Technology Investigations."
146. "Guilty Plea for Illegal Exports."
147. "Bellevue Man Sentenced for Violating Arms Export Act."
148. U.S. District Court for the District of Oregon, 2011, *United States of America v. Wan Li Yuan and Jiang Song*—indictment.
149. Hannas, Mulvenon, and Puglisi, *Chinese Industrial Espionage*, 79.
150. "Overseas Talents Wooed to Improve Social Management," *Xinhua News Agency—CEIS*, February 23, 2012, http://search.proquest.com/docview/923237960/abstract/387BA67931074398PQ/17.
151. "China Engages Foreign Experts in Rural Development," *Xinhua News Agency—CEIS*, December 31, 2006.
152. "New Programs Envisioned to Import Foreign Experts," *China Today*, March 5, 2012, http://search.proquest.com/docview/1222299381/citation/E8BF44F3B18F4C87PQ/107.
153. Han Ximin, "Over 4,500 Overseas Exhibitors at CIEP," *Shenzhen Daily*, April 15, 2016, 500, http://search.proquest.com/docview/1785209702/abstract/E8BF44F3B18F4C87PQ/221.
154. "China to Recruit up to 1,000 High-Caliber Overseas Experts in 10 Years," *Xinhua News Agency—CEIS*, January 10, 2012, http://search.proquest.com/docview/915067667/abstract/E8BF44F3B18F4C87PQ/51.
155. Authors' interviews, Washington, DC, June 2016.
156. Department of Justice, "Sinovel Corporation and Three Individuals Charged in Wisconsin with Theft of AMSC Trade Secrets," https://www.justice.gov/opa/pr/sinovel-corporation-and-three-individuals-charged-wisconsin-theft-amsc-trade-secrets.
157. "Sinovel Corporation and Three Individuals Charged."
158. "Sinovel Corporation and Three Individuals Charged."
159. Federal Bureau of Investigation, "Three Sentenced to Federal Prison for Illegally Exporting Highly Sensitive U.S. Technology to China," https://www.fbi.gov/losangeles/press-releases/2009/la080409.htm.
160. Kaitlin Gurney, "Pair Accused of Exporting Sensitive Goods to China," *Philadelphia Inquirer*, July 30, 2004.
161. Graham, "Camden Firm Pleads Guilty."
162. "U.S. Charges Five Chinese Military Hackers for Cyber Espionage Against U.S. Corporations and a Labor Organization for Commercial Advantage,"

accessed September 23, 2016, https://www.justice.gov/opa/pr/us-charges-five-chinese-military-hackers-cyber-espionage-against-us-corporations-and-labor.

163. Martin, "Unraveling the Great Chinese Corn Seed Spy Ring."
164. Eligon and Zuo, "U.S. Suspects Chinese in Theft of Seed Research."
165. Federal Bureau of Investigation, "Six Chinese Nationals Indicted for Conspiring to Steal Trade Secrets from U.S. Seed Companies," https://www.fbi.gov/omaha/press-releases/2013/six-chinese-nationals-indicted-for-conspiring-to-steal-trade-secrets-from-u.s.-seed-companies.
166. U.S. District Court for the Eastern District of Virginia, 2008, *United States of America v. Wavelab, Inc.*—Plea Agreement.
167. "Summary of Major U.S. Cases (January 2009 to the Present)."
168. Department of Justice, "Woman Sentenced for Illegally Exporting Electronics Components Used in Military Radar, Electronic Warfare and Missile Systems to China," https://www.justice.gov/usao-ma/pr/woman-sentenced-illegally-exporting-electronics-components-used-military-radar-electronic; Department of Justice, "Two Chinese Nationals Convicted of Illegally Exporting Electronics Components Used in Military Radar and Electronic Warfare," https://www.justice.gov/opa/pr/two-chinese-nationals-convicted-illegally-exporting-electronics-components-used-military.
169. "Two Chinese Nationals Convicted of Illegally Exporting Electronics Components Used in Military Radar and Electronic Warfare."
170. "Two Chinese Nationals Convicted of Illegally Exporting Electronics Components"; Federal Bureau of Investigation, "Chinese National Sentenced for Illegally Exporting Military Electronics Components," https://www.fbi.gov/boston/press-releases/2013/chinese-national-sentenced-for-illegally-exporting-military-electronics-components.
171. United States Attorney's Office, Eastern District of Virginia, "Chinese Nationals Sentenced 24 Months for Illegally Attempting to Export Radiation-Hardened Microchips to the PRC," September 30, 2011, https://www.justice.gov/archive/usao/vae/news/2011/09/20110930Chinesenr.html; "Two Chinese Nationals Charged with Illegally Attempting to Export Military Satellite Components to the PRC."
172. U.S. District Court for the District of New Jersey, *United States of America v. Bing Xu*, INDICTMENT.
173. Department of Justice, "Chinese National Sentenced to 22 Months in Prison for Trying to Buy Night Vision Technology for Export to China," July 1, 2009, https://www.justice.gov/sites/default/files/usao-nj/legacy/2013/11/29/xu0701%20rel.pdf.

174. Backover, "Feds: Trio Stole Lucent's Trade Secrets"; "New Indictment Expands Charges Against Former Lucent Scientists Accused of Passing Trade Secrets to Chinese Company."

175. Gold, "Firm Guilty of Stealing Lucent Information."

176. John Shiffman and Sam Wood, "7 Indicted in Export of Military Circuitry," *Philadelphia Inquirer*, July 2, 2004.

177. "Four Owners/Operators of Mount Laurel Company Sentenced for Illegally Selling National-Security Sensitive Items to Chinese Interests," *U.S. Federal News Service*, May 1, 2006.

178. "Four Owners/Operators of Mount Laurel Company Sentenced."

179. "Summary of Major U.S. Cases (January 2009 to the Present)."

180. Terry Baynes, "Ex-CME Programmer Pleads Guilty to Trade Secret Theft," *Reuters*, September 20, 2012, http://www.reuters.com/article/us-cme-theft -plea-idUSBRE88J02U20120920.

181. Kim Janssen, "Chinese Immigrant Spared Prison for Chicago Merc Trade Secrets Theft," *Chicago Sun-Times*, March 3, 2015, http://chicago.suntimes .com/news/chinese-immigrant-spared-prison-for-chicago-merc-trade-se crets-theft/.

182. "Major U.S. Export Enforcement Prosecutions."

183. Mike Carter, "Woodinville Man Pleads Guilty to Attempted Sale of Banned Technology to China," *The Seattle Times*, March 24, 2011, http://www.seat tletimes.com/seattle-news/woodinville-man-pleads-guilty-to-attempted- sale-of-banned-technology-to-china/; Federal Bureau of Investigation, "Washington Man Charged in Connection with Attempts to Ship Sensitive Military Technology to China Man Arrested in FBI Sting Operation After Attempting to Smuggle Parts Out of United States," https://www.fbi.gov /seattle/press-releases/2010/se120610.htm.

184. Sindhu Sundar, "Wash. Man Gets 18 Months for Satellite Smuggling Plan," *Law 360*, October 28, 2011, http://www.law360.com/articles/281685/wash- man-gets-18-months-for-satellite-smuggling-plan.

185. "Major U.S. Export Enforcement Prosecutions."

186. Gibson, "Chinese Nationals Held in Attempted Export of Encryption Devices."

187. Marquis, "2 Arrested in Case on Selling Encryption Device"; Joe Eaton, "Court Upholds Convictions of Men Who Tried to Export Military Goods to China," *Capital News Service*, April 15, 2004, https://cnsmaryland .org/2004/04/15/court-upholds-convictions-of-men-who-tried-to-export -military-goods-to-china/.

188. Howard Mintz, "Former Silicon Valley Engineers Sentenced for Trying to Sell Technology Secrets to China," *The Mercury News*, November 21, 2008, https://www.mercurynews.com/2008/11/21/former-silicon-valley-engi neers-sentenced-for-trying-to-sell-technology-secrets-to-china-2/.

189. Ariana Eunjung Cha, "Even Spies Embrace China's Free Market: U.S. Says Some Tech Thieves Are Entrepreneurs, Not Government Agents," *Washington Post*, February 15, 2008, http://www.washingtonpost.com/wp-dyn/con tent/article/2008/02/14/AR2008021403550.html.

190. Richtel, "Handful of Indictments Over Technology."

191. Richtel.

192. *United States of America v. Wan Li Yuan and Jiang Song.*

193. "Summary of Major U.S. Cases (January 2009 to the Present)."

194. Basil Katz, "U.S. Charges Chinese Man with NY Fed Software Theft," *Reuters*, January 19, 2012, http://www.reuters.com/article/us-nyfed-theft-idUSTRE80H27L20120119; Jonathan Stempel and Nate Raymond, "Chinese Man Avoids Prison for New York Fed Cyber Theft," *Reuters*, December 4, 2012, http://www.reuters.com/article/us-usa-crime-fed-idUS BRE8B30WF20121204.

195. Federal Bureau of Investigation, "Two Men Arrested in Connection with the Illegal Export of Sensitive Technology to China Without a License, and Conspiracy to Purchase Counterfeit Electronic Components," January 21, 2009, https://www.fbi.gov/losangeles/press-releases/2009/la012109a.htm.

196. "Summary of Major U.S. Cases (January 2009 to the Present)."

197. "Chinese National Pleads Guilty to Attempting to Illegally Export Aerospace-Grade Carbon Fiber to China," https://www.justice.gov/usao-edny /pr/chinese-national-pleads-guilty-attempting-illegally-export-aerospace-grade-carbon-fiber.

198. Robert Beckhusen, "Chinese Smuggler Tried to Sneak Carbon Fiber for Fighter Jets, Feds Claim," *Wired*, September 28, 2012, https://www.wired .com/2012/09/carbon-fiber/.

199. Christie Smythe, "Chinese Man Gets Almost Five Years for Export Scheme," *Bloomberg.com*, December 10, 2013, http://www.bloomberg.com/news/arti cles/2013–12–10/chinese-man-gets-almost-five-years-for-export-scheme.

200. Eligon and Zuo, "U.S. Suspects Chinese in Theft of Seed Research."

201. "California Resident Convicted of Conspiring to Illegally Export Fighter Jet Engines and Unmanned Aerial Vehicle to China."

202. "California Resident Convicted."

203. Minnick, "China Accused of Trying to Acquire Fighter Engines, UAV."

204. "Chinese Exports Case Lands in Spokane," *Spokesman.com*, http://www
    .spokesman.com/blogs/sirens/2012/aug/01/chinese-exports-case-lands-
    spokane/.

205. "Chinese Exports Case Lands in Spokane."

206. Dinesh Ramde, "Researcher Stole Cancer Data for China, Says Prosecu-
    tor," *Associated Press*, April 3, 2013, https://www.bostonglobe.com/news
    /nation/2013/04/02/prosecutor-researcher-stole-cancer-data-for-china
    /MSEYuIprfxWcPE5mUZmlcM/story.html.

207. Ramde.

208. "Former Silicon Valley Engineers Sentenced for Trying to Sell Technology
    Secrets to China," *The Mercury News*, November 21, 2008, http://www.mer
    curynews.com/2008/11/21/former-silicon-valley-engineers-sentenced-for-
    trying-to-sell-technology-secrets-to-china/.

209. Cha, "Even Spies Embrace China's Free Market."

210. Cha.

211. U.S. Department of Commerce, "Don't Let This Happen to You! An Intro-
    duction to U.S. Export Control Law: Actual Investigations of Export Con-
    trol and Antiboycott Violations," September 2010, https://www.bis.doc.gov
    /index.php/forms-documents/doc_view/535-don-t-let-thishappen-to-you.

212. Chawkins, "Thousand Oaks Arms Exporter Is Sentenced"; "Select ICE Arms
    and Strategic Technology Investigations."

Chapter 5. Espionage during the Revolution and the Early People's Republic

1. Jonathan Unger, *Using the Past to Serve the Present: Historiography and
    Politics in Contemporary China* (Armonk, NY: M. E. Sharpe, 1994), 6–7.

2. MacFarquhar, *The Origins of the Cultural Revolution*, vol. 2, 408; Gao Yuan,
    Born Red: A Chronicle of the Cultural Revolution (Stanford, CA: Stanford
    University Press, 1987), 121.

3. Tong, *Fengyu sishinian*, 403–4.

4. Tong, 404–5.

5. Tong, 405–6.

6. MacFarquhar and Schoenhals, *Mao's Last Revolution*, 98.

7. *Zhou Enlai nianpu 1949–1976*, vol. 3, 137.

8. *Zhou Enlai nianpu 1949–1976*, vol. 3, 138.

9. MacFarquhar and Schoenhals, *Mao's Last Revolution*, 97–98; *Zhou Enlai
    nianpu 1949–1976*, vol. 3, 151.

10. G. C. Allen, *Western Enterprise in Far Eastern Economic Development: China
    and Japan* (New York: MacMillan Company, 1954), 217; Felix Patrikeef,

"Railway as Political Catalyst: The Chinese Eastern Railway and the 1929 Sino-Soviet Conflict," in *Manchurian Railways and the Opening of China: An International History*, ed. Bruce Elleman and Stephen Kotkin (New York: Routledge, 2015), 90–92.

11. Viktor Usov, *Soviet Intelligence Services in China in the Early 1920s* (Moscow: Olma Press, 2002); Henry Wei, *China and Soviet Russia* (New York: Van Nostrand Company, 1956), 67–70; C. Martin Wilbur and Julie Lien-ying How, *Documents on Communism, Nationalism, and Soviet Advisors in China, 1918–1927: Papers Seized in the 1927 Peking Raid* (New York: Columbia University Press, 1956), 8–10.

12. Robert T. Pollard, *China's Foreign Relations: 1917–1931* (New York: Macmillan Company, 1933), 336–37.

13. *Renmin Ribao*, May 11, 2007, http://theory.people.com.cn/GB/40534/5717 308.html.

14. Gu, *Gong'an Gongzuo*, 53; Dujmovic, "Extraordinary Fidelity"; video, "Extraordinary Fidelity," https://www.youtube.com/watch?v=Z0Mh7EiXRJI.

15. Jiang, *Zhonggong zai Xianggang*, vol. 1, 29–39; Christine Loh, *Underground Front: The Chinese Communist Party in Hong Kong* (Pokfulam: Hong Kong University Press, 2010), 47–53.

16. Jiang, *Zhonggong zai Xianggang*, 92–94.

17. Wang, *Liao Chengzhi zhuan*, 43–44.

18. Yin, *Pan Hannian de qingbao shengya*, 93.

19. Wang, *Liao Chengzhi zhuan*, 44, 91.

20. Wang, 142–45; Chan Sui-jeung, *East River Column* (Hong Kong: Hong Kong University Press, 2009), 41–43.

21. *Kangri zhanzheng shiqide Zhongguo renmin jiefangjun* [The Chinese People's Liberation Army During the Anti-Japanese War] (Beijing: Renmin Chubanshe, 1953), 169–72; Wang, *Liao Chengzhi zhuan*, 127–31, 145, 150.

22. Chan, *East River Column*, 41–43, 50–55.

23. Wang, *Liao Chengzhi zhuan*, 129–131; *Kangri zhanzheng shiqide Zhongguo renmin jiefangjun*, 172–73; Chan, *East River Column*, 17, 63–64, 83–84.

24. Chan, *East River Column*, 50, 57–61; Wang, *Liao Chengzhi zhuan*, 149.

25. Near Lechang, Shaoguan County. Wang, *Liao Chengzhi zhuan*, 153.

26. Wang, 139, 143–47, 149–53; Chan, *East River Column*, 20–23.

27. Wang, *Liao Chengzhi zhuan*, 145.

28. Tod Hoffman, *The Spy Within* (Hanover, NH: Steerforth Press, 2008), 158–59.

29. Cathy Zhou Jinyu, *Wode zhangfu Jin Wudai zhi si* [The death of my husband Jin Wudai] (Taipei: Dong Huang Wenhua Chuban Shiye Gongsi, 1998), 49, 164, 267, 272, 307–13, 340–42, 447.

30. Hoffman, *The Spy Within*, 42–67; James R. Lilley, "Blame Clinton, Not China, for the Lapse at Los Alamos," *Wall Street Journal*, March 17, 1999, http://www.aei.org/publication/blame-clinton-not-china-for-the-lapse-at-los-alamos/print/.

31. Li Hong, "The Truth Behind the Kashmir Princess Incident," in *Selected Essays on the History of Contemporary China*, ed. Zhang Xingxing (Leiden: Brill, 2015), 234; Steve Tsang, "Target Zhou Enlai: The 'Kashmir Princess' Incident of 1955," *The China Quarterly* 139 (September 1994): 766–82.

32. Li, "The Truth," 237; Tsang, "Target Zhou Enlai," 774–75.

33. Tsang, "Target Zhou Enlai," 767–70; Li, "The Truth," 237–38.

34. "Waijiao bu jie mi mi 'Keshenmi'er gongzhu hao' Zhou Zongli zuoji bei zha an" [Ministry of Foreign Affairs unveils secret case on the bombing of Zhou Enlai's plane the Kashmir Princess], Xinhuanet, July 20, 2004, http://news.xinhuanet.com/newscenter/2004–07/20/content_1616252.htm.

35. Tsang, "Target Zhou Enlai," 770–73.

36. Tsang, 770, 780–81.

37. Tsang, 775–76.

38. Gu, *Gong'an Gongzuo*, 82, entry for March 21–31, 1955.

39. Gu, 82–84, entry for March 21–April 11, 1955; Kai, *Li Kenong*, 426.

40. Interview with former U.S. diplomat, 2004.

41. Peter Wesley-Smith, *Unequal Treaty 1898–1997: China, Great Britain, and Hong Kong's New Territories* (Hong Kong: Oxford University Press, 1980), 17–19, 32, 36.

42. Wesley-Smith, 123.

43. Authors' interview with Hong Kong Police officers at the Walled City, November 1989.

44. Frederick Forsyth, *The Outsider: My Life in Intrigue* (New York: Putnam, 2015), 270–73.

45. Interview, 2017. See entry on Pan Jing'an for details.

46. http://www.discoverhongkong.com/us/see-do/culture-heritage/historical-sites/chinese/kowloon-walled-city-park.jsp.

47. Gunn, *Encountering Macau*, 96, 99; Steve Tsang, *Hong Kong: An Appointment with China* (London: I. B. Tauris and Co., 1997), 70.

48. João Guedes, *Macau Confidencial* (Macau: Instituto Internacional Macau, 2015), 113–19; Gunn, *Encountering Macau*, 96, 112–13, 116n60.

49. Gunn, *Encountering Macau*, 117–18.

50. "Japan Wants to Buy Macao from Portugal," *The Daily Mail*, May 15, 1935. See also Macau Antiga, May 6, 2017.

51. João F. O. Botas, *Macau 1937–1945, os Anos da Guerra* [Macau 1937–1945, the war years] (Macau: Instituto Internacional de Macau, 2012), 293–94, 323.

52. Guedes, *Macau Confidencial*, 147–49; Gunn, *Encountering Macau*, 118–28.

53. Xiao, *Zhonggong Tegong*, 205–6. Thanks to Dr. David Chambers for this reference.

54. Guedes, *Macau Confidencial*, 166–67.

55. Gunn, *Encountering Macau*, 128–29.

56. Gunn, 174.

57. Marques and Borges, *O Ouro no Eixo Hong Kong Macau, 1946–1973*, 183, 217, 237, 246, 488.

58. Fernando Lima, *Macau: as duas Transições* [Macau: The Two Transitions] (Macau: Fundação Macau, 1999), 600–5.

59. Lima, 606–8.

60. Interview.

61. Barbara Demick, "Macau Bank Freeze Angers North Korea," *Los Angeles Times*, April 7, 2006; Chris McGreal, "China Feared CIA Worked with Sheldon Adelson's Macau Casinos to Snare Officials," *The Guardian*, July 22, 2015; James Ball and Harry Davies, "How China's Crackdown Threatens Big U.S. Casino Moguls," *The Guardian*, April 23, 2015; Sands China, Inc., "Findings of a Discreet Consulting Exercise in Macau, Hong Kong, and Beijing," June 25, 2010, http://www.documentcloud.org/documents/2170141-sands-asia-cia-report-redacted.html#document/p1. Thanks to João Guedes for his comments.

62. Choe Sang-Hun, "North Korea Revives Coded Spy Broadcasts After 16-Year Silence," *New York Times*, July 21, 2016.

63. STC booklets have been sold for decades at PRC post offices, and STC was used from the early twentieth century in telegraphic messaging. See Zhonghua Renmin Gonghe Guo You Dian Bu [PRC Ministry of Posts and Telegraph], *Biaozhun dianma ben* [Standard Telegraphic Code Book] (Beijing: Ministry of Posts and Telegraph, 1983).

64. *The Americans*, FX Productions.

65. *Zhou Enlai nianpu 1949–1976*, vol. 2, 666; Schoenhals, *Spying for the People*, 109; Joyce Wadler, "Shi Beipu, Singer, Dies at 70," *New York Times*, http://www.nytimes.com/2009/07/02/world/asia/02shi.html.

66. Joyce Wadler, "Shi Beipu." The Shi-Boursicot relationship is detailed in Wadler, *Liaison*, and in Hoffman, *The Spy Within*, 68–80. Public Radio International, "At 83, the embassy worker at the center of the 'M. Butterfly' story is still an

enigma," September 21, 2017, https://www.pri.org/stories/2017-09-21/83-embassy-worker-center-m-butterfly-story-still-enigma.

67. Kai, *Li Kenong*, 2.

68. Kai, 2.

69. Kai, 9; Hao, *Zhongguo mimi zhan*, 9; Mu, *Yinbi zhanxian tongshuai Zhou Enlai*, 104.

70. Kai, *Li Kenong*, 8–10, 12; Hsu, *The Invisible Conflict*, 59–60.

71. Mu, *Chen Geng Tongzhi zai Shanghai*, 34–40; Kai, *Li Kenong*, 15, 34–40.

72. Hsu, *The Invisible Conflict*, 67–69. This practice, but not the specific incident, is discussed in Mu, *Yinbi zhanxian tongshuai Zhou Enlai*, 16.

73. Yin, *Pan Hannian de Qingbao Shengya*, 4–5; Hsu, *The Invisible Conflict*, 58–59, 62.

74. Mu, *Chen Geng Tongzhi zai Shanghai*, 82–85; Jin, *Chen Yun zhuan*, 104; Wakeman, *Spymaster*, 42–45; Hsu, *Chou En-lai, China's Gray Eminence*, 128; Liu, *Zhou Enlai da cidian*, 31–32; Barnouin and Yu, *Zhou Enlai, A Political Life*, 45–48.

75. Zhou departed Shanghai in December 1931. Shen, *Zhongyang Weiyuan*, 540; Liu, *Zhou Enlai da cidian*, 32.

76. Hao, *Zhongguo mimi zhan*, 106.

77. Schoenhals, *Spying for the People*, 65.

78. John Kenneth Knaus, *Orphans of the Cold War: America and the Tibetan Struggle for Survival* (New York: Public Affairs, 2000), 147–48; Mikel Dunham, *Buddha's Warriors: The Story of the CIA-Backed Tibetan Freedom Fighters, the Chinese Communist Invasion, and the Ultimate Fall of Tibet* (New York: Jeremy Tarcher Inc., 2014), 227–31; Schoenhals, *Spying for the People*, 24–25.

79. "Memorandum for the 303 Committee, 26 January 1968, Tibet," in Harriet Dashiel Schwar, ed., *Foreign Relations of the United States, 1964–1968*, vol. 30, *China* (Washington, DC: Government Printing Office, 1998), 741.

80. Shu Yun, *Luo Ruiqing dajiang* [General Luo Ruiqing] (Beijing: Jiefang Jun Wenyi Chubanshe, 2005), 304–9; Gu, *Gong'an Gongzuo*, 92.

81. Liu Gengsheng, *Hui Rui baguan yu wenge* [Hai Rui Dismissed from Office and the Cultural Revolution] (Taipei: Yuan Liou Publishing Company Ltd., 2011), 320; Shu, *Luo Ruiqing dajiang*, 306–7.

82. Shu, *Luo Ruiqing dajiang*, 309–10.

83. Shu, 310.

84. Li, *The Private Life of Chairman Mao*, 203.

85. Li, 476.

Chapter 6. Espionage during China's Rise

1. Dual-use technology refers to software, hardware, and other items that may be employed for both civilian and military purposes. Examples include electronics, aerospace designs, artificial intelligence applications, sophisticated machine tools, chemical engineering processes, night vision equipment, and nuclear technology.

2. Christoph Giesen and Ronen Steinke, "Wie chinesische Agenten den Bundestag ausspionieren," *Süddeutsche Zeitung*, July 6, 2018, https://www.sueddeutsche.de/politik/einflussnahme-auf-politiker-wie-chinesische-agenten-den-bundestag-ausspionieren-1.4042673.

3. Hiroko Nakata, "China Slammed Over Cryptographer Honey Trap Suicide," *Japan Times*, April 1, 2006, https://www.japantimes.co.jp/news/2006/04/01/national/china-slammed-over-cryptographer-honey-trap-suicide/#.Wbi-dxmGPrc.

4. Authors' interview, June 2012.

5. Department of Justice, "Former Defense Department Official Sentenced to 57 Months in Prison for Espionage Violation," July 11, 2008; David Wise, *Tiger Trap: America's Secret Spy War with China* (New York: Houghton Mifflin Harcourt, 2011), 222–24.

6. "U.S. Contractor Gets 7 Years for Passing Secrets to Chinese Girlfriend," *Reuters*, September 17, 2014; authors' interviews, December 2016, June 2017.

7. "Retired Officers Sentenced for Helping to Recruit Spies for China," Central News Agency (Taiwan), February 21, 2014, http://focustaiwan.tw/search/201402210015.aspx; Rich Chang and Chris Wang, "Three Ex-Officers Arrested for Spying," *Taipei Times*, October 30, 2012, http://www.taipeitimes.com/News/front/archives/2012/10/30/2003546431; "Retired Naval Officer Gets 15 Years for Spying for China," Central News Agency, December 15, 2014, http://focustaiwan.tw/news/aipl/201412150021.aspx.

8. Jason Pan, "High Court Rules in Favor of Chen Chu-fan in Spy Case," *Taipei Times*, May 19, 2016, http://www.taipeitimes.com/News/taiwan/archives/2016/05/19/2003646621.

9. Pan.

10. "The Supreme Court Upholds Ex-major's Jail Term for Spying," Central News Agency (Taiwan), October 14, 2014, http://www.taipeitimes.com/News/taiwan/archives/2014/10/14/2003602029.

11. J. Michael Cole, "Former Officer Gets 12 Life Terms in China Spy Case," *Taipei Times*, February 7, 2013, http://www.taipeitimes.com/News/taiwan/archives/2013/02/07/2003554439.

12. Chen Chao-fu and Sofia Wu, "Ex-Naval Officer in Taiwan Given Jail Term for Spying for China," Central News Agency (Taiwan), March 1, 2013, http://focustaiwan.tw/news/aipl/201303010028.aspx.

13. Jason Pan, "Six Indicted in Chinese Espionage Ring Case," *Taipei Times*, January 17, 2015, http://www.taipeitimes.com/News/front/archives/2015/01/17/2003609431; P. C. Tsai and Lillian Lin, "Chinese Spy Ring to Be Sentenced on Sept. 1," Central News Agency (Taiwan), August 29, 2015, http://focustaiwan.tw/news/aipl/201508290015.aspx.

14. Department of Justice, "FBI Employee Pleads Guilty to Acting in the United States as an Agent of the Chinese Government," August 1, 2016, https://www.justice.gov/opa/pr/fbi-employee-pleads-guilty-acting-united-states-agent-chinese-government.

15. Nate Raymond and Brendan Pierson, "FBI Employee Gets Two Years in Prison for Acting as Chinese Agent," Reuters, January 20, 2017, https://www.reuters.com/article/us-usa-china-fbi/fbi-employee-gets-two-years-in-prison-for-acting-as-chinese-agent-idUSKBN1542RO.

16. Department of Justice, "State Department Employee Arrested and Charged with Concealing Extensive Contacts with Foreign Agents," March 29, 2017, https://www.justice.gov/opa/pr/state-department-employee-arrested-and-charged-concealing-extensive-contacts-foreign-agents.

17. Criminal Complaint, *United States of America v. Candace Marie Claiborne*, U.S. District Court for Washington, DC, No. 1:17-mj-00173, March 28, 2017.

18. Robert David Booth, *State Department Counterintelligence: Leaks, Spies, and Lies* (Dallas, TX: Brown Books Publishing Group, 2014).

19. Department of Justice, "Defense Department Official Sentenced to 36 Months for Espionage, False Statement Charges," January 22, 2010, https://www.justice.gov/opa/pr/defense-department-official-sentenced-36-months-espionage-false-statement-charges; Department of Justice, "Defense Department Official Charged with Espionage Conspiracy," May 13, 2009, https://archives.fbi.gov/archives/washingtondc/press-releases/2009/wfo051309.htm.

20. Affidavit in Support of an Application for a Search Warrant, U.S. District Court for the District of Maryland, No. 14–2641, November 17, 2014.

21. "Tibetan Charged in Sweden Denies Spying for China," Radio Free Asia, April 18, 2018, https://www.rfa.org/english/news/tibet/spying-04182018133403.html.

22. Jan M. Olsen, "Swedish Court Finds Man Guilty of Spying for China," Associated Press, June 15, 2018, https://apnews.com/2c3ed87f9eec48d786b4f57f5c8c8b9e.

23. Criminal Complaint, *United States of America v. Ron Rockwell Hansen*, U.S. District Court for Utah, No. 2:18-mj-00324-PMW, June 2, 2017.

24. Authors' interviews, December 2016, June 2017.

25. Lin Chang-shun and Bear Lee, "Taiwanese Businessman Indicted for Spying for China," Central News Agency (Taiwan), April 15, 2010, http://focustai wan.tw/news/aall/201004150035.aspx.

26. Jason Pan, "Second Suspect Investigated in Spy Case," *Taipei Times*, May 11, 2017, http://www.taipeitimes.com/News/taiwan/archives/2017/05/11 /2003670361.

27. Pan.

28. Pan, "Six Indicted in Chinese Espionage Ring Case"; Yu Kai-hsiang and Elizabeth Hsu, "Ex-PLA Spy Fails Appeal in Taiwan after 4-Year Sentence," Central News Agency (Taiwan), April 27, 2016, http://focustaiwan.tw/news /acs/201604270006.aspx.

29. Department of Justice, "Chinese Intelligence Officers and Their Recruited Hackers and Insiders Conspired to Steal Sensitive Commercial Aviation and Technological Data for Years," October 30, 2018, https://www.justice.gov /opa/pr/chinese-intelligence-officers-and-their-recruited-hackers-and-insiders-conspired-steal; Department of Justice, "Chinese National Arrested for Allegedly Acting Within the United States as an Illegal Agent of the People's Republic of China," September 25, 2018, https://www.justice.gov /opa/pr/chinese-national-arrested-allegedly-acting-within-united-states-illegal-agent-people-s; Department of Justice, "Chinese Intelligence Officer Charged with Economic Espionage Involving Theft of Trade Secrets from Leading U.S. Aviation Companies," October 10, 2018, https://www.justice .gov/opa/pr/chinese-intelligence-officer-charged-economic-espionage-in volving-theft-trade-secrets-leading.

30. Jason Pan, "Top Navy Brass Gets 14 Months in Prison for Spying for China," *Taipei Times*, October 3, 2014, http://www.taipeitimes.com/News/taiwan /archives/2014/10/03/2003601166; Philip Dorling, "Australian Man Shen Ping-kang Jailed in Taiwan for Spying for China," *Sydney Morning Herald*, October 4, 2014, http://www.smh.com.au/national/australian-man-shen-pingkang-jailed-in-taiwan-for-spying-for-china-20141003–10pxk7.html.

31. "Ex-Air Force Officer Accused of Spying for Chinese Network," Central News Agency (Taiwan), June 23, 2015, http://www.taipeitimes.com/News/ front/archives/2015/06/23/2003621353.

32. Matthew Strong, "Taiwan Air Force Hero Charged with Spying for China," Taiwan News, March 3, 2017, https://www.taiwannews.com.tw/en/news /3110600.

33. Wise, *Tiger Trap*, 221.

34. Affidavit.

35. Wise, *Tiger Trap*, 226.

36. David Hammer, "Businessman's Spy Case Stuns Associates," *The Times Picayune*, February 12, 2008, https://www.nola.com/news/index.ssf/2008/02/businessmans_spycase_arrest_st.html; Bruce Alpert, "Spy for China with N.O. Ties is Back in Federal Court," *The Times Picayune*, September 22, 2009, https://www.nola.com/crime/index.ssf/2009/09/spy_for_china_is_back_in_feder.html.

37. Criminal Indictment of Jerry Chun Shing Lee, U.S. District Court for the Eastern District of Virginia, No. 1:18-cr-89, May 8, 2018.

38. Bill Gertz, *Enemies: How America's Foes Steal Our Vital Secrets—and How We Let It Happen* (New York: Crown Forum, 2006), 23.

39. Gertz, 24–39, 43–46; Federal Bureau of Investigation, Office of the Inspector General, "A Review of the FBI's Handling and Oversight of FBI Asset Katrina Leung," May 2006, https://oig.justice.gov/special/s0605/.

40. Amy Argetsinger, "Spy Case Dismissed for Misconduct; Plea Deal Silenced Defendant's Ex-Lover," *Washington Post*, January 7, 2005, http://www.washingtonpost.com/wp-dyn/articles/A54571-2005Jan6.html.

41. "Shuang mian die Li Zhihao" [Double agent Li Zhihao], *China Times*, October 11, 2015, http://www.chinatimes.com/cn/newspapers/20151011000278–260106; "China Releases Taiwanese Spies," Central News Agency (Taiwan), December 1, 2015, http://www.taipeitimes.com/News/front/archives/2015/12/01/2003633726.

42. Strong, "Taiwan Air Force Hero Charged with Spying for China."

43. Authors' interview, Washington, DC, July 2012.

44. Dorling, "Australian Man Shen Ping-kang Jailed in Taiwan for Spying for China"; "China Lured General with Sex," Taiwan News, February 11, 2011, http://www.taipeitimes.com/News/taiwan/archives/2011/02/11/2003495608/1.

45. "Life Term for China Spy Justified: Ministry of Defense," Central News Agency (Taiwan), January 19, 2014, http://www.taipeitimes.com/News/taiwan/archives/2014/01/19/2003581633.

46. Y. F. Low, "Retired Officers Sentenced for Helping to Recruit Spies for China," Central News Agency (Taiwan), February 21, 2014, http://focustaiwan.tw/search/201402210015.aspx.

47. "Sweden Jails Uighur Chinese Man for Spying," Reuters, March 8, 2010, https://www.reuters.com/article/us-sweden-china-spy/sweden-jails-uighur-chinese-man-for-spying-idUSTRE6274U620100308; Paul O'Mahony, "Pensioner Indicted over China Spy Scandal," Agence France Presse, December 15, 2009, https://www.thelocal.se/20091215/23864.

48. Wise, *Tiger Trap*, 217.

49. Department of Justice, "Chinese Agent Sentenced to Over 24 Years in Prison for Exporting United States Defense Articles to China," https://www.justice.gov/archive/opa/pr/2008/March/08_nsd_229.html; Edward M. Roche, *Snake Fish: The Chi Mak Spy Ring* (New York: Barraclough, 2008), 1–21, 29–31, 50, 87–89, 143, 184–86.

50. Roche, *Snake Fish*; Gertz, *Enemies*, 68.

51. Criminal complaint, *United States of America v. Kevin Patrick Mallory*, U.S. District Court for the Eastern District of Virginia, No. 1:17MJ-288, June 21, 2017; Josh Gerstein, "Ex-CIA Officer Charged with Spying for China," *Politico*, June 22, 2017, http://www.politico.com/story/2017/06/22/kevin-mallory-ex-cia-officer-arrested-spying-china-239877.

52. Peter Mattis, "Everything We Know about China's Secretive State Security Bureau," *The National Interest*, July 9, 2017, http://nationalinterest.org/feature/everything-we-know-about-chinas-secretive-state-security-21459.

53. Pan, "Top Navy Brass Gets 14 Months in Prison for Spying for China"; Dorling, "Australian Man Shen Ping-kang Jailed in Taiwan for Spying for China."

54. David Wise, "Mole-in-Training: How China Tried to Infiltrate the CIA," *The Washingtonian*, June 7, 2012, https://www.washingtonian.com/2012/06/07/chinas-mole-in-training.

55. Wise, *Tiger Trap*, 23.

56. Nate Thayer, "China Spy," *Asia Sentinel*, July 4, 2017, https://www.asiasentinel.com/politics/china-spy/; authors' interview, June 2017. The authors also had access to all of the communications between Thayer and the SSSB officers who pitched him.

57. Sophie Yang, "Taiwan Ex-Vice President's Bodyguard Arrested as Chinese Spy," *Taiwan News*, March 16, 2017, https://www.taiwannews.com.tw/en/news/3118435; Chen Wei-han, "Ex-Agent Detained Amid Spy Allegations," *Taipei Times*, March 17, 2017, http://www.taipeitimes.com/News/front/archives/2017/03/17/2003666922.

58. Cole, "Former Officer Gets 12 Life Terms in China Spy Case."

59. Pan, "Six Indicted in Chinese Espionage Ring Case"; Strong, "Taiwan Air Force Hero Charged with Spying for China."

60. Jason Pan, "Ex-Student Held for Espionage," *Taipei Times*, March 11, 2017, http://www.taipeitimes.com/News/front/archives/2017/03/11/2003666539; "周泓旭涉共諜案 北檢起訴 [Chinese Communist Spy Zhou Hongxu to be Prosecuted]," Central News Agency (Taiwan), July 6, 2017, http://www.cna.com.tw/news/firstnews/201707060093-1.aspx.

Chapter 7. Intelligence and Surveillance in China, Then and Now

1. Dutton, *Policing Chinese Politics*; Schoenhals, *Spying for the People*; Hannas, Mulvenon, and Puglisi, *Chinese Industrial Espionage*. We also look forward to Faligot, *Chinese Spies* (forthcoming, 2019).

2. Xue Yu, "Guanyu zhonggong zhongyang teke nuogan wenti de tantao," 1–4; Hao, *Zhongguo mimi zhan*, 5–8; Mu, *Zhou Enlai*, 11.

3. Hao, *Zhongguo mimi zhan*, 9; Mu, *Zhou Enlai*, 104.

4. Yin, *Pan Hannian de Qingbao Shengya*, 4–5; Hsu, *The Invisible Conflict*, 62.

5. Yin, *Pan Hannian de Qingbao Shengya*, 55, 72.

6. Pantsov and Levine, *Mao: The Real Story*, 283–88; Yang Shilan, "Deng Fa," 359.

7. Zhang Jiakang, "Wang Ming yu Zhongyang fengting kangli de shi ge yue" [Wang Ming and the ten month rivalry in the Central Committee], *Shiji Fengcai*, October 27, 2010, cpc.people.com.cn; Pantsov and Levine, *Mao: The Real Story*, 315–16; Kuo, *Analytical History*, vol. 3, 340; Zhonggong zhongyang shuji chu [CCPCC Secretariat], "Guanyu chengli shehui bu de jueding" [Concerning the Decision to Establish the Central Social Affairs Department], February 18, 1939, in Zhonggong zhongyang shehui bu [CCP Central Social Affairs Department], *Kangzhan shiqi chubao wenjian* [Documents on Digging Out Traitors and Protection in the Anti-Japanese War], December 1948. Thanks to David Chambers for this document. For the duties of Li and Pan, see Hao, *Zhongguo mimi zhan*, 54, 59.

8. Chen Yun, "Gonggu dang zai dahoufang ji dang zhanqu de mimi zuzhi" [Strengthen Secret Party Organizations in the Main Rear Area and in Enemy Occupied Areas], in *Chen Yun Wenxian, 1926–1949* [Works of Chen Yun, 1926–1949] (Beijing: Renmin Chubanshe, 1984), 136–37, 203–4. For an official English rendition that is slightly different, see Chen Yun, *Selected Works of Chen Yun, 1926–1949* (Beijing: Foreign Languages Press, 1988), 133–39; Liu Shaoqi, "Speech at the Security Personnel Training Class at Yancheng, April 29, 1941," in Kuo, *Analytical History*, vol. 4, 475–76.

9. Pantsov and Levine, *Mao: The Real Story*, 341–42.

10. Teiwes and Sun, "From a Leninist to a Charismatic Party," 372; "Spies are like hemp" (*tewu ru ma*, 特务如麻), Jin Chongji (ed.), *Mao Zedong Zhuan* [Biography of Mao Zedong] (Beijing: Zhongyang Wenxian Chubanshe, 1996), 676.

11. Gao Hua, *Hong taiyang zenyang shengqi de*, 465–66; Gao Wenqian, *Wannian Zhou Enlai*, 82; Pantsov and Levine, *Mao: The Real Story*, 337–39.

12. "Kang Sheng," in *Zhongguo Xiandaishi Renwu Zhuan*, 733; Kai Cheng, *Li Kenong*, 279.

13. Central Intelligence Agency, "Departure for Canton of Chinese Communist Agents of Central Social Affairs Department" (Langley, VA: Central Intelligence Agency, November 3, 1952; CIA-RDP82–00457R014500390010–2), available at CIA.gov/library/reading room.

14. Chambers, "Edging in from the Cold"; Li Kwok-sing (Li Gucheng), *Zhongguo dalu zhengzhi shuyu* [A Glossary of Political Terms of the People's Republic of China] (Hong Kong: The Chinese University of Hong Kong Press, 1992), 501–2; Kai, *Li Kenong*, 406–8.

15. *Yang Shangkun Riji*, vol. 1, 337, 352, 359–60; vol. 2, 79.

16. "Memorandum for the 303 Committee, 26 January 1968 (Tibet)," in Schwar, *Foreign Relations of the United States,* 741.

17. Schoenhals, *Spying for the People,* 24–25.

18. Schoenhals, "A Brief History of the CID of the CCP"; *Zhongyang Weiyuan,* 111; Kai Cheng, *Li Kenong,* 417–18.

19. MacFarquhar and Schoenhals, *Mao's Last Revolution,* 32–51, 89–91, 96–98; Yang and Yan, *Deng Xiaoping Nianpu, 1904–1974,* vol. 2, 1917; Xia Fei, "Xie Fuzhi Zhege Ren" [This Person, Xie Fuzhi], *Dushu Wenzhai,* no. 10, 2004, xuanju.org; Gu, *Gong'an Gongzuo,* 317; *Zhou Enlai nianpu 1949–1976,* 138.

20. Chambers, "Edging in from the Cold," 34.

21. Directorate of Intelligence, "China: Reorganization of Security Organs" (Washington, DC: Central Intelligence Agency, August 1, 1983, declassified copy, U.S. Library of Congress); Peter Mattis, "The Analytic Challenge of Understanding Chinese Intelligence Services," *Studies in Intelligence* 56, no. 3 (September 2012).

22. Confidential interviews and documents.

23. Lin Nian, "Gaogan zidi zai Xianggang lunwei waiguo jiandie" [Son of senior cadre in Hong Kong becomes foreign spy], Renmin Bao [People's News], December 18, 2003, http://m.renminbao.com/rmb /articles/2003/12/18/29152m.html; State Council Document 692, "Zhonghua Renmin Gongheguo Fan Jiandie Fa Shishi Xize" [PRC Counterespionage Law Detailed Regulations], December 6, 2017, http://www.gov.cn/zhengce /content/2017–12/06/content_5244819.htm; Lilley and Lilley, *China Hands,* 344, 347; Gu, *Gong'an Gongzuo,* 828; Kim Zetter, "Google Hackers Targeted Source Code in More than 30 Companies," *Wired,* January 13, 2010, https:// www.wired.com/2010/01/google-hack-attack/; Peter Mattis, "Shriver Case Highlights Traditional Chinese Espionage," *China Brief* 10, issue 22 (November 5, 2010); Mark Mazzetti et al., "Killing C.I.A. Informants, China Crippled U.S. Spying Operations," *New York Times,* May 20, 2017, https://www .nytimes.com/2017/05/20/; Nichole Perlroth, "Hackers in China Attacked

the Times for Last Four Months," *New York Times*, January 31, 2013; Ned Moran and Mike Oppenheim, "Darwin's Favorite APT Group," September 3, 2014, https://www.fireeye.com/blog/threat-research/2014/09 /darwins-favorite-apt-group-2.html 3.

24. Authors' interview with Chinese security official, 2009.

25. Mara Hvistendahl, "You Are a Number," *Wired*, January 2018, 50–59; Forbes profile of Lucy Peng, https://www.forbes.com/profile/lucy-peng/.

26. "Ali shouxi fengxian guan Shao Xiaofeng: dui fubai ling rongren taidu buhui bian" [Alibaba CRO Shao Xiaofeng: Zero Tolerance for Corruption Will Not Change], *Renmin Wang People*, June 8, 2012, http://finance.people.com.cn /GB/70846/18123177.html.

27. Interviews, 2016, 2017.

28. "New Personal Details Form Arrives at Phuket Immigration," *The Phuket News* (Thailand), May 21, 2016, https://www.thephuketnews.com /new-personal-details-form-arrives-at-phuket-immigration-57510 .php#aEbA3ZgPtrQ7y38J.97.

29. Interview, 2017.

30. Matthew Brazil, "Addressing Rising Business Risk in China," *China Brief* 16, issue 8 (May 2016).

◆ Selected Bibliography ◆

In addition to the sources that follow, we relied upon a broad set of publicly available court documents, articles primarily from local and regional newspapers, governmental press releases, and general Chinese-language online reference tools, such as selected biographical entries on *Baidu's* online encyclopedia when they appeared reliable. Also instrumental were research databases, including ProQuest, LexisNexis, and China National Knowledge Infrastructure. These databases, in some cases, offered English translations of Chinese articles that have long since disappeared from the Internet.

Chinese-Language Sources
Books
Ba Lu Jun Huiyi Shiliao [Eighth Route Army Memoirs and Historical Materials, vol. 3]. Beijing: Jiefangjun Chubanshe, 1991.

Biaozhun dianma ben [Standard Telegraphic Code Book]. Beijing: Ministry of Posts and Telegraph, 1983.

Chen Hanbo. *Wo zenyang dangzhe Mao Zedong de tewu* [How I Became a Spy for Mao Zedong]. Hong Kong: Ziyou Chubanshe, 1952.

Chen Jingtan. *Xie gei Xianggang ren de Zhongguo xiandai shi* [Modern History of China for Hong Kong People]. Hong Kong: Zhonghua Shu Ju Youxian Gongsi, 2014.

Chen Shaochou. *Liu Shaoqi zai baiqu* [Liu Shaoqi in the White Areas]. Beijing: Zhonggong Dangshi Chubanshe, 1992.

Chen Yung-fa. *Zhongguo Gongchandang qishi nian* [Seventy Years of the Chinese Communist Party]. Taipei: Linking Books, 1998.

Deng Jiarong. *Nan Hancheng zhuan* [The Biography of Nan Hancheng]. Beijing: Zhongguo Quanrong Chubanshe, 1993.

Deng Lijun. *Zhongguo Gang Ao Tai diqu mimi zhencha zhidu yanjiu* [Research on the secret investigation systems of the Hong Kong, Macau, and Taiwan regions of China]. Beijing: Zhongguo Shehui Kexue Chubanshe, 2013.

Dong Xiafei and Dong Yunfei. *Shenmi de hongse mushi, Dong Jianwu* [The Mysterious Red Pastor, Dong Jianwu]. Beijing: Beijing Chubanshe, 2001.

Fan Shuo. *Ye Jianying zai guanjian shike* [Ye Jianying in Crucial Moments]. Shenyang: Liaoning Renmin Chubanshe, 2001.

Fang Ke. *Zhonggong qingbao shou nao, Li Kenong* [Chinese Communist Intelligence Chief, Li Kenong]. Beijing: Zhongguo Shehui Kexue Chubanshe, 1996.

Gao Hua. *Hong taiyang shi zenme shengqi de: Yan'an zhengfeng yundong de lai long qu mai* [How Did the Red Sun Rise Over Yan'an: A History of the Rectification Movement]. Hong Kong: Chinese University Press, 2000.

Gao Wenqian. *Wannian Zhou Enlai* [Zhou Enlai's Later Years]. Hong Kong: Mirror Books, 2003.

Gu Chunwang. *Jianguo yilai Gong'an gongzuo da shi yaolan* [Major Highlights in Police Work Since the Founding of the Nation]. Beijing: Qunzhong Chubanshe, 2003.

Hao Zaijin. *Zhongguo mimi zhan—Zhonggong qingbao, baowei gongzuo jishi* [China's Secret War—The Record of Chinese Communist Intelligence and Protection Work]. Beijing: Zuojia Chubanshe, 2005.

He Jinzhou. *Deng Fa zhuan* [Biography of Deng Fa]. Beijing: Zhonggong Dangshi Chubanshe, 2008.

He Lin, ed. *Chen Geng zhuan* [Biography of Chen Geng]. Beijing: Dangdai Zhongguo Chubanshe, 2007.

Hu Jie. *Zhongguo xibu mimi zhan.* [Western China's Secret War]. Beijing: Jincheng Chubanshe, 2015.

Hu Wenlin, ed. *Qingbao xue* [The Study of Intelligence]. Taipei: Zhongyang Junshi Yuanxiao, 1989.

Huan Yao and Zhang Ming. *Luo Ruiqing zhuan* [The Biography of Luo Ruiqing]. Beijing: Dangdai Zhongguo Chubanshe, 2007.

Jiang Guangsheng. *Zhonggong zai Xianggang, Shang* [The Chinese Communists in Hong Kong, vol. 1]. Hong Kong: Cosmos Books, Inc., 2011.

Jin Chongji, ed. *Chen Yun zhuan* [The Biography of Chen Yun]. Beijing: Zhongyang Wenxian Chubanshe, 2005.

_____. *Mao Zedong zhuan 1893–1949* [Biography of Mao Zedong, 1893–1949]. Beijing: Zhongyang Wenxian Chubanshe, 1996.

Kai Cheng. *Li Kenong, Zhonggong yinbi zhanxian de zhuoyue lingdao ren* [Li Kenong: Outstanding Leader of the CCP's Hidden Battlefront]. Beijing: Zhongguo Youyi Chubanshe, 1996.

Kangri zhanzheng shiqi de Zhongguo Renmin Jiefangjun [The Chinese People's Liberation Army During the Anti-Japanese War]. Beijing: Renmin Chubanshe, 1953.

Li Kwok-sing (Li Gucheng). *Zhongguo dalu zhengzhi shuyu* [A Glossary of Political Terms of the People's Republic of China]. Hong Kong: The Chinese University of Hong Kong Press, 1992.

Li Li. *Cong mimi zhanxian zouchu de kaiguo shangjiang huainian jiafu Li Kenong* [Remembering My Father Li Kenong, the General Who Emerged from the Secret Battlefront at the Founding of the Nation]. Beijing: Renmin Chubanshe, 2008.

Li Songde. *Liao Chengzhi* [Liao Chengzhi]. Singapore: Yongsheng Books, 1992.

Li Weihan. *Huiyi yu yanjiu* [Reminiscences and Investigations]. Beijing: Zhonggong Dangshi Ziliao Chubanshe, 1986.

Li Yimin and Huang Guoping, *Li Yimin huiyilu* [The Memoirs of Li Yimin]. Changsha: Hunan Renmin Chubanshe, 1980.

Li Zengqun, ed. *Shiyong Gong'an xiao cidian* [A Practical Public Security Mini-Dictionary]. Harbin: Heilongjiang Renmin Chubanshe, 1987.

Lin Qingshan. *Kang Sheng Zhuan* [Biography of Kang Sheng]. Jilin: Jilin Renmin Chubanshe, 1996.

Liu Gengsheng. *Hai Rui baguan yu wenge* [Hai Rui Dismissed from Office and the Cultural Revolution]. Taipei: Yuan Liou Publishing Company Ltd., 2011.

Liu Wusheng, ed. *Zhou Enlai da cidian* [The Big Dictionary of Zhou Enlai]. Nanchang: Jiangxi Renmin Chubanshe, 1997.

Liu Zonghe and Lu Kewang. *Junshi qingbao: Zhongguo junshi baike quanshu (di er ban)* [Military Intelligence: China Military Encyclopedia (Second Edition)]. Beijing: Zhongguo Da Baike Quanshu Chubanshe, 2007.

Melton, H. Keith. *Zhongji jiandie* [Ultimate Spy]. Translated by Lu Tan and Wu Xiaomei. Beijing: Zhongguo Lvyou Chubanshe, 2005.

Mu Xin. *Chen Geng tongzhi zai Shanghai* [Comrade Chen Geng in Shanghai]. Beijing: Wenshi Zike Chubanshe, 1980.

_____. *Yinbi zhanxian tongshuai Zhou Enlai* [Zhou Enlai, Commander of the Hidden Battlefront]. Beijing: Zhongguo Qingnian Chubanshe, 2002.

Ni Xingyang, ed. *Zhongguo Gongchandang chuangjian shi* [A History of the Establishment of the CCP]. Shanghai: Shanghai Renmin Chubanshe, 2006.

Quan Yanchi. *Zhongguo miwen neimu* [Secrets and Insider Stories of China]. Lanzhou: Gansu Wenhua Chubanshe, 2004.

Sa Su. *Dongfang tegong zai xingdong* [Special Operations of the East in Action]. Shanghai: Wenhui Chubanshe, 2011.

Shi Zhe. *Zai lishi juren shenbian, Shi Zhe huiyi lu* [At the Side of History's Great People, the Memoirs of Shi Zhe]. Beijing: Zhongyang Wenxian Chubanshe, second ed., 1995.

Shu Yun. *Luo Ruiqing Dajiang* [General Luo Ruiqing]. Beijing: Jiefangjun Wenyi Chubanshe, second ed., 2011.

Sima Lu. *Zhonggong Lishi de Jianzheng* [Witnessing the Secret History of the Communist Party of China]. Hong Kong: Mirror Books, 2004.

Suimengqu Gonganshi changbian [A Public Security History of Suiyuan and Inner Mongolia in Draft]. Hohhot: Neimenggu Gongan Ting Gongan Shi Yanjiu Shi, 1986.

Sun Zi bing fa baihua jianjie [An Introduction to Sun Zi the Art of War in Colloquial Chinese]. Taipei: Wenguang Chubanshe, 1986.

Tian Changlie, ed. *Zhonggong Jilin shi Dangshi renwu* [Personalities in Party History in Jilin Municipality]. Jilin: Dongbei Shida Chubanshe, 1999.

Tong Xiaopeng. *Fengyu Sishinian (dierbu)* [Forty Years of Trials and Hardships, vol. 2]. Beijing: Zhongyang Wenxian Chubanshe, 1996.

Wang Fang. *Wang Fang huiyilu* [Memoirs of Wang Fang]. Hangzhou: Zhejiang Renmin Chubanshe, 2006.

Wang Junyan. *Liao Chengzhi zhuan* [The Biography of Liao Chengzhi]. Beijing: Renmin Chubanshe, 2006.

Yan Jinzhong, ed. *Junshi qingbao xue, xiuding ban* [Military Informatics, Revised Edition]. Beijing: Shishi Chubanshe, 2003.

Yin Qi. *Pan Hannian de qingbao shengya* [The Intelligence Career of Pan Hannian]. Beijing: Renmin Chubanshe, 1996.

Yu Botao. *Mimi zhencha wenti* [Issues of secret investigations]. Beijing: Zhongguo Jiancha Chubanshe, 2008.

Yu Tianming. *Hongse jiandie—daihao Bashan* [Red Spy—Code Name Bashan]. Beijing: Zuojia Chubanshe, 1993.

Zhang Shaohong and Xu Wenlong. *Hongse guoji tegong* [Red International Agents]. Haerbin: Haerbin Chubanshe, 2005.

Zhang Yun. *Pan Hannian zhuan* [Biography of Pan Hannian]. Shanghai: Shanghai Renmin Chubanshe, 1996.

Zhao Yongtian. *Huxue shuxun* [In the Lair of the Tiger]. Beijing: Junshi Kexue Chubanshe, 1994.

Zhong Kan. *Kang Sheng Pingzhuan* [A Critical Biography of Kang Sheng]. Beijing: Hongqi Chubanshe, 1982.

Zhonggong dangshi ziliao [Materials on CCP Party History]. Beijing: Zhonggong Dangshi Ziliao chubanshe, 1981.

Zhonggong zhongyang dangshi yanjiushi, Zhongguo Gongchandang lishi 1921–1949 [History of the Chinese Communist Party, 1921–1949]. Beijing: Zhonggong Zhongyang Dangshi Yanjiu Chubanshe, 2011.

Zhongguo ershi shiji jishi benmo [China's 20th Century History from Start to Finish, vol. 1, 1900–1926]. Jinan: Shandong Renmin Chubanshe, 1999.

Zhongguo Gongchandang lingdao jigou yange he chengyuan minglu [Directory of Organizations and Personnel of the Communist Party of China During the Revolution]. Beijing: Zhonggong Dangshi Chubanshe, 2000.

Zhongguo Gongchandang zuzhi shi ziliao, vol. 4, 1945.8–1949 [Materials on CCP Organizational History, vol. 4, August 1945–1949]. Beijing: Zhonggong Dangshi Chubanshe, 2000.

Zhongguo Renmin jingcha jianshi [A Brief History of Chinese People's Policing]. Beijing: Jingguan Jiaoyu Chubanshe, 1989.

Zhu Jiamu, ed. *Dangdai Zhongguo yu tade fazhan daolu* [Contemporary China and Its Developmental Road]. Beijing: Xiandai Zhongguo Xueyuan, Zhongguo Shehui Kexue Xueyuan, 2010.

Periodicals and Journals

Bainianchao [The Hundred Year Tide]. Beijing: Zhonggong Zhongyang Dangshi Yanjiushi, 1997.

Dang de wenxian [The Party's Documents]. Beijing: Zhongyang Wenxian Chubanshe, 1988.

Dangdai Zhongguoshi yanjiu [Contemporary Chinese History Research]. Beijing: Dangdai Zhongguo Chubanshe, 1994.

Zhonggong dangshi tongxun [CCP History Bulletin]. Beijing: Zhonggong Dangshi Chubanshe, 1989–96.

Zhonggong dangshi yanjiu [The Study of Chinese Communist History]. Beijing: Zhonggong Dangshi Chubanshe, 1988.

Articles

Ding Ke. "Tegong-minyun-Falungong: yi ge shengming de zhenshi gushi" [Secret Agent–Democracy Movement–Falungong: The True Story of a Life]. *Ming Hui Net*, September 12, 2003, http://www.minghui.org/mh/articles/2003/9/12/57232.html.

"Guo'an bu die bao renyuan 10 wan ren: guowai 4 wan duo guonei 5 wan duo" [Ministry of State Security espionage personnel number 100,000 with more than 40,000 abroad and 50,000 at home]. *China Digital Times*, June 1, 2015, https://chinadigitaltimes.net/chinese/2015/06/内幕 | 国安部谍报人员10万人：国外4万多国内5万多/.

Hui Guisong. "Aomen Zhonggong dixia dang ren Ke Lin" [Ke Lin of the Macau CCP Underground Party]. *Guangxi Shenji*, no. 5 (1999): 34.

Luo Yanming. "Chen Yun, Kang Sheng yu Yan'an ganbu shencha" [Chen Yun, Kang Sheng, and the Yan'an Cadre Examination]. *Dangshi bolan*, no. 8, 2010.

Sun Guoda. "Wo Dang qingbao shishang de yici da jienan" [A catastrophe in the history of our party's intelligence services]. *Beijing Ribao*, August 31, 2009, http://blog.sina.com.cn/s/blog_4447da480102x97r.html.

"Waijiao bu jie mi 'Keshenmi'er gongzhu hao' Zhou Zongli zuoji bei zha an" [Ministry of Foreign Affairs unveils secret case on the bombing of Zhou Enlai's plane the Kashmir Princess]. China.com. http://www.china.com.cn/chinese/TR-c/614445.htm.

Xue Yu. "Guanyu Zhonggong Zhongyang Teke ruogan wenti de tantao" [An investigation into certain issues regarding the CCP Central Committee Special Branch]. *Zhonggong Dangshi Yanjiu* [The Study of Chinese Communist History] no. 3, 1999.

Reference Works

Chen Yun. *Chen Yun wenxian, 1926–1949* [Works of Chen Yun, 1926–1949]. Beijing: Renmin Chubanshe, 1984.

_____. *Chen Yun wenxian, di 3 juan* [Selected Works of Chen Yun, vol. 3]. Beijing: Renmin Chubanshe, 1995.

Chen Yun nianpu, 1905–1995, xia juan [Annals of Chen Yun, 1905–1995, vol. 3]. Beijing: Zhongyang Wenxian Chubanshe, 2000.

Kang Sheng. "Qiangjiu shizu zhe—Kang Sheng zai Zhongyang zhishu dahui de baogao" [Rescue Those Who Have Lost Their Footing—Kang Sheng's Report to Units Subordinate to the Central Committee], July 15, 1943. In Zhongguo Renmin Jiefangjun Guofang Daxue Dangshi Dangjian Zhonggong Jiaoyan Shi, ed. *Zhonggong Dangshi Jiaoxue Cankao Ziliao* [Reference Materials for the History of the CCP, vol. 17]. Beijing: n.p., n.d.

Liu Shufa, ed. *Chen Yi nianpu* [The Annals of Chen Yi, vol. 2]. Beijing: Renmin Chubanshe, 1995.

Shen Xueming, ed. *Zhonggong diyi jie zhi diwu jie Zhongyang weiyuan* [Central Committee Members from the First CCP Congress to the Fifteenth]. Beijing: Zhongyang Wenxian Chubanshe, 2001.

Wang Jianying, ed. *Zhongguo Gongchandang zuzhi shi ziliao huibian* [Compilation of Materials on CCP Organizational History]. Beijing: Hongqi Chubanshe, 1983.

Xiao Zhihao. *Zhonggong tegong* [Chinese Communist Special Operations]. Beijing: Shidai Wenxian Chubanshe, 2010.

Xu Zehao, ed. *Wang Jiaxiang nianpu* [Annals of Wang Jiaxiang]. Beijing: Zhong-yang Wenxian Chubanshe, 2001.

Yang Shangkun. *Yang Shangkun riji, Shang* [The Diary of Yang Shangkun, vol. 1]. Beijing: Zhongyang Wenxian Chubanshe, 2001.

Yang Shengqun, ed. *Deng Xiaoping nianpu, 1904–1974* [Annals of Deng Xiaoping, 1904–1974]. 3 vols. Beijing: Zhongyang Wenxian Chubanshe, 2009.

Zeng Qinghong, ed. *Zhongguo gongchandang zuzhishi ziliao* [Materials on Chinese Communist Organizational History, vol. 4, no. 1]. Beijing: Zhongguo Gongchandang Zuzhishi Ziliao Bianshen Weiyuanhui, 2000.

Zhonggong dangshi dashi nianbao [Chronology of Major Events in CCP History]. Beijing: Renmin Chubanshe, 1987.

Zhonggong dangshi renwu zhuan [Biographies of Personalities in Chinese Communist Party History]. Vols. 1–60: Xi'an: Shaanxi Renmin Chubanshe, 1980–96; Vols. 61 onward, Beijing: Zhongyang Wenxian Chubanshe, 1997.

Zhonggong zhongyang wenjian xuanji [Selected Documents of the CCP Central Committee]. Beijing: Zhonggong Zhongyang Dangxiao Chubanshe, 1992.

Zhongguo gongchandang zuzhi shi ziliao [CCP Materials on Organizational History]. Beijing: Zhonggong Dangshi Chubanshe, 2000.

Zhonghua renmin gonghe guo di er jixie gongye bu [PRC Second Ministry of Machine Building], ed. *Zhongyao wenjian huibian* [Assembly of Important Documents]. Beijing: Second Ministry of Machine Building, July 1955.

Zhou, Jinyu Cathy. *Wode zhangfu Jin Wudai zhi si* [The death of my husband Jin Wudai]. Taipei: Dong Huang Wenhua Chuban Shiye Gongsi, 1998.

Zhou Enlai nianpu 1898–1949 [Annals of Zhou Enlai, 1898–1949]. Beijing: Zhongyang Wenxian Chubanshe, 1989.

Zhou Enlai nianpu 1949–1976 [Annals of Zhou Enlai, 1949–1976]. 3 vols. Beijing: Zhongyang Wenxian Chubanshe, 1997.

Online Sources

The Chinese Mirror: A Journal of Chinese Film History. http://www.chinesemirror.com/.

Ding Shaoping. "Mao Zedong zhishi zhuzhi yisheng shishi 'yaowu zhuzhe duhai' Wang Ming?" [Did Mao Zedong Order Attending Physicians to Gradually Poison Wang Ming?], December 29, 2011. http://history.people.com.cn/GB/205396/16752903.html.

"Hongse tegong Qian Zhuangfei" [Red Special Agent Qian Zhuangfei]. *Renmin-wang,* http://dangshi.people.com.cn/GB/144964/145470/8859544.html.

"Mao Zedong zan hongse tegong Zeng Xisheng: meiyou tade erju, jiu meiyou Hongjun" [Mao Zedong Praised Red Special Agent Zeng Xisheng: Without

His 2d Bureau There Would Be No Red Army]. Beijing Ribao, March 22, 2010, https://wenku.baidu.com/view/b22235b91a37f111f1855b4b.html.

"On Questions of Party History—Resolution on Certain Questions in the History of Our Party Since the Founding of the People's Republic of China," June 27, 1981. *Zhongguo Gongchandang xinwen wang* [CCP News Network], http://english.cpc.people.com.cn/66095/4471924.html.

Xu, Aihua. "Zhongguo de Fu'er Mosi: Yuan Gongan buzhang Zhao Cangbi de Yan'an baowei gongzuo" [China's Sherlock Holmes: Former MPS Minister Zhao Cangbi's Protection Work in Yan'an]. *Renminwang*, November 12, 2009, http://dangshi.people.com.cn/GB/85038/10366238.html.

"Yifen juemi qingbao cushi hongjun tiaoshang changzhenglu" [Secret Intelligence Prompted Red Army to Embark on Long March]. *Zhongguo Gongchandang xinwen wang* [CCP News Network], http://dangshi.people.com.cn/GB/144956/9090941.html.

Films and Television Programs

Chen Yingqi, director. *Guojia mimi* [State Secrets]. Jiangsu Tianlong Culture Media Development (Skylong.com.cn), 2004. A television series in twenty-four episodes.

Nv jiaotong yuan [The Woman Courier]. Changchun dianying zhipian chang, 1978.

Zhang Xin, director. *Zhonggong dixia dang* [The Chinese Communist Underground], 2008. A television series in twenty episodes.

Primary Chinese Sources in English
Books and Monographs

Chen Yun. *Selected Works of Chen Yun, 1926–1949*. Beijing: Foreign Languages Press, 1988.

Chiang Kai-shek. *Soviet Russia in China*. New York: Farrar, Straus and Cudahy, 1957.

Compton, Boyd, ed. *Mao's China, Party Reform Documents, 1942–1944*. Seattle: University of Washington Press, 1952.

Ji Chaozhu. *The Man on Mao's Right*. New York: Random House, 2008.

Kuo, Warren. *Analytical History of the Chinese Communist Party*, 4 vols. Taipei: Institute of International Relations, 1968, 1970, 1971.

Li Zhisui. *The Private Life of Chairman Mao: The Memoirs of Mao's Personal Physician*. London: Chatto and Windus, 1994.

Mao Tse-tung [Mao Zedong]. *Selected Military Writings of Mao Tse-tung*. Beijing: Foreign Languages Press, 1963.

_____. *Selected Works of Mao Tse-tung,* vol. 1. Beijing: Foreign Languages Press, 1965.

_____. *Selected Works of Mao Tse-tung,* 5 vols. New York: International Publishers, 1954.

Saich, Tony, ed. *The Rise to Power of the Chinese Communist Party: Documents and Analysis.* Armonk, NY: M. E. Sharpe, 1996.

Schram, Stuart, Nancy Hodes, and Stephen C. Averill. *Mao's Road to Power: Revolutionary Writings, 1912–1949,* vol. 4. Armonk, NY: M. E. Sharpe, 1992.

T'ang Liang-li. *Suppressing Communist Banditry in China.* Shanghai: China United Press, 1934.

Wilbur, C. Martin, and Julie Lien-ying How. *Documents on Communism, Nationalism, and Soviet Advisors in China, 1918–1927: Papers Seized in the 1927 Peking Raid.* New York: Columbia University Press, 1956.

Xu Enzeng [U. T. Hsu]. *The Invisible Conflict.* Hong Kong: China Viewpoints, 1958.

Zhang Guotao [Chang Kuo-t'ao]. *The Rise of the Chinese Communist Party, 1928–1938.* Lawrence: University Press of Kansas, 1972.

Secondary Sources

Books and Monographs

Allen, Maury. *China Spy: The Story of Hugh Francis Redmond.* New York: Gazette Press, 1998.

Andrew, Christopher, and Vasili Mitrokhin. *The Sword and the Shield: The Mitrokhin Archive and the Secret History of the KGB.* New York: Basic Books, 1999.

Barme, Geremie R. *In the Red: On Contemporary Chinese Culture.* New York: Columbia University Press, 1999.

Barnouin, Barbara, and Yu Changgen. *Chinese Foreign Policy during the Cultural Revolution.* London: Kegan Paul International, 1998.

_____. *Zhou Enlai: A Political Life.* Hong Kong: Chinese University of Hong Kong, 2006.

Barrett, David D. *Dixie Mission: The United States Army Observer Group in Yenan, 1944.* Berkeley: University of California Center for Chinese Studies, 1970.

Benton, Gregor. *New Fourth Army: Communist Resistance Along the Yangtze and Huai, 1938–1941.* Richmond, Surrey: Curzon Press, 1999.

Booth, Robert David. *State Department Counterintelligence: Leaks, Spies, and Lies.* Dallas, TX: Brown Books Publishing Group, 2014.

Botas, João F. O. *Macau 1937–1945, os Anos da Guerra* [Macau 1937–1945, the war years]. Macau: Instituto Internacional de Macau, 2012.

Brady, Anne-Marie. *Making the Foreign Serve China: Managing Foreigners in the People's Republic.* Lanham, MD: Rowman and Littlefield, 2003.

Braun, Otto. *A Comintern Agent in China, 1932–1939.* St. Lucia, Australia: University of Queensland Press, 1982.

Byron, John, and Robert Pack. *The Claws of the Dragon: Kang Sheng—The Evil Genius Behind Mao—and His Legacy of Terror in People's China.* New York: Simon and Schuster, 1992.

Carl, Leo D. *CIA Insider's Dictionary of U.S. and Foreign Intelligence, Counterintelligence, and Tradecraft.* Washington, DC: NIBC Press, 1996.

Chan Lau Kit-ching. *From Nothing to Nothing: The Chinese Communist Movement in Hong Kong, 1921–1936.* New York: St. Martin's Press, 1999.

Chan Sui-jeung. *East River Column: Hong Kong Guerrillas in the Second World War and After.* Hong Kong: Hong Kong University Press, 2009.

Conquest, Robert. *The Great Terror: A Reassessment.* New York: Oxford University Press, 1991.

_____. *Inside Stalin's Secret Police: NKVD Politics 1936–1939.* London: MacMillan Press Ltd., 1985.

Deacon, Richard. *The Chinese Secret Service.* New York: Taplinger Publishing, 1974.

DeVore, Howard. *China's Intelligence and Internal Security Forces.* Coulsdon, UK: Jane's Information Group, 1999.

Dunham, Mikel. *Buddha's Warriors: The Story of the CIA-Backed Tibetan Freedom Fighters, the Chinese Communist Invasion, and the Ultimate Fall of Tibet.* New York: Jeremy Tarcher Inc., 2014.

Dutton, Michael. *Policing Chinese Politics.* Durham and London: Duke University Press, 2005.

Dzhirkvelov, Ilya. *Secret Servant: My Life with the KGB and the Soviet Elite.* London: Collins, 1987.

Dziak, John J. *Chekisty: A History of the KGB.* Lanham, MD: Lexington Books, 1988.

Easton, Ian. *The Chinese Invasion Threat: Taiwan's Defense and America's Strategy in Asia.* Arlington, VA: Project 2019 Institute, 2017.

Eftimiades, Nicholas. *Chinese Intelligence Operations.* Annapolis, MD: Naval Institute Press, 1994.

Fairbank, John K., ed. *The Cambridge History of China*, Vols. 12 and 13, *Republican China 1912–1949, Parts I and II.* Cambridge: Cambridge University Press, 1983.

_____. *The Cambridge History of China*, Vol. 15, *The People's Republic, Part 2: Revolutions Within the Chinese Revolution 1966–1982.* Cambridge: Cambridge University Press, 1991.

_____. *The Great Chinese Revolution 1800–1985*. New York: Harper and Row, 1986.

Faligot, Roger. *Les Services Secrets Chinois de Mao aux Jo* [The Chinese Secret Services of Mao and Zhou]. Paris: Nouveau Monde, 2008.

Faligot, Roger, and Remi Kauffer. *The Chinese Secret Service*. London: Headline Book Publishing, 1990.

Forsyth, Frederick. *The Outsider: My Life in Intrigue*. New York: Putnam, 2015.

Gao Wenqian. *Zhou Enlai: The Last Perfect Revolutionary*. New York: BBS Public Affairs, 2007.

Garside, Roger. *Coming Alive! China after Mao*. New York: McGraw-Hill, 1981.

Garver, John W. *Chinese-Soviet Relations, 1937–1945: The Diplomacy of Chinese Nationalism*. New York: Oxford University Press, 1988.

Gertz, Bill. *Enemies: How America's Foes Steal Our Vital Secrets—and How We Let It Happen*. New York: Crown Forum, 2006.

Gleason, Gene. *Hong Kong*. New York: John Day Company, 1963.

Guedes, João. *Macau Confidencial*. Macau: Instituto Internacional Macau, 2015.

Gunn, Geoffrey C. *Encountering Macau: A Portuguese City-State on the Periphery of China, 1557–1999*. Boulder, CO: Westview Press, 1996.

Guo Xuezhi. *China's Security State: Philosophy, Evolution, and Politics*. Cambridge: Cambridge University Press, 2012.

Hannas, William, James Mulvenon, and Anna B. Puglisi. *Chinese Industrial Espionage: Technology Acquisition and Military Modernization*. New York: Routledge, 2013.

Hart, John N. *The Making of an Army "Old China Hand": A Memoir of Colonel David D. Barrett*. Berkeley: University of California Institute of East Asian Studies, 1985.

Haynes, John Earl, and Harvey Klehr. *In Denial: Historians, Communism, and Espionage*. San Francisco: Encounter Books, 2003.

_____. *Venona: Decoding Soviet Espionage in America*. New Haven, CT: Yale University Press, 1999.

Hoffman, Tod. *The Spy Within*. Hanover, NH: Steerforth Press, 2008.

Hsu Kai-yu. *Chou En-lai, China's Gray Eminence*. New York: Doubleday, 1968.

Hyman, Bruce G. *Chinese-English English-Chinese Information Technology Glossary, Second Edition*. Springfield, VA: Dunwoody Press, 2013.

Johnson, Chalmers, ed. *Ideology and Politics in Contemporary China*. Seattle: University of Washington Press, 1973.

Klehr, Harvey, John Earl Haynes, and Fridrikh Firsov. *The Secret World of American Communism*. New Haven, CT: Yale University Press, 1993.

Knaus, John Kenneth. *Orphans of the Cold War: America and the Tibetan Struggle for Survival.* New York: Public Affairs, 2000.

Kotani, Ken. *Japanese Intelligence in World War II.* Oxford: Botely Publishing, 2009.

Lampton, David, ed. *The Making of Chinese Foreign and Security Policy in the Era of Reform, 1978–2000.* Stanford, CA: Stanford University Press, 2001.

Lee Chae-Jin. *Zhou Enlai: The Early Years.* Stanford, CA: Stanford University Press, 1994.

Leonard, Raymond W. *Secret Soldiers of the Revolution.* Westport, CT: Greenwood Press, 1999.

Li Tien-min. *Chou En-lai.* Taipei: Institute of International Relations, 1970.

Li Xiaobing. *China at War: An Encyclopedia.* Santa Barbara, CA: ABC CLIO, 2012.

Lindsay, Jon R., Tai-ming Cheung, and Derek S. Reveron. *China and Cybersecurity: Espionage, Strategy, and Politics in the Digital Domain.* New York: Oxford University Press, 2015.

Lilley, James, and Jeffrey Lilley. *China Hands: Nine Decades of Adventure, Espionage, and Diplomacy in Asia.* New York: Public Affairs, 2004.

Lima, Fernando. *Macau: as duas Transições* [Macau: The Two Transitions]. Macau: Fundação Macau, 1999.

Lindsay, Michael. *The Unknown War: North China 1937–1945.* London: Bergstrom and Boyle Books, 1975.

Loh, Christine. *Underground Front: The Chinese Communist Party in Hong Kong.* Pokfulam: Hong Kong University Press, 2010.

MacFarquhar, Roderick. *The Origins of the Cultural Revolution,* Vol. 2: *The Great Leap Forward 1958–1960.* New York: Columbia University Press, 1983.

_____. *The Origins of the Cultural Revolution,* Vol. 3: *The Coming of the Cataclysm 1961–1966.* New York: Columbia University Press, 1997.

MacFarquhar, Roderick, ed. *The Politics of China: Sixty Years of the People's Republic of China.* Third ed. Cambridge: Cambridge University Press, 2011.

MacFarquhar, Roderick, and Michael Schoenhals. *Mao's Last Revolution.* Cambridge, MA: Harvard University Press, 2006.

Marques, Vasco Silverio, and Anibal Mesquita Borges. *O Ouro no Eixo Hong Kong Macau, 1946–1973* [The Gold on the Axis of Hong Kong and Macau, 1946–1973]. Macau: Instituto Português do Oriente, 2012.

May, Ernest, ed. *Knowing One's Enemies: Intelligence Assessment before the Two World Wars.* Princeton: Princeton University Press, 1986.

McGregor, Richard. *The Party: The Secret World of China's Communist Rulers.* London: Penguin Press, 2010.

McReynolds, Joe, ed. *China's Evolving Military Strategy*. Washington, DC: The Jamestown Foundation, 2016.

Meisner, Maurice. *Mao's China and After: A History of the People's Republic*. New York: The Free Press, 1999.

Nathan, Andrew, and Andrew Scobell. *China's Search for Security*. New York: Columbia University Press, 2012.

Nelson, Steve, James R. Barrett, and Rob Ruck. *Steve Nelson, American Radical*. Pittsburgh: University of Pittsburgh Press, 1981.

Ownby, David, ed. *Secret Societies Reconsidered: Perspectives on the Social History of Modern South China and Southeast Asia*. Armonk, NY: M. E. Sharpe, 1993.

Pantsov, Alexander V., and Steven I. Levine. *Deng Xiaoping: A Revolutionary Life*. New York: Oxford University Press, 2015.

———. *Mao: The Real Story*. New York: Simon and Schuster, 2002.

Perry, Elizabeth. *Shanghai on Strike: The Politics of Chinese Labor*. Stanford, CA: Stanford University Press, 1993.

Pollpeter, Kevin, and Kenneth W. Allen, eds. *The People's Liberation Army as Organization 2.0*. Vienna, VA: DGI Inc., 2015.

Polmar, Norman, and Thomas B. Allen. *The Encyclopedia of Espionage*. New York: Gramercy Books, 1997.

Pomfret, John. *The Beautiful Country and the Middle Kingdom*. New York: Henry Holt, 2016.

Porter, Edgar A. *The People's Doctor: George Hatem and the Chinese Revolution*. Honolulu: University of Hawaii Press, 1997.

Richelson, Jeffrey T. *A Century of Spies: Intelligence in the Twentieth Century*. New York: Oxford University Press, 1997.

Rittenberg, Sidney, and Amanda Bennett. *The Man Who Stayed Behind*. New York: Simon and Schuster, 1993.

Roche, Edward M. *Snake Fish: The Chi Mak Spy Ring*. New York: Barraclough, 2008.

Saich, Tony, and Hans Van de Ven, eds. *New Perspectives on the Chinese Communist Revolution*. Armonk, NY: M. E. Sharpe, 1995.

Salisbury, Harrison E. *The Long March: The Untold Story*. New York: Harper and Row, 1985.

Schell, Orville, and John Delury. *Wealth and Power: China's Long March to the Twenty-First Century*. New York: Random House, 2013.

Schoenhals, Michael. *Spying for the People: Mao's Secret Agents, 1949–1967*. New York: Cambridge University Press, 2013.

Schwar, Harriet Dashiell, ed. *Foreign Relations of the United States, 1964–1968.* Vol. 30: *China.* Washington, DC: Government Printing Office, 1998.

Shambaugh, David. *Modernizing China's Military: Progress, Problems, and Prospects.* Berkeley: University of California Press, 2002.

Share, Michael. *Where Empires Collided: Russian and Soviet Relations with Hong Kong, Taiwan, and Macao.* Hong Kong: Chinese University Press, 2007.

Short, Philip. *Mao: A Life.* New York: Henry Holt, 2000.

Snow, Edgar. *Random Notes on Red China (1936–1945).* Cambridge, MA: Harvard University Press, 1957.

_____. *Red Star Over China.* London: Victor Gollancz Ltd., 1938.

Soeya, Yoshihide. *Japan's Economic Diplomacy with China, 1945–1978.* Oxford: Clarendon Press, 1998.

Spence, Jonathan D. *The Search for Modern China.* New York: W. W. Norton and Co., 1999.

Sun Shuyun. *The Long March: The True History of Communist China's Founding Myth.* New York: Doubleday, 2006.

Swaine, Michael D., and Zhang Tuosheng with Danielle F. S. Cohen, eds. *Managing Sino-American Crises: Case Studies and Analysis.* Washington, DC: Brookings Institution Press, 2006.

Taylor, Jay. *The Generalissimo: Chiang Kai-shek and the Struggle for Modern China.* Cambridge, MA: The Belknap Press of Harvard University, 2009.

Teiwes, Frederick C. *Politics and Purges in China: Rectification and the Decline of Party Norms, 1950–65.* Armonk, NY: M. E. Sharpe, 1979.

_____. *Politics at Mao's Court: Gao Gang and Party Factionalism in the Early 1950s.* Armonk, NY: M. E. Sharpe, 1990.

Teiwes, Frederick C., and Warren Sun. *The Formation of the Maoist Leadership: From the Return of Wang Ming to the Seventh Party Congress.* London: Contemporary China Institute Research Notes and Studies, 1994.

_____. *The End of the Maoist Era: Chinese Politics During the Twilight of the Cultural Revolution.* Armonk, NY: M. E. Sharpe, 2007.

Trahair, Richard. *Encyclopedia of Cold War Espionage, Spies, and Secret Operations.* Westport, CT: Greenwood Press, 2004.

Unger, Jonathan, ed. *Using the Past to Serve the Present: Historiography and Politics in Contemporary China.* Armonk, NY: M. E. Sharpe, 1994.

Van de Ven, Hans. *War and Nationalism in China 1925–1945.* London: Routledge Curzon, 2003.

_____. *Warfare in Chinese History.* Boston: Brill, 2000.

Vladimirov, Peter. *China's Special Area, 1942–1945*. Bombay: Allied Publishers, 1974.

_____. *The Vladimirov Diaries, Yenan, China: 1942–1945*. New York: Doubleday and Company, 1975.

Wadler, Joyce. *Liaison: The Real Story of the Affair that Inspired M. Butterfly*. New York: Bantam Books, 1994.

Wakeman, Frederic, Jr. *Policing Shanghai 1927–1937*. Berkeley: University of California Press, 1995.

_____. *Spymaster: Dai Li and the Chinese Secret Service*. Berkeley: University of California Press, 2003.

Wasserstein, Bernard. *Secret War in Shanghai*. London: Profile Books, 1998.

Wasserstrom, Jeffrey S., ed. *Twentieth Century China: New Approaches*. London: Routledge, 2003.

Weatherly, Robert. *Mao's Forgotten Successor: The Political Career of Hua Guofeng*. New York: Palgrave Macmillan, 2010.

Werner, Ruth. *Sonya's Report*. London: Chatto and Windus, 1991.

Wesley-Smith, Peter. *Unequal Treaty 1898–1997: China, Great Britain, and Hong Kong's New Territories*. Hong Kong: Oxford University Press, 1980.

Westad, Odd Arne. *Decisive Encounters: The Chinese Civil War, 1946–1950*. Stanford, CA: Stanford University Press, 2003.

Whiting, Kenneth R. *The Soviet Union Today: A Concise Handbook*. New York: Praeger, 1966.

Whymant, Robert. *Stalin's Spy: Richard Sorge and the Tokyo Espionage Ring*. New York: St. Martin's Press, 1996.

Wise, David. *Tiger Trap: America's Secret Spy War with China*. New York: Houghton Mifflin Harcourt, 2011.

Wortzel, Larry, and Robin Higham. *Dictionary of Contemporary Chinese Military History*. Santa Barbara, CA: ABC CLIO, 1999.

Yang, Benjamin. *Deng: A Political Biography*. Armonk, NY: M. E. Sharpe, 1998.

Yeh Wen-hsin, ed. *Wartime Shanghai*. London: Routledge, 1996.

Yick, Joseph Y. S. *Making Urban Revolution in China: The CCP-GMD Struggle for Beiping and Tianjin, 1945–1949*. Armonk, NY: M. E. Sharpe, 1995.

Yu Maochun. *The Dragon's War: Allied Operations and the Fate of China, 1937–1945*. Annapolis: Naval Institute Press, 2006.

_____. *OSS in China: Prelude to Cold War*. New Haven, CT: Yale University Press, 1996.

Zhang Shu Guang. *Deterrence and Strategic Culture: Chinese-American Confrontations, 1949–1958*. Ithaca: Cornell University Press, 1992.

Articles and Chapters

Bakken, Børge, "Transition, Age, and Inequality: Core Causes of Chinese Crime," delivered at the 20th International Conference of the Hong Kong Sociological Association, Chinese University of Hong Kong, December 1, 2018.

Bernstein, Richard. "At China's Ministry of Truth, History Is Quickly Rewritten." *New York Times*, June 12, 1989.

Bickers, Robert. "Changing Shanghai's 'Mind': Publicity, Reform, and the British in Shanghai, 1928–1931." China Society Occasional Papers no. 26, 1992.

Branigan, Tania. "Authorities in Lhasa Parade Repentant Rioters on TV." *The Guardian* (London), March 20, 2008.

Brazil, Matthew. "Addressing Rising Business Risk in China." *China Brief* 16, issue 8, May 2016.

———. "China." *The Encyclopedia of Intelligence and Counterintelligence.* Armonk, NY: M. E. Sharpe Reference, 2005.

Burns, John. "The Structure of Communist Party Control in Hong Kong." *Asian Survey* 30, no. 8, August 1990.

Chambers, David. "Edging in from the Cold: The Past and Present State of Chinese Intelligence Historiography." *Studies in Intelligence* 56, no. 3 (2012).

"Communist Party's Vengeance, Wholesale Murders, Amazing Story from Shanghai." *Straits Times* (Singapore), December 9, 1931, http://newspapers.nl.sg /Digitised/Article/straitstimes19311209.2.73.aspx.

Dujmovic, Nicholas. "Two CIA Prisoners in China, 1952–1973: Extraordinary Fidelity." *Studies in Intelligence* 50, no. 4, 2006.

Giffin, Peter. "*The Vladimirov Diaries* by Peter Vladimirov." *The Western Political Quarterly* 29, no. 3, September 1976.

Gill, Bates, and James Mulvenon. "Chinese Military-Related Think Tanks and Research Institutes." *The China Quarterly*, no. 171, September 2002.

Hoffman, Samantha, and Peter Mattis. "Managing the Power Within: China's Central State Security Commission." *War on the Rocks*, July 18, 2016, https:// warontherocks.com/2016/07/managing-the-power-within-chinas-state-security-commission/.

Kania, Elsa, and Peter Mattis. "Modernizing Military Intelligence: Playing Catchup (Part Two)." *China Brief* 16, issue 9, December 21, 2016.

Kelton, Mark. "Putin's Bold Attempt to Deny Skripal Attack." *The Cipher Brief*, September 19, 2018, https://www.thecipherbrief.com/putins-bold-attempt-to-deny-skripal-attack.

Lam, Willy Wo-Lap. "Jiang and Li Grasp Control of Security; Proteges of President and Premier Moved Up." *South China Morning Post*, March 2, 1998.

_____. "Meeting Endorses New Leadership for Army; Seal of Approval for New Military Lineup." *South China Morning Post*, October 19, 1992.

_____. "Security Boss Tipped to Leap Forward." *South China Morning Post*, May 29, 1997.

_____. "Surprise Elevation for Conservative Patriarch's Protégé Given Security Post." *South China Morning Post*, March 17, 1998.

_____. "Zhu Cabinet a Blend of Four Generations; Leaders Have Say in Achieving Factional Balance." *South China Morning Post*, March 19, 1998.

Li Hong. "The Truth Behind the Kashmir Princess Incident." In Zhang Xingxing, ed., *Selected Essays on the History of Contemporary China*. Leiden: Brill, 2015.

Link, Perry. "Waiting for Wikileaks: Beijing's Seven Secrets." *The New York Review of Books*, August 19, 2010.

Litten, F. S. "The Noulens Case." *The China Quarterly*, no. 138, 1994.

Louie, Genny, and Kam Louie. "The Role of Nanjing University in the Nanjing Incident." *The China Quarterly*, no. 86, 1981.

Mattis, Peter. "The Analytic Challenge of Understanding Chinese Intelligence Services." *Studies in Intelligence* 3, no. 56, September 2012, https://www.cia.gov/library/center-for-the-study-of-intelligence/csi-publications/csi-studies/studies/vol.-56-no.-3/pdfs/Mattis-Understanding%20Chinese%20Intel.pdf.

_____. "Assessing the Foreign Policy Influence of the Ministry of State Security." *China Brief* 11, issue 1, January 14, 2011, https://jamestown.org/program/assessing-the-foreign-policy-influence-of-the-ministry-of-state-security/.

_____. "Everything We Know About China's Secretive State Security Bureau." *The National Interest*, July 9, 2017, http://nationalinterest.org/feature/everything-we-know-about-chinas-secretive-state-security-21459.

_____. "New Law Reshapes Chinese Counterterrorism Policy and Operations." *China Brief*, January 25, 2016, https://jamestown.org/program/new-law-reshapes-chinese-counterterrorism-policy-and-operations/.

_____. "PLA Personnel Shifts Highlight Intelligence's Growing Military Role." *China Brief*, November 5, 2012, https://jamestown.org/program/pla-personnel-shifts-highlight-intelligences-growing-military-role/.

Moore, Paul. "Chinese Culture and the Practice of 'Actuarial' Intelligence." http://www.asiancrime.org/pdfdocs/Actuarial_Intelligence_by_Paul_Moore.pdf.

Sapio, Flora. "*Shuanggui* and Extralegal Detention in China." *China Information* 22, no. 8, 2007, http://cin.sagepub.com/content/22/1/7.

Schoenhals, Michael. "A Brief History of the CID of the CCP" (in Chinese). In Zhu Jiamu, ed. *Dangdai Zhongguo yu tade fazhan daolu* [Contemporary China and Its Development Road]. Beijing: Contemporary China Institute and Chinese Academy of Social Sciences, 2010.

Schwarck, Edward. "Intelligence and Informatization: The Rise of the Ministry of Public Security in Intelligence Work in China." *The China Journal* 80, July 1, 2018.

Seybolt, Peter J. "Terror and Conformity, Counterespionage Campaigns, Rectification, and Mass Movement, 1942–1943." *Modern China* 12, no. 1, January 1986.

Teiwes, Frederick C. "Mao Zedong in Power (1949–1976)." In William A. Joseph, ed., *Politics in China: An Introduction*. Oxford: Oxford University Press, 2010.

———. "Political Personae, Biographical Profiles." In Colin Mackerras, ed., *Dictionary of the Politics of the People's Republic of China*. London: Routledge, 2001.

Tsang, Steve. "Target Zhou Enlai: The 'Kashmir Princess' Incident of 1955." *The China Quarterly* no. 139, September 1994.

Wylie, Ray. "The Vladimirov Diaries. Yenan, China: 1942–1945 by Peter Vladimirov." *Slavic Review* 36, no. 2, June 1977.

Biographical Directories

Bartke, Wolfgang. *Who's Who in the People's Republic of China*. Armonk, NY: M. E. Sharpe, 1981.

Boorman, Howard L. *Biographical Dictionary of Republican China*. 4 vols. New York: Columbia University Press, 1970.

Chang Jun-mei, ed. *Chinese Communist Who's Who*. 2 vols. Taipei: Institute for International Relations, 1970.

Klein, Donald W., and Anne B. Clark. *Biographic Dictionary of Chinese Communism 1921–1965*. 2 vols. Cambridge, MA: Harvard University Press, 1971.

Lamb, Malcolm. *Directory of Officials and Organizations in China: A Quarter-Century Guide*. Armonk, NY: M. E. Sharpe, 1994.

Who's Who in Communist China. Hong Kong: Union Research Institute, 1966.

Unpublished MA Theses

Mattis, Peter L. "Chinese Intelligence Operations Reconsidered: Toward a New Baseline." Georgetown University, April 2011.

Reynolds, David Anthony. "A Comparative Analysis of the Respective Roles and Power of the KGB and the Chinese Intelligence/Security Apparatus in Domestic Politics." Brown University, May 1984.

Miscellaneous Original Sources

Benson, Robert L. *The Venona Story.* Fort Meade, MD: Center for Cryptologic History, undated, https://www.nsa.gov/Portals/70/documents/about/crypto logic-heritage/historical-figures-publications/publications/coldwar/ven ona_story.pdf.

Central Intelligence Agency. "Beijing Institute for International Strategic Studies Established," December 14, 1979, CIA Electronic Reading Room, https:// www.cia.gov/library/readingroom/docs/DOC_0001257059.pdf.

_____. "Communist China: The Political Security Apparatus." POLO 35, February 20, 1969 (declassified).

◆ Index ◆

◆ About the Authors ◆

Peter Mattis is the deputy staff director of the Congressional Executive Commission on China (CECC). He previously was a fellow at The Jamestown Foundation and edited its biweekly *China Brief* from 2011 to 2013. He also worked as a counterintelligence analyst at the Central Intelligence Agency.

Matthew Brazil, PhD, is a nonresident Fellow at The Jamestown Foundation. He worked in Asia for more than twenty years as an Army officer, American diplomat, and corporate security investigator. He is the account manager for a security firm at an American technology company in the San Francisco Bay area.

The Naval Institute Press is the book-publishing arm of the U.S. Naval Institute, a private, nonprofit, membership society for sea service professionals and others who share an interest in naval and maritime affairs. Established in 1873 at the U.S. Naval Academy in Annapolis, Maryland, where its offices remain today, the Naval Institute has members worldwide.

Members of the Naval Institute support the education programs of the society and receive the influential monthly magazine *Proceedings* or the colorful bimonthly magazine *Naval History* and discounts on fine nautical prints and on ship and aircraft photos. They also have access to the transcripts of the Institute's Oral History Program and get discounted admission to any of the Institute-sponsored seminars offered around the country.

The Naval Institute's book-publishing program, begun in 1898 with basic guides to naval practices, has broadened its scope to include books of more general interest. Now the Naval Institute Press publishes about seventy titles each year, ranging from how-to books on boating and navigation to battle histories, biographies, ship and aircraft guides, and novels. Institute members receive significant discounts on the Press' more than eight hundred books in print.

Full-time students are eligible for special half-price membership rates. Life memberships are also available.

For a free catalog describing Naval Institute Press books currently available, and for further information about joining the U.S. Naval Institute, please write to:

Member Services
U.S. Naval Institute
291 Wood Road
Annapolis, MD 21402-5034
Telephone: (800) 233 8764
Fax: (410) 571-1703
Web address: www.usni.org